The Family with a Handicapped Child

Understanding and Treatment

The Family with a Handicapped Child

Understanding and Treatment

Edited by

Milton Seligman, Ph.D.

Professor, Program in Rehabilitation Counseling
University of Pittsburgh
Pittsburgh, Pennsylvania

G&S

GRUNE & STRATTON, INC.
Harcourt Brace Jovanovich, Publishers
Orlando   New York   San Diego   Boston   London
San Francisco   Tokyo   Sydney   Toronto

Library of Congress Cataloging in Publication Data
Main entry under title:

The Family with a handicapped child.

  Bibliography
  Includes index
  Contents: The handicapped and their families/
Joseph Newman—Legal issues that affect parents/
Bonnie Strickland—Lost, then found/Stefi Rubin and
Noreen Quinn-Curran—[etc.]
  1. Handicapped children—United States—Family
relationships—Addresses, essays, lectures. 2. Handi-
capped children—Care and treatment—United States—
Addresses, essays, lectures. I. Seligman, Milton.
[DNLM: 1. Handicapped—Psychology. 2. Family.
3. Family therapy. 4. Child, Exceptional—Psychology.
WS 105.5.H2 F198]
HV888.5.F35   1983   362.8′2   83-5531
ISBN 0-8089-1561-4

Grune & Stratton, Inc.
Orlando, Florida 32887

Distributed in the United Kingdom by
Grune & Stratton, Ltd.
24/28 Oval Road, London NW 1

Library of Congress Catalog Number 83-5531
International Standard Book Number 0-8089-1561-4
Printed in the United States of America

86 87   10 9 8 7 6 5 4 3

Contents

v

III. FAMILY DYNAMICS

IV. INTERVENTIONS

Preface

A LAN ROSS's book, *The Exceptional Child in the Family,** provided professionals with the first comprehensive analysis of the effects of a handicapped child on the family. To a modest degree, the 1960s and especially the 1970s heralded a period of increased parent involvement and advocacy, signified not only by the passage of landmark legislation but also by the publication by parents of their own experiences with their handicapped sons and daughters. A considerable amount of interest in exceptional families marked the 1970s as a number of books and articles appeared in the professional literature. Many of the contributions were made not only by parents, but also by educators who were responding to the emerging training emphasis in education (particularly special education) to help teachers better understand and collaborate with the parents of the children they teach.

Much of the published work and professional training has taken place in education, although there is presently an awakening in fields such as social work and pediatrics. As advances in knowledge continue, albeit slowly, professionals who will be increasingly sought out as service providers for families, such as psychologists, counselors, psychiatrists, and social workers, need to be better informed about the character and dynamics of family life when a handicapped child is present. They not only require a better understanding of such families but also need to be better prepared to provide psychological services for them.

The early work in this field, modest as it is, has been augmented by recent contributions that helped to identify important areas of study. This volume is an effort to explore the family from a number of perspectives, including external influences such as legislation, the community, and the attitudes of health-care providers. In addition, various treatment ap-

---

*Ross, A. O. *The exceptional child in the family.* New York: Grune and Stratton, 1964.

proaches are examined in this book—interventions that have shown promise in the amelioration of psychosocial problems often faced by families.

It is not always clear how interest in certain areas of study has evolved. The present day focus on families of handicapped children had its roots in the widely held attitudes toward those considered "deviant" by society. Contributions by professionals in fields such as sociology, psychology, and education have sharpened our understanding of societal responses to deviance. Further, legislation has had a profound impact on the provision of present day services to handicapped children and adults. Joseph Newman, in Chapter 1, traces three converging themes as he explores the historical building blocks of the current interest in handicapped children and their families.

Landmark legislation, P.L. 94-142, the Education for All Handicapped Children Act, has had profound implications for greater parental involvement in their child's development. Although P.L. 94-142 has generally had a favorable effect on children and parents, this act is not without its drawbacks. In Chapter 2, Bonnie Strickland briefly reviews both the favorable and unfavorable implications of P.L. 94-142. She also examines the psychological impact of the due process hearing, which is an important appeal process parents may elect to exercise when they consider educational placements unsuitable for their child.

In Chapter 3, Stefi Rubin and Noreen Quinn-Curran explore in detail the effects that the extended family and community attitudes and support have on the family. They also examine processes by which parents can successfully negotiate the incredibly complex network of available community services and how they can engage natural helping networks.

Parents and the professionals who serve them do not always enjoy comfortable and productive working relationships. In some instances, parent–professional relationships may be characterized by mistrust, misunderstanding, and hostility. In Chapter 4, Rosalyn Benjamin Darling reviews the present status of parent–professional relationships and provides an incisive analysis of the factors that contribute to poor rapport.

With much of the attention paid to mother–child bonding and theories of child development that emphasize mother–child relationships, the parenting role of the father is often ignored. The significant parenting contribution of fathers, however, has come into prominence in recent years. Michael Lamb, in Chapter 5, reviews the research and commentary made on the role of fathers and their influence in families with a handicapped child.

Like fathers, siblings of handicapped children have not been accorded sufficient attention. Milton Seligman notes in Chapter 6 that the identified client or patient in the family, the handicapped youngster, is often not the family member in greatest distress—the real client may be the nonhandicapped sibling. This chapter explores the many factors that affect the psychological adjustment of siblings.

A major area of study in the past has been the families' response to the presence of a handicapped child. This book further explores the presumed effect a handicapped child has on the family. Chapters 7 (Rebecca Fewell and Steven Gelb) and 8 (Steve Lyon and Annie Preis) highlight the impact that a handicapped child has on the family. These authors lend credence to the notion that family reaction or adjustment is not necessarily determined by the nature or severity of the child's handicap but is more aptly considered a complex arrangement of numerous factors that affect the family unit.

Chapters 9, 10, and 11 explore specific therapeutic interventions that can be employed with exceptional families. June Mullins, in Chapter 9, reviews the key issues in using bibliotherapy as a therapeutic intervention. In her contribution, Dr. Mullins cautions that the inappropriate application of this potentially useful approach can intensify family problems instead of ameliorating them. The rationale of bibliotherapy and models of implementation are examined in this chapter.

Chapter 10 (Peter Randell Laborde and Milton Seligman) discusses three primary approaches: educative, facilitative, and advocacy. Common issues and useful individual counseling interventions are examined. Roberta Meyerson, in Chapter 11, notes that group support, encouragement, and feedback may be the preferred mode of therapeutic intervention for many parents. In considering the effect a handicapped child may have on the family, Dr. Meyerson argues that family therapy may prove useful for intact families who are open to such treatment. She reviews a number of group and family therapy strategies in this chapter.

The chapters in this volume, which cover a series of topics related to exceptional families, are designed to help broaden and deepen the reader's understanding of this underserved population. It is hoped that an increased understanding of such families will help professionals work effectively and compassionately with them so that they may lead full and rich lives.

Contributors

ROSALYN BENJAMIN DARLING, Ph.D.
Director, In-Home Services Program
City–County Clinic in Johnstown, Inc.
Johnstown, Pennsylvania

REBECCA R. FEWELL, Ph.D.
Professor, College of Education
Area of Special Education
University of Washington
Seattle, Washington

STEVEN A. GELB, M.Ed.
Graduate Student
College of Education
Area of Educational Psychology
University of Washington
Seattle, Washington

PETER RANDELL LABORDE, M.Ed.
Research Graduate Assistant
Rehabilitation Counseling Program
University of Pittsburgh
Pittsburgh, Pennsylvania

MICHAEL E. LAMB, Ph.D.
Professor, Departments of Psychology, Psychiatry and Pediatrics
University of Utah
Salt Lake City, Utah

STEVE LYON, Ph.D.
Assistant Professor
Special Education Program
University of Pittsburgh
Pittsburgh, Pennsylvania

ROBERTA C. MEYERSON, Ph.D.
Assistant Professor
Counselor Education Program
University of Pittsburgh
Pittsburgh, Pennsylvania

JUNE B. MULLINS, Ph.D.
Professor, Special Education Program
University of Pittsburgh
Pittsburgh, Pennsylvania

JOSEPH NEWMAN, Ph.D.
Professor Emeritus
Rehabilitation Counseling Program
University of Pittsburgh
Pittsburgh, Pennsylvania

ANNIE PREIS, Ph.D.
Assistant Professor
Bethany College
Bethany, West Virginia

NOREEN QUINN-CURRAN, M.A.
Senior Associate in Parent Advocacy and Training
Federation for Children with Special Needs
Boston, Massachusetts

STEFI RUBIN, Ph.D.
Associate Professor
Preschool Special Needs Graduate Program
Wheelock College and
Clinical Psychology Fellow
Department of Psychiatry
Harvard Medical School
Boston, Massachusetts

MILTON SELIGMAN, Ph.D.
Professor, Program in Rehabilitation Counseling
University of Pittsburgh
Pittsburgh, Pennsylvania

BONNIE STRICKLAND, Ph.D.
Clinical Assistant Professor
Division of Special Education
School of Education
University of North Carolina
Chapel Hill, North Carolina

The Family with a Handicapped Child

Understanding and Treatment

I

FOUNDATIONS

1

Handicapped Persons and Their Families: Philosophical, Historical, and Legislative Perspectives

JOSEPH NEWMAN

BIOGRAPHICAL SKETCH

Joseph Newman, Ph.D., is Professor Emeritus in the School of Education, University of Pittsburgh. He is a psychologist who has devoted virtually his entire professional career as a clinician and teacher to the field of rehabilitation. He is active with numerous community groups concerned with the problems created by handicapping conditions. He has contributed articles to professional journals and books in the field.

The skilled editorial assistance and review by my wife, Sylvia Newman, were invaluable. Her participation in the preparation of this chapter is warmly acknowledged.

A FTER A HISTORY of slowly relinquishing the care, treatment, and education of their handicapped* children to institutions, professionals, and schools, parents have been reversing that process. On every level they are active participants in programs for handicapped children. In fact, parental participation is regarded as so fundamental a component of these programs that it was mandated by federal legislation in the Education for All Handicapped Children Act (P.L. 94-142, 1975).

But the shift back to family involvement does not represent a return to the times when the family bore the entire burden of care for the handicapped member with virtually no resources available for help. When such help was developed beginning in the 19th century, parents were passive recipients of whatever became available. These services resulted from the humanitarian efforts not of the parents of the handicapped but of public-spirited individuals working through their charitable and voluntary organizations. As the formation of organizations dedicated to coping with the problems of the handicapped continued into the 20th century, parents began to join these organizations, eventually becoming their chief supporters and workers (Stanhope & Bell, 1981). These groups have become the leading advocates for the initiation, improvement, and extension of services for the handicapped. Moreover, they do not restrict their concerns solely to children but assist all age groups in recognition of the necessity to plan for the future lives of the handicapped.

Over the years, the activities of these humanitarian movements were important forces in the development and wide acceptance of two concepts basic to support of programs for the handicapped: societal responsibility for the handicapped and recognition of the constitutional rights of the handicapped. The observance of these concepts has led to scrutiny of existing programs and agitation for their improvement; missing essential services have been pressed for. Of necessity these activities involved litigation and political activism to promote legislation. Ineluctably the organizations have been drawn into activism by retrogressive budgets which in times of ecomonic stringency raise serious problems, such as the threat of curtailment of services. In these circumstances the question of the role of government in providing for the handicapped is vigorously reintroduced. This and other related issues have their roots in the past century and earlier, and a review of these backgrounds will provide a clarifying perspective.

---

*In practice, the care, treatment, and education of handicapped children frequently cannot be separated into these components; usually any intervention contains elements of all three. For this reason the three terms will be used virtually interchangeably in this discussion. Also, the term *handicapped* will refer to persons of all ages to reflect the current philosophy that treatment should include attention to future as well as to present problems.

THREE GUIDING PHILOSOPHIES

The treatment accorded its handicapped members by any society has been guided by a basic philosophy that was appropriate to the historical period and circumstances of that society. Probably the first such philosophy was an early form of what came to be known as *utilitarianism*. Its central doctrine was that usefulness to society determines the value of some thing or person. This concept has had somewhat different emphases in different societies and different eras, but its primary tenet stood: usefulness to society is the criterion for value (Windelband, 1958).

Among many primitive and ancient societies, usefulness took on a very direct meaning—usefulness in the struggle for survival. That struggle was constant and intense in an environment that was hostile and filled with dangers. Diseased and disabled persons were seen as burdens to the group because they could not contribute to the welfare of the group or could do so only in a limited fashion. Similarly, children and the aged could only contribute to the group in negligible ways. When times were hard the sick, the disabled, the aged, and the children became burdens the group could not bear and had to dispose of. The result was abandonment, rejection, or being killed. Infants were likewise low on the scale of human value since they were most helpless; female infants had a usefulness potential that was lower than that of male infants and were even more frequently destroyed. These expressions of a utilitarian philosophy among many primitive and ancient cultures are now considered barbaric and cruel but were seen by those cultures as necessary to their survival (Abt, 1965).

With the greater security afforded through advances in physical and economic existence, a more humane view toward society's weaker members became possible; with the advent of Christianity, all human life was regarded as sacred, and compassion was stressed as a moral force. Nevertheless, the focus of early Christian doctrines upon a future heavenly life in distinction to the present earthly one did not lead to significant change in the treatment of human "burdens." While infanticide was interdicted, the Church was indifferent to the lot of children. Forces of change were nascent, however, and in time new ideas developed that, during the Renaissance, grew into the philosophy of humanism. This philosophy attached primary importance to human beings and their situations, to their affairs, aspirations, and well-being. Life before death became the focus, rather than existence after death. Each individual had personal worth, and people were not to be subordinated to political or biological theories. These ideas formed the basis of *humanitarianism,* the second of the philosophies guiding society's treatment of the handicapped (Salt, 1914).

While humanitarian ideas permitted individual benevolent and charitable deeds, changes toward more benign general treatment were slow in coming. The climate for change was nevertheless developing, as could be inferred from the art of the Renaissance period that exalted motherhood and infancy, particularly through depicting the Madonna and the Christ Child. Change was also signaled by the work of St. Vincent de Paul in the 17th century in establishing homes and hospices for abandoned children. But for the masses of weak or impoverished people, utilitarian considerations remained dominant. Life was beset with hardships of every sort, and in such straitened circumstances children were burdens and were frequently abandoned or sold (Abt, 1965).

At the same time, the arts and literature flourished, and the foundations of the modern era were laid, especially the beginnings of modern science and medicine. The development of scientific medical care affected in a fundamental way the treatment of disability and the diseases that led to disability. The ability to reduce disease and disability rates and to treat individuals so as to enable survival could not but modify the existing negative views toward handicapped persons. Advances in medical care slowly helped to fortify the humanitarian approach.

Scientific progress during the Renaissance and later periods led to the development of technology and its application to the production of goods, which marked the Industrial Revolution. Concurrently there ensued social and political changes—the creation of the factory system, growth of cities and movement away from rural life, and new ideas about political relationships and authority. Humanistic theories (e.g., natural rights and social contract) had flourished during the Enlightenment and traditional theories had been questioned. Existing religious doctrines had been challenged from the Reformation on, and many new religious groups had come into existence. The New World had been colonized, and the gradual unfolding of a democratic philosophy had had a significant impact on societal institutions and, in particular, on the family.

Improvements in social and economic conditions lagged, however, and poverty and wretched living circumstances persisted when the factory system with its exploitative child labor practices, low wages, and long hours of work brought on a welter of public health problems leading to disease and disability. These conditions of life drew the attention of persons with humanistic beliefs and led to efforts toward alleviating social distress. The humanitarian movement grew and reached its ascendancy during the 19th century. Its first efforts led to the establishment of places of refuge, hospices, and hospitals to shelter and care for the cast-offs of society—the sick, the disabled, the disturbed, the retarded, and the abandoned. Numerous charitable, benevolent, philanthropic, and reform groups came into existence, and some played pioneering roles in improving the treatment of the handicapped (Kauffman, 1981).

The third philosophy guiding society's treatment of the handicapped, the concept of *rights,* is based directly upon law, in this country specifically on the Constitution and the Bill of Rights, the 5th and 14th Amendments with guarantees of rights, equal protection, and due process (fair and proper legal procedures). To be sure, the rights philosophy has elements of humanism in its emphasis on the intrinsic value of the individual. But it moves beyond humanism in its insistence that individuals exercise active roles in reaching decisions on matters that affect them, a realization of the democratic ideal. The movement to gain these rights for the handicapped began in the 1950s and developed rapidly in the ensuing years, culminating in legislation enacted in the 1970s in which the rights of the handicapped to protection against discrimination and other forms of unjust treatment were further elaborated (Bateman & Herr, 1981).

Three recent pieces of legislation form the core of this thrust in the United States. We have already mentioned the Education for All Handicapped Children Act; the others are Title V (Section 504) of the Rehabilitation Amendments of 1973 (P.L. 93-112) and the Developmentally Disabled Assistance and Bill of Rights Act (P.L. 94-103, 1975). Essentially the legislation provides statutory safeguards in (1) protection against discrimination in federally assisted programs, (2) access to facilities and programs supported by or operated by the federal government, and (3) the right to a free appropriate education (see Chapter 2). Further legislation was enacted in 1980 that permitted the federal government to initiate civil suits against states to protect the rights of the mentally retarded and other institutionalized individuals (Summary of Existing Legislation Relating to the Handicapped, 1980).

The rights movement has been influenced by a number of allied and related movements: civil and minority rights; women's rights; children's rights; consumer rights. The spheres of activity are the courts and the legislatures, and the objectives are to bring the governmental apparatus into a protagonist role in establishing and protecting the rights of aggrieved groups. This role of the government is one that is being challenged, and that challenge, if successful, would radically affect the entire structure of human services, including services to the handicapped, created in the past 100 years (The rights of children, 1974).

The three major philosophies function and interact concurrently in present-day endeavors and proposals to initiate and guide plans for the handicapped. For example, the utilitarian approach has constituted the strongest and most productive argument for programs for the handicapped—to institute such programs would convert handicapped persons from "tax consumers" to taxpayers, and eventually they would repay many times over the costs of their rehabilitation. Similarly, the deinstitutionalization drive was fueled by the promise to reduce the mounting costs of operating large institutions. Consistently, no matter how desirable the goal, it must be "practicable" and "cost effective."

The argument for support additionally includes humanitarian ideas about the essential worth of the individual and the need for compassion for the less fortunate. Present, too, is the plea to rise above materialistic considerations, since helping people cannot be measured in such terms.

The rights philosophy goes directly to the issue of social responsibility, as expressed through the governmental structure. It starts with the position that the handicapped have not received the same rights extended to the nonhandicapped. It is the responsibility of the state to affirm or reaffirm those rights through judicial and legislative actions. But utilitarian factors often play a strongly influencing role, as in the continuing troublesome and expensive problem of providing access for the handicapped in buildings and in transportation. The crucial terms used are "reasonable costs" and "budgetary restraints." These utilitarian arguments have cogency and must be taken into account. Also implicated in the problem of access are political values and philosophies, liberal versus conservative views on the role of the state, the role of the "private sector," and the role of voluntarism.

INFLUENCES FOR CHANGE IN THE TREATMENT OF THE HANDICAPPED

The great advances in productivity in all kinds of goods and the improvements in living conditions and in health that have taken place over the past two centuries in American society have drastically reduced the potency of survival considerations in the treatment of the handicapped. Societal betterment overall made it possible to tolerate and follow more benign practices with the handicapped; the great easing of economic stringency over time permitted the influences of humanitarianism to be heeded and the rights philosophy to unfold. The focus of utilitarianism became limited in contemporary economic life to financial or cost–benefit factors.

Astounding advances were made in medical sciences as well. Progress in the treatment and understanding of disease and disability changed the epidemiologic picture of human disease and disability. Rates of survival and longevity increased; for example, in 1900 life expectancy in this country was 48 years, whereas today it is more than 70 years (Straus, 1965). Dramatic reductions were achieved in infant and maternal mortality rates. At the same time survival rates increased for persons with congenital anomalies, birth injuries, and those disabled through accidents and by disease. In prior decades (and centuries), relatively few disabled persons survived until adulthood. The establishment of pediatrics as a medical specialty in the late 1800s, closely followed by a similar status for obstetrics, signified the rising medical recognition that children required special attention (Abt, 1965). But this cognizance extended only to healthy or intact children; medicine did not as yet display any great interest in the care of the handicapped. When medical science acquired the capability for effective intervention and alleviation of disabling conditions, the medical profession began to take note of handicapped children. Nevertheless, it was the humanitarian movement that first assumed social responsibility for the care of the handicapped and used its influences to induce public acceptance of that responsibility (Bremner, 1970).

The lack of significant public attention to and interest in handicapped children until this century can be attributed not only to utilitarian considerations and medical ignorance but also to the persistence of naive, superstitious, and animistic beliefs about handicaps. To understand this we must again consider the distant past. In early societies, illness and disability were seen as the work of evil demons and supernatural forces. These occult powers controlled life and intervened in childbirth. They could substitute one of their own as a changeling and thus create a defective infant or monster. Twins were frequently killed as being unnatural or uncanny or the result of adulterous intercourse. If a child was born on an "unlucky" day, it was killed, as were children born with some abnormality. Witches and sorcerers were believed to cast spells or the child was subjected to the "evil eye." When the child was not killed or abandoned, the treatments pursued were in accord with such bizarre beliefs. Medicine men or their equivalents administered an array of prayers, incantations, exorcisms, and ritualistic sacrifices along with the use of "holy relics," charms, amulets, and talismans. These practices extended well into the Middle Ages in Western societies. Magic was still widely utilized as, for instance, a sick or rachitic child would be passed through clefts or arching roots of trees, holes in large stones, ladders, and the like (Abt, 1965). Nevertheless, it was during the Middle Ages that more humane treatment was begun sporadically by religious orders in Switzerland and in France (Juul, 1981).

The medieval church, however, did little to advance medical science (Abt, 1965). As in the Judaic and the Islamic faiths, Christianity saw disease and disability as the scourges of God, as punishment for sin, or as disciplines to be endured. In some orders, priests and monks were forbidden to study medicine and even to see doctors and take medicine. At the same time, the church opposed the magic practiced by witches, and it is believed that witches were put to death by the thousands.

Despite the passage of years well into the Renaissance, progress toward scientific treatment methods was slow in coming. By the 18th century, although a good many of the superstitious ideas had changed, treatment had not, and abandonment and casting out prevailed, which along with high mortality rates from disease reduced survival (Johnson, 1967). That century saw the blossoming of scientific thought and reason and was called the Age of Enlightenment. Now the forces of change quickened; there were periodic steps to help the blind, the deaf, and the retarded. These efforts were to establish institutions, a movement that proliferated during the 19th century to include not only the handicapped but dependent children of all types; hospitals for children began to be founded as well. Medical interest in handicapped children and the development of scientific knowledge about them advanced at a quickened pace early in the 20th century (Bremner, 1970).

The focus of the groups active with the handicapped was to reach those children. Public schools were obvious sites to begin the search, and eventually the schools came to share the responsibility for the care and health of fragile, sickly, and handicapped children. This role was enlarged over subsequent years to encompass special education, and some of the first achievements were to establish special classes for children regarded at risk for the development of illnesses, such as tuberculosis. The early 20th century also saw the growing awareness of the crucial role of the family in matters of health. Also, recognition of the importance of psychological factors in the care of the handicapped child was influenced by the establishment and spread of child guidance clinics (Bremner, 1971).

Beginning in the 1930s, great advances took place in pediatrics, social legislation, and attention to handicapped children, and the federal-state system for health care and social security was established. There was wide recognition and acceptance of the fact that social problems in most, if not all, areas were beyond the capabilities of philanthropic organizations and the voluntary private sector. That is not to say that there was no opposition to development of governmental programs; social and health legislation was denounced as being "socialistic," as being unconstitutional and in violation of states' rights, as being destructive invasions of the privacy of family life, as the meddlesome preoccupation of "bleeding hearts," and as encouraging the perpetuation of "inferior stock." Added to these charges, which are still heard, is the continuing apprehension of creating a permanent dependent underclass of those receiving different types of governmental assistance.

This last issue tends to erupt during periods of economic distress. Utilitarian arguments, always present, are then forcefully asserted, accepted, and implemented. Strong governmental leadership in human services becomes restrained in the face of budgetary problems. Loss and curtailment in services occurs generally, not only for the handicapped, but also for other groups benefitting by social legislation. At such times it is important to recognize that the leadership role of the government is a phenomenon that slowly and continuously evolved. It is not something that was instituted within the last few decades and that can be abruptly terminated in disregard of the experiences that form its history. We shall now trace that history.

THE STATE AND THE HANDICAPPED CHILD

As discussed earlier, the status of any individual in olden Western cultures depended upon the value of the individual to the survival of his society. Intact male adults had high value since they could make fundamental contributions economically and militarily. In contrast, those who could make only few or no contributions—the crippled, the infirm, the aged, children, and infants—were expendable in terms of their utilitarian value. As we have described, in times of hardships and want, these became threats to group survival and were subject to elimination (Barclay, 1959). This practice had the sanction of the "government" or leadership of the society. Moreover, the child was not regarded as a person and had no rights. He could achieve personhood and move directly into adult society when he began to be able to perform adult tasks. Essentially the child was viewed as chattel, as an economic or natural resource (Aries, 1962). Handicapped children were worth little as a resource. It is doubtful that handicapped children survived to any significant extent in early societies, given the primitive and superstitious medical understanding and treatment of the times and the high rates of infant and child mortality, although some ancient cultures, such as those of Egypt, Babylon, Israel, and Athens, did not treat their children as harshly.

Whatever were the practices pursued with children, they must have had the direct or indirect sanction of what constituted the state or "government" and, in this sense, intervention by the state in the "interests" of its children was present in ancient times. As societies became more organized intervention became more direct and formal, as in Egypt, Israel, and Athens, which established schools for governmental or military or religious purposes. In Sparta and Rome, a form of eugenics was widely practiced in order to produce vigorous offspring for the military. Puny, sickly, or deformed infants and excess female children were abandoned or killed. While this policy was eventually abolished, unwanted children continued to be exposed, abandoned, or sold into slavery up through the Middle Ages (Abt, 1965). During this period the state did not directly intervene in the care of children; it was essentially passive.

The child, as chattel, could be dealt with as any piece of property; hence the custodial rights of the parents included transfer or sale. The right to custody appeared to have had an economic basis, and custodial right was mainly a property right. As economic objects, children were open to abuse. With the continuing influence of the Church and the rise of more humane ideas, the state was induced to act when it was deemed necessary to protect the child. There arose in England in the 17th century the doctrine of *parens patriae*. Under this doctrine, the state had the power to intervene to protect children but only under unusual circumstances. The parents were recognized as having the right to custody unless shown to be unfit. With time the doctrine of *parens patriae* changed, and the emphasis shifted from the property theory of custody to the personal status theory, which held that the parents because of their relationship to the child were the custodians best suited to serve the child's needs (Katz, 1971).

Although humanizing forces became manifest during and after the Renaissance, there were marked social class differences in how their influences took effect. Humanist ideas mainly affected the upper social strata, and indeed these are the population groups about whom information in this respect exists. The lives of the common people—the artisans and peasants—did not change in any meaningful way from the poverty, ignorance, callousness, and cruelties of the Middle Ages. For this large mass of the population, it is likely that the hardships and high infant mortality did not permit bonds of affection toward offspring to develop, especially when the probability was high that the child would be lost at an early age. Aries (1962) describes this as an indifference—that is, regret but no great sorrow—akin to that displayed when an animal pet dies. Moreover, a fatalistic approach to life was widespread.

The first evidences, then, of change in the treatment of children were to be found among the literate and economically favored classes. Also, the aristocracy, as the ruling class, did have a tradition of protecting their "subjects" and the doctrine of *parens patriae* was seen as being derived from the sovereign's prerogative in protecting defenseless subjects such as infants and incompetents (Katz, 1971). The state also acted out of concern for other special groups of subjects. In the England of the 15th and 16th centuries, when seapower was so fundamental to the economy, the government took steps to insure an adequate supply of manpower for the dangerous and unattractive occupation of seaman by establishing a program of (in today's terms) compulsory health and disability insurance for the men of the Royal Navy and the merchant fleet. The men and their families would be provided for should the men be disabled or killed in the course of duty. Later, marine hospitals were established, and other seapowers did the same. The new American nation also established marine hospitals soon after it was founded. These early expressions of societal acceptance of responsibility for certain groups were in accordance with the utilitarian philosophy and therefore deemed necessary (Straus, 1965).

The protective role of the state slowly expanded. The idea of the child as the private property of the parents and under their exclusive control diminished. The power of the government began to penetrate family life—a process that has been viewed generally as benevolent. A policy of intervention was followed in England for dependent, abused, and neglected children of "incompetent parents." Such children were "bound out," that is, placed in the community with families with whom they lived and worked for a specified period. This practice relieved the authorities of the need for support, and benefits presumably accrued to the children in terms of stability in living conditions (although there are records of proceedings against masters who abused their charges). This early protective policy was an illustration of the subordination of the authority of the natural parents to the welfare of the child and the good of the community—the fact that economic motivation was uppermost notwithstanding. Similar policies were followed in colonial America (Bremner, 1970).

The great flowering of humanitarianism in the 19th century in Europe was reflected in the young American republic, where it was marked by an acceleration of philanthropic and social reform activities. The reformers came from the dominant social groups—the middle and upper classes, persons with ties to influential circles. Attention was directed to the "unfortunates" of society, and increasingly the state was induced to bring the neglected, the abused, and the handicapped child under the protection of the public authorities. The state began to intervene more frequently on behalf of such children. Legislation was passed for compulsory school attendance, moral education, prohibition of physical abuse, and age restrictions in child labor. This legislation advanced governmental authority and in general reduced the authority of parents and guardians, albeit only in specific areas of social concern.

To be sure, such developments aroused opposition on the part of economic, political, ethnic, and religious groups, and each group had its own rationale for opposition. Some adhered to traditional points of view toward parental authority and the place of children in society, and they deplored trends that appeared to diminish parental authority. Others feared the advancement of governmental authority and clung to the Jeffersonian-Jacksonian credo, "the less government the better." Still others were influenced strongly by the Social Darwinism developed by the English philosopher, Herbert Spencer. Spencer, a fervent promoter of evolutionary theory as propounded by Charles Darwin, applied the notions of the extinction of the unfit and the survival of the fittest to social life despite the fact that they had been developed from observations of biological life. These ideas were applied not only to the handicapped but also to the great numbers of immigrants who had been recruited to work in the vastly expanding industrial establishment. Social Darwinism gave rise to the eugenics movement, whose ultimate purpose was to eliminate the unfit (Kauffman, 1981). These ideas served well the political and religious groups that believed that personal misfortune was the result of defects in the individual rather than in society.

Nevertheless, significant legislative steps continued to be made; one such change came in 1912 when the U.S. Children's Bureau was established. Bremner (1971) regards this event as the single most important development in child and maternal health and welfare in the early 20th century. It signified the acceptance by the federal authorities of the responsibility for promoting the health and welfare of the young. The Children's Bureau grew from a research and information center to one that was charged with administration of laws relating to child labor, child health, and child welfare. Beginning in the 1910s, a series of social legislative measures were promulgated that directly affected families and their welfare: workmen's compensation, unemployment, and health insurance, housing laws, antidiscrimination and equal opportunity legislation, rehabilitation of the handicapped statutes, and measures for education of handicapped children. These legislative acts were a fulfillment of an early principle of the Children's Bureau that the wellbeing of children could be best achieved through the economic security of the family (Bremner, 1974).

In the years prior to all these events there was controversy around the issue of foster home care versus institutional care, despite the prevailing belief that the poorest home was superior to the best institution. Moreover there seemed to be little hesitation in removing children from homes deemed unfit by economic and moral standards. Because economic considerations alone were no longer sufficient, the authorities applied the "suitable home" concept (Katz, 1971). The interpretation of the suitability of a home was highly discretionary but was usually along social class lines. Although it was presumed that the state wanted to do what was in the "best interests" of the child, intervention was more readily carried out when the families were poor, nonwhite, and unconventional, that is, families that were politically, economically, or psychologically powerless (Rodham, 1974).

Parents have certain obligations to fulfill. These include financial security, maintenance of the child's health, ensurance of education, and inculcation of values such as morality and respect for authority. Failure in any of these areas constitutes neglect and creates a basis for state intervention. Beyond these obligations, there is no comprehensive statement in law as to the full range of responsibilities of parents to children, such as, for example, to handicapped children. Neglect and abuse have been, historically, the occasions for state intervention. Both are regarded as lower-socioeconomic-status (SES) phenomena. But that view has come to be regarded as being mainly the expression of middle-class bias. The apparent greater frequency of neglect and abuse among lower-SES families may well be the function of the additional scrutiny these families receive because of the increased contacts they have with official service agencies. Indeed, families in high-SES classes may be equally "irresponsible" and "neglectful," but they are able to escape official scrutiny because of their greater access to services from private professionals and agencies. There are many lower-SES families that provide adequate child care or could do so if some support services were available (Katz, 1971).

Over the years, the ability of the state to be an adequate substitute parent has come to be seriously questioned. Opposition to that parental role has emerged from the increased assertion of rights by parents and custodians. In addition, there has been greater recognition that the prevailing assumption that a child's interests were identical to those of parents did not hold (Rodham, 1974). One outcome of this recognition has been the rise of the advocacy movement for the rights of children, which has led to the introduction and intensification of the political elements in child care issues.

Traditionally, the relationships between parents and children function under parental dominance. In this view, parents are held responsible for their own children and exercise primary control. The state steps in only when parental control and care are not exercised. Children need not or should not participate in making decisions affecting their lives (Worsfold, 1974).

The advocates of children's rights raise questions about the above assumptions and insist that children have rights that are essentially the same as those of adults. It is recognized, however, that children are not capable of fulfilling the responsibilities that go along with rights because of their dependency. Exercise of rights for children is seen as taking place within a context of love and protection by adults that is seen as a fundamental need of children.

There is much ambiguity in the matter of children's rights. How should children's rights be conceptualized? As adult rights granted to children, or should the special needs and interests of children be recognized as rights? Should the minority status of children be abolished? Should procedural rights—the Bill of Rights guarantees—be granted? Should the "best interests of the child" standard followed by the state for intervention be abandoned? (Katz, 1971).

These questions have been much discussed, and some changes in attitude have evolved. Adults are being seen as not necessarily having an adequate conception of children's interests; they may have interests and preferences that do not coincide with those of children. Moreover, the child may suffer from adverse consequences if adults have unlimited discretion in the name of children's "special needs." There is a growing acceptance of the equal protection clause of the 14th Amendment as applying to children.

The development of the concept of children's rights owes much to the influence of the White House Conferences on Children which began in 1909. These conferences were convened periodically, and it was the Conference of 1930 that drew up a Children's Charter that spoke of "the rights of the child as the first rights of citizenship." Subsequent White House conferences issued similar pronouncements, and the 1970 Conference endorsed a Children's Bill of Rights. Previously, in 1959, the United Nations had promulgated a Declaration of the Rights of the Child. The 1970 report of the Joint Commission on Mental Health of Children emphasized family life as crucial to the fulfillment of the rights of children and further advanced the conviction that the quality of parental care had important mental health consequences. The report marked the emergence of the unique concept of present-day Western culture that children form a distinct group of citizens (Bremner, 1974).

It should be noted that the active appearance of the children's rights movement occurred in the same decades as did the movements for the rights of minorities, women, and the handicapped, and there were many cross influences. For example, children are a minority in the most literal sense. Like racial minorities and women, they have not had full status under the law. However, the analogies between children's rights and adult minority rights cannot be carried to extremes, since there are many real problems if unperceptive impartiality or equality is pursued. Children should not be made to serve as instruments for satisfying the interests of others, usually the parents, nor should they be treated as nonpersons who are to be molded according to adult preconceptions.

An important component of advocacy for the rights of children has been litigation and the ready use of the courts. This has led to a limited use of governmental intervention in order to avoid charges of unreasonable interference. A major factor in this judicial reluctance has been the numerous court decisions affirming the need to recognize the integrity and security of the family (Lilly, 1979).

Children's rights today have moved in two major directions: education and deinstitutionalization (mainstreaming or normalization). The right to education was spurred by the landmark 1954 United States Supreme Court decision in *Brown* v. *Board of Education*. In that decision, the Supreme Court established the legal entitlement to equal educational opportunity for racial minorities, a concept central to the later decisions of the lower federal courts that extended similar rights to handicapped children. This case betokened the successful use of courts for the advancement of children's rights and signaled a shift that was inevitable because of the key role schools came to play in American society. Education became the vehicle for sharing in the national image of individual liberty, social equality, and personal fulfillment as well as for the social need to develop and maintain a common outlook. We have referred previously to the role schools also came to play in health and welfare matters. Schools could not avoid becoming involved in the broad social problems of the post-World War II decades. *Brown* v. *Board of Education* thrust schools into the midst of the ongoing and developing rights movements (Oberman, 1980).

Implicit in the *Brown* v. *Board of Education* decision was that school segregation constituted denial of educational opportunities. Segregation was practiced not only with black and other minority children but with handicapped children as well. It was to be expected that the same constitutional issues would be faced by the handicapped children's advocates. The eventual outcome was P.L. 94-142, the Education for all Handicapped Children Act, which with its "least restrictive setting" provision was concerned with desegregation and pointed toward normalization (Martin, 1979).

The constitutional issues raised by the school desegregation movement could not help but direct attention to the most severely segregated of the handicapped—the institutionalized. The state, in placing handicapped persons in institutions, relied upon the *parens patriae* doctrine that enables the state to act in the interest of an individual or on the police powers doctrine which enables the state to act in order to protect the safety and well-being of society in general. The court decisions that were handed down limited both doctrines in accordance with the due process clause of the 14th Amendment. Two principles were enunciated to guide treatment of the handicapped: the least restrictive alternative and the right to treatment (Soskin, 1977).

Deinstitutionalization came into full force in the 1970s. Up to that time meager attention had been paid to the rights and needs of thousands of mentally or emotionally disabled persons confined in public institutions. There was little in federal and state legislation that protected the rights of those institutionalized persons. Institutions had been used with virtually no challenge for over 100 years. Modern social and psychological theories did not, however, view mental and emotional disabilities as static and hopeless conditions; much progress and change could occur given treatment and "normal" living conditions—conditions usually lacking in institutions. Federal courts have ruled that residents of institutions suffer "an extraordinary deprivation of liberty" despite the fact they have committed no crime against society. The courts have also held that the residents of institutions have a "constitutional right to treatment." Both of these principles have not been squarely determined as yet by the Supreme Court. Nevertheless there has evolved a reluctance on the part of the judiciary in general to commit persons to institutions. The conviction has grown that large institutions have ceased to be viable means for treating the handicapped. The speed with which the deinstitutionalization drive took hold was fueled by utilitarian as well as rights motives. The mounting costs of maintaining institutions made them attractive cost-cutting targets to budget-minded legislators, as in California beginning in 1969 and in other states (Mickenberg, 1980).

Unfortunately, effective means to achieve deinstitutionalization and the establishment of community alternatives have not come into being readily. Closing institutions or discharging residents did not automatically assure better care or services. These consequences and realizations thrust parents and families into the deinstitutionalization fray. It became apparent that there were many legal details to be clarified and worked out as well as principles to be fully accepted and expressed in court decisions. A host of community zoning, licensing, and other regulatory measures would have to be enacted, and funds would have to be appropriated, before a stable and adequate system of community services could be created (Oberman, 1980).

Opponents of deinstitutionalization point to these problems as justification for a more deliberate and considered course. They emphasize that certain groups of handicapped persons are not capable of benefitting from the treatment necessary for returning them to the community and that they require continued institutional life. The problems, issues, and controversies surrounding deinstitutionalization directly affect parents and families, as do the many similar issues and problems confronting "mainstreaming" in special education.

THE FAMILY AND THE HANDICAPPED CHILD

We now turn to our central concern of this work—the contemporary American family and the treatment of the handicapped child. We have identified and traced the important forces, concepts, and trends that have shaped the present-day societal approach to the handicapped child. We have delineated the major philosophies that have guided society in that respect. We shall now examine the family's role and record some of the changes that have occurred in that role over time.

Today's American family is not the family of its European forebears, nor, for that matter, is it the family of the early years of the nation. As a social institution, the family is molded by the culture in which it exists, and as that culture changes so does the family. The changes that have occurred in the family have been quite varied in nature and extent: for most families they were fundamental, for some they were moderate or fragmentary, and for some they were minimal or absent. In contrast to European families, the American family changed at a greater rate. While we can speak generally of an American family, the pluralistic nature of American society leads to a variety of family life patterns—some innovative, some polymorphous, some inconsistent, and many traditional to a greater or lesser extent (Groves & Groves, 1947).

Essentially the colonies followed English institutions. Thus the English (and European) patriarchal family was established in which the father was master. Women and children occupied subordinate positions and discipline was stern and harsh. Because information about colonial life derives mainly from middle class sources, there is little information about families on the lower socioeconomic levels. The early settlers were mainly individuals, not families, and as communities were established there were organized efforts to promote the formation of families. Life for the settlers was filled with hardships and most people had a low standard of living. It was necessary that everyone in the family contribute to its economic upkeep, mainly in the form of physical work. Moreover, work had both religious and moral values as well.

There existed in the colonies a large "floating" population comprised mainly of persons of lower socioeconomic status. Included in this population were numbers of children and youth who, for one reason or another, had become separated from their families. The communities saw these individuals as dependents and undertook to control the problem. They were attached to families, following the English practice of "binding out," since there were no special facilities for young offenders and runaways. As in England, the youngsters received their maintenance and performed work or chores out in the colonies and were provided at least a minimal education. The practice of binding out relieved the communities of the necessity to support dependents. Binding out was also followed for children of "incompetent" parents who neglected them, following the English doctrine of *parens patriae* in that the authority of the parents was subordinated to the welfare of the child and to the good of the community. The governmental bodies in the colonies undertook to supervise the moral and ethical behavior of the members of the communities (Stern, 1938).

Colonial families carried the responsibility for the moral and ethical behavior of their members. This was one of the many social and economic functions they performed. Families were the chief educational force not only for morals and ethics and the fundamentals of literacy but for respect for public laws and domestic manners. The homes maintained an authoritarian atmosphere and strong discipline, leading many young people to flee, usually to join the floating population.

There was a constant temptation to flee the rigidly controlled lives of the established Eastern towns to the freedom of the ever-present frontier of the West. This influence and the migration it stimulated were some of the forces in American life that led to changes in the family. Change was indeed inevitable when we consider the lure of the New World for the many people who had left or fled the onerous social, economic, political, and religious circumstances of their lives in the Old World in the hope of improving their situations (Butts, 1955).

In those years, the 18th and early 19th centuries, no reference could yet be made to a "typical American family." Families varied greatly according to religious, social class, ethnic, and economic characteristics. Certain common forces can, however, be identified. Clearly family life began to be permeated by ideas of an individualistic, laissez-faire, white democracy. The hierarchical family was slowly leveled culturally by democratic social principles, and children assumed a more enhanced role in the family. Children were allowed to become increasingly independent, individualistic, assertive, and challenging. These traits were strengthened by the influences of the frontier—aggressive individualism, desire for independence, egalitarianism, elevation of women's status, and emphasis on physical and moral qualities. Doctrines of human improvement and perfectibility prevailed, especially for the young. There was a sense, derived from evangelistic Calvinism, that people attain "heaven" or "hell" through their own decisions and actions. In time, however, this religious orientation eroded, and materialistic views of life came to prevail. This was due largely to the development of our industrial society (Burgess & Locke, 1953).

The factory system brought women and children into the industrial work force. This was not radically different from colonial practice, which had been inspired by Puritan ideology. Work in both settings had the encouragement of the religious doctrine of the sanctity of work and the fear of idleness as the Devil's opportunity. Two systems of employment prevailed: one in which entire families, mainly rural, worked, and the other in which children, mainly girls, worked in textile factories and the parents continued to live on the farm. The working hours were alike: regardless of the setting, every member of the family above the age of seven years worked from sunrise to sunset.

The effects of working in factories were drastic for the family. It was no longer a self-contained economic unit. Children, albeit exploited, were paid, at the rate of 25–50 cents a day, but this was different from being bound out; they were not protected by the traditional roles of apprenticeship. There were no controls over abuse, nor was the need for protection diminished; the only source of protection was paternalism. The child now had two masters—the father and the foreman. The long working day left little time for school or recreation. By 1830 the use of children in factories was common, and it continued through the middle of the century (Bremner, 1970).

During these years, child labor was not a major concern of humanitarian reformers. Children were expected to work, and their labor was viewed as being socially productive and individually beneficial. Some states became concerned about the lack of education for working children and passed compulsory school attendance laws, as did Massachusetts in 1857. But these laws were widely ignored. The factory system involved other problems as well, mainly of disease and poor public health. The turn of the century saw the many reform movements influencing changes toward the improved economic, health, welfare, and educational status of the family. Especially fundamental was the acceptance of responsibility in these matters on the part of the government because this was a precondition for social legislation—an undertaking that was to increase in momentum in the coming decades (Bremner, 1971).

Changes in the status and the development of services for the handicapped, both adults and children, came more slowly; they came first for adults. After World War I, legislation was enacted for the vocational rehabilitation of handicapped soldiers in 1918. This was followed in 1920 by legislation that created a system of vocational rehabilitation for handicapped civilians. Further developments were few until the 1930s, when the beginnings of the present social security system were established. Then, in the 1940s, rehabilitation made significant advances in providing services to the nonphysically handicapped. Under the impact of the experiences of World War II, the present veterans' rehabilitation program was formed (Sussman, 1965).

Parallel changes in services to handicapped children lagged somewhat, but attention to their needs was present with the increased activity of insistent interest groups, especially of parent organizations such as the National Association for Retarded Children and its affiliates. Those groups and analogous groups for other types of handicapped children were the direct results of transformations that had occurred in the family and in the role of parents in the handicapped children movement since the early years of the 20th century (Gallagher, 1980).

The European family had become altered in America; it was no longer predominantly patriarchal, authoritarian, and duty-bound with an overriding economic preoccupation. It was now essentially democratic, and emphasized relationships characterized by concensus, companionship, and affection. The child's role changed from being a chattel to occupying a central place in the family with special characteristics and needs. Increasingly expressed was recognition of the child's rights, as a citizen in a democratic society, to freedoms of expression, assembly, petition, and conscience (Burgess & Locke, 1953).

At the outset of this chapter we referred to the significant change whereby parents have moved from passive roles to being active participants in programs for the handicapped. These activities marked the introduction of political factors into the handicapped children's movement: the family was no longer a private, nonpolitical unit (Bohrer, Breedon, & Weikert, 1979). Moreover, the social character of such reform movements, which traditionally had been mainly middle class, now began to reflect the inclusion of working-class families as active members. The spread of democratic orientation tended to provide families with a greater sense of control over their lives and to instill a sense of hope for the future of their handicapped children (Lilly, 1979).

In their active roles, parents have also begun to be more directly involved in programs for their own handicapped children. Many have participated through parent education and as observers. In progressively more active roles, they have served in home training, in group training, and as classroom helpers. It has been observed that on any level some parental involvement enhances the child's developmental progress and that it helps meet the family's emotional needs. On the broader program level, parents have served as decision makers (Turnbull & Blacher-Dixon, 1980; Wehman & McLaughlin, 1981).

However, parental involvement in programs for handicapped children has not been without criticism. The underlying assumption that parental involvement is beneficial is not seen as fully established. In addition there are the professional versus parent or status considerations. Some feel that roles as agents of school systems could interfere with roles as parents. Others believe that parents need a respite from the strains of difficult parenting and hence should not be involved in classroom activities or home instruction. Nevertheless, the prevailing opinion appears to be that parental involvement has been a positive factor in terms of child performance, parent satisfaction, and program effectiveness, and that the problems noted are indicative not so much of the inherent deficiencies of parent involvement as of its developing nature (Kirk, 1962; Wegerink, Hocutt, Posante-Loro, & Bristol, 1980).

SUMMING UP AND SOME PROGNOSTICATIONS

From a historical perspective, despite the progress that has been achieved in the treatment of handicapped children, there are still persisting residues of negative attitudes of avoidance, exclusion, sequestration, and rejection and actions instigated by ignorance, stereotyping, and superstition. Gellman (1950) has stated that existing prejudices have their roots in long-standing supernatural beliefs and are present on all socioeconomic levels and in all regions. Research studies of today confirm that a handicap, like any other characteristic that is different, is negatively tinged and stigmatized (Siller, 1976). These views support the social forces that continue to cast out the handicapped, utilizing rationalizations derived from utilitarianism to justify such actions. They are especially damaging in the current climate of budgetary retrenchment and imminent political change in reversing the past leadership role of the federal government in providing human services. Narrowly conceived utilitarian considerations predominate. There is recognition among the advocates of handicapped rights that the existence of legislation does not automatically insure that the rights of a handicapped person will be secure (if indeed the handicapped person will be seen as having such rights—for example, the right to access). Laws do not enforce themselves, and the implementation of legislative and judicial mandates requires persistent monitoring (Soskin, 1980).

The increased emphasis on narrow, utilitarian concerns about costs comes at a time in which several critical questions have been raised by legislation and judicial opinion. The answers to these questions are being searchingly pursued by activists in the handicapped children's movement—professionals, lawyers, and parents. Some of the questions are as follows:

1. What is the scope of public education? For the common good? For social equality?
2. What is an "appropriate" education?
3. What are the limits of educability? Are all children to be educated? Are the severely handicapped to be included?
4. What is a "free" education?
5. What is the "least restrictive" environment?
6. What is the proper role of government in education?
7. What intervention is desirable?
8. How do due process procedures fit into the educational system? (Kauffman, 1981; Oberman, 1980).

Parents have come to play a central role in seeking answers to these questions and to other serious challenges facing the education and general treatment of handicapped children. The present role of parents has evolved out of the convergence of the historical trends we have traced, and therefore it does not seem likely that that role will be easily relinquished.

REFERENCES

Abt, A. F. *Abt-Garrison history of pediatrics*. Philadelphia: W. B. Saunders, 1965.

Aries, P. *Centuries of childhood*. New York: Knopf, 1962.

Barclay, W. *Train up a child*. Philadelphia: Westminster Press, 1959.

Bateman, B. D., & Herr, C. M. Law and special education. In J. M. Kauffman & D. P. Hallahan (Eds.), *Handbook of special education*. Englewood Cliffs, N.J.: Prentice-Hall, 1981.

Bohrer, T. S., Breedon, L., & Weikert, R. J. On lay advocacy. *Amicus*, 1979, *4*, 82–85.

Bremner, R. H. (Ed.). *Children and youth in America: A documentary history* (Vol. 1). Cambridge, Ma.: Harvard University Press, 1970.

Bremner, R. H. (Ed.). *Children and youth in America: A documentary history* (Vol. 2). Cambridge, Ma.: Harvard University Press, 1971.

Bremner, R. H. (Ed.). *Children and youth in America: A documentary history* (Vol. 3). Cambridge, Ma.: Harvard University Press, 1974.

Burgess, E. W., & Locke, H. J. *The family* (2nd ed.). New York: American Book Co., 1953.

Butts, R. F. *A cultural history of western education*. New York: McGraw-Hill, 1955.

Gallagher, J. J. (Ed.). *Ecology of exceptional children*. San Francisco: Jossey-Bass, 1980.

Gellman, W. Roots of prejudice against the handicapped. *Journal of Rehabilitation*, 1959, *25*, 4–6.

Groves, E. R., & Groves, G. H. *The contemporary American family*. Philadelphia: Lippincott, 1947.

Johnson, R. W. *Disease and medicine*. London: B. T. Batsford, 1967.

Juul, K. D. Special education in Europe. In J. M. Kauffman & D. P. Hallahan (Eds.). *Handbook of special education*. Englewood Cliffs, N.J.: Prentice-Hall, 1981.

Katz, J. N. *When parents fail*. Boston: Beacon Press, 1971.

Kauffman, J. M. Introduction: Historical trends and contemporary issues in special education. In J. M. Kauffman & D. P. Hallahan (Eds.). *Handbook of special education*. Englewood Cliffs, N.J.: Prentice-Hall, 1981.

Kirk, S. A. *Educating exceptional children*. Boston: Houghton Mifflin, 1962.

Lilly, S. *Children with exceptional needs*. New York: Holt, Rinehart & Winston, 1979.

Martin, R. *Educating handicapped children: The legal mandate*. Chicago: Research Press, 1979.

Mickenberg, N. H. A decade of deinstitutionalization. *Amicus*, 1980, *5*, 54–63.

Oberman, C. A. The right to education for the handicapped. *Amicus*, 1980, *5*, 44–53.

The rights of children. *Harvard Educational Review*, 1974, Reprint Series No. 9.

Rodham, H. Children under the law. *Harvard Educational Review*, 1974, Reprint Series No. 9, 1–28.

Salt, H. S. Humanitarianism. In J. Hastings (Ed.). *Encyclopedia of religion and ethics* (Vol. 6). New York: Scribner, 1914.

Siller, J. Attitudes toward disability. In H. Rusalem & D. Malikin (Eds.). *Contemporary vocational rehabilitation*. New York: New York University Press, 1976.

Soskin, R. M. The least restrictive alternative: In principle and in application. *Amicus*, 1977, *2*, 29–32.

Soskin, R. M. *Handicapped advocacy: A last hurrah? Amicus*, 1980, *5*, 69–71.

Stanhope, L., & Bell, R. Q. Parents and families. In J. M. Kauffman & D. P. Hallahan (Eds.). *Handbook of special education*. Englewood Cliffs, N.J.: Prentice-Hall, 1981.

Stern, B. J. *The family: Past and present*. New York: Appleton-Century, 1938.

Straus, R. Social change and the rehabilitation concept. In M. B. Sussman (Ed.). *Sociology and rehabilitation*. Washington, D.C.: American Sociological Association, 1965.

Summary of existing legislation relating to the handicapped (U.S. Department of Education Publication No. E-80-22014). Washington, D.C.: U. S. Government Printing Office, 1980.

Sussman, M. B. (Ed.). *Sociology and rehabilitation*. Washington, D.C.: American Sociological Association, 1965.

Turnbull, A. P., & Blacher-Dixon, J. Preschool mainstreaming: Impact on parents. In J. J. Gallagher (Ed.). *Ecology of exceptional children*. San Francisco: Jossey-Bass, 1980.

Wegerink, R., Hocutt, A., Posante-Loro, R., & Bristol, M. Parent involvement in early education programs for handicapped children. In J. J. Gallagher (Ed.). *Ecology of exceptional children*. San Francisco: Jossey-Bass, 1980.

Wehman, P., & McLaughlin, P. J. *Program development in special education*. New York: McGraw-Hill, 1981.

Windelband, W. *A history of philosophy* (Vol. 2). New York: Harper & Row, 1958.

Worsfold, V. L. A philosophical justification for children's rights. *Harvard Educational Review*, 1974, Reprint Series No. 9, 29–44.

2

Legal Issues That Affect Parents

BONNIE STRICKLAND

BIOGRAPHICAL SKETCH

Bonnie Strickland, Ph.D., is Clinical Assistant Professor with the Division of Special Education, University of North Carolina at Chapel Hill. She has authored several articles in the area of parental involvement and due process and currently serves as a hearing officer for the state of North Carolina.

THE FAMILY WITH A HANDICAPPED CHILD
All rights of reproduction in any form reserved.

ISBN 0-8089-1561-4
Copyright © 1983 by Grune & Stratton

A S MENTIONED in Chapter 1, P.L. 94-142 (the Education for All Handicapped Children Act) has required unprecedented change in the delivery of public education to handicapped students. It has provided legal assurance that all handicapped students will be educated at public expense, that they will be evaluated in a nondiscriminatory manner, that an individualized education program including needed special education and related services will be written, and that the student will be educated in a setting with nonhandicapped students whenever possible and appropriate (*Federal Register,* 1977). In addition, parents are provided the opportunity to participate in all educational decisions regarding their child. These legal assurances are safeguarded by the right to due process, which enables the parents of the handicapped student to protest unjust discriminatory practices concerning their child.

The principles of P.L. 94-142, while mandating the accountability of public agencies in regard to implementing the provisions of this legislation, also place additional pressure upon parents to initiate steps to take advantage of these guarantees. Parents must interact increasingly with service delivery personnel in order to insure that the intended benefits are realized. Such interaction is not always easy to initiate for parents, and could, in many cases, be described as stressful, tense, and time-consuming (Strickland, 1982a). This chapter examines the impact of P.L. 94-142 on the parent seeking access to the legal entitlements of this legislation. The nature and impact of dispute settlement mechanisms, namely the due process hearing, are discussed and methods of parental support considered.

THE IMPACT OF P.L. 94-142 ON THE PARENTS OF HANDICAPPED CHILDREN

Degree of Impact on Parents

In the midst of much ambiguity surrounding P.L. 94-142, there is little doubt of the clear intention that parents should be involved in decisions made concerning their child. P.L. 94-142 sets the minimal criteria for the acceptable involvement of parents by establishing for public agencies requirements related to notification, consent, and participation of parents in decision-making. However, P.L. 94-142 specifies only what public agencies, specifically public schools, must do. There are no corresponding mandates governing the reciprocal action of parents. Thus parental response to the mandates of this legislation and the degree to which they are affected by its provisions may vary greatly.

Most parents appear to be quite satisfied with the services being provided their handicapped children (Barbacovi, 1977). Hutchinson (1978) found that parents were satisfied both before and after legislative mandates to serve handicapped school children appropriately. Over 70 percent of these parents reported that school personnel made them feel like an important part of their child's education and listened to their concerns. Parents also reported that the schools provided much of the information they required regarding the legal provisions of state legislation (Hutchinson, 1978). For the majority of these parents the impact of P.L. 94-142 has been positive and appears to have enhanced an already positive working relationship with the service provider, primarily the public school.

Other parents may be minimally, if at all, involved in negotiating and monitoring the services their children receive. This is often true of poor and minority families, primarily as a result of inaccessability to the educational system (U.S. Dept. HEW, 1979). Budoff (1979) has noted that the way in which these parents interact with the system is quite different than that of the middle-class parent. According to Budoff, low-income persons are usually less well educated, may have language problems, and probably have different ways of conceiving the problems of their child than service delivery personnel. Thus it is unlikely that these parents would interact with or press the schools for the most appropriate services, unless provided with considerable outside support (Budoff, 1979). These parents, in all probability, are unfamiliar with the potential benefits of P.L. 94-142 and recognize minimal if any effect that might be attributed specifically to this law.

Still other parents may simply choose not to become involved. They may be dissatisfied with the educational services but unwilling to tackle the educational procedures that are necessary to voice their concerns. Thus they, by choice, are minimally affected by the provisions of P.L. 94-142, except as they are positively or negatively affected by the unilateral decisions made and implemented by the public school in regard to their child.

Finally, some parents, dissatisfied with the services provided their child, negotiate one hurdle after another in almost compulsive pursuit of the entitlements of P.L. 94-142. Indeed, it is likely that in some respects educational matters were a great deal simpler for these parents before the advent of specific educational rights and detailed procedures for exercising those rights. These parents have often felt both the positive and negative impacts of P.L. 94-142. They have elected to obtain the services to which they feel they are legally entitled through involvement in the educational system. While high levels of parental involvement may prove to be an effective means of achieving appropriate educational services, such involvement often takes its toll on these parents. New laws have precipitated new knowledge, which in turn has necessitated additional parental skill and responsibility in obtaining their legislative entitlements.

Increased Skills Required

For those parents who choose to take full advantage of their rights, varied and often unfamiliar skills are required. These include skills related to knowledge of the provisions of P.L. 94-142, negotiation with service providers, and monitoring of educational services.

Knowledge

The guarantees of P.L. 94-142 and related legislation may be little more than unfulfilled promises if parents of handicapped children are not familiar with them. Many parents either do not know or do not understand the educational entitlements contained in P.L. 94-142 (Budoff, 1979; Hutchinson, 1978; U.S. Dept. HEW, 1979). Often parents must go to great lengths to obtain information regarding the services to which their handicapped child is entitled. Research to date indicates that communication systems provided by public schools have not fully achieved their desired effect (Budoff, 1979). Parents report understanding little regarding their rights other than the fact that they may have a hearing if they disagree with the school's proposed action (Hutchinson, 1978; Mitchell, 1976; Wallington, 1979; Yoshida, 1979).

Parents must often discover sources of information for themselves. These sources are often parent groups, private service agencies, and attorneys (Strickland, 1982b). Thus, obtaining the necessary knowledge to exercise their legal rights can be a time-consuming and often frustrating experience for parents of handicapped children.

Another related problem that parents encounter at this point is the ambiguity that surrounds the specifications of P.L. 94-142. The information parents obtain may vary with its source. This may be because the already ambiguous regulations of P.L. 94-142 are open to many interpretations (Turnbull, Turnbull, & Strickland, 1979). For example, because the parameters of "appropriate education" are not specifically defined (i.e., what level of service is appropriate for a *particular* child), parents may find themselves dealing with several different versions of what their child is actually entitled to. Such differences in perspective are apparent when parents consider a private school program appropriate whereas the local public school considers its own "less restrictive" environment appropriate. Public schools generally consider any placement decision in terms of the concept of the least restrictive educational setting. That is, it is preferred that children be placed in or as close to the regular classroom as possible for as great a period of time as possible. As a result, in the presence of two possibly appropriate placements, the school will choose the one closest to the regular classroom. Parents, on the other hand, are often more concerned with intensity and specialization of services. Thus, for them, *appropriate* is often defined in those terms. Public school programs often consist only of part-time special instruction; yet parents may perceive a private full-time program to be appropriate. This controversy continues to cause friction between public schools and parents and is a source of frustration, especially for parents who feel that despite their legal entitlements and their own strenuous efforts they have been duped by the school system. This ambiguity at the knowledge level is often the source of frustrations at other levels of participation as parents attempt to apply the knowledge they have acquired (Turnbull, et al., 1979).

Negotiation

P.L. 94-142 has not only sanctioned parent participation in decision making but has specified when and how parents are to be involved. In addition to the minimal rights to be notified of and to approve services or changes in the program provided, parents are to be involved in educational meetings concerning their child (*Federal Register,* 1977). While many parents welcome the opportunity to have a voice in the education of their handicapped child, active participation can (1) be difficult to achieve, (2) require a great deal of time, and (3) be a difficult and emotionally stressful experience (Mitchell, 1976; Strickland, 1982b).

Despite the desire to participate, parental involvement may be limited to mere attendance at educational meetings with little substantive input in decision making (Goldstein, Strickland, Turnbull, & Curry, 1980). One reason for this may be that parents lack strategies for negotiating with professional service providers. They are often unfamiliar with the established procedures used in the system, the educational terminology, and the application of the law to the level of services to be provided.

One of the most frequently occurring negotiation problems concerns the provision of related services—those services that are necessary in order for the child to benefit from special education. Examples of such services include counseling, speech therapy, physical therapy, and transportation. In order to insure the provision of these services parents must negotiate the amount of service needed, the schedule for receiving the service, the identity of the service provider (sometimes other than the public school), and the duration of the service. Beyond participation in educational meetings, parents who initiate further action on their own must negotiate access to educational records, responsibility for independent evaluations, and requests for due process hearings, to mention a few. Considering the scarcity of programs to train parents for active involvement in educational decision making (NEA,1978; Strickland, 1982b), it is not surprising that parents infrequently venture beyond the planning stage and that many parents, even at this level, continue to feel removed from the decision making process (Yoshida, Fenton, Kaufman, & Maxwell, 1978).

Active negotiation also takes considerably more time than simply attending planning meetings. Thus parents who possess strategies for negotiation invest a substantial amount of time negotiating educational services. Some parents report initiating contact with service delivery personnel at least once or twice monthly to discuss the provision of educational services. These contacts are in addition to regular communication with the service provider (Strickland, 1982b). For parents with families and responsibilities other than the handicapped child, this investment of time over a number of years is substantial.

In addition to the lack of negotiation strategies and the time required for active participation, some parents report that when they do attempt to play an active part in planning, their negotiations with service delivery personnel are not positive. They report being made to feel as though they are not qualified to help in developing an educational plan (Budoff, 1975; Yoshida et al., 1978). Parents who later become involved in due process hearings have often reported experiencing stress related to planning meetings (Mitchell, 1976; Strickland, 1982b). In some instances they have reported sensing intentional noncompliance on the part of the school, withholding of information altogether, difficulty in scheduling meetings, low levels of trust, and patterns of unresponsive, condescending, misleading, or dishonest communication (Mitchell, 1976). As all of these parents were subsequently involved in a due process hearing, they represent only a specific subpopulation of parents with similar experiences and are not representative of parent–school relationships in general. Nonetheless, for the small number of parents who become so involved the effects may be devastating.

Inability to negotiate over extended periods of time may result in lack of confidence between parents and service providers (Yoshida, 1979). Such confidence is not easily restored by conciliatory conferences or due process hearings (Mitchell, 1976; Yoshida, 1979). After years of attempting to negotiate with service providers, parents may simply withdraw their children from school rather than continue to work within a system that is perceived to be unresponsive.

Monitoring

Acquiring adequate knowledge of one's rights and effectively negotiating their appropriate application obviously requires a great deal of parental time and energy. These activities, however, are not always sufficient for insuring an appropriate education for handicapped children and educational peace of mind for their parents. Because they are heavily invested in the success of the educational program, parents usually maintain active interest in program implementation once the initial planning phase has been completed. Even when knowledge acquisition and negotiations in program planning have been tedious and frustrating for the parent, successful implementation of the subsequent educational program can result in positive feelings regarding the benefits of P.L. 94-142. Conversely, continued failure to implement an agreed upon program may negate positive relationships that may have been established between parents and schools during planning meetings and may lead to increasing mistrust between the parties most vitally involved in the education of the handicapped child, namely the parent and the school.

P.L. 94-142 requires that each state educational agency develop monitoring procedures to insure that appropriate implementation occurs (*Federal Register,* 1977). This requirement suggests the use of parents as members of monitoring teams. Nevertheless, although parents are legally permitted to participate in organized monitoring activities, their solicited and active involvement has been minimal thus far (U.S. Dept. of Education, 1980). This may be due to many factors, including preconceived notions regarding the limitations of parental involvement and the lack of parental strategies for dispelling these notions.

Service delivery personnel in many cases perceive the role of the parent in educational planning to be limited to tasks such as information gathering, rather than curriculum judging and decision making (Yoshida et al., 1978). Thus it is unlikely that schools have actively solicited parental input in monitoring activities or provided training for parents to develop their skills in regard to this process. In addition, the monitoring function of schools in general is not sufficiently developed to encompass measurement of the substantive compliance of this legislation. Even at the procedural level many states have had difficulty in fully complying with monitoring requirements (U.S. Dept. of Education, 1980). Since it is often the monitoring aspect of parental involvement that ultimately determines the level and quality of the impact of P.L. 94-142 on its consumers, it is unfortunate that this dimension of P.L. 94-142 has been limited primarily to procedural compliance rather than to substantive compliance, which includes representation by the population it is intended to serve.

Parents lack strategies for necessary monitoring. Skills associated with analyzing evaluation materials used to document progress and methods for documenting program effectiveness are not generally available to parents. Furthermore, the relationship between the written IEP and actual classroom practice is difficult to determine. That they may lack encouragement and specific strategies does not, however, mean that parents will not use what knowledge they have as a basis for program evaluation. It is reasonable to assume that parents will indeed employ a monitoring strategy of their own choosing, namely that based on the amount of achievement they perceive occurring. When not included in a systematic and informative monitoring plan, parents have no alternative than to rely on the informal information they acquire. When relying only on information provided by report cards or yearly reviews it is likely that, unless the child is achieving, their view of the success of the prescribed program will be negative.

While most parents are quite satisfied with the services provided their handicapped children, some parents, specifically those who consider requesting the due process hearing, report years of frustration due to inappropriate implementation of programs (Mitchell, 1976; Strickland, 1982b). Some of these parents express feelings of frustration that the IEP promises everything but delivers nothing. That is, the IEP itself may be appropriately written; but, in effect, its implementation either is not achieved or does not occur as agreed. Some common implementation problems that parents encounter in their efforts to monitor include failures to (1) provide the supplementary aids and materials necessary to achieve success in an agreed-upon placement; (2) provide agreed-upon related services such as physical and occupational therapy; (3) teach according to the specific goals and objectives developed for the child; and (4) coordinate and communicate with parents and other professionals (Strickland, 1982b). Even when obvious problems exist it appears that, in many cases, once the IEP has been written there is seldom another conference for the purpose of revising it until the legally required annual review and revision occurs (Hutchinson, 1978). While such a review schedule is sufficient when a program is progressing as planned, failure to acknowledge the need for more frequent review and perhaps modification can result in an ineffective educational program and thus cause parents to lose confidence in the ability or the sincerity of the school to provide an appropriate program.

Seldom can one element of P.L. 94-142 implementation be identified as explaining the impact of this legislation on parents. Positive or negative impact is heavily dependent on the cumulative success parents have in dealing with schools at each of the levels of knowledge acquisition, negotiation, program implementation, and review. This is to say that the parent who has been most negatively affected has, in most cases, experienced not one but a series of negatively perceived incidents over a period of time. On the other hand, parents who have been most positively affected have had a primarily successful cumulative experience in obtaining the benefits they feel are appropriate for their handicapped child.

The following section considers a very specific aspect of the provisions of P.L. 94-142—the due process hearing. After brief identification of the legislated provisions for the hearing, the nature and impact of this experience on the parents who participate is discussed.

PARENTS AND THE DUE PROCESS HEARING

The Due Process Hearing Provisions

The due process mechanism established by P.L. 94-142 is primarily and most importantly a mechanism for insuring that handicapped children receive an appropriate education. When parents and public school representatives cannot agree, P.L. 94-142 essentially provides for an informed third party to decide what does or does not constitute appropriate education and services for a particular child.

The parent or a public educational agency may initiate a hearing whenever the public agency proposes or refuses to initiate or change the identification, evaluation, or educational placement of the child or the provision of a free appropriate public education (*Federal Register,* 1977). Thus the hearing is the central mechanism within the regulations for protecting the educational rights of handicapped children and their parents.

The regulations governing the due process hearing are minimally specified by law, being limited to a description of the (1) qualifications of the hearing officer, (2) rights of each party in regard to the hearing, and (3) procedures for appeal and review of decisions rendered. The due process hearing may therefore be an informal meeting or a formal procedure similar to courtroom proceedings. In addition, the procedures governing the due process hearing differ from state to state in regard to whether the hearing is to be conducted by the local school system or by the state educational agency.

The qualifications of the person or persons conducting the hearing also vary from state to state. In some states only attorneys preside at due process hearings, whereas in other states any individual meeting the criteria of impartiality may conduct a hearing. The regulations of P.L. 94-142 regarding the qualifications of hearing officers specify that a hearing cannot be conducted by anyone who

1. Is employed by an agency involved in the education or care of the child, or
2. Has a conflicting personal or professional interest that would interfere with his or her objectivity.

Since the criteria for selection of hearing officers are vague, and because it is this individual who will make the decision subsequent to a due process hearing, parents and advocates should make certain that the hearing officer selected meets the minimum criteria of impartiality.

P.L. 94-142 guarantees that any party participating in a due process hearing may

1. Be accompanied and advised by counsel and by individuals with special knowledge or training with respect to the problems of handicapped children,
2. Present evidence and confront, cross-examine, and compel the attendance of witnesses,
3. Prohibit the introduction of any evidence at the hearing that has not been disclosed to that party at least five days before the hearing,
4. Obtain a written or electronic verbatim record of the hearing, and
5. Obtain written findings of facts and decisions (*Federal Register,* 1977, p. 42495).

In addition, parents involved in a due process hearing must be given the right to have their child present, to have the hearing open to the public, and to have the hearing conducted at a time convenient to the parents and child involved.

During the period before a final decision is reached the child must remain in his or her present setting, unless the parents and the public agency agree otherwise. If the complaint involves initial admission to public school, the child, with the consent of the parent, must be placed in the school program until after the hearing proceedings are concluded. This period includes the time during which a decision is being appealed or civil action is being taken.

In order to insure that the rights of the child are protected, P.L. 94-142 provides for the appointment of a surrogate parent in cases when the child's parent cannot be identified, when the parents cannot be located, or when the child is a ward of the state (*Federal Register,* 1977). In selecting the surrogate parent, the public agency must assure that the individual selected has no interest that conflicts with the interest of the child and will be able to represent the child adequately in matters relating to the provision of an appropriate education.

The decision of the hearing officer must be mailed to each of the parties no later than 45 days after receipt of a request for a hearing. The hearing officer can, however, grant specific extensions of time beyond the 45-day limit at the request of either party. If either party is dissatisfied with the decision, a request for review may be made to the state educational agency. If an appeal is not made or civil action is not taken, the decision of the hearing officer is final.

Nature of the Due Process Hearing

Parents, educators, and others concerned with the due process procedures as they currently exist express fear that the due process hearing has, in some ways, compounded existing problems. Preliminary research regarding the due process hearing indicates that the due process hearing (1) is adversarial in nature (Budoff, 1976; NASDSE, 1978; Yoshida, 1979), (2) is accessible primarily to parents with money and education (NASDSE, 1978; Strickland, 1982b), and (3) is an expensive endeavor for both parents and school systems (Budoff, 1976; NASDSE, 1978).

Adversarial Nature of Hearings

Conflict between the parent and the school may actually originate years before the event of the due process hearing (Yoshida, 1979; Mitchell, 1976). The hearing may be a result of an already existing disagreement between the parent and the school. Thus the due process hearing may be reflective of that prior conflict rather than responsible for creating it. Nonetheless, research indicates that the hearing is not viewed as an agreeable procedure by the parents involved (Budoff, 1976; Strickland, 1982b; Yoshida, 1979). Issues occurring during the hearing that may influence parent perceptions of the hearing appear to include the formality and length of the hearing, the issue and number of participants involved, the presence of an attorney, and the background of the hearing officer.

The perceived formality of the hearing may contribute to its adversarial nature. Most school systems report formal due process hearings (Budoff, 1979; U.S. Dept. HEW, 1979). Perhaps this is because the regulations monitoring the due process hearing require a hearing officer who acts as a judge and both parties have the right to be represented by counsel, to present evidence, and confront, cross-examine, and compel the attendance of witnesses (*Federal Register,* 1977). In a study of hearings in Pennsylvania after the precedent-setting PARC (*Pennsylvania Association for Retarded Children* v. *the Commonwealth of Pennsylvania*) decree, Mitchell (1975) indicated that the requirements for hearings made it virtually impossible for them to remain informal. And yet, most parents and professionals seem to prefer an informal hearing, perhaps because the looser structure holds promise of mutually equitable means of problem solving and decision making (Bersoff, 1979; Budoff, Mitchell, & Kotin, 1976; Buss, Kirp, & Kuriloff, 1975; Kotin & Eager, 1977; NASDSE, 1978; U.S. Dept. HEW, 1979). The alternative that many states have preferred is mediation procedures that, while not designed to delay the due process hearing, are considered by many to be more conducive to conflict resolution. The process of mediation, however, often perceived as less formal and thus often preferred, has been noted by Yoshida (1979) to be equally as adversarial, formal, and costly as the due process hearing.

Parents generally come to the due process hearing because there appears to be no other way to obtain satisfaction concerning their child's education (Mitchell, 1976). They come believing that the hearing is indeed an impartial means of settling disputes. As noted, they are frequently apprehensive and unfamiliar with the procedures to be used in the hearing (Mitchell, 1975; Yoshida, 1979). Likewise, they are relatively unfamiliar with the legal intricacies that are often involved. The school system representative, on the other hand, is usually knowledgeable regarding legal parameters and has the added leverage of experience in educational hearings or mediation. It appears that the school may be in a better position to present its case and win, and that parents may find themselves overwhelmed and hesitant to pursue the issue to a satisfying conclusion.

Both parents and schools indicate that one of the major problems with due process hearings is the time involved (Budoff, 1976; Lay, 1977). The average length of due process hearings as reported by NASDSE (1978) is from six to eight hours, during which six to ten people testify. While this does not appear to be an unreasonable amount of time, it must be remembered that the hearing is the climax of perhaps months of preparation and therefore can be a psychologically stressful occasion representative of only a small portion of the time and energy actually invested. Furthermore, the hearing procedure may extend beyond the initial hearing if a review of the original decision is requested. Rather than considering the hearing in terms of a one-day affair, then, it is probably more accurate to consider the procedure in terms of months.

It appears that most due process hearings center around the issue of appropriate placement, with parents requesting more specialized educational services than the school considers adequate or appropriate (Lay, 1977; Mitchell, 1976; NASDSE, 1978; Yoshida, 1979). This issue itself engenders adversarial relationships between the parents and the school as a result of the different perceptions of the intent of P.L. 94-142 regarding the term appropriate. The parents may feel that appropriate means the best possible educational program to meet the needs of their child, whereas the school interprets appropriate to mean that it must provide an adequate program to meet those needs (Jacobs, 1979; Shrybman & Matsoukas, 1978). As yet there has been no decisive definition provided pertaining to the educational significance of the word appropriate (NASDSE, 1978). The lack of procedural guidelines and definitions in regard to the issues brought to the due process hearing may serve to irritate relations between the parents and the school further.

There is some indication that numerous participants for one party with few witnesses for the other party may negatively influence the perceptions of the under-represented party in regard to the other (Mitchell, 1976). In one study (Mitchell, 1976) parents were reported as referring to the hearing as "a lonely citizen fighting a lonely battle. The school brings in all its big guns. . . . "

Parents also seem to view the school as having the resources to bring in "as many witnesses as they want" (Mitchell, 1976; Silberberg, 1979). Thus, if indeed the school is represented by many witnesses, the perception of the parents may be reinforced. In reporting results of data collected in Massachusetts, NASDSE (1978) indicated that public schools were generally represented by from six to eight people, including the director of special education, four or five key staff, and one or two teachers. The only reference to the number of representatives for the parents was an indication that, in private school issues, parents usually brought several representatives from the private school. Aside from the probability that more representatives increases the length of the hearing, the presence of a number of representatives may be intimidating to either side and, in the case of parents, may reinforce the concept of the school as a bureaucracy, unresponsive to the educational needs of their children.

The presence of advocates or attorneys on behalf of either the parent or the school system may have an effect on the adversarial nature of the due process hearing. According to Jacobs (1979), there is no question that attorneys have frequently played the role of escalator of the adversarial level between parents and school systems. Parents are often encouraged by attorneys to engage legal service at a very early point in a disagreement. Jacobs (1979) notes that it is this encouragement by attorneys of an adversarial position on the part of parents that most educators resent.

Parents report that their reasons for retaining attorneys for the due process hearing center around the need to depend on such a person for advice and emotional support. Parents also report feeling that they lack the skills needed to effectively use their procedural safeguards, need protection from what is perceived to be heavy-handed and arbitrary action by the school, and lack knowledge about school practices concerning diagnosis and programing (Mitchell, 1976; Yoshida, 1979). According to Silberberg (1979), an attorney for the National Center for Law and the Handicapped, parents are at a disadvantage, despite their legal rights, because they are facing the school system, which has time, money, resources, and determination on its side.

Representation by attorneys is not uncommon according to studies completed in Massachusetts and Connecticut. In Massachusetts, half the parents and half the schools used attorneys (NASDSE, 1978). In a study conducted in Connecticut (Yoshida, 1979), three-fourths of the parents were represented by attorneys at mediation conferences or hearings. The remaining parents either were represented by advocates or expressed a need for such support. The results of this study indicated that parents may be incapable of representing their children at due process hearings or mediations because of the complex nature of the hearing. Thus, while the presence of an attorney may increase the adversarial nature of the relationship between parents and schools, the absence of representation may place parents at a considerable disadvantage.

Parents are reported to react negatively to the legal procedures and language during the hearing. They report resenting being cross-examined under oath by an attorney. Because of the highly legalistic courtroom procedures to which most attorneys are accustomed, it appears likely that highly legal procedures will dominate the due process hearing when attorneys are present. If these procedures create an adversarial hearing model, then according to Budoff (1979) patterns of negative relationships between parents and schools may be created that may adversely affect the long-term development of the handicapped child.

Finally, the hearing officer may exert considerable influence on the climate of the hearing and its impact on parents. Although there are many pertinent issues surrounding the qualifications of hearing officers (Turnbull et al., 1979) mention will be made here of two rather basic considerations.

First, hearing officers, in many instances, are selected and paid by the local school system or by the state educational agency. Parents who report feeling that the hearing officer was partial to the school often cite selection and payment criteria as their reasons for such feelings (Strickland, 1982b). Even if the officer's decision is, in fact, impartial, parents may come to feel that although the due process hearing is intended to provide a mechanism for the parent formally to take issue with school decisions or procedures, it may in reality only serve formally to sanction actions taken by the schools. Parents who have expended a great deal of money come to feel that the system is "rigged" (Budoff, 1976) and may develop feelings of frustration and futility toward the procedure as well as hostility toward a system that they perceive to have provided an illusion rather than the reality of fairness.

Second, the way in which the hearing officer conducts the hearing may make the occasion more or less stressful for the parent. In some instances it appears that parental apprehension dissipates during the hearing as a result of the hearing officer making the participants feel at ease (Mitchell, 1976). In other situations, however, the hearing procedure appears to contribute to adversarial feelings. Lack of organization in the procedure, inability to control the hearing, and lack of knowledge on the part of the hearing officer are, in many cases, associated with reported parental stress during the hearing (Mitchell, 1976; Strickland, 1982b).

Thus, rather than being a mechanism for resolving the issue at hand, the hearing may serve only to intensify differences between the parent and the school.

Limited Accessibility

According to the report of a due process criteria study panel commissioned by the Department of Health, Education and Welfare (1979), now the Office of Education, the due process system is accessible primarily to parents with money. The panel reports an infrequency of due process hearings for poor and minority families, primarily as a result of lack of access to the system.

Budoff (1979) noted that, in addition to lacking the resources with which to understand the complexities of P.L. 94-142, low income and minority parents may have different ways of conceiving their child's problem than school personnel or perhaps parents of middle and upper incomes. They may, for example, consider good school performance irrelevant in terms of future occupations that do not necessarily require such performance.

It is unlikely, according to Budoff, that these parents would consider a due process hearing unless given considerable outside support. When poor and minority parents do participate in due process hearings they often do so with representation by a third party such as advocacy councils, parent coalitions, or other organizations and agencies involved in the issue (Strickland, 1982b). As will be discussed later, agencies representing clients in this capacity must often determine whether they are in fact representing the best interest of the parent and the family rather than using their situation to promote a controversial issue.

Cost of the Hearing

There is unanimous agreement in the literature regarding the high cost of the due process hearing. Such cost for the parent may include attorney's fees, reproduction of materials, independent evaluations, telephone calls, time off from work, and perhaps payment of witnesses (Mitchell, 1976). Estimates of costs to parents as reported by NASDSE (1978) were as high as $4000, the average cost of a lawyer for a hearing being $800 to $1000. Yoshida (1979) reports that parents engaged attorneys at a cost ranging from $300 to $1500.

Many parents cannot afford the cost involved in preparing a case against the school system and yet are not familiar enough with their rights and the due process procedures to prepare the case themselves. Parents report that retaining private counsel placed a heavy financial burden on them (Budoff, 1976; Mitchell, 1976; Yoshida, 1979). Human costs are also a factor to be considered and may do more to enhance or destroy the parents' positive perception related to the hearing than any other variable. Such costs may occur during but outside of the proceedings of the hearing: in a study reported by Budoff (1976) 20 percent of parents involved in a due process hearing indicated that their child's attitude toward school deteriorated during the process.

In addition it appears that feelings of conflict between the home and the school are intensified during the hearing (Mitchell, 1976; Yoshida, 1979). Some parents report that they would not go through the process again under any circumstances (NASDSE, 1978). It should be remembered that many parents may be unable to foresee the possible cost of the due process hearing in reference to its effect on themselves and their family. Dealing with the unexpected stress of the hearing procedures in addition to normal daily routines may become quite difficult for the parent. Nonetheless, once involved in the procedure they are likely to see it through. The cost both financial and otherwise becomes more apparent, however, when parents, upon losing an initial decision, fail to pursue the matter further through the review process or the courts. At this point some parents either accept an undesirable decision or take their child out of the school system altogether (Strickland, 1982b).

Despite dismal reports on the due process hearing itself, the impact of the hearing is not always negative. The ultimate impact of the due process hearing is probably most conclusively determined by whether the parent is satisfied with the decision of the hearing officer and whether that decision is appropriately implemented. For example, parents who have had years of unsatisfying experience with day-to-day negotiations may find a long-term solution in the due process hearing. A hearing may result in the provision of private educational services for a handicapped child or may require the school to provide a long-needed program. In such a case the parents may report that the impact was favorable even though the hearing was adversarial. Likewise, a host of other outcomes are possible, some negative, some positive. Ultimately, for parents, the due process hearing provides a new starting point, a basis for future educational services. Parents must still, as before the hearing, participate, negotiate, and monitor the services provided to their child and question their appropriateness again if necessary.

Focusing on P.L. 94-142 and the impact of the due process hearing represents only one aspect of a multitude of variables that uniquely affect the parents of handicapped children. Because school plays a major role in the growth and development of the handicapped child, it is not surprising that one of the most obvious ways in which parents advocate for their handicapped child is through the provisions of educational legislation such as P.L. 94-142. But, as noted earlier in this chapter, parents vary greatly in the degree in which they take advantage of and are affected by these provisions. Efforts to provide supportive services to these parents must consider their different needs and concerns. The final section of this chapter considers various levels of support that might be considered in working with parents of handicapped children.

ASPECTS OF PARENTAL SUPPORT

When disagreement between parents and schools extends over a period of time, effective working relationships may be impaired. Discrepancies between parents and schools may lose all positive value when they fail to be constructively focused. Thus, a support system apart from the emotional tensions that may pervade the parent–school relationship is sometimes necessary. At such times the assistance of individuals and agencies outside the public school may be necessary to support the efforts of parents on behalf of their handicapped child.

It should be recognized and emphasized that the support needs of families are not always of the same kind or degree. Support for parents may range from simply being a good listener at a crucial time to accompanying a parent of a handicapped child to meetings to discuss special education services to be provided. Different types of problems, children, and families require varying types of support. Reciprocally, different agencies are suited to providing varying types of support.

In general, supportive efforts should provide parents with the means to advocate for themselves whenever possible, since it is primarily the parent and the family who "own" the situation and must maintain a continuing relationship with the school. Taking over an educational problem for the parent may result in over-reliance on the advocacy structure or encourage the parent to assume a peripheral posture, thus preventing the parent from gaining the necessary skills to maintain a central role in negotiating with the school. In addition, the method and level of support established by someone other than the parent may not be the type most suitable for that parent to maintain on a continuing basis. It must be remembered that the presence of a handicapped child is a way of life with the family of that child and that the level of support must be one that is consistent with the life of the family. Thus, when both parents in a family work full-time and there are other children in the family, the type of support needed may be different than for couples where only one parent works and there are no other children in the family.

Types of support that might be provided include provision of information, development of negotiation strategies, attendance at educational meetings, representing parents at school meetings or due process hearings, and the provision of psychological intervention through appropriate therapeutic strategies (see Chapter 10 and 11). The appendix to this chapter provides suggestions for assisting parents in negotiating and exercising their rights in regard to the provisions of P.L. 94-142.

Provision of Information

In many instances parents need various types of information in order to work with the school system. For example, many parents of handicapped children are not familiar with federal or state regulations that govern the provision of education to their children. They may need assistance in obtaining a copy of state or federal regulations either by requesting a xerox copy from the school system or by purchasing copies from the state department of public instruction. They may also need information regarding the nature of their child's handicap or professional counseling in establishing realistic expectations for their child. Counseling might further assist parents in locating other sources of support, such as the Association for Retarded Citizens and the Association for Children with Learning Disabilities. Parents and advocates for handicapped children have often found that alignment with other parents provides a welcome and effective support system. However, parental support groups are not available in every locality, and even where they do exist parents often find it difficult to attend scheduled meetings of the group. In such instances, the availability of an individual support system may assist parents in obtaining necessary information related to the handicapped child in the family.

Helping parents to secure needed information may provide all that is necessary for them to work effectively with the school without the involvement of additional support personnel. In many cases, however, parents need assistance in developing strategies for negotiation.

Development of Strategies

Because some parents may be unaccustomed to interacting with school personnel on educational issues, it may be necessary to go beyond the provision or location of information. Helping parents to develop strategies for using the information they have acquired in their dealings with the school may provide the focus of support efforts. Strategies for how to best approach the school, through which administrative channels, and whether in individual or group conferences may differ depending on the issue and the individual preferences of the parents. It is important for parents to become familiar with various appropriate means of interacting in order to make certain that their concerns are heard and considered while at the same time they maintain a cooperative working relationship with the school. If strategy development is determined to be the primary need of the parent, suggestions as to effective means of communication with the school might be provided. Again, the strategy employed depends on the identified needs of the parent. If, for example, the parents were considering a due process hearing, the strategy of interaction with the school system might, of necessity, be more legally oriented, thus requiring referral to free or low-cost legal aid agencies. The primary benefit of assisting parents in developing effective means of interacting with school personnel is that these methods may set a positive tone for continual cooperation with the school and can enhance the parents' confidence in their ability to negotiate educational issues.

Attending Educational Meetings

Yet another level of support requires the presence of an advocate at meetings held to discuss the education of a handicapped child. Even with appropriate information and strategies for working with school personnel, many parents feel the need for active support when meeting with school representatives on potentially controversial issues. In such cases a counselor-advocate may attend meetings with the parent to provide support, actively advocate during the meeting, mediate differences between the parent and the school, or provide information on behalf of the parent.

If a third party is to attend educational meetings it is necessary that a decision be made before the meeting to clarify the role this person will assume. Both parents and their advocates need to know what to expect from each other in such a meeting. Careful planning must occur to insure that the advocate assumes a role that supports, rather than overwhelms, that of the parent. If, at the meeting, the advocate is perceived as monopolizing the conversation, speaking unnecessarily for the parent, or assuming an accusing posture, relations between the parent and the school may suffer, an outcome directly opposed to the concept of advocacy.

The school should be notified if an advocate will accompany the parents to an educational meeting. The role of this individual should also be clarified to the school.

Representing Parents at Meetings or Hearings

A final level of support is apparent when an individual assumes the full responsibility for representing the parents. In this role the advocate becomes the central figure in promoting the rights of the parents and the handicapped child. This arrangement is most often found in due process hearings (discussed previously in this chapter) and less often in meetings with the school.

This type of arrangement requires that the advocate have highly developed skills in the area in which he is representing the parent. Often these skills are of a legal nature, since parents sometimes feel inadequate to advocate for themselves on legal matters involving the school and may feel that the presence of an advocate with legal training provides them with leverage that would otherwise be lacking. At this level the concept of advocacy might be broadened to include volunteer legal representation by attorneys or paralegals.

When no parent can be identified for a handicapped child, when parents cannot be located after reasonable efforts, or when the child is a ward of the state, a surrogate parent may be appointed to represent the parent and the educational interest of the child. Service as surrogate parent can be considered a form of advocacy at this level of representation.

Each of the preceding forms of advocacy may be appropriate for the same parents at different or coinciding points in the handicapped child's educational career. It should again be emphasized that, in order to be most effective, advocacy efforts should be a means of supporting parents and schools in their positive interaction with one another. Even after educational problems have been resolved and the immediate need for strong advocacy has diminished, parents often must continue to work within the structure of the school system. Promoting a positive climate for continuing cooperation is therefore essential. Effective advocacy and support services can provide a crucial element in enabling parents and schools to work together within a framework of better understanding.

SUMMARY

This chapter attempts to characterize the increasing responsibilities and support needs of parents of handicapped children in regard to the educational entitlements of P.L. 94-142. Specific consideration is given to discussion of the nature of the due process hearing and its impact on parents. While providing an administrative mechanism for dispute settlement, the due process hearing has also produced a laboratory for exploring the significant parameters of appropriate education. The role of parents has evolved to one requiring sophisticated skills for negotiating within the administrative arena. Providing parents with strategies to deal effectively with the specific and cumulative problems that may arise during a child's educational experience is considered an essential element in the network of resources necessary to fulfill the promise of P.L. 94-142 for parents and their handicapped children.

REFERENCES

Barbacovi, D. R. A study of parent advisory committee members' experiences with due process and their attitudes toward the educational planning and placement committee meeting (Doctoral dissertation, Michigan State University, 1977). *Dissertation Abstracts International, 1977, 38,* 1325A.

Bersoff, D. N. Procedural safeguards. In Department of Health, Education, and Welfare, Office of Education, *Due process: Developing criteria for the evaluation of due process procedural safeguards provisions.* Philadelphia: Research for Better Schools, Inc., 1979.

Budoff, M. Engendering change in special education practices. *Harvard Educational Review,* 1975, *45,* 507–526.

Budoff, M. Implementing due process safeguards: From the user's point of view. In Department of Health, Education, and Welfare, Office of Education, *Due process: Developing criteria for the evaluation of due process procedural safeguards provisions.* Philadelphia: Research for Better Schools, Inc., 1979.

Budoff, M., Mitchell, S., & Kotin, L. *Procedural due process: Its application to special education and its implications for teacher training.* Cambridge, Mass.: Research Institute for Educational Problems, Inc., 1976.

Buss, W. G., Kirp, D. L., & Kuriloff, P. J. Exploring procedural modes of special classification. In N. Hobbs (Ed.). *Issues in the classification of children* (Vol. 2). San Francisco: Jossey-Bass, 1975.

Federal Register. Washington, D.C.: U.S. Government Printing Office, August 23, 1977.

Goldstein, S., Strickland, B., Turnbull, A. P., & Curry, L. An observational analysis of the IEP conference. *Exceptional Children,* 1980, *46*(4), 278–285.

Hutchinson, D. H. Has Chapter 766 accomplished its goals? The views of parents of children with special needs (Doctoral dissertation, University of Massachusetts, 1978). *Dissertation Abstracts International,* 1978, *39,* 2180A. (University Microfilms No. ISSN 0419-4209)

Jacobs, L. J. Hidden dangers, hidden costs. *Amicus,* 1979, *4*(2), 86–88.

Kotin, L., & Eager, N. B. *Due process in special education: A legal analysis.* Cambridge, Mass.: Research Institute for Educational Problems, Inc., 1977.

Lay, C. A. Due process in special education. (Doctoral dissertation, Boston University, 1977). *Dissertation Abstracts International,* 1977, *37,* 7687A.

Mitchell, S. Preliminary report of findings on the due process hearing model in Pennsylvania (Project on Student Classification and the Law, NIE Project No. NE6-00-192). Unpublished report, University of Pennsylvania, July 1975.

Mitchell, S. *Parental perceptions of their experiences with due process in special education: A preliminary report.* Cambridge, Mass.: Research Institute for Educational Problems, 1976 (ERIC Document Reproduction Service No. Ed. 130 482).

National Association of State Directors of Special Education. *The implementation of due process in Massachusetts.* Washington, D.C.: Author, 1978.

National Education Association. *A study report: Education for all handicapped children: Consensus, conflict and challenge.* Washington, D.C.: National Education Association, 1978.

Shrybman, J., & Matsoukas, G. The principal and the special education hearing. *National Elementary Principal,* 1978, *58*(1), 30–33.

Silberberg, N. G. Schools have home court advantage. *Amicus,* 1979, *4*(2), 89–90.

Strickland, B. Parent participation, school accountability and due process. *Exceptional Education Quarterly,* 1982, *3*(2) 41–49. (a)

Strickland, B. *Perceptions of parents and school representatives regarding their relationship before, during, and after the due process hearing.* Doctoral dissertation, University of North Carolina at Chapel Hill, 1982. (b)

Turnbull, H. R., Turnbull, A. P., & Strickland, B. Procedural due process: The two-edged sword that the untrained should not unsheath. *Journal of Education,* 1979, *161*(3), 40–59.

U.S. Department of Education. *Second annual report to congress on the implementation of P.L. 94-142: The education for all handicapped children act to assure the free appropriate public education for all handicapped children.* Washington, D.C.: U.S. Department of Education, 1980.

U.S. Department of Health, Education and Welfare, Office of Education. *Progress toward a free appropriate public education.* Washington, D.C.: U.S. Government Printing Office, 1979.

Wallington, C. J. The compliance between 1972 and 1977 by the District of Columbia public schools with the special education hearing requirements of the *Mills* decision (Doctoral dissertation, George Washington University, 1979). *Dissertation Abstracts International, 40,* 1412A. (University Microfilms No. ISSN 0419-4209)

Yoshida, R. *Developing assistance linkages for parents of handicapped children.* U.S. Department of Health, Education, and Welfare, Bureau of Education for the Handicapped, 1979.

Yoshida, R., Fenton, K., Kaufman, M. J., & Maxwell, J. P. Parental involvement in the special education pupil planning process: The school's perspective. *Exceptional Children,* 1978, *44,* 531–533.

APPENDIX: REQUIREMENTS OF P.L. 94-142 AND SUGGESTIONS FOR PARENTS AND ADVOCATES

APPENDIX A. Identification, Location, and Evaluation of Handicapped Children

Requirements of School System	Suggestions for Advocates
Locate all handicapped children, regardless of severity of the handicap, within the jurisdiction, including children in private schools and institutions.	If there is no indication that the school system knows of the child, inform the school in writing with a copy to the director of special education of the location, age, and type of handicap of the child.
	Ask for a meeting to discuss the school system's responsibility for the child.
Determine which children are receiving needed special education and related services and which ones are not.	Inform the school of the type of setting in which the child is currently placed and what special education is currently being provided.
	Provide names of contacts in child's current placement (if arfy) that the public school representative may call for information.
Establish a multidisciplinary evaluation team (including someone with knowledge in the area of suspected disability) to evaluate each child who is not receiving an education or is in school but in need of evaluation.	Request the names and positions of those individuals comprising the multidisciplinary evaluation team.
	Determine the suspected area of disability and ascertain who on the committee is knowledgeable in that area.
Fully inform the child's parent of the evaluation procedure, in compliance with the requirements for providing notice.	Check to be sure that all required information is provided.
	Write down and ask all questions regarding the procedure to be followed.
Obtain written consent to conduct a preplacement evaulation.	Read the consent form fully before granting or denying permission for evaluation.
	Remember that consent is voluntary and may be withdrawn at any time.

(continued)

Requirements of School System	Suggestions for Advocates
Evaluate the child in all areas related to the suspected disability.	Make certain that the child is evaluated within a reasonable time after being referred for evaluation.
	If evaluation is not performed, obtain an independent educational evaluation.
Select and administer evaluation materials so that they are not racially or culturally discriminatory.	Review procedures for evaluation as well as test used if child is of a cultural or racial minority. Ask what measures are taken to alleviate such bias.
Establish evaluation procedures that insure, at a minimum, that evaluation materials are (1) administered in the child's native language or other mode of communication, (2) are valid for the purpose for which they are being used, and (3) are administered by trained personnel according to the instructions of the test producer.	Ask school representative (perhaps teacher or psychologist) what steps have been taken to insure that evaluation criteria are met.
	Ask for qualifications of personnel administering the tests.
	Inform school representative if child is to be tested in a language or mode other than oral English.
Insure that no single procedure is used to determine an appropriate educational program for a child. Tests must include those designed to assess specific areas of educational need, not simply those yielding an intelligence quotient.	Obtain a list of tests to be administered and what specifically is measured by each instrument. Insure that these areas are educationally relevant and will be helpful in educational planning.

Requirements of School System	Suggestions for Advocates
Establish an IEP committee for the purpose of developing an IEP for each handicapped child. This committee must consist of the child's teacher, the parents, a representative of the school system, and the child, when appropriate. (For children being evaluated for the first time, a member of the evaluation team or someone else knowledgeable about the child's evaluation is present).	Review IEP notice with parents to insure that required information is included and that all required members are included. If members are listed who are not required, ask school for clarification of their role. Clarify the parent's role as a member of the IEP committee. Insure that the IEP is not already developed by the school before the IEP meeting.
Hold an IEP meeting within 30 days of a determination that the child needs special education and related services.	Insure that deadline is met and that meeting is scheduled at a convenient time and place. Obtain copies of evaluation information and other records for use at the IEP meeting. Request an interpretation of evaluation information if necessary.
Have an IEP in effect before special education and related services are provided.	Assist the parent and school in teaching augmentation placement based on the IEP. Review with parents, if necessary, the option of temporary placement as a part of the evaluation process.
Hold an IEP meeting to review the IEP and revise as often as necessary, but at least annually.	Develop with the parent a regular schedule and method for reviewing the IEP. Determine the school policy on monitoring, reviewing, and revising the IEP. Attend review meetings with the parent.
Insure that an IEP is developed for all handicapped children placed in private schools by the public school and/or receiving special education or related services from a public school.	Work with the school, private agency, and parents in determining a workable method of IEP development and coordinate communication between these parties.

(continued)

Requirements of School System	Suggestions for Advocates
	Discuss with parents and public school means of providing special education and related services to children in private schools or institutions.
Take whatever action is necessary to insure that parents understand the proceedings at the meeting.	Coordinate efforts with school to conduct the IEP meeting in a way conducive to parental understanding and involvement. This is especially necessary for parents with communication difficulties (deaf, blind, or illiterate).
Take steps to insure that one or both of the child's parents are present at the IEP meeting. These include sufficient notice, telephone calls, correspondence, or visits to the home or place of employment.	Assist the school in convincing parents to attend the IEP meeting. Insure that school has exhausted all means of soliciting parental involvement before holding an IEP meeting without them. If the parents cannot attend, facilitate other means of parent participation.
Insure that the IEP includes all required information the school is committed to provide to document education and services.	Review with the parent all components of the IEP to insure compliance with requirements and the understanding and satisfaction of the parents. Point out discrepancies or vague items on the IEP.
Insure that there is not undue delay in implementing IEP once it is finalized.	Facilitate the immediate implementation of the IEP. If delay is necessary, document the reasons and establish the implementation date of the portion of the IEP that is delayed.
Insure that all special education and related services are provided in accordance with the IEP.	Review with the parent which services and the amount of those services are to be provided and how they will be provided. Facilitate the resolution of problems arising from the inability of the school to provide needed services. Explore with the parent and school options outside the public school.

APPENDIX C. Least Restrictive Appropriate Placement

Requirements of School System	Suggestions for Advocates
Insure that the various alternative placements are available to the extent necessary to implement the individualized education program for each handicapped child.	Assist parents in determining a placement preference based on documented needs rather than services available in the school.
	Review placement options within the school system to determine whether an appropriate placement option exists.
	Gather information regarding placement options outside the public school if no appropriate placement is available within the public school.
Carefully consider and document a variety of services in making a placement decision (aptitude and achievement tests, teacher recommendations, physical condition, social and cultural background, and adaptive behavior).	Review with parents (and placement committee) all evidence available for making a placement decision.
	Determine what additional evidence is necessary and make arrangements for obtaining it.
	Assist parents in obtaining an independent educational evaluation if necessary.
Insure that the placement decision is made by a group of people with knowledge about the child, the meaning of evaluation information, and the various placement options.	Review the credentials of those determining placement for the child.
	Suggest additional members or consultants to the group making the placement decision.
	Assist parents in negotiating an acceptable placement decision.
	Assist parents in implementing due process procedures if agreement cannot be reached.
Insure that the handicapped child is placed with nonhandicapped children to the maximum extent appropriate, and that removal of the handicapped child from the regular classroom occurs only when education in the regular class, even with supplemental aids and services, cannot be achieved satisfactorily.	Gather documentation that the placement selected is both least restrictive and most appropriate for the child.
	Determine supplemental aids or adaptation to be made in the child's placement or method of instruction.
	Present alternative placement options if an agreeable placement decision cannot be made.
	Assist parents in implementing due process procedures if agreement cannot be reached.

(continued)

Requirements of School System	Suggestions for Advocates
Make provisions for services such as resource room or itinerant instruction to be provided in conjunction with regular class placement.	Determine and review exactly which supplemental services have been agreed upon by the committee, and monitor periodically.
	Consider the provision of supplemental services in regard to amount of time provided, how often provided, at what time of day, and which other subject is replaced by service.
	Determine method of transportation if it is necessary to change schools to receive services.
Insure that handicapped children participate with nonhandicapped children in nonacademic and extracurricular services and activities.	Make arrangements for placement in art, music, and physical education if nonhandicapped students receive these activities.
	Advocate for inclusion of child in other nonacademic activities such as clubs, athletic teams, and special courses.
Insure that handicapped children participate in the regular physical education program unless a child needs specially designed physical education or is enrolled fulltime in a separate facility.	Insure that the child's schedule includes physical education that is provided on the same basis as that of nonhandicapped children unless otherwise specified in the IEP.
	Insure that, if special physical education is necessary, the public school either provides it or makes arrangements and pays for the program through other private or public facilities.
Insure that, if placement in a public or private residential program is necessary to provide an appropriate education, that program, including nonmedical care and room and board, is at no cost to the parent.	Assist parents in determining what costs they will incur as a result of residential placement.
	Meet with school representatives to determine distinction between medical and nonmedical care.
	Determine what, if any, insurance coverage may help offset the cost to parents. The parents' insurance benefits are not required to be used to cover costs that are the responsibility of the school system.

Requirements of School System	Suggestions for Advocates
Provide notice to parents whenever it proposes or refuses to change or initiate the placement, classification, or evaluation of a handicapped child.	Assist parent in understanding the notice provided, insuring that the notice contains all necessary information.
	Assist parent in identifying pertinent questions regarding the notice.
	Assist parents in understanding their legal rights as presented in the notice.
Obtained informed and written consent from parents whenever a preplacement evaluation is conducted or placement in a special education program is made.	Insure that parent is fully informed regarding the activity proposed before granting or denying permission.
	Help the parent understand the possible consequences of the action proposed by the school and the consequences of denying or granting permission for that action.
Actively encourage parental involvement at the IEP conference by scheduling the meeting at a convenient time and place, using alternative methods of involving parents, documenting the failure to gain parental involvement, and providing a copy of the IEP to the parent upon request.	Determine the preferences of the parents in regard to their child's educational program and at which level they wish to be involved in the development of the IEP.
	Help the parents understand the purpose of the IEP meeting and the subsequent educational plan.
	Attend the IEP meeting with the parent if necessary.
	Assist the parent in preparing for the IEP meeting by writing down items the parent wishes to discuss.
	Encourage the parent to ask questions during the meeting and obtain a copy of the child's IEP.
Provide an opportunity and information for parents to obtain an independent educational evaluation, if necessary.	Obtain from the school or other community agencies names of sources of independent evaluations.
Provide an opportunity for parents to inspect all records of their child.	Encourage parents to inspect all records before an IEP meeting or before a due process hearing and to obtain copies of records for subsequent meetings.

(continued)

Requirements of School System	Suggestions for Advocates
	Assist parents in obtaining reasonable requests for explanations and interpretations of the records.
	Serve as a parent representative to inspect and review records.
Make the local plan for providing services to handicapped children available to the public, and provide an opportunity for public participation in implementing the plan.	Help the parents in locating and obtaining the local education agency plan for the purpose of review.
	Assist parents in reacting to the plan and in making comments to the public agency regarding its implementation.
Make available to parents the opportunity to disagree with educational procedures by way of a due process hearing.	Help the parents become familiar with the mechanisms and issues related to the due process hearing.
	Contact other parents involved in due process hearings to discuss their experiences with the procedure.

APPENDIX E.   The Due Process Hearing

Requirements of School System	Suggestions for Advocates
Conform with regulations for conducting a due process hearing as determined under state statute, state regulation, or written policy of the state educational agency.	Obtain and review with the parent the state regulations for conducting a due process hearing. In some states initial hearings are held at the local level, while in others the hearing is conducted at the state level.
	Assist parent in the proper procedure for requesting and preparing for the hearing.
	Encourage parents and school to opt for mediation if possible.
	Talk with other parents who have been involved in due process hearings.
Inform parents of any free or low-cost legal and other relevant services in the area if the parent requests the information or requests a due process hearing.	Obtain information on low-cost services in the area and assist the parents in locating and engaging these services.
	Help the parents determine the extent of their need for legal or other support services.
	Determine fees and indirect cost for services.
	Assist parents in developing material for presentation at the hearing if legal services are not used.
Keep a list of impartial persons who serve as hearing officers and the qualifications of each.	Request a list of the qualifications of hearing officers serving the school system.
	Review qualifications of the hearing officer who will hear the case.
	Request another hearing officer if it appears that the officer is not fully qualified.
Transmit the findings and decision of the hearing officer to the state advisory panel with all personally identifiable information deleted.	Request from school the person to whom the decision is sent.
	Document points in the hearing officer's decision with which the parents disagree if an appeal is to be requested.

(continued)

Requirements of School System	Suggestions for Advocates
Insure that no later than 45 days after the receipt of a request for a hearing a final decision is reached and a copy of the decision is mailed to each of the parties.	Determine when the hearing decision is to be completed and encourage parents to do their part in the prompt scheduling of the hearing. (It often takes at least 20 days to receive a transcript of a hearing and roughly a week to review it and reach a decision.) If delays are necessary, request an explanation and agree on a date for completion of the hearing procedure. File a complaint with the state educational agency if a decision is unnecessarily delayed.
Insure that the hearing is conducted at a time and place that are reasonably convenient to the parents.	If parents work, encourage and support their request for an evening hearing. If parents are reluctant to have the hearing held at school offices, assist in arranging a more suitable or neutral meeting place.
Maintain the child in his or her present educational placement during the duration of the hearing process unless the parent and the school agree otherwise.	Insure that parents are aware of the requirement to maintain the child's current educational placement for the duration of the hearing process unless otherwise agreed, and help in negotiating a temporary alternative with the school system if necessary. Advise parents that if their child is out of school at the time the hearing is requested, then the school must enroll the child.
Disclose to parents all evidence to be presented at the hearing at least five days before the hearing.	Assist parents in the selection and development of the material to be presented at the hearing. Disclose to school system all evidence to be presented at the hearing at least five days before the hearing, and review with the parent evidence presented by the school system.
Obtain a written or electronic verbatim record of the hearing.	Insure that a copy of the record of the hearing is available to the parent.

Requirements of School System	Suggestions for Advocates
Provide parents the opportunity to have their handicapped child present at the hearing and to have the hearing open to the public.	Determine with parents whether the child's presence at the hearing is appropriate to the issue involved. Determine whether the hearing should be restricted to the parties involved or whether it should be heard by the public.

If the decision is not satisfactory, either party may appeal to the state educational agency (if the state did not conduct the initial hearing). In such a case the state must

Conduct an impartial review by reviewing the record of the initial hearing, insuring that the procedures used were correct and seeking additional information if necessary.	Assist parent in requesting an impartial review if the decision of the initial hearing decision is not satisfactory. Document in writing why the decision was not satisfactory as well as any incorrect procedures used during the initial hearing procedure. Assist parent in collecting additional information if requested by the review official. Assess qualifications of review office.
Allow the parties an opportunity for oral or written argument at the discretion of the review official.	Obtain a copy of the transcript of the initial hearing so that testimony may be reviewed and supplemented where necessary. Assist parent in developing oral or written arguments upon request of the review office.
Make an independent decision, a copy of which is given to the parties involved. This must be done within 30 days of the receipt of a request for a review unless an extension has been granted by the review office.	Monitor deadline on which decision should be reached. If delay is necessary, determine an alternate deadline. Review decision with parent to determine satisfaction with decision. Assist parent in working cooperatively with school to emplement decision. If parent is not satisfied, explore the feasibility of further appeal through civil action.

II

PARENTS, THE COMMUNITY, AND SERVICE PROVIDERS

3

Lost, Then Found: Parents' Journey Through the Community Service Maze

STEFI RUBIN
NOREEN QUINN-CURRAN

BIOGRAPHICAL SKETCH

Stefi Rubin, Ph.D., is a licensed psychologist and Associate Professor and former director of the preschool special needs graduate program at Wheelock College, Boston. At present she is Clinical Psychology Fellow in child and family therapy in the Department of Psychiatry, Harvard Medical School. Dr. Rubin has conducted research on the role of educational television and discussion groups for training family day care providers. She has collaborated with a team of parents and special educators to produce an instructional videotape and discussion guide, "Living with a Special Needs Child." Dr. Rubin has also contributed articles to professional special education journals and currently serves as Associate Editor for the journal Exceptional Children.

Noreen Quinn-Curran, formerly Codirector of the Parent Information Project, Boston public schools, is presently a Senior Associate in Parent Advocacy and Training at the Federation for Children with Special Needs. She is the parent of two children, one of whom has Down's syndrome with mild to moderate special needs. Ms. Quinn-Curran has translated her own experiences as a parent who has searched for services into workshops, courses, and written materials for other parents. Trained as a teacher, Ms. Quinn-Curran has designed and taught parent advocacy courses through the Massachusetts Department of Education and through Wheelock College. She has also lectured at Lesley College, Northeastern University, Suffolk University, Tufts University, and at medical centers and human service agencies. Ms. Quinn-Curran also works privately as an educational consultant/special needs advocate.

ISBN 0-8089-1561-4
Copyright © 1983 by Grune & Stratton

THE EVOLUTION OF POLICIES, PRACTICES, AND ATTITUDES

Changing Policies

Children with special needs share a century-old legacy of injustices: exclusion, misclassification, and arbitrary and inadequate programming. Doggedly, their parents have battled for their right to minimum services while many of them, inconsequential names on lengthy waiting lists, languished in custodial institutions or at home. While their inclusion into public school special education classes had begun prior to World War II, it was not until after the war that their parents witnessed a substantial increase in services stemming initially from the need to rehabilitate disabled veterans. The freshly imported Scandanavian concept of "normalization" further captured their imagination at a time when many parents of children with special needs were organizing themselves into advocacy groups. Prompted both by their own frustration and by their awareness of a shifting political climate toward people with disabilities, they filed class-action suits to end the all too routine violations of their children's constitutional rights to equal protection and equal educational opportunity.

As with the challenges to discrimination brought on behalf of other minority groups, the courts successfully bolstered the rights of children with special needs during the early 1970s. These legal precedents gathered momentum and culminated in congressional passage in 1975 of P.L. 94-142, the Education for All Handicapped Children Act. It is noted elsewhere in this volume but bears repeating that P.L. 94-142 is landmark legislation for several reasons. It establishes the rights of children with special needs, ages 3 to 21, to a free, appropriate public education in the least restrictive environment. It specifies their right to a written, individualized educational plan and their parents' rights to due process and to participation in educational decision making. Furthermore, it authorizes federal funding to states and localities to assist in implementing the law's requirements.

Despite optimism for the reform this law presages, neither its letter nor its spirit has yet been fully realized. Part of this failure can be assigned to the educational establishment's own general resistance to organizational innovation (Joiner & Sabatino, 1981). Part can be traced to the "top-down" process by which P.L. 94-142 was introduced to the school systems, which lacked enough preliminary planning time to gather broad popular support. Part can be understood in terms of the decrease in resources for which communities must aggressively compete. But part must also be attributed to the still-pervasive negative attitudes among all segments of our society toward children and adults with disabilities. As Dr. Edwin Martin (1982), former Assistant Secretary for Special Education and Rehabilitative Services in the U.S. Department of Education, has commented:

> In providing education, employment and access to buildings, the United States has come a long way. But we have not yet arrived. If one assumes that this history of discrimination is not an accident, that there are forces within us, perhaps unconscious fears of death and disability, that keep us from fully including disabled people in our society, there is no reason to weaken our national resolve nor to ignore the lessons we have so recently learned (Martin, 1982).*

Lagging Attitudes

Negative attitudes toward people with disabilities reflect a psychological response to differences. When there is misinformation or the lack of information and experience, troublesome feelings and attitudes emerge. These can range from outright mistrust, dislike, and bigotry to fear and condescension. Such reactions function as defensive shields that literally and figuratively keep people who are different at a safe distance.

People with special needs threaten their nondisabled peers, often by arousing the latter's unconscious anxiety about the possibility of loss of control in terms of human aggression, sexuality, and independence. Consequently, nondisabled people may erect barriers to ward off "contamination" or to suppress their own feelings of vulnerability. Such barriers need not be tangible ones in order to contain, control, or even punish people with special needs; attitudinal barriers are invisible yet potent forces that can produce these effects.

From a sociological perspective, fear and hostility are bred when instability is introduced into routine patterns of behavior or thought. Negative attitudes may arise or be exacerbated during periods of unsettling change within an organization's power structure; or they may reflect a protest against externally imposed changes in ingrained values and norms. Sometimes professionals who are themselves feeling exploited in their workplace will displace their anger onto their clients rather than onto the oppressive system. Their anger can then fuel actions that in the long run serve to perpetuate the stereotyping and segregation of people with special needs. The conventional myths about them have historical roots. As myths, they reveal our beliefs about the causes of disabilities and about the value and efficacy of various treatment methods.

Facets of Handicapism

In their interactions with professionals as well as with peers, parents of children with special needs are inevitably drawn into the nature versus nurture controversy about the etiology of deviant behavior and development. There are several theoretical models that attempt to account for developmental deviance. Some of these models emphasize organic or intrapsychic factors. Others emphasize interpersonal or environmental factors. These models may compete side by side within the same agency or within the same individual. Each model offers a different lens through which to see, understand, and address a child's special needs. Because the medical model has been preeminent, it is important to examine its tenets and their implications for parents and professionals alike.

The medical model focuses on determining, or diagnosing, underlying pathology or disease, of which symptoms are but isolated signals. Diagnosis proceeds linearly. Diagnostic categories are themselves static, unitary entities that tend to reduce an individual person to a mere representative of a disease process that has a predictable course, treatment, and prognosis of its own. A treatment protocol is used to attack the disease process as an aberrant element within the patient, with little consideration for the patient's psychosocial needs. When treatment fails to produce a "cure," the strict adherent to this model may "write off" a patient, as in the notorious cases (see Turnbull & Turnbull, 1978) in which pediatricians have urged institutionalization of children with mental retardation.

In a series of forceful articles Elizabeth Pieper (1979, 1980), herself a parent of a child with special needs, has elucidated the evolution of the medical model within the field of developmental disabilities. Pieper observes that the medical model has been linked to a moral code since ancient times. People with special needs have been viewed as but one kind of "degenerate" (among sinners, felons, and delinquents) whose suffering is perceived as a kind of punishment (Pieper, 1979). (This attitude is discussed by Newman in Chapter 1.) The medicalization of developmental disabilities and, more recently, of behavior problems such as hyperactivity, derives both from this view as well as from what Sarason (1981) called medicine's "tradition-conferred leadership role" within the helping professions.

Such pernicious beliefs have also provided the basis for some of the insidious attitudes revealed in our contemporary language about people with disabilities. Pieper strikes home with a number of graphic examples: one is a "victim" of a disease, "suffers" from Down's syndrome (despite the absence of pain), or experiences "attacks" as if controlled by an external force. A person born with hydrocephalus becomes a hydrocephalic; a person with epilepsy, an epileptic (Pieper, 1980).

Our terminology works to highlight a person's impairment or disability as if it were the person's sole or salient feature. By singling out an aspect of a person's physique or behavior and making it synonymous with that person's identity, we stigmatize and ultimately dehumanize that individual. Rather than saying a person is paralyzed, Pieper (1980) suggests that we might learn to say that she cannot move her legs. Because it is more cumbersome to tell how a person is affected by paralysis, "paralyzed" or "paraplegic" become convenient shortcuts that unfortunately are rarely augmented by specific descriptions of behavior.

Furthermore, Sameroff (1975) has eloquently described the ethical implications of diagnostic labeling:

> When people are treated as if a constitutional or genetic deficit remains as an unchanging characteristic they are being treated as a thing. When any abnormality in functioning is treated as intrinsic to that person and taken out of the social and cultural context in which that person is living, that person is being treated as a thing. . . . Whenever retrospective research has pointed to a variable which was thought to be causal to some adverse behavioral outcome, prospective research has shown that individuals with exactly the same characteristics or experience have not had the adverse outcome. . . . Why is it then that in the face of this negative data we continue to believe that premature children, difficult children, or handicapped children will all have poor developmental outcomes? I would suggest it is because we here do not have the necessary developmental perspective. As long as we believe that labels are received rather than given we will be confronted with this problem. When we come to see that not only is the label something we have attributed to the child but also the initial ingredient in a self-fulfilling prophecy, will we really come to the heart of primary prevention. (p. 23)[†]

The issue of labeling is but one facet of handicapism. Defined by Biklen and Bogdan (1977, p. 206) as a "theory and set of practices that promote unequal and unjust treatment of people because of apparent or assumed physical or mental disability," handicapism manifests itself in our personal and professional lives and in our social policies.

> If you are labeled "handicapped," handicapism is your biggest burden. It is a no-win situation. If you fulfill the stereotype, you are pegged as a poor, pathetic, sad, forever childlike and dependent person, someone who should be spoken for rather than to, someone with an unending need for pity and charity. If you succeed in challenging, or even escaping the stereotype, you

---

[†]Reprinted with permission from Sarason, S., & Doris, J. *Educational handicap, public policy, and social history. A broadened perspective on mental retardation.* New York: The Free Press, 1979, p. 23.

may be objectified in another way, as an unusual, rare case, amazing. You are not simply an ordinary person (Biklen & Bogdan, 1977, p. 208.)‡

Thus, the medical model runs the risk of making assumptions about the degree to which a person's impairment may interfere with his or her functioning. For too long society has made a handicapped person of a person who happens to have a disability. It has been presumed that, as if with cap in hand, a so-called handicapped person was uneducable and unemployable. Professionals have cultivated a jargon that legitimizes their profession, gives it prestige and control, and maintains a comfortable distance between them and their clients.

Practitioners sensitive to handicapism have become more vocal in recent years as representatives of a developmental, transactional model. Within pediatrics, some doctors are beginning to interpret dysfunction as

the end result of particular constitutional predispositions such as uneven patterns of development, individual cognitive styles, or specific temperament profiles interacting with social or environmental factors . . . e.g., parental styles, cultural values, and critical events (Oberklaid, Dworkin, & Levine, 1979, p. 1126).

Multiple factors are seen as contributing to a disability in this transactional model. Strengths, interests, and rights are considered in addition to weaknesses and needs. Emphasis is placed on how interactions with environments may exaggerate disabilities or, by contrast, promote a person's attainment of his or her full potential. Individuals sharing a type of disability are viewed as differing from one another as do people in general.

Invisible Barriers

Despite such an enlightened view, outmoded attitudes linger. Labels detrimental to a child are applied to his or her parents. Inevitably, parents are made to feel responsible for their child's problems. The parents' genes, poor prenatal care, or neuroses are all targets. Guilt is not merely one of several initial parental reactions to the discovery of a child's special needs; it is also later amplified by professionals who have the power to induce parental self-doubt. As Schliefer (1981) notes, diagnostic formulations, unsuccessful placements, or inaccessible facilities can each be used to point a finger at parents who are told their expectations are unrealistic, their acceptance of their child's disability is incomplete, or their behavior is uncooperative. Sometimes thwarted in the constructive ex-

‡Reprinted with permission from Biklen, D., & Bogdan, R. Handicapism in America. In B. Blatt, D. Biklen, & R. Bogdan (Eds.). *An alternative textbook in special education, people, schools, and other institutions*. Denver: Love, 1977.

pression of their legitimate anger over the unavailability of services or over procrastination in the delivery of services, parents may turn their anger inward upon themselves. Or they may go numb. These responses may be useful defenses against being labeled a troublemaker. When reinforced by professionals, however, these reactions can immobilize parents. The possibility of genuine collaboration with professionals then becomes a dashed hope.

Once parents are identified as having a child with special needs, they are often perceived differently by relatives, friends, neighbors, and service providers. For example, friends may have difficulty handling their own feelings about the child's disability. Their awkwardness with their own feelings may be shown in several ways. Some might feel so flustered that they withdraw; others, at the opposite extreme, may intrude and become overindulgent.

Beyond the intimate circle of family and friends, parents will encounter programs in their community that vary enormously in their philosophy and in their approach to parent participation. One dimension that differentiates programs is the degree to which they perceive and treat parents as active or passive persons who are or are not capable of making meaningful contributions to their child's program. Programs based on perceptions of parents as having little to offer tend to relegate parents to a "patient" role. Parents are seen as dependent upon the program for its superior expertise and guidance. Other organizations will go so far as to recognize the parent as a consumer or as a client. Some amount of bargaining is expected in order to arrive at a mutually satisfactory service delivery plan.

Further along this scale, other programs may view parents as competent case managers. Parental authority is respected because parents are the only adults who are constantly involved in their child's service delivery plan. Parents seen from this perspective are expected to want and to need to participate in planning services and even to advocate alterations in them. Still other organizations presume that parents play a critical role in teaching their own children or in teaching less experienced parents such intricacies as preparing for an interdisciplinary team meeting. Programs that are most receptive to the potential contributions of parents may organize themselves so that parents are hired as staff, administrators, or members of the board of directors. Parents who are so empowered may threaten the traditional power, job security, and self-esteem that professionals have, and so these more active roles for parents are less commonly seen.

How actively parents participate in their child's program and the decision-making process will also vary according to each individual parent's "own needs, desires, skills or personal situations" (Gordon & Breivogel,

1976). Divisions of labor between mothers and fathers may be observed in which, for example, the mother may seek out a chance to serve on a board while the father prefers more informal activity, such as making equipment. It is a wise program that gives parents room to explore a diversity of roles and permission to participate to whatever degree they wish. Training and support services tailored for parents may also be offered so that parents who would like to broaden the nature of their participation can gain the confidence and prerequisite knowledge and skills to do so.

The reality, however, is that the majority of parents of children with special needs will encounter a pervasive skepticism about their potential contributions. Parents' interactions with a fragmented service delivery system will exacerbate their sense of being unwelcome. It is unfortunate that, in confronting the obstacles inherent in a frequently inadequate service delivery system, parents often begin to invalidate their own perceptions and underrate their own abilities. Self-doubt becomes one of the hidden traps into which parents all too easily fall. Some might even argue that fostering self-doubt is an outcome compatible with a service delivery system that depends upon the compliance of its users.

It is not only parents who are victims of these hidden traps. Professionals who have been deprived of opportunities to work *with* parents, rather than either for or against them, also suffer. With the implementation of P.L. 94-142, the balance of power between parents and professionals has finally begun to change. Parents and professionals who relate to one another as adversaries are at least implicitly elevating the parents to a status of pseudo-equals who have the right to challenge the professionals' views. Others are relating to one another as genuine equals who can trust and work together as partners. Professionals who cling to an impairment model of disability and to a pathology model of parents of children with special needs are missing out on an historic opportunity to join with parents who are learning what it means to act on their own behalf.

THE DYNAMICS OF THE SEARCH
FOR SERVICES

Discovering the Service Delivery Maze

Approaching the service delivery system for children with special needs is akin to negotiating a massive maze. Parents are confronted by a number of agencies, all ostensibly designed to serve their children and families. Yet, the services specifically for families of children with special needs are not well integrated into the general array of services. Parents may also be impeded by a host of problems such as the services' differing priorities and mandates, their overlapping geographic boundaries, their contrasting administrative structures, or even their incomprehensible acronyms.

In preparing to enter the maze, parents inevitably find themselves asking questions that have more to do with administrative issues than with parenting issues. "Which pathway of this maze do I take for which service? Are the pathways organized by special needs, disability, severity, age, income, or geography?" When parents arrive at dead ends in their search, they must save face by trying again, which produces a stressful and ultimately frustrating and anger-provoking situation. Such parents are often told that they are "looking for services that do not exist." They can be made to feel that they are "crazy" or ignorant simply because they insist on continuing their search.

Parents new to the search for services may not be clear about how to label the service they are seeking. All they may know is that a family member needs assistance. There are three steps a parent must go through to gain access to services. First, parents need to identify what their needs are—e.g., someone else to take over for a while so they can get some rest. Second, they need to translate their needs into the proper service label—e.g., "respite care." Third, they need to contact the appropriate agency that delivers that service. Only the first step in this process is familiar to the average parent. In the second and third steps, parents must rely on the knowledge they have acquired, their memory, resourcefulness, and persistence.

Getting Lost

In addition to grappling with the external mazes, many parents also experience internal, psychic mazes as they ponder the affordability of services, their rights to services, and their own adequacy as providers for their children. Patterns of circular thinking leading to self-defeating inaction and eventually to "learned helplessness" (Heifetz, 1980) will develop unless parents are assertive or psychologically astute enough to combat these "side effects." When professionals are supportive of the parents' search for services, parents are more likely to think clearly and retain their determination.

Theories about stages in parental adjustment to having a child with special needs commonly identify a series of emotional states parents presumably experience: denial, anger, hopeful bargaining, depression, and acceptance (see Chapter 11). But these psychologically oriented theories tend to overlook parents' concomitant reactions to an inadequate service delivery system. Parents' feelings are intensified each time they must deal with a system that is fragmented, hierarchical, intimidating, and demeaning. The frustrations inherent in using such a system may amplify parents' grief reactions and leave parents feeling even more vulnerable and exposed.

In their quest for services, parents may convey their ambivalance to professionals. They may feel inadequate about not being able to fulfill more of their child's needs. They may feel overwhelmed in not being "up to" the constant task. They may feel angry about having to rely on agencies for financial or direct assistance. Or they may feel betrayed, having learned to accept their child's special needs only then to discover that there are no services. On the other hand, they may realize they need assistance in a number of areas that other families would probably never require, and they may feel grateful for whatever help is provided, however limited or inappropriate that help may be.

In the early stages of being a "new" parent, they may feel dependent upon the "experts" for the answers and for many of the supports. As parents move from a fairly dependent state to one of increasing independence, they may feel angry about their former dependent state, especially in terms of decisions engineered or perceived to be made by others. Usually parents want to gain more control over decisions affecting their child and family. They are often willing to learn vast amounts of information, increase their skills, and become familiar with a variety of resources. Eventually parents are able to evaluate more clearly, think more independently about their child's needs, and advocate more effectively.

It is important to understand parents in the context of what has already happened in their lives and the issues with which they live daily. As Featherstone (1980) shows, the reality of living with a child with special needs changes the parents' perception of what that child will be like and what their lives will be like, today, tomorrow, and always. The parents' ability to predict and to exercise control over the future is altered. Parents often experience sorrow, confusion, and a blow to their self-esteem, as well as anger over their loss of control.

When parents regain personal control and can regulate the number of changes in their lives, they often feel more comfortable in their interactions with professionals. They begin to see themselves as equals, and as partners in the care of their child. Profound growth can take place on both planes. When professionals experience, even secondhand, the parents' reasons for distress, they are better equipped with the knowledge and sensitivity to enable parents to find their way through the mazes to the services. They can help parents demystify the service delivery system and see the mazes for what they are, with their limitations, negative assumptions, and institutional barriers. Together parents and professionals can plan, implement, and evaluate needed services. They can co-advocate on many levels for better services. In this regard, *Parents Speak Out*

(Turnbull & Turnbull, 1978) is an excellent book for parents and professionals alike to read in order to foster a more empathic view of parents.

How successful the transaction is between parents and professionals often depends on how well the professionals understand both the parents' perspectives and feelings and their own. The effectiveness with which parents' approach an agency and gain access to services may depend on how far along they are in the process of integrating the child with special needs into their lives, physically and psychically. Their effectiveness may also depend on how sensitive the professionals are to the complexities that parents face when they approach the service delivery system. Coming to grips with ambivalent feelings is as important for professionals as for parents.

Parents, Too, Are Labeled

Sometimes professionals assign labels to parents, perhaps partly as a response to their own frustration in not being able to deliver comprehensive and high-quality services. There are several popular, though derogatory, labels typically applied to parents which can be relinquished once their origins are understood. Several of these labels deserve analysis.

"Stupid and lazy" parents often have not been given the necessary information to explain articulately their situation and to make decisions about their child. The lack of information on the parents' part often leads to their being dismissed as uncaring and uninterested, whereas in fact they are making a valiant attempt to make a decision but have not been given a chance to gain information through direct contact with a professional, a parents' workshop, a parents' group, or written materials.

Seeing the parents as "the problem" assumes that the parents are emotionally disturbed. Professionals under seige sometimes begin to fall back on this perception of parents to justify their desire to excuse themselves from their responsibility for responding to parents' concerns. It is crucial to distinguish between the possibly excessive emotional responses of parents, if they do exist, and the legal, procedural, and substantive issues to which the parents may be reacting and about which they may rightly feel distressed.

"Greedy" parents, who "shop for services," are seen as dissatisfied, hypercritical, and unaccepting of their child's disability. In actuality "shopping" entails investigating other programs and services and provides parents with information upon which to base observations of their own child, in relation to others, as well as the kinds and quality of services and programs. By shopping, parents can come to a better understanding of their own child's needs, of their rights to services, and of the nature of those services that could meet their needs. Professionals should remember that very seldom do parents have knowledge before the child's birth about their child's disability or about programs and services. It is all learned on the job, often at the expense of a great deal of time and personal resources. Shopping for services can be a legitimate method that parents use to gain essential information.

"Angry, defensive" parents are ones who rapidly alienate professionals. Yet parents are often made legitimately angry by what they are subjected to in order to obtain services. There are mounds of forms to be filled out; each agency has its own form but may ask parents for the same upsetting and otherwise private information over and over again. Parents often experience these encounters as an assault and as an invasion of their privacy. For example, a child might be diagnosed at birth as having Down's syndrome, with doctors' medical diagnoses of mental retardation in the records, and recent, adequate school testing to verify special needs. Yet the Supplemental Security Income procedure subjects the parents and their child to another day of intelligence testing at the hands of a totally unknown tester. In such cases parents have a right to be angry. It is the only appropriate response. This is an unfortunate situation that is demeaning to the family, yet comparable situations occur every day. Even within the same agency parents may be subjected to several interviews with professionals from various disciplines, each asking similar questions. Not only is this insensitive but it is indicative of poor management. The parents' often painful memories are needlessly stirred up.

If the parents have felt exploited or rejected during assessment procedures in the past, their pain may be especially deep. Parental anxiety about confidentiality and about the accuracy of the information that is recorded about them is often misinterpreted by professionals as undue suspiciousness, hostility, or uncooperativeness. If the professional believes that the parents are "privileged" to receive services or "privileged" to be able to ask for them, and parents come to the transaction with anger or trepidation, then the transaction is not going to be a fruitful one for either party. The burden is on the professional to lift some of the weight off of the parents' shoulders!

"Demanding" parents are seen as exploiters of the taxpayers' money, abusers of privileges, and nuisances. In reality parents have a right to services and realize that they must assert themselves repeatedly to be taken seriously. Experienced parents reaffirm this truth with their own storehouse of horror tales. "You have to fight for services!" they advise. When systems cannot respond to requests for services, it is assumed that there is something wrong with the parents rather than with the systems that cannot or will not respond.

"Conniving" is an adjective used about parents who underhandedly manipulate and scheme to get what they want. In reality parents who want to be most effective in obtaining services do have to learn the channels, the contacts, the best approaches, and the auxiliary techniques and resources. They do become quite expert in mastering the special services environment. Parents have much more in their environment with which to deal and consequently control. Learning how to operate within the system is therefore an adaptive skill to cultivate and one that professionals ought to encourage rather than criticize.

GETTING SMART AND UNLEARNING HELPLESSNESS

Initial Contacts Between Parents and Agencies

Parents living in urban centers are especially at risk for not receiving the services they need. Although resources may seem more plentiful in cities, access is usually more difficult because the mazes are more complex, the bureaucratic layers of administrators are more dense, and the services are more obscured by urban anonymity. Parents need direct assistance in order to counteract these hindrances. Anticipating parents' needs is a valuable strategy to enable them to "get smart" and avoid learning helpless behavior patterns.

In their quest for services, parents need assistance with four components of their search: clarification, support, information, and action. The following typical excerpt from a telephone call from an inexperienced mother who has called a parent information specialist at the citywide Information, Assistance, and Resource Project for parents of students with special needs in the Boston public schools illustrates how these components are integrated into the professional's response.

Parent: "Hello, I want to know what school my son is going to. Mrs. Hurley said he would be changing schools but Mr. Dennison said he could stay in his same school."

A humane and successful interaction with this parent would require the professional to take a moment to thoughtfully analyze the parent's request in order to respond constructively. For example, the professional might think that all parents care as much as they are able to about their children; this one seems distressed because she does not know where her son will be going to school. She detects a contradiction among professionals; she doesn't know the special education process; she is oriented to her individual situation and not to the organization and distribution of services. How can I help her?

The intake worker might start with a supportive statement for the parent and then ask basic questions to elicit more information before action can be taken. The dialogue continues:

Parent Information Specialist: "Well, of course, it is very important to know which school he will be going to. Let me ask you some questions that will help in getting you an answer. Did your son have a special needs evaluation?"

Parent: "Yes, last spring, about May."

Parent Information Specialist: "What was the recommendation?"

Parent: "That he needed a special needs program."

Parent Information Specialist: "Did you agree with that recommendation?"

Parent: "Yes."

Parent Information Specialist: "Do you know what kind of program he is supposed to be placed in—a small, structured class or a resource room?"

Parent: "Yes, a small class that is separate."

Parent Information Specialist: "Can you tell me what his special needs are?"

Parent: "Yes, some. He has a very short attention span; he writes letters backwards; he can't read even though he is almost nine, but he is smart in other ways."

Parent Information Specialist: "Yes, I'm sure. Did the evaluation team mention a learning disability class?"

Parent: "Yes."

Parent Information Specialist: "Let me ask you some basic background information—your name and address. Now if you can hold for just a minute, I'll check the files to make sure all the paper work is up-to-date and then I will give you the name and number of the person who makes the learning disability assignments. In that way, if you have any questions about the assignment or program, you can discuss them directly with the person in charge of the program. If, after that point, you have any questions or concerns, you can call me back and I will try to assist you further. We do have a booklet for parents on Chapter 766, our state's special education law, which will give you more information on special needs and your rights as a parent. Also, I can send you some printed information on learning disabilities and, if you are interested in being on a mailing list, we can let you know about upcoming workshops for parents."

The intake worker must perceive signals the parent may send out that indicate a parent's need for information or for reassurance. It is a rare parent, either quite experienced in special education or knowledgeable about obtaining services, who can automatically give relevant, complete information upon the initial contact. The following excerpt from another conversation is offered to highlight how a sophisticated parent initiates a request for services.

Parent: "Hello, this is Amanda Jones, of 40 Webster Street, Dorchester. My eight-year-old son, Darrell, had a special education evaluation last spring when he was in the second grade. The recommendation was that he go to a special needs program for children with learning disabilities. I agreed with that recommendation by signing the educational plan but have not yet received an official assignment. Could you tell me who I should speak with to get that information?"

TABLE 3-1. Accessing Community Services: Some
Questions for Parents to Ask

- Is this a need my child has?
- Who/what can help me in obtaining this service?
- Is this an informal service of which we might be able to take advantage?
- Is there a law, regulation, or policy that covers this service and safeguards my child's eligibility?
- What is the best way to obtain this service?
    By telephone?
    By letter?
    By requesting a meeting?
- What action shall I take if the service is denied?
    Prepare tone of voice?
    Prepare alternate or compromise plan, if appropriate?
    Prepare back-up resources?
    Prepare information on my due process rights and on procedures for mediation or appeal?

This articulate, well-informed parent not only is bound to receive better services for her child on a long-term basis but also will be treated more professionally by those with whom she comes into contact. Having accurate information, communication skills, and some knowledge of resources is essential for all parents, but particularly for those who live in a city.

Two vastly different styles of communication that parents use to convey their needs and a step-by-step method the professional must use to ferret out information have been described. The professional or other intake worker should be careful not to intimidate or embarrass the parent by using jargon but instead should use ordinary language. Any exchange of information adds to the parent's repertoire for the next contact. Replacing the parent's confusion and anxiety with hope and confidence is crucial. It is most beneficial to the parent for the professional to be aware of all the resources available, to listen sensitively for expressions of the parent's or their child's needs, and then to suggest an appropriate referral.

Ways to Simplify the Parents' Task

Some parents may need help in organizing themselves to approach agencies effectively. Basic communication and organizational skills that professionals take for granted may have to be taught or at least reviewed with many parents. These are consumer skills that parents need to acquire or sharpen in order to effectively advocate for their child. For example, there are several questions that parents might first ask as they contem-

TABLE 3-2. Tips for Parents in Contacting
Community Services

Method	Suggestion
The *telephone* is a good place to begin to assert yourself.	● Give your name, ask for the appropriate person or state the reason for calling. If the person to whom you wish to speak is not available, leave your name, phone number, and a message. ● Find out approximately when your call will be returned. ● Obtain the name of the person answering.
A *letter* often becomes a necessary form of communication, particularly when verbal communication has not worked.	● Be brief and to the point. ● Address to the proper person. ● Send carbon copies to all the involved parties. ● Keep a carbon copy for yourself.
Record-keeping helps you to stay organized and develop confidence as your child's case manager.	● Obtain copies of school, medical, and other relevant records. ● Use a log sheet, listing who was contacted, when, and the outcome. (See Figure 3-3). ● Compile in a folder a listing of names, titles, addresses, and telephone numbers of people you often contact. ● Prepare a standard background sheet that includes your child's developmental milestones, health and medical history, and history of contacts with other service providers. This sheet may be given to each agency routinely, avoiding the repetition of painful memories, and saving you time.

plate matching their child's needs to an existing service. Table 3-1 outlines these. Table 3-2 provides guidelines for parents who wish to maximize their effectiveness when using the telephone, correspondence, or records to either convey or collect information in their search for services. Figure 3-1 illustrates a form that can aid parents in keeping records of telephone conversations. A useful handbook for parents and professionals alike is Cutler's *Unraveling the Special Education Maze: An Action Guide for*

Person I Talked to	Telephone	Date
Question/Information		
Follow-up—What do I do next?		

Person I Talked to	Telephone	Date
Question/Information		
Follow-up—What do I do next?		

FIGURE 3-1. Telephone log. (Reprinted with permission from Celuzza, P., & Clayton, S. (Eds.). *Connections: A directory of services for Children with special needs in the Boston Public Schools.* Boston: Public Schools Department of Special Services, 1979.)

Parents (1981), which elaborates the steps parents must take to insure that their children receive the services to which they are entitled.

Some special needs parent organizations and other human service agencies are now offering assertiveness training and advocacy courses for parents. Nationwide Parent Information Centers (PICs) have staff, libraries, and workshops to assist parents of children with special needs as well as professionals.

When mental health workers validate the parent's search by being supportive, providing information, and offering assistance, they are providing parents with a crucial service in itself. Professionals can assist parents in expressing their feelings of ambivalence, uncertainty, and anger that are normally stirred up by the search for services. Parents need to know that "they're okay" and that "it's okay" to need assistance. They should not be expected to do it alone.

MATCHING PARENTS TO COMMUNITY SERVICES

Conducting Needs Assessments

In matching parents to community services, a number of preliminary issues must be explored during the needs assessment phase. Prior to addressing the problems in the service delivery system itself, it behooves professionals to take the time to have parents discuss the daily realities of raising their child. Clarifying the nature and the extent of a child's disability and the parents' perceptions of it gives professionals an understanding of how the parents have come to terms with their child's special needs. Determining how the child's disability affects the family's everyday life and identifying the parents' expectations of the child and of themselves will also be helpful. Professionals ought not to be surprised by the seemingly remarkable ability that some families have to cope with and integrate differences into their household or to find community resources on their own. In one representative case, the parents of a teenager with Down's syndrome have encouraged her to act independently and to attend after-school activities with her peers from the neighborhood, while they have proceeded to locate supplementary resources and continued to work full-time outside the home. Families like these strike a balance in their lives by capitalizing on their own strengths and on those of the community.

It is important to take stock of the resources that are available to a family and to assess the extent to which the family can use them. Professionals and parents must also evaluate which of their needs cannot be met by existing resources; this will extend the search for services into other districts, lead to the modification of current services, or stimulate the creation of new ones.

For some parents, having a needs assessment interview to express their needs and to receive emotional support and a guarantee of concrete assistance when needed may suffice. These parents may prefer to activate services by themselves and enlist the mental health staff on an as-needed basis only. Others may want direct, immediate assistance. Some may feel most comfortable discussing their needs in a parent group led by a parent and a professional; the group can also function as a way to pool information based on personal experiences with agencies and thus fulfill a matchmaking role as well.

The Range of Available Services

When parents first learn that their child has special needs, most have little idea about the types of services that might be utilized to intervene, rehabilitate, or reconstruct. It is through experience and through receiving information that parents learn about the range of available services in education, medicine, social work, mental health, law, employment, housing, and recreation. Table 3-3 is a synopsis of these services and their legal underpinnings.

TABLE 3-3. Laws Stipulating Specific Services

	Section 504* of the Rehabilitation Act of 1973	P.L. 94-142†	SSI‡
Social Services			
Welfare	X		X
Day care	X		X
Respite care	X		X
Foster care	X		X
Legal Assistance		X	
Due process	X	X	X
Financial			X
Residential	X	X (If educationally related)	
Transportation	X	X	
Mental health			
Counseling	X	X (If educationally related)	
Parent groups		X	
Sibling groups			
Respite care			
In home			
Out of home			
Medical	X		X
Dental	X		X
Public health	X		
Nutritional	X		
Educational	X	X	
Recreational	X	X (If required for over-all development)	
Vocational	X	X	
Employment	X		
Psychological	X ⎫ If	X	
Occupational therapy	X ⎪ related	X	
Physical therapy	X ⎪ to	X	
Speech therapy	X ⎬ education	X	
Vision resources	X ⎪	X	
Hearing resources	X ⎪	X	
Adaptive physical education	X ⎪	X	
Parent/child education	X ⎭	X	

*Section 504 of the Rehabilitation Act of 1973 is a federal civil rights provision that applies to people of all ages and that makes it illegal to discriminate on the basis of an actual or alleged handicap in areas such as employment, education, public transportation, and access to public buildings. It applies to any activity or program that receives federal assistance of any kind.

†P.L. 94-142, the Education for All Handicapped Children Act, requires that a free appropriate education be provided for all handicapped children between the ages of 3 and 21. It establishes a major program of federal financial assistance that flows through the state to the local school systems in order for them to provide increased services to meet the law's requirements. A key concept of P. L. 94-142 is that of related services. The act defines related services as

> transportation, and such developmental, corrective and other supportive services (including speech pathology and audiology, psychological services, physical and occupational therapy, recreation, and medical and counseling services, except that such medical services shall be for diagnostic and evaluation purposes only) as may be required to assist a handicapped child to benefit from special education, and includes the early identification and assessment of handicapping conditions in children.

P.L. 94-142 requires the following:

1. All handicapped children must be identified, located, and evaluated.
2. Special education services must be provided in conformity with an "individualized educational program" that is developed and written for each child. Each "individualized educational program" must be implemented without cost to the parents.
3. Parents must be afforded procedural safeguards, such as notice of meetings, access to records, the right to have the child independently evaluated, and the right to a hearing if they dispute the child's educational program.
4. Testing and evaluation procedures must be nondiscriminatory. Wherever possible, the child's native language must be used in the testing and evaluation process.
5. Children must be placed in the "least restrictive" educational setting that meets their special needs. To the greatest extent possible, children with special needs should be educated with children who do not have special needs.
6. Procedures must be established to protect the confidentiality of data and information.

‡Supplementary Security Income (SSI) is a national program that provides a basic minimum income for blind or disabled children who have limited income or resources. Children may receive a monthly check, Medicaid coverage, and other social and health services. Parents may complete application forms at their local Social Security office. They have the right to request the legal basis for any determination and to appeal if the application is denied.

Securing Referrals

Referrals for services require systematic monitoring and followup to insure that services are provided in a sensitive, efficient, and timely manner. All too often bureaucracies lack smooth coordination. Information collected and decisions rendered at any point in the cycle (intake, assessment, matching, implementation) can get stalled or lost. When parents feel stranded in their search for services, they have in essence been given another opportunity to mistrust agencies or to feel helpless. Yet where the system works well and parents do receive services, they will be the best promoters and advocates when funding and legislative issues arise. This is another aspect of the true partnership between parents and professionals.

FAMILY, FRIENDS, NEIGHBORS, AND PLAYMATES

Mobilizing Natural Networks

Too often both parents and professionals take it for granted that once a family is linked to a public or private community service, the family's needs have been met. A successful referral can be invested with the power of a magical solution. However, linking families to community services is only half the story. The other half involves linking families to their natural networks of relatives, friends, and neighbors.

Attempting to raise a child with special needs singlehandedly is a formidable task. To counteract the certain hurdles such a task poses, many families strive to build a reliable support system for themselves. Depending upon formal agency supports becomes a necessary but insufficient dimension of their effort. The insufficiency stems from the reality that human service agencies are usually low priorities in our state and federal budgets. They are hampered by unsatisfactory working conditions and as a result are subject to an endemic pattern of high employee turnover. Repeatedly a staff member disappears and is replaced by someone new to the case who needs time to "pick up the pieces." Families, in turn, learn to expect instability and discontinuity in the services they receive.

To tolerate the cycle of broken relationships, some families become jaded and wary. They become cautious and do not hope for too much. They stint their emotional investment. To the professionals, they may seem apathetic, whereas in fact they are weary of having to remain alert to impending changes or gaps in their child's services from year to year. Others are less able to subdue their anger and impatience. These families may seem belligerent and inflexible to the professionals.

In addition to the fluctuations and uncertainties in service delivery related to staff turnover, families of children with special needs must engage agencies that are, in some cases, oblivious to each other's existence or, in other cases, rivalrous of each other's accomplishments. The consumers of the services, families, can easily get caught in the middle or lost in the process. Furthermore, agencies may be geographically scattered. The decentralization of services (or a limited quantity or range of ser-

vices) confronts families with practical and logistic exigencies like transportation costs. Instead of reflecting a planned mechanism for facilitating
community control, decentralization may be a euphemistic reference to a
service delivery system that is fragmented and out of control. Thus whatever fragile continuity a family can muster is indeed an achievement,
given the likelihood of their changing needs, the erratic availability of
services, and the competitiveness that characterizes some agencies.

The wear and tear on families of children with special needs is real. In
their attempts to cope with unresponsive systems, professionals in the
human services succumb to "burnout." So, too, do parents. Parental
burnout (that is, emotional, physical, and attitudinal deterioration due to
job-related stress) has not been given the attention that professional burnout has, perhaps because it is felt that these families have either deserved
or must learn to "accept" whatever extra stresses and strains that arise.
These parents are expected to have unlimited reserves of patience, forti-
tude, and good humor. They are often expected to be super-parents, not
ordinary human beings.

It is imperative that professionals take into account the entire family
constellation, its "life space," when assessing a family's strengths, needs,
and resources. Professionals must evaluate to what extent a family does
or could at some time participate in an "informal" support system. Just as
a child's needs do not exist in a vacuum but coexist with those of his or
her family, so too do a family's needs stand in relationship to the kind and
quality of human resources available to them by virtue of kinship, friend-
ship, or simple neighborliness. Helping families make use of the familiar
resources of relatives, friends, and neighbors may in fact be a goal as
important as gaining families access to agency-sponsored programs. The
search for alternative resources is an adaptive one and will ultimately
strengthen the family and provide them with a more comprehensive support system. The literature on family network therapy and on "network-
ing" among human service professionals themselves has demonstrated
that mobilizing natural networks is an effective approach (Sarason, Carroll, Maton, Cohen, & Lorentz, 1977; Speck & Attneave, 1973).

Involving Relatives

Extended family members may initially retreat upon the diagnosis of
a child's special needs. At the very time when parents need maximum
support, they may find themselves abandoned. The self-protective withdrawal of bewildered family members may turn out to be a merely tempo-
rary aberration, but it can seem like a painful wound that only slowly
heals. Other extended family members may harness their energies and
unite to support the parents.

Professionals in the human services have tended to downplay the potential resourcefulness of the extended family. The possibility that the extended family has needs of its own has also been neglected. Often grandparents need help in understanding the nature of a child's disability and the ways in which they can be helpful. Family conferences that include grandparents may be valuable in helping a family work out its responses to the changes called for by the child's special needs. Support groups for grandparents, or grandparent-to-grandparent buddy systems, may prove to be common in the years ahead. Pairing grandparents with each other as well as with children who lack living, biological grandparents of their own would be a mutually beneficial procedure. The national Foster Grandparents volunteer program and films such as *Sharing the Experience with Gavin* (National Institute on Mental Retardation, 1981) exemplify how much elder citizens have to offer children with special needs. The unique position of grandparents in the family hierarchy presents them with cross-generational issues of how to best communicate and reach out to their sons and daughters.

Brothers and sisters within the family have a unique position, too. Feelings of jealousy over the parents' attention, confusion about their sibling's disability, sadness for the reduction in their parents' availability for them, dismay at social taunting, and anxiety about their responsibilities that lurk in the future may predominate (see Chapter 6 for an in-depth discussion of siblings). Time-limited support groups for siblings of children with special needs as well as training for them in how to teach their siblings new skills have been reported (Miller & Cantwell, 1976). Concern for the mental health of siblings of children with special needs as well as recognition of their contributions within the family have even led to the inauguration of a sibling network and newsletter (Powell, 1981).

Involving People in the Community

Outside the family, parents' relationships with their friends and neighbors can be jeopardized if there is a stigma attached to having a child with special needs. The parents' need to maintain some semblance of a social life may be in jeopardy as they cope with the taxing demands that a child's special needs may make. Friends represent a trustworthy "oasis." They can nourish parents who are in need of "recharging." Friends can meet the parents' need for relaxation, both by functioning as a legitimate reason to get away and take a break and by occasionally offering respite care so that the parent can go shopping unencumbered. For some parents a new set of friends is made among other parents of children with special needs encountered in hospital or clinic waiting rooms, agency lobbies, school open-houses, or parent groups.

Parents keep a watchful eye on their children's own emerging friendships. Fostering the development of their child's social network may be stressful if the neighborhood children shun, tease, or express curiosity about their child's special needs. Often the child's teachers will be talented at "matchmaking." For example, they might promote friendships among families whose children share interests or who travel to school on the same bus. Teachers can also offer parents matter-of-fact ways of talking about a child's disability with peers or they can introduce parents to the growing body of storybooks (Chesler, 1979) geared for children interested in mainstreaming. Mental health and social service personnel can benefit from inservice training and role-playing to increase their sensitivity to the affronts that children with special needs experience.

In summary, family members, friends, and people in the community may play influential roles in helping parents of children with special needs make adjustments and cope successfully.

BUILDING BRIDGES: HOME, SCHOOL, AND COMMUNITY CONNECTIONS

Respecting the Family's Life Cycle

Human service professionals traditionally have been trained to pay attention to individual, child, or adult developmental issues and so are often oblivious to issues related to stages in the family life cycle. Yet the integrity of the family as a human group with its own developmental tasks must be recognized and responded to. This is particularly important when a family's usual problem-solving strategies and coping style fail to work. At that time they are plunged into a crisis state causing disequilibrium. The human service professional may see family regression, chaos, or paralysis. It is often at such a juncture that a family seeks outside help. Either the family presents itself or a referral is generated by a family member's behavior that is sufficiently disturbing to gain the attention of referring agents such as schools or courts.

For families with a child with special needs, the passage through normal developmental stages may become more complicated and difficult because of a poor "fit" between their family's needs and the nature of the available community services. For example, during adolescence the issues of sexuality, identity, and autonomy are prominent. Yet these issues may be overshadowed by a family's questions about their teenager's readiness to resolve these issues maturely. If the teenager's readiness is compromised by chronic moderate special needs, then the family is caught in a dilemma between trying to pave the way for their child's increasing autonomy and investigating alternative residential and vocational opportunities in the community. The parents are attempting to lay a groundwork that will allow themselves to move on to the next stage in their personal development. Martha Ufford Dickerson, a social worker at the Institute for the Study of Mental Retardation and Related Disabilities at the University of Michigan and a foster parent of teenage boys with mental retardation, has eloquently described this nexus between individual and family developmental stages in the case of parents of children with severe special needs, whose dependency on the family may be lifelong (Dickerson & Brown, 1978).

> Many parents begin to experience some loss of health, security or relationship during the middle years. . . . Their problems become compounded because they have one child who is not going to release them from responsibility. It gets to be a very big worry. Who is going to support this child? Who will pay the bills? Provide him a good home? Supervise his leisure time and his participation in the sheltered workshop or educational class? Who is going to keep him out of trouble, keep him from being misused? The parents find that they need to make long-term arrangements for the disabled child in the event of their deaths. They may become extremely depressed, and old guilt feelings may resurface. (p. 85)[§]

In addition to the anxiety aggravated by such realistic questions about the future, parents of teenagers with special needs will encounter impediments and postponements due to problems in the service delivery system itself. Perhaps most disconcerting for these families at this time is the experience of losing the systematic provision of educational and related services that had been sponsored through the schools. For the child, a secondary loss occurs with the termination of classes and the disbanding of his or her school-based peer group. For many families, the loss of the school as a "gatekeeper" and monitor of their child's services is tantamount to falling into a frightening abyss. Services for young adults with special needs tend to suffer from a greater degree of fragmentation than those for school-age children, which at least cohere around concerns of schooling. Given the dearth of personal home care attendants, restrictive program eligibility criteria, or program inaccessibility due to physical barriers, disappointments and setbacks are likely to characterize this transitional phase. Another hindrance may be an even greater public disdain toward grown-up than toward young sons or daughters with special needs, who simply by virtue of their age lack the appeal they may have had as children. The public's lowered expectations and skepticism about

---

[§]Reprinted with permission from Dickerson, M., & Brown, S. A search for a family. In S. Brown & M. Moersch (Eds.), *Parents on the team.* Ann Arbor: University of Michigan Press, 1978.

the economic productivity of young adults with special needs may also make this phase difficult. Communities may prove to be especially hostile to families of children with special needs now that towns are strapped with financial problems related to our country's recession and federal budget cuts.

Thus, the transition from childhood to adulthood for the maturing child with special needs involves the entire family in a number of adjustments. Both the family's resourcefulness and the condition of its community services will affect how easily these adjustments are made. There is a risk that the family will face considerable difficulty if the family's needs are not met by appropriate services.

Human service professionals can apply preventive mental health principles by teaching families how to anticipate roadblocks in the service delivery system and how to make forecasts about which routes will most likely lead to the acquisition of necessary services. As children with special needs come of age, families that are emotionally fortified and already armed with practical information will be better equipped to search for services and wisely guide their children's decision making.

This discussion about how families master this particular developmental challenge is but one illustration of the ways in which having a child with special needs can be stressful. Professionals have been shown to perceive inaccurately both the normalcy and the chronicity, albeit periodic, of the parent's dormant sorrow that is often awakened when an expected developmental milestone is delayed or not attained. Wikler, Wasow, and Hatfield (1981) found that social workers overestimated how upsetting the early experiences of parents of children with mental retardation were and underestimated how upsetting their later experiences were, such as the celebration of a child's 21st birthday. An implication of this study and of the issues in general surrounding the life cycle of families of children with special needs is the need for a continuum of services planned around these predictable periods of developmental change.

Allying Professionals with Parents

Unlike many families whose contacts with human service professionals are few and far between, families of children with special needs are routinely dependent upon the benevolence of human service staff and upon the vitality of the organizations that employ them. In particular, low-income families of children with special needs are involved in a multitude of associations with agencies and professionals, since welfare or other assistance payments typically originate from separate offices. Families that do not include a child with special needs often can confine their entanglements with human service agencies to periods of disruption precipitated by events such as job layoffs, divorce, or illness. By contrast, families of children with special needs often have little choice but to rely continually on these agencies as sources of essential, specialized care and assistance, sometimes spanning their child's lifetime.

These families consequently undergo a socialization process akin to conditioning in which they learn, first and foremost, that their family's boundaries will need to become highly permeable. That is, in order to get help their children require, they will have to submit themselves to interrogations about childrearing methods and family history. What for some families might be considered private information shifts into a semipublic sphere as professionals collect data for the ostensible purpose of planning appropriate services. While this purpose may be legitimate and laudable, some families are interviewed in an impersonal, even accusatory manner. Because their compliance with the interviewing may be correctly perceived as a precondition for receiving services, few parents, no matter how offended, will draw the line and criticize the professionals' disrespectful attitude. Thus the second aspect of the family's socialization is their relative powerlessness in the face of a bureaucratic structure shored up by reams of rules and regulations that are unfamiliar, if not incomprehensible, to most families.

While families of children with special needs learn to let others into their lives to provide help, they also must learn how to enter the human service professionals' world. They position themselves at a crossroads, regulating the flow of information and services. Entrance into the professionals' world entails participating in help-seeking and help-sustaining activities such as phone calling, reviewing records, attending conferences, and surveying programs. These activities cannot be taken for granted as part of the parents' natural repertoire of skills. They must learn what it takes to get, use, evaluate, monitor, and change services.

Some families fare better than others in managing the tasks of finding and orchestrating services and of fostering positive relationships with the professionals. They discover that their socialization into the role of "parents of a child with special needs" means that expectations of them are different from those of parents of nondisabled children. For example, they "should" be able to acknowledge their own helplessness by asking public agencies for help. Likewise, they should "cooperate" with professionals and carry out home tutoring or therapy. These moral imperatives place families of children with special needs in a quandary. While the presence of children with special needs can create burdens for families, the presumed burdensomeness of these children may stem less from the children's disabilities per se and more from the inadequacies of our services and from the ingrained attitudes held by the community.

Flaws in our service delivery system predispose it to hamper and at times obstruct the provision of adequate services to families of these children. Some parents nevertheless rise to the occasion and develop an assertive style, gain insight into how the system works, and focus a keen eye on their child's strengths and weaknesses. They will advocate for their child, but at a cost to their time, energy, and finances. For others the frequency of having to deal with professionals may hardly alleviate their dread. The situation becomes one to avoid. Families of children with special needs vary in terms of their level of interest, comfort, and skill in working with professionals and agencies. All, however, may find themselves settling for less than what they and their children are entitled to.

Because parents of children with special needs will be in contact with innumerable human service professionals, it behooves these professionals to understand this reality and to aim to empower parents, children's best advocates, rather than to diminish or dismiss them. Bartlett and Schlesinger (1976, p. 192) discuss several facets of professional accountability in this regard. They suggest that mental health professionals can "enfranchise" parents, first by "giving away their expertise, enabling consumers to ask more intelligent and pertinent questions of the providers," and secondly by creating "informal and formal mechanisms" to monitor the relationships between professionals and parents. A third step toward increased accountability would be for professionals to join with parents and interpret their complaints not as personal criticisms but as valid indictments against an imperfect system encompassing them both.

P.L. 94-142 dramatically empowered parents of children with special needs by specifying their rights. Empowerment, however, does not rest solely on legislative decree. Ultimately, legal reforms provide a framework and a philosophy that service providers (in conjunction with consumers) interpret and shape through their actions in classrooms, therapy offices, or service centers. Weatherly and Lipsky (1978) have called this less-publicized side of policy making "street-level bureaucracy."

One aspect of this policy making that is significant for human service professionals is the way in which public schools have pioneered methods of interdisciplinary assessment, planning, and curriculum development. At best, an interdisciplinary approach is a responsive, flexible, organic vehicle for service delivery. Parents' perceptions and recommendations are valued and actively tapped. Parents are engaged not only at the starting point of diagnosis and planning, but also through the phases of program implementation and evaluation.

To clarify the distinctions between the proposed "empowering" model and that of the conventional medical model, a brief appraisal of each follows. The medical model's definition of a team hinges upon the concepts of specialization and hierarchy. At one extreme, a single discipline asserts its expertise by conducting a unidisciplinary evaluation in which the evaluation questions, methods, results, and recommendations rest solely upon that discipline's autonomous judgment. Interaction with other disciplines is nonexistent. When disciplines unite to form a team, at minimum, a multidisciplinary approach may be employed. That is, each discipline keeps its respective tasks compartmentalized, yet recognizes the need for some contact with their counterparts in allied disciplines. Typically, there is no preevaluation dialogue by the team about which areas of the child's development will warrant careful examination, but there may be a pooling of results after each evaluation has been carried out independently. Integrating and translating these results into a language that is comprehensible to parents is rarely a priority. Parents are often excluded from these team meetings.

An advancement over the multidisciplinary approach is an interdisciplinary one in which representatives of several disciplines are committed to working together as members of a group to conduct and follow-through on evaluations. Noteworthy features of this approach include: (1) leadership that is determined by the priorities relevant within a case, rather than solely by a person's years of training, degrees, or prestige, (2) membership that includes parents in the deliberations, (3) colleagues from different disciplines who jointly preplan their evaluations and who work interdependently, (4) team conferences shaped by a sensitivity to communication issues in group process and mutual problem solving, and (5) collaborative program implementation.

Taken a step further, so-called transdisciplinary teams attempt to cut across or go beyond the boundaries that define any single discipline. Early intervention programs have successfully piloted transdisciplinary teams, for example, that involve an exchange of roles, called "role release," and "arena" assessments (Haynes, 1976). Role release enables one discipline to share its skills with others, frequently parents, through systematic supervision in the natural environment; arena assessment refers to an evaluation of a child that is conducted simultaneously by a pair or small number of professionals who may be assisted by the child's parents. Clearly, parent participation is affected by the ethos and structure of any team model being employed as well as by deliberate actions professionals take to elicit and reinforce parent participation. Research (Goldstein & Turnbull, 1982) has begun to indicate that the attendance and participation of parents of children with special needs in IEP meetings can be increased by such straightforward steps as completing premeeting questionnaires or by adding a parent advocate to the meeting.

From a policy perspective, mental health and social service agencies have much to learn from their educator peers who have been obliged by P.L. 94-142 to work out definitions of teamwork and parent participation. Although schools have differed in how narrowly or broadly they have carried out these fundamental elements of that law, there are compelling examples of nonhierarchical, democratically run teams that merit the attention of administrators and staff in the human services. We are beginning to witness the spread of an interdisciplinary approach (stimulated by the activities within special education) into pediatrics itself (Guralnick, 1982). A promising model for collaboration between health care personnel and educators has been used in Massachusetts. There the Department of Education Division of Special Education Early Childhood Project compiled regional community resource directories that were then presented in workshops for pediatricians who happily passed along their new information to the parents of their young patients (Taylor, 1980). Communities will find that regular meetings of a council representing the array of agencies affecting the lives of families of children with special needs can promote a liberating sense of shared responsibility and can simplify methods for cost sharing, coordination, and continuity of care.

A Look to the Future

Parents supporting each other have at times been maligned by professionals as amateurish. Yet banding together has been a crucial way for parents of children with special needs to take pride in their identity, to ward off fatigue and despair, to build a community, and to bring about change through collective action. Parents of children with special needs may remain psychologically and socially isolated unless they are introduced to other families whose experiences have parallels to their own. Of course each family's situation must be evaluated individually; but, in general, providing preliminary information about the availability of hotlines, toy-lending libraries, babysitter exchanges, parent groups, and disability and advocacy organizations at least gives families the chance to later involve themselves, in their own time and in their own way.

Within community mental health centers, it would be ideal to create a comfortable, welcoming space for parents of children with special needs to have refreshments, talk informally with other parents, and peruse brochures and bulletin board announcements. Resource directories of services would be available for parents to read alone or in consultation with a parent services coordinator, who might also be a parent of a child with special needs. Parents would be encouraged to jot down on index cards their ratings of services they have used. These cards would be compiled and made available in a file for parents to review. This kind of rating service would not only remind agencies of their need for accountability but would also enable parents to select services in a more personal manner. The friendly atmosphere in a parents' lobby might also make it easier for some parents to confide in others about their concerns or to make a decision to contact a new service.

An enlightened parent is one who is aware of the political circumstances governing the distribution of services in his or her locality. Documenting needs that are not being met produces data that is a persuasive tool in seeking funds or new legislation. Human service professionals have also found it strategic to join with parents to organize special needs coalitions and lobbies to keep legislators alert to grassroots sentiment (Biklen, 1974). Professionals can assist parent self-help groups by serving as speakers, consultants, coleaders, endorsers, and disseminators of timely information. Teaching parents and paraprofessionals how to carry out parts of service delivery plans and training future trainers across a state will in the long run have more of an impact through creating a "ripple" effect than the concentration of expertise among an elite group (Guerney, 1969).

Community mental health, in its best sense, is a public practice of psychology. Professionals must look beyond the preservation of their own turf and work to protect and nurture the human and material resources that families of children with special needs urgently require and deserve.

REFERENCES

Bartlett, D., & Schlesinger, S. Toward an enlightened consumer: Professional accountability in behavioral assessment. In G. Koocher (Ed.), *Children's rights and the mental health professions*. New York: Wiley, 1976.

Biklen, D. *Let our children go, an organizing manual for advocates and parents.* Syracuse, N.Y.: Human Policy Press, 1974.

Biklen, D., & Bogdan, R. Handicapism in America. In B. Blatt, D. Biklen, & R. Bogdan (Eds.), *An alternative textbook in special education, people, schools, and other institutions*. Denver: Love, 1977.

Celuzza, P., & Clayton, S. (Eds.). *Connections: A directory of services for children with special needs in the Boston Public Schools*. Boston: Public Schools Department of Special Services, 1979.

Chesler, B. *Mainstreaming through the media*. (The Early Childhood Project.) Boston: Massachusetts Department of Education, 1979.

Cutler, B. *Unraveling the special education maze: An action guide for parents*. Champaign, Ill.: Research Press, 1981.

Dickerson, M., & Brown, S. A search for a family. In S. Brown & M. Moersch (Eds.), *Parents on the team*. Ann Arbor: University of Michigan Press, 1978.

Featherstone, H. *A difference in the family, life with a disabled child*. New York: Basic Books, 1980.

Goldstein, S., & Turnbull, A. Strategies to increase parent participation in I.E.P. conferences. *Exceptional Children*, 1982, *48*, 360–361.

Gordon, I., & Breivogel, W. *Building effective home–school relationships*. Boston: Allyn & Bacon, 1976.

Guerney, G. B. (Ed.). *Psychotherapeutic agents: New roles for nonprofessionals, parents, and teachers*. New York: Holt, Rinehart, & Winston, 1969.

Guralnick, M. Pediatrics, special education, and handicapped children: New relationships. *Exceptional Children,* 1982, *48,* 294–295.

Haynes, V. *Staff development handbook: A resource for the transdisciplinary process.* New York: United Cerebral Palsy Association, 1976.

Heifetz, L. From consumer to middleman: emerging roles for parents in the network of services for retarded children. In R. Abidin (Ed.), *Parent education and intervention handbook.* Springfield, Ill.: Charles C Thomas, 1980.

Joiner, E., & Sabatino, D. A policy study of P.L. 94-142. *Exceptional Children,* 1981, *48,* 24–33.

Martin, E. W. Aid for disabled is defended. *New York Times* Winter Survey of Education, Section 13, January 10, 1982.

Miller, N., & Cantwell, D. Siblings and therapists: A behavioral approach. *American Journal of Psychiatry,* 1976, *133,* 447–450.

National Institute on Mental Retardation, Canada. *Sharing the experience . . . with Gavin.* Santa Monica, Calif.: The Stanfield House, 1981. (Film: 16 mm, color, 28 minutes.)

Oberklaid, F., Dworkin, P., & Levine, M. Developmental-behavioral dysfunction in preschool children: Descriptive analysis of a pediatric consultative model. *American Journal of Diseases of Children,* 1979, *133,* 1126–1131.

Pieper, E. The medical-moral model and people with disabilities. *Education Unlimited,* 1979, *1,* 38–39.

Pieper, E. Labels, language, and self-image. *Education Unlimited,* 1980, *2,* 43–44.

Powell, T. Sibling information network newsletter. Department of Educational Psychology, Box U-64, The University of Connecticut, Storrs, Connecticut, 1981.

Sameroff, A. J. Concepts of humanity in primary prevention. Paper presented at the Vermont Conference on the Primary Prevention of Psychopathology, Burlington, Vermont, June 1975.

Sarason, S. An asocial psychology and a misdirected clinical psychology. *American Psychologist,* 1981, *36,* 827–836.

Sarason, S., Carroll, C., Maton, K., Cohen, S., & Lorentz, E. *Human services and resource networks.* San Francisco: Jossey-Bass, 1977.

Sarason, S., & Doris, J. *Educational handicap, public policy, and social history. A broadened perspective on mental retardation.* New York: The Free Press, 1979, p. 23.

Schliefer, M. Let's all stop blaming the parents. *The Exceptional Parent,* 1981, *11,* 16–19.

Speck, R., & Attneave, C. *Family networks.* New York: Pantheon Books, 1973.

Taylor, A. Personal communication, 1980.

Turnbull, A., & Turnbull, H. R. *Parents speak out: Views from the other side of the two-way mirror.* Columbus, Ohio: Charles Merrill, 1978.

Weatherly, R., & Lipsky, M. Street-level bureaucrats and institutional innovation: Implementing special education reform. *Harvard Educational Review,* 1977, *47,* 171–197.

Wikler, L., Wasow, M., & Hatfield, E. Chronic sorrow revisited: Parent vs. professional depiction of the adjustment of parents of mentally retarded children. *American Journal of Orthopsychiatry,* 1981, *51,* 63–70.

4

Parent–Professional Interaction: The Roots of Misunderstanding

ROSALYN BENJAMIN DARLING

BIOGRAPHICAL SKETCH

Rosalyn Benjamin Darling, Ph.D., is Director of the In-Home Services Program at the City–County Clinic in Johnstown, Pennsylvania, which serves handicapped infants and preschool children, and is an adjunct faculty member at the University of Pittsburgh at Johnstown. She is a medical sociologist who teaches courses in various aspects of the sociology of the health care system. She is also a member of the Professional Advisory Council of the Spina Bifida Association of America.

Dr. Darling is the author of two books, Children Who Are Different: Meeting the Challenges of Birth Defects in Society, *a textbook for professionals (with husband, Jon) and* Families Against Society: A Study of Reactions to Children with Birth Defects, *as well as several articles on sociological aspects of handicapping conditions in children.*

ISBN 0-8089-1561-4
Copyright © 1983 by Grune & Stratton

It's somebody's tragedy. I can find good things in practically every-thing—even dying—but birth defects are roaring tragedies. . . . There's nothing interesting about it. . . . Death doesn't bother me, but the living do.*

—a pediatrician

They told me it would be a long, hard road with nothing but heart-aches. . . . It hasn't been that way at all. . . . She's my baby, and I love her and I wouldn't trade her for another child.*

—the parent of a child with Down's syndrome

WORLDVIEWS AND THEIR SOURCES

Sociologists employ the concept of worldview to describe the way individuals and groups perceive and define the events they encounter in everyday life. Members of the same cultural group tend to have similar worldviews. To the extent that their life experiences differ, however, individuals may have views that diverge markedly from those of others. The quotes above illustrate such divergent views in the case of handicapped children. Because their life experiences and consequent expectations differ, parents and professionals often see handicapped children in different lights. As a result, parent–professional interaction is strained, and conflict is a common outcome. As Freidson (1961) has written, "the separate worlds of experience and reference of the layman and the professional worker are always in potential conflict with each other (p. 175).

Knowledge, beliefs, attitudes, and opinions about a subject are learned through experience—at home, at school, on the job. Many parents have little knowledge of children before they have children of their own. The parenting experience is a powerful means of socialization that shapes parents' views of child development and appropriate parental behavior. Similarly, physicians and other professionals acquire their views from their educational training and subsequent professional experience, as well as from the experience derived from their nonprofessional roles in society. A professional who is not a parent cannot "understand" parenthood from the same perspective as the parent of five children. Similarly, a parent of a typical child cannot "understand" the experience of parenting a handicapped child in the same way as the handicapped child's parent.

The differing worlds of experience of parents and professionals is illustrated by the following account related by the mother of four multiply handicapped children:

---

*Reported in Darling, 1979, pp. 215, 166, 169.

I told my doctor I was always tired, and he said, "It's your nerves." . . . It got to the point where I thought, "Nobody wants to help me." . . . I saw a psychologist on TV . . . and I called him. . . . He said, "Don't you think someone else could take care of your children as well as you can?" I said, "It's not a matter of someone else. It's a matter of being able to pay somebody." . . . He said, "Go to work." . . . I'm not qualified. I've been home for 20 years. . . . I'm seeing someone else now. He's kind of giving me the blame for the way I am: "It's your fault you feel the way you do about things." I don't *want* to feel this way. . . . He says, "You create your own problems." My problem is that I have four handicapped children, and that has nothing to do with the fact that I had an unhappy childhood. . . . I'm nervous because I have reason to be nervous. . . . That night we were supposed to go someplace, and the van at the CP center broke down, so suddenly we had four kids to worry about. . . . We had to change our plans . . . . *That's the problem with these professionals.* . . . They have a job. . . . *They don't live with the parents 24 hours a day.* What sounds nice at the office just doesn't work in real life (emphasis added). (Darling, 1979, p. 179–180)†

Similarly, a mother of a spina bifida child explains,

The doctor says "Don't put her in diapers," and comes down hard on me when I do. . . . The last time I tried [putting her in panties], we both ended up being embarrassed in public. . . . Medical professionals see things only one way. They have no idea how the problem affects the family. (Spina Bifida Association of America, 1982)

In one study (Wolraich, 1980), a majority of pediatric practitioners reported *no* nonprofessional contact with developmentally disabled individuals, and in another small sample of pediatricians (Darling, 1979), less than seven percent had an immediate family member who was handicapped.

In this chapter the differing worldviews of parents of handicapped children and the professionals who work with them are examined. The sources of both parental and professional attitudes and behavior are explored, and an attempt is made to suggest some strategies for reconciliation, with the aim of improving the treatment of the handicapped child.

THE PROFESSIONAL (CLINICAL) WORLDVIEW

Many different professionals are involved with families of handicapped children. Depending on the child's disability, treatment professionals may include primary care and special physicians, nurses, and oth-

---

†Reprinted with permission from Darling, R. B. *Families against society: A study of reactions to children with birth defects.* Beverly Hills, Calif.: Sage Publications, 1979.

er medical personnel, educators, various therapists, social workers, psychologists, or other counselors, among others. Each of these professionals has a unique worldview associated with professional training and practice as well as with everyday social experience. In the past, the major shapers of the professional worldview have been (1) socialization in a stigmatizing society and (2) training in the clinical perspective. Each of these forces will be discussed in turn.

Social Stigma

Professionals are, first of all, people. As a result, they are exposed to the same social influences as others in society. From the time they are small they see uncomplimentary images of disabled people on television or read uncomplimentary accounts in books (literary villains, such as Long John Silver, have been classically depicted as disabled or disfigured), they hear unfavorable epithets, such as "retard" or "crip," and most have little informal, direct social contact with disabled individuals in their everyday lives. Media images *are* slowly changing, and the disabled *are* becoming a more vocal and visible minority in American society. Most professionals practicing today, however, have grown up with negative images of the disabled that are not always readily amenable to change.

As Goffman stated in his classic work on the subject (1963), the predominant social attitude toward those who are "different" is one of *stigma,* and stigmatized individuals are regarded as morally inferior to those who are "normal." Goffman's observations have been supported by a number of studies which found that individuals with various disabilities were not accepted by "normals." (See, for example, Kleck, Ono, & Hastorf, 1966; Richardson, 1970; Richardson, Goodman, Hastorf, & Dornbusch, 1961.) Discrimination against the disabled has been well documented in educational, occupational, recreational, and other settings.

Almost all of the general public's exposure to handicapping conditions is negative. Even when the disabled are shown in a "positive" light, they are typically depicted as objects of pity rather than as happy, fulfilled human beings. Considering such exposure, this pediatrician's view of handicapped children is not surprising:

> There are personal hang-ups. You go home and see three beautiful, perfect children; then you see this "dud." You can relate more easily to those with three beautiful perfect kids. . . . If somebody comes in with a cerebral palsy or a Down's, I'm not comfortable. . . . It's hard to find much happiness in this area. The subject of deformed children is depressing. Other problems I can be philosophic about. As far as having a Mongoloid child, I can't come up with anything good it does. There's nothing fun or pleasant. (Darling, 1979, pp. 214–215)

Such negative attitudes could be counteracted by professional training. However, as the following section will show, stigma may actually be reinforced by education in medical schools and other professional training programs.

The Clinical Perspective

The clinical perspective is shared by a variety of professionals, including physicians, social workers, and psychologists. Not all professionals are exposed to the clinical perspective to the same extent, and many changes are taking place in professional education. A majority of the professionals practicing today, however, have had some exposure to the perspective, and their attitudes and behavior have been shaped by it as a result.

The clinical perspective has a number of components, including (1) a belief in psychologistic theories of human behavior that locate the causes of all problems within the victim's personality or other individual traits, (2) the medicalization of all human problems based on an acute infectious disease model, (3) a belief in the need for professional dominance, and (4) a tendency to accept the restrictions imposed by the bureaucratic context of clinical work. These components are learned both formally and informally in the course of professional education and in professional practice. Each component will be discussed separately.

Blaming the Victim

Much clinical work involves changing the individual who has a problem. In the traditional medical model, the physician examines the patient, and not the patient's environment, to locate the cause of an illness. Similarly, when a child performs poorly in school, the child is often evaluated by an educational psychologist to determine the cause of the problem. Not many would suggest that the school or teacher be evaluated instead of the child. In the same way, a juvenile convicted of theft is sent to a training school to be rehabilitated; the juvenile's parents are not usually sent to prison. Education for clinical work, thus, tends to focus on the patient or client to the exclusion of the social framework within which the client operates.

The behavioral science training that is part of many professional education programs often has an individualistic focus as well. Training in the psychoanalytic perspective in particular locates the source of most human problems within the psyche of the client (or the client's parents). Subconscious motives are sought as explanations for pathologic behavior and, in some cases, *all* behavior is attributed to subconscious motives.

The clinical literature regarding parents of handicapped children is replete with such psychologistic interpretations. The major motivational force in these cases is believed to be parental guilt over having given birth to an imperfect child (see, for example, Forrer, 1959; Powell, 1975; Zuk, 1959). When such an interpretive framework is used, expressions of parental love are sometimes defined as "idealization," attention to a child's needs becomes "overprotection," and treating a child as normal is seen as "denial." Regardless of whether parents apparently accept or reject their children, their actions are believed to stem from a similar guilt-based source.

Professionals who accept such explanations seem to have difficulty believing that parents of handicapped children can *really* love their offspring in the same way as parents of typical children. Yet at the same time parents are expected to "cope" with their situation, regardless of the availability of physical, social, or financial supports to help them. When parents fail to cope, then, their failure is blamed on a supposed neurotic inability to accept the child. *Real* needs for financial aid, help with child care, or medical or educational services tend to be discounted and attributed to parental inadequacy rather than to a lack of societal resources.

Although some parents certainly *do* have neurotic tendencies, the victim-blaming model is inadequate to account for the many problems faced by parents of handicapped children. These problems stem largely from the fact that society is structured for typical families and goods and services for the handicapped are usually difficult, if not impossible, to find. Parental counseling does little to relieve parents of the burdens of daily care associated with having a handicapped child in the home. Yet most textbooks in the field persist in stressing guilt-based theories of parental behavior, and many new professionals come away from their training with the belief that the parents of handicapped children are responsible for their own problems.

The Medical Model

The primary focus of medical education is curing. Diseases that are readily amenable to cure provide the greatest rewards for medical students and physicians and enhance the physicians' feelings of self-worth and success. When physicians in one study (Mawardi, 1965) were asked which aspects of their careers they found most satisfying, they typically said "good therapeutic results or a large percentage of successful cases." Similarly, in a study of medical students, Ford (1967) found unfavorable attitudes toward "severely disabled" and "hopelessly ill" patients.

Pediatricians, in particular, have been trained to cure the acute illnesses of childhood, and most have chosen their specialty because of an appreciation for the qualities of typical, healthy children. As one pediatrician said, "our business is a pleasant business—going into the hospital to see a mother who has just had a (normal) baby" (Darling, 1979, p. 211). In one study of a small group of practicing pediatricians, Ford (1967) found that none of the respondents especially liked chronically ill patients and 46 percent definitely disliked the chronic cases.

The character of pediatric practice has changed over the years with the advent of modern antibiotics and immunization techniques. The emphasis on the curable has consequently shifted from severe infectious illnesses to high technology management of life-threatening situations. The neonatal intensive care unit marks this shift. The ultimate goal, however, remains *the maintenance or restoration of normalcy of function*. This goal does not take the child who cannot be made "normal" into account.

Because of its stress on the typical child, pediatric education has traditionally neglected the area of developmental disabilities. One study of practicing pediatricians (Powers and Rickert, 1979) found that only 27 percent felt that medical school and residency training had prepared them adequately to work with handicapped children. Similarly, Wolraich (1980) found that pediatric practitioners had less knowledge of developmental disabilities than residents with one month of special training in this area. Finally, Kelly and Menolascino (reported in Wolraich, 1982) found that most physicians were unaware of associations of parents of handicapped children, and many were unfamiliar with mental retardation services. Thus, most physicians leave their training with little knowledge of developmental disabilities and with the idea that permanently disabling conditions are not interesting, not important, or too depressing for further involvement. As one pediatrician (reported in Darling, 1979) said,

> I don't enjoy it. . . . I don't really enjoy a really handicapped child who comes in drooling, can't walk, and so forth. . . . Medicine is geared to the perfect human body. Something you can't do anything about challenges the doctor and reminds him of his own inabilities. (p. 215)

Sometimes the emphasis on curing has even led physicians to refuse to treat children with severe, permanent disabilities. Lorber (1971) and Duff and Campbell (1973) have presented strong arguments for nontreatment in some cases, and Todres, Krane, Howell, and Shannon (1977) have reported that more than half of the pediatricians they studied felt that newborns with Down's syndrome should not receive life-saving surgery. Similarly, two-thirds of the surgeons in another study (Shaw, Randolph, & Manard, 1977) would not consent to surgery for intestinal obstruction if their own child had Down's syndrome. The argument for nontreatment is the ultimate natural outcome of a model that stresses curing when curing is defined as making perfect.

Some have suggested the need for a new model in pediatric practice. Those who cannot be cured can still be treated. Treatment methods go beyond traditional medical practice and include educational and advocacy techniques. Pediatrics *is* slowly coming to recognize the need for more and better education in this area (Guralnick, 1981; Guralnick and Richardson, 1980), and Bennett (1982) has suggested that the pediatrician's role in the future will involve being "an active advocate for the 'whole' child in the family, community, and society." Recent trends in pediatric education are further discussed later in this chapter.

Professional Dominance

The professional-client relationship involves power and subordination. Traditionally, the professional's expertise has created a situation of "professional dominance" (Freidson, 1970), in which the "helpless" client or patient accepts whatever treatment the professional prescribes. Examples of professional dominance can be found in all fields. Most parents sign without question the individual education plans presented by their children's teachers, and most patients do not question their physicians' diagnoses (at least not while they are still in the doctor's office).

Professional dominance does differ somewhat in various professional fields. By virtue of their education and training and their high social status in the community, physicians have greater dominance than other professionals. Teachers, on the other hand, are more vulnerable and more likely to feel threatened by parents. As Lortie (reported in Seligman, 1979) notes, parents in America enjoy considerable rights in controlling their children's education. The enhancement of these rights by recent legislation (P.L. 94-142) has been regarded as a challenge to their professional expertise by many teachers.

Professional dominance serves to reinforce the professional's self-esteem at the expense of that of the client. As Slack (1977) has written, "For centuries, the medical profession has perpetrated paternalism as an essential component of medical care and thereby deprived patients of the self-esteem that comes from self-reliance." In order to maintain their self-esteem, professionals have traditionally felt a need to be "in control" of the interaction situation. Such control is enhanced by the settings in which such interactions generally occur—in the professional's office, school, hospital, or clinic—and only rarely in the client's home or office.

Professional dominance is learned in the process of professional education. As Haug and Lavin (1981) have noted, "the training of physicians lays heavy stress on their taking responsibility for their patients, which would seem to require the authority to be in charge and, if necessary, to take control in order to carry out that responsibility despite patient objections" (p. 218).

Further, Wolraich (1982) has written, "Medical training often neglects to teach physicians how to say 'I don't know' in a manner that will not reflect poorly on their competence. In fact, during medical school and residency training any lack of knowledge is frequently viewed as poor performance" (p. 325). Thus, the physician (and other professionals) learns to speak authoritatively as a mark of responsibility, competence, and expertise.

One way that professionals can maintain their dominance is to control the amount of information that the client receives. As Crozier (reported in Waitzkin and Stoeckle, 1976) has written, "A physician's ability to preserve his or her own power over the doctor-patient relationship depends largely on the ability to control the patient's uncertainty." Numerous examples exist in the literature of physicians' withholding information about prognosis in the case of serious, permanent, or terminal conditions (see, for example, Darling, 1979; Davis, 1960; Glaser and Strauss, 1965; Quint, 1965). When curing is not possible, the professional's dominance is threatened, and power is maintained only as long as the client or patient does not recognize the professional's inability to control or change the ultimate outcome.

In the case of permanent birth defects, for example, physicians commonly engage in stalling techniques such as avoidance, hinting, mystification, or passing the buck (see Darling, 1979, pp. 212–213, for a further explanation of these terms) in order to delay informing the parents. These techniques are usually rationalized with statements about parents' inability to handle emotion-laden information, as seen in these pediatricians' remarks (Darling, 1979):

> Birth is a traumatic experience. For 24 to 48 hours after birth the mother has not returned to a normal psychological state, so I just say everything is O.K., even if it isn't.

> It's not wise to go into all sorts of possibilities. I don't want to raise anxiety. Emotionally, they're in shock. They're really not listening.

> With cerebral palsy, I sort of lead them into it. I say, "Wait and see." I hedge. Usually I don't call in specialists for two or three months. It depends on parental pressure.

> I go slowly. . . . I don't seek a consultation right away. Usually the mothers want to see a specialist right away. They want the uncertainty removed. (pp. 205, 208)

Freidson (1970) argues that the client is believed to be "too ignorant to be able to comprehend what information he gets and . . . is, in any case, too upset at being ill to be able to use the information he does get in a manner that is rational and responsible" (p. 42).

Gliedman and Roth (1980) have noted that parents of handicapped children are typically caught between victim-blaming and professional dominance: "As for the parent, . . . he finds himself in a double bind: either submit to professional dominance (and be operationally defined as a patient) or stand up for one's rights and risk being labeled emotionally maladjusted (and therefore patientlike)" (p. 150). The clinical perspective is thus difficult to escape.

The Bureaucratic Context

Professional–client relationships reflect their societal context. The traditional model of the country doctor who makes house calls to a patient who is an old friend is no longer valid. As Bloom and Summey (1978) and others have noted, the patient today engages the services of a professional institution rather than a professional person. Increasing bureaucratization has diminished the interpersonal bond between professional and client. The bureaucratic context is apparent in this mother's report (Darling, 1979): "We went to the clinic at _____ Children's Hospital. . . . We saw a different doctor every time and we always had to wait a long time. One time, Kathy was so fussy by the time they got around to examining her, they couldn't even examine her. . . . The doctors treated her like a 'thing' "(p. 152).

The professional sees many clients with similar problems, and individual clients are only rarely regarded as special or unique. As Freidson (1961) has written, "The routine of practice not only makes varied elements of experience equivalent—it also makes them *ordinary*" (p. 176). With regard to teachers, Waller (reported in Seligman, 1979) has noted that the child is just one member of the category "student," and parents' requests for special treatment are regarded as presumptuous because their child is no different from the other pupils in the class. Gliedman and Roth (1980) note, similarly, that although an appointment with a professional may be the highlight of a parent's day, for the professional, it is routine.

Although the parent sees the child in many different contexts (home, school, neighborhood, etc.), the professional looks at the child only within the context of a particular specialty, such as medicine or education. Roth (1962) has written: "The goals of the professional in his relationship to the client tend to be highly specialized . . . whereas the goals of the client include goals generated by all of his roles in addition to that of client of a given professional person" (p. 577).

Professional training teaches the student to see the client as a "case" rather than a person. With regard to medical education, Straus (1978) has written,

> In [medical education] . . . a preoccupation with the intensely gratifying rewards associated with modern medical miracles has tended to focus values on impersonal techniques, substances, organs, systems, and procedures and to obscure the continuing importance of knowledge about the patient and the vital need for effective personal relationships with the patient. (p. 416)

Wolraich (1982) notes, too, that communication skills have traditionally been regarded as part of the "art" of medicine and have not been stressed in medical education.

As part of increasing bureaucratization, our professional care system has been marked by increasing specialization. Thus, as Pratt (1978) has noted, although the client may expect total care from a given professional, the professional's expectations may include only limited involvement with the client. A physician, for example, may have little or no interest in a child's school adjustment, or even in the child's medical problems that fall outside his or her field of specialization. Parents are not always aware of these distinctions between specialists.

The professional worldview is an ideal type. Not all professionals necessarily accept all of its tenets; in fact, many would reject some or all of them. Haug and Lavin (1981) have shown, for example, that some physicians do try to accommodate their patients' wishes rather than playing a dominant role, and even within the bureaucratic context, a few professionals *do* develop close, personal relationships with their clients.

Although the ideal type may not fit any given professional individual, it describes the subculture of norms, values, attitudes, and beliefs to which most professionals are exposed in the course of their training, practice, and collegial associations. The professional worldview characterizes the *professional community as a whole* but allows for variation within the whole. The worldview thus typifies what parents are likely to encounter when they interact with professionals concerning their handicapped children.

THE PARENT WORLDVIEW

Parents' worldviews generally change over time. Before their children are born, most parents of disabled children hold the same stigmatizing views of the handicapped as others in society. The experience of giving birth to and parenting a child who is "different," however, usually has a profound effect on parents' beliefs, values, and attitudes. Changing parental worldviews over a course of four time periods will be discussed: (1) prenatal, (2) infancy, (3) childhood, and (4) adolescence. These periods describe stages in the life of parents of congenitally handicapped children. Although parental reactions will be the same, these time periods will differ in the cases of handicaps that occur later in childhood or in later-appearing birth defects.

Prenatal Views

Most parents anticipate the birth of a healthy newborn. Although many do express concerns about the health of their unborn offspring, these concerns are generally rationalized away by the time the birth is imminent. Obstetricians and childbirth education classes usually assume that the baby will be normal, and the possibility of birth defects is not mentioned.

Parents enter the delivery room, then, with a set of expectations revolving around the birth of a normal baby. In the case of obvious birth defects, these expectations are not fulfilled. Although few physicians tell parents about a defect immediately, most arouse suspicion by their behavior:

> The doctor did not say anything at all when the baby was born. Then he said, "It's a boy," and the way he hesitated, I immediately said, "Is he all right?" And he said, "He has ten fingers and ten toes," so in the back of my mind I knew there was something wrong. (Mother of a Down's syndrome child, reported in Darling, 1979, p. 129.)

Sometimes, parents' suspicions continue to be aroused well into the postpartum period when physicians continue to deny the existence of a problem. Most parents are aware of an abnormality before they are informed by their pediatrician. However, as noted in the last section, physicians generally use various stalling techniques before acknowledging that parents' suspicions are correct. The result is bitterness toward the physician:

> I always thought they told you the truth in the hospital and if you wanted to know anything you should ask. I really thought her ears looked funny and I had this funny feeling, so I asked the doctor, "Is there anything wrong?," and he looked right at me and said, "No." . . . The next morning he told me she was retarded. . . . I was very bitter about it. (Mother of a Down's syndrome child, reported in Darling, 1979, p. 131)

> [The neurologist said] "I think I know what's wrong with your son but I'm not going to tell you because I don't want to frighten you." Well, I think that's about the worst thing anyone could say. . . . We didn't go back to him. . . . We insisted that our doctor refer us to _____ Children's Hospital, but the doctor said, "He's little. Why don't you wait? You don't need to take him there yet." . . . Everyone was pablum-feeding us, and we wanted the truth. (Mother of a child with cerebral palsy, reported in Darling, 1979, p. 147)

Before they are given a truthful diagnosis, then, many parents of congenitally disabled children feel a great deal of anomie in the form of meaninglessness. They know that *something* is wrong with their baby and they fear the worst. When professionals refuse to confirm their suspicions, they sometimes develop pathologic reactions, such as blaming the baby's delayed development on their own inadequacies as parents. They rarely challenge their physicians because they have been socialized to respect their professional dominance. In the end, however, parents' confidence in the physician is likely to be eroded.

Infancy

When parents are first informed about their children's disabilities they are likely to feel shock, disappointment, grief, sorrow, and remorse. Such reactions are understandable in light of the fact that, typically, parents' only prior exposure to handicapping conditions has been negative. As one mother said, "I was thinking of all the retarded people I'd seen. I wasn't thinking about my little girl anymore" (Darling, 1979, p. 135). Another mother said, "I remember thinking, before I got married, [having a handicapped child] would be the worst thing that could ever happen to me" (Darling, 1979, p. 124).

Strongly negative reactions are usually short-lived, however. Most parents receive encouragement and support from close friends and family members, but the strongest shaper of parental feelings is usually the handicapped infant itself. As parents live with their children, they learn to love them. Most parents leave the postpartum period with the desire to do all they can for their children, because, like parents of typical children, their self-esteem as parents is based in some measure on their children's accomplishments. Although parents' goals may have to be adjusted (the physically handicapped child may not become a star athlete, and the mentally handicapped child will not become a great scientist), most parents are able to find meaning and pleasure in the goals their children *can* accomplish, no matter how small.

In our society, "good" parents do all they can for their children. As a result, most parents are strongly motivated to find appropriate treatment programs that will maximize their children's achievements. Parents' quests, however, are sometimes thwarted by professionals who see little merit in training handicapped children who will never be "normal" to achieve small objectives. Consequently, meaninglessness is replaced by feelings of powerlessness, and parents continue to feel anomie because they are not in control of their children's lives and have no definite plan of action.

Because many pediatricians are not aware of services for handicapped children even when they do see the value of such services, parents often embark on long and elaborate searches to find information about their children's problems, infant stimulation and preschool training programs, physical therapy, special equipment, and community resources of various kinds. As one mother said "I was looking for a door at that point—somebody who could give us any help at all. Dr. _____ didn't even tell us there was a state agency that dealt with mental retardation" (Darling, 1979, p. 149).

For many parents, the first source of real help is other parents of similarly disabled children. In parents' groups mothers and fathers receive emotional support as well as practical information about child rearing techniques, resources, and services. As one mother said: "I met other parents of the retarded after we moved here. I felt that made the biggest difference in my life. . . . Down there (where we lived before) . . . I felt that I was just singled out for something, that I was weird. I felt a lot of isolation and bitterness. . . . Meeting other parents you get practical hints—like how someone got their child to chew—that normal parents take for granted" (Darling, 1979, pp. 162–163).

Parents' groups serve too as a forum for exchanging "horror stories" about bad experiences with professionals. Favorite stories usually involve the situation of first information about a child's problem and some professionals' lack of caring or concern for handicapped children. When parents hear other stories similar to their own they realize that their experiences are shared and their definitions of events are supported. As a result, some parents become more assertive in advocating their rights and their children's rights in interactions with professionals.

During the preschool years, most parental advocacy involves medical professionals. Professionals often argue that parents of handicapped children "shop around" in search of a miracle cure. However, most "shopping" usually involves, rather, a search, first, for a correct diagnosis, and second, for a practitioner who is eager or even willing to have the child as a patient. One family with a severely handicapped child describes how they became involved with an alternative treatment program:

> My pediatrician kept after me to put him away (in an institution). (We finally changed pediatricians). Our new pediatrician gushed all over us at first. . . . But then, he never touched Billy. I always had to move him for him. We were never left in the waiting room. It was like I was an embarrassment. . . . It's like when you take your dog to the vet. . . . Not many doctors pick him up and try to communicate with him as a child.
>
> Because nothing was happening, and I was just sitting there with this baby, we got involved with the patterning program. . . . It was the first time that anyone had reacted to him as Billy: "Billy is a person, and we'll help Billy." We were never told he would be cured. They were the first people who reacted to Billy as a person or called him by name. Up to that time he had done nothing. My pediatrician said, "You're just looking for hopes." I said, "No, I'm just looking to *do* something for him. I'm sitting at home doing nothing." (Darling, 1979, pp. 151, 152)

Parents of handicapped children are probably more likely than other parents to play an active role in their children's medical treatment because of repeated negative experiences with medical professionals. Handicapped children are more likely to require frequent hospitalization, and parents are more likely to come into contact with a variety of medical professionals, not all of whom will be sympathetic toward the handicapped child. These parents begin to feel as though their child is becoming the "property" of the hospital and the medical professional and come to resent their loss of control over their own child and their own lives. As one mother of a spina bifida child said, "We were always going back and forth to _____ Children's Hospital. . . . It was a constantly pulling away. We could never be a family. . . . We got to the point where we hated doctors, we hated _____ Children's Hospital" (Darling, 1979, p. 154).

Parents' expressions of dissatisfaction with medical treatment have been encouraged by the recent growth of the consumer movement in health care. As Reeder (1972) has noted, the consumer-provider relationship is not as one-sided as it was in the past, and bargaining and negotiation are now part of the interaction process. Haug and Lavin (1979) found that most people are *willing* to challenge a physician's authority today; however, most people have never done so. The strongest impetus to *actual* challenge appears to be *the experience of medical error* (Haug and Lavin, 1981), an experience that is certainly common among parents of handicapped children. (Parent activism is further discussed later in this chapter.)

By the end of the preschool years, most parents have obtained an accurate diagnosis of any early-appearing handicap and have found a pediatrician who is willing to treat the child. Many have also found emotional support from family, friends, and especially, from other parents of handicapped children. The lifestyle of such parents is usually not very different from that of other young parents in American society.

Childhood

By the beginning of the school years, most parents have adopted a stance of *realistic acceptance* toward their situation. They remain unhappy about their children's handicaps but they are able to see positive aspects in their children's lives. As one mother said, "I'm not sorry. I think it's opened a whole new world for me—you don't get involved until it strikes home" (Darling, 1979, p. 185). Although they would prefer that their children were not handicapped, most parents love their children in spite of their handicaps. Some phrases used by one sample of parents (Darling, 1979) to describe their disabled sons and daughters included: "a joy to me and her family," "retarded but can learn," " a binding force in the family as a whole," "a beautiful child," and "a teacher of compassion and love."

Voysey (1975) has suggested that the ideology of realistic acceptance is learned from professonals, voluntary associations, and the popular culture. In our society, parents of handicapped children are *supposed* to accept their situation. "Success stories" and other images of parents who are coping well are commonly presented in the media, and parents are expected to emulate these models. Most parents do live up to such expectations and learn to "make the best" of their difficult situation. In attempting to achieve a lifestyle that is as close to normal as possible, these parents often look to professionals to provide needed supports. When such supports are not forthcoming, conflict results.

As indicated in the previous section, most parent–professional conflict during the preschool years involves medical professionals. During later childhood the focus of conflict tends to shift to the field of education. Because our educational system is structured primarily for typical children, it often fails to meet the needs of the exceptional child. Thus, parents once again come to play the role of advocate in attempting to secure an appropriate educational program for their children.

The most common educational problem faced by these parents is the placement of the child in an inappropriate program. Usually such placements are made for the convenience of the school system rather than to meet the needs of the child. As one mother of a spina bifida child explained:

> When Ellen entered kindergarten, she was in a special needs class in the morning and mainstreamed in the afternoon. . . . [In the special needs class], she was with children whose needs were much more demanding than Ellen's. . . . Some were retarded. . . . At the end of the year we had a meeting. The first grade was on the second floor . . . [Ellen was in a wheelchair]. They said we should keep her in the special needs class. I was furious. . . . She had done so well in the mainstreaming class. . . . I wanted her in a regular first grade and I suggested moving the class downstairs. . . . They wanted Ellen in the special needs class, because it was easier for *them,* not for any other reason. (Darling & Darling, 1982, p. 140)

Sometimes, *no* appropriate placement exists, as revealed in this account by the mother of four multiply handicapped teenagers:

> At Children's Hospital, Tony was in a class with bright, active kids. . . . He just sat in the corner and played in the sandbox. . . . Then he went to the School for the Blind, which is geared for the totally blind child. . . . They mostly concentrated on teaching Braille. Finally, Tony and Jean had to leave the school. They said they were retarded. . . . The teachers were not trained in learning disabilities. . . .
>
> After Tony and Jean were labeled retarded by the School for the Blind, they started in the [city] Public School System, but they had no appropriate program either. . . . After three years, we started fighting. . . . The Board of Education said, "We've got all kinds of retarded programs. We'll just put them in one of those." . . . I visited the programs, and there wasn't one child in a wheelchair. . . . I said, "How are my children going to get around? How are they going to go on these stairs?" . . . They told us we had the only multiply handicapped teenagers in the city. . . . I said, "We have the only *siblings,* but you've got a lot of *misplaced* multiply handicapped children." I knew them all. (Darling, 1979, pp. 176–177)

The parents of these children continued to write letters to school system administrators, and a program was finally established. As another parent explained, "You eventually get what you need . . . if you're very persistent, but they always leave you with the feeling that they're doing you a favor . . . to provide your son with an education" (Darling & Darling, 1982, p. 138).

Another common concern involves a lack of coordination among educational services (Orenstein, 1979). Because current legislation mandates that handicapped children be "mainstreamed" in regular classes as much as possible, many children are served by special education teachers or therapists for part of the school day and by regular classroom teachers the rest of the day. Regular teachers who have not been trained to work with handicapped children are often not involved with special education programming, and, as Scanlon, Arick, and Phelps (1981) have noted, most do not attend parent conferences. Some of these teachers resent their exclusion by special education staff; however, parents may come to feel that regular class teachers and other school personnel are not interested in their children's education.

Finally, some parents engage in controversies with school systems over the provision of ancillary services, such as in-school physical therapy or catheterization. In some cases, long court battles have resulted from parents' challenging the school's denial of such services to their children. Catheterization of a spina bifida child, for example, is a simple procedure that can be performed by a school nurse. When nurses do not perform the procedure, the parent must come to the school every day to do it. This daily requirement is burdensome to parents, especially those who do not have transportation, and usually generates resentment toward the administrators who refuse to assign the procedure to school personnel.

Sometimes parents are afraid that if they challenge the school system their children will be removed from a mainstream situation and placed in special classes or that the children will be hurt in other ways. As one mother said, "I'm always afraid that if I start making any waves, then they will reflect this on Ellen. I want her to be accepted" (Darling & Darling, 1982, p. 141).

As Seligman (1979) has noted, parents may also feel intimidated by teachers for other reasons. They may feel inferior educationally or socially. The teacher may be older than the parent or of a different sex. Most parents are nervous in the conference situation anyway because they are likely to hear negative evaluations of their child. Such fears do not encourage open communication between parents and school personnel.

By the end of the school years, many parents of handicapped children do become more assertive as a result of repeated negative experiences with the school system. Professional dominance in the educational realm is challenged for the same reasons as dominance in the medical realm: parents are trying to secure services that will permit them to enjoy a normalized lifestyle, one similar to that of families with typical children.

Normalization is the prime motivating force for parents of handicapped children. For some families normalization is relatively easy to attain because of supportive physicians, cooperative school systems, and other family and community supports. Other families attain normalization only after a series of struggles to obtain needed services. A few families whose children have unusual, continuing needs or who are socially or geographically isolated never attain normalization at all; for them the primary mode of adaptation is continued "crusadership" to create needed services, or resignation to their fate. Most commonly, however, families do achieve normalization by the end of the childhood years. As one father described this adaptation, "Retardation is not number one around here. It's just something that Karen has" (Darling, 1979, p. 190).

Adolescence

The bubble of normalization may be burst as adolescence and impending adulthood approach. Typical children become increasingly independent as they grow. They eventually leave home and establish independent lifestyles. For the moderately or severely handicapped child such independence is problematic, and parents who have been living "one day at a time" must once again begin to search for solutions as their children's adulthood approaches.

Because concern about the future is highly salient to parents at this time, their interactions with professionals may reflect this concern. Parents may look to professionals for help in finding appropriate living arrangements, occupational placements, or legal or financial advice for their adult handicapped children. When professionals are not able to provide the information and advice that parents seek at this stage in their children's lives, parents may turn to nonprofessional sources such as parents' associations for help.

Parents' worldviews, then, tend to change over the course of their children's life cycles. During the prenatal period most hold somewhat negative views of the handicapped and somewhat positive views of professionals. In the immediate postpartum period negative views of the handicapped generally continue, but professionals may come to be regarded negatively as well. During later infancy and childhood views of the handicapped typically change; as they live with and come to love their

TABLE 4-1. Ideal–Typical Role Patterns of Professionals and Parents

Professional	Parent
Achieved	Ascribed
Universalistic	Particularistic
Functionally specific	Functionally diffuse
Affectively neutral	Affective
Dominant	Anomic

own children, parents are able to view handicapped individuals in a favorable light and to see some positive aspects of their own life situations. Views of professionals are likely to remain unfavorable, however, as negative interactions with medical, educational, and other professionals continue to occur. Eventually some parents do encounter professionals who are helpful to them, but negative attitudes will continue to prevail as long as large numbers of professionals are uninformed about, uninterested in, or unconcerned about the needs of handicapped children and their parents.

THE CLASH OF PERSPECTIVES

Because parents and professionals hold such divergent worldviews, when they meet in various interaction situations each is likely to define the other in a negative way. Although parents and professionals generally do not openly discuss these negative views with one another, the resulting lack of mutual respect is likely to affect the quality of care that the handicapped child receives.

The opposing worldviews of parents and professionals that have been described can be summarized by a typology suggested by Parsons (1951). According to Parsons, the role of the professional in our society is characterized by the traits of achievement, universalism, functional specificity, and affective neutrality. When the Parsonian typology is applied to parents of handicapped children (or clients or patients in general) their role can be characterized by the traits of ascription, particularism, functional diffuseness, and affectivity. In addition, the professional role is marked by dominance, and the client role is marked by anomie and submission (see Table 4-1). Although these are ideal–typical traits that do not always apply to individual professionals or parents, they describe the normative expectations that accompany the parent and professional *roles* in American society today.

Achievement/Ascription

The status of professional is *achieved,* and the status of parent of a handicapped child is *ascribed.* Because professionals *choose* their careers, they are likely to expect the freedom to practice in a manner that is interesting and rewarding to them. As a result, many do not want to be "bothered" with the problems of handicapped children. Parents, on the other hand, have little choice; they have given birth to a child with a problem whose care they are expected to assume. Although parenthood is an achieved status, if given a choice virtually no parents would want their children to be handicapped. Most, however, are able to love their child and accept society's expectations about good parenting and doing everything possible to help their child. These parents become frustrated when they interact with professionals who do not share their parental enthusiasm.

Universalism/Particularism

The professional is concerned with all cases of a particular type, while the parents are concerned with only one case—their own child. The universalistic orientation of the professional is reflected in the bureaucratic structure of clinical practice and the tendency to treat all clients in a like manner, regardless of each client's unique personal situation. Professionals tend to categorize clients on the basis of clinical theory and past personal and clinical experience. Resulting generalizations may lead them to treat all parents or parents of a given class similarly. Pieper (in Darling & Darling, 1982) notes anecdotally, for example, a case in which a professional gave parents a long lecture about their guilt over having given birth to a handicapped child, only to learn that the child who was the subject of their discussion was adopted.

Parents resent universalistic treatment. For them, *this* child is important. These parental reports are typical:

> Whenever there's something wrong, our pediatrician says, "I don't know what I can do for you. That's her condition." . . . He blames all of her [medical] problems on retardation instead of treating them. (Mother of a severely retarded child)‡

> She had a problem with her knee, and we took her to _____ Children's Hospital. . . . They said, "There's nothing we can do with one of *these* children." (Father of a child with Down's syndrome)‡

> [Our pediatrician] treated her as an article in a medical journal. (Mother of a child with a rare congenital syndrome)‡

---

‡Reported in Darling, 1979, pp. 151, 152.

Specificity/Diffuseness

As Mercer (1965) has noted, clients may be regarded from either a clinical or a social system perspective. In the clinical perspective, the client is defined in terms of his or her problem; in the social system perspective, all of the client's roles—in addition to the role of "client with a problem"—are taken into account. Most professionals employ a clinical perspective, in which the client's specific presenting problem or symptoms become paramount and the other roles played by the client in the community are ignored. Thus the hospital patient becomes "the gall bladder in Room 32," even though he is also a husband, a father, a carpenter, and a churchgoer. One adult with cerebral palsy noted that the message constantly communicated by professionals was, "Your weakest point is what is most important to us, we don't care about the rest of you" (Richardson, 1972, p. 533). Similarly, the father of a retarded child with cerebral palsy remarked, "The pediatrician . . . would keep him alive but he wasn't interested in Brian as a *person*" (Darling, 1979, p. 152).

Parents see their children playing a variety of social roles: loving son or daughter, sibling, grandchild, playmate, and student, as well as child with a problem. Their relationship to their child is diffuse, involving all of these roles. Sometimes, when a child's handicap does not conflict with the roles played by the child in the family setting, parents do not define the child as handicapped at all. A child with a learning disability, for example, may be regarded as perfectly normal at home and in the neighborhood. The parents of such a child may resent a label applied by professional educators that is not relevant to their experience. Professionals sometimes accuse such parents of denying reality; their unidimensional perspective prevents them from realizing that the parents' "reality" may be very different from their own.

Affective Neutrality/Affectivity

Professional training stresses the instrumental nature of the professional role, and the professional is cautioned about becoming too emotionally involved with the client. Overinvolvement is believed to impair the professional's instrumental effectiveness. Consequently, many professionals seek to maintain some emotional distance between themselves and their clients. Stacey (1980) notes, further, that professionals are often not trained in techniques of counseling or supportive communication.

Clients, on the other hand, generally expect professionals to satisfy their socioemotional needs. Freidson (1961) found that patients expected their physicians to be *both* technically competent and able to satisfy emotional needs. Many questioned their physicians' competence in the socioemotional area. Many parents interpret professionals' affective neutrality to mean that these professionals do not care about their children. Some parents become involved in unconventional or sometimes even unethical treatment programs because these programs are likely to provide greater emotional satisfaction. Parents who love their children resent teachers, physicians, and other professionals who appear to be indifferent and do not show any appreciation for their children's positive qualities.

Professional Dominance/Anomie

Generally, both professionals and parents have a need to be in control of their situations of mutual interaction. Typically, however, professionals retain control. The ritualized routine of clinical practice supports the professional's dominance. Parents, on the other hand, are likely to feel powerless and resent the professional's control over their lives.

Parents only rarely challenge professional dominance openly, however. As Strong (1979) noted in a study of two hospital outpatient departments, "Many parents disagreed strongly with the doctors' verdict at one time or another. Nevertheless all but a handful made no direct challenge to their authority. Most maintained an outward pose of agreement with what they were told" (p. 87). Stimson and Webb (1975) explain patients' reticence to challenge the physician as follows:

> Our observations and interviews lead us to suggest that the doctor is aided in his ability to exert control over the information he gives and in his way of acting towards patients by their desire to please him, to emerge from the encounter without loss of face. (p. 127)

Parents *do* often complain about professionals after they have left the clinical setting. Parents' groups serve an important function by providing a forum for storytelling. As a result of interaction in such groups, many parents change physicians or explore various treatment modes against the advice of professionals. As Stimson and Webb (1975) have noted, "Whilst the patient's ability to control the outcome of the consultation is limited, he has considerable ability to control what happens after he has left the doctor's presence." (p. 87). Parents who do not have access to supportive interactions outside of the clinical setting may continue to feel anomie, however. Parents who reside in isolated rural areas or feel inferior in social class status are especially likely to remain powerless in the face of professional dominance.

NEW DIRECTIONS IN PROFESSIONAL TRAINING AND PARENTAL ACTIVISM

Are the worldviews of parents and professionals hopelessly in conflict? Until recently little effort was made, either by professionals or by parents, to change attitudes. Within the past few years, however, parents have become actively involved in social movements to bring about change; and even more recently, new professional training curricula are being designed to promote awareness of the needs of handicapped children and their families.

Parental Activism

Consumerism in general has been growing in recent years. Various minority groups have also become more vocal in demanding their rights. As part of this larger social movement, parents of handicapped children have become more active in asserting their demands for programs and services for their children. This new assertiveness has been aided by legislation such as the Education for All Handicapped Children Act and by a number of recent publications that instruct parents in organizing techniques (see, for example, Biklen, 1974, and Markel & Greenbaum, 1979).

So far, most parental challenges have occurred within the realm of education. With the support of recent legislation, parents are confronting school administrators with demands for appropriate educational programs for their children. Challenges in the medical realm are not as widespread and have tended to take place quietly, on a case-by-case basis rather than as part of a larger social movement. Most parents are still intimidated by medical authority and are reluctant to confront physicians directly with their concerns. Consumerism in the health care field has been increasing, however, and parents will be more likely to challenge the medical profession directly as support for such challenges grows.

Changing Professional Attitudes

While parents have become more involved in advocacy movements, some professionals have become similarly involved. Although some continue to question the correctness of such involvement and its implied threat to the affective neutrality of the professional role (see, for example, Adams, 1973, and Kurtz, 1975), more and more professionals are arguing that advocacy is a necessary extension of helping, an inherent function of their role (see Council for Exceptional Children, 1981). Parsons (1951) has suggested that, in addition to being affectively neutral, achieved, specific, and universalistic, the professional role is also *collectivity-oriented,* that is, the professional has a mission to help the client. When this mission conflicts with other aspects of the role, the professional must decide which aspect is most important. Consequently, some professionals are choosing to become involved in advocacy on behalf of their clients.

Medical school curriculum has also been undergoing some changes in recent years. Because the acute infectious diseases of childhood are now largely treatable or preventable, pediatricians and family physicians have been turning their attention to other areas. Although most pediatric curricula do not stress chronic, handicapping conditions, a new interest in developmental disability is apparent in a recent statement issued by the Task Force on Pediatric Education (1978). In addition, curricula on handicapped children are being developed for pediatric residents and physician inservice training (Guralnick et al., 1982; Powers and Healy, 1982). New techniques of instruction employing videotapes, trained parents, and experience with handicapped children are also being used to make professionals more aware of the parent worldview (see, for example, Richardson, Guralnick, & Tupper, 1978; Stillman, Sabers, & Redfield, 1977). Finally, a recent textbook for professionals (Darling & Darling, 1982) stresses the importance of taking the parents' perspective into account in treating the handicapped child.

Is Rapprochement Possible?

Will all these recent efforts bring parents and professionals closer together? In one report (Stacey, 1980), professionals who were made aware of parents' dissatisfaction did not change their behavior at all. However, as Richardson et al. (1978), Wolraich (1979), and others have reported, pediatricians and residents exposed to training programs in developmental disabilities did have more favorable attitudes toward handicapped children as a result. Only the future will reveal whether the worldview gap between parents and professionals has been narrowed by recent efforts. Certainly, neither group will ever share the other's experiences completely. As long as human beings are capable of empathy, however, change in the direction of greater mutual understanding is possible.

REFERENCES

Adams, M. Science, technology, and some dilemmas of advocacy. *Science,* 1973, *180,* 840–842.

Bennett, F. C. The pediatrician and the interdisciplinary process. *Exceptional Children,* 1982, *48,* 306–314.

Biklen, D. *Let our children go: An organizing manual for advocates and parents.* Syracuse, N.Y.: Human Policy Press, 1974.

Bloom, S. W., & Summey, P. Models of the doctor–patient relationship: A history of the social system concept. In E. B. Gallagher (Ed.), *The doctor–patient relationship in the changing health scene.* Washington: U.S. Government Printing Office, 1978.

Council for Exceptional Children. Editor's note. *Exceptional Children,* 1981, *47,* 492–493.

Darling, R. B. *Families against society: A study of reactions to children with birth defects.* Beverly Hills, Calif.: Sage Publications, 1979.

Darling, R. B., & Darling, J. *Children who are different: Meeting the challenges of birth defects in society.* St. Louis: C.V. Mosby, 1982.

Davis, F. Uncertainty in medical prognosis, clinical and functional. *American Journal of Sociology,* 1960, *66,* 41–47.

Duff, R. S., & Campbell, A. G. M. Moral and ethical dilemmas in the special-care nursery. *New England Journal of Medicine,* 1973, *289,* 890–894.

Ford, A. B. *The doctor's perspective: Physicians view their patients and practice.* Cleveland: The Press of Case Western Reserve University, 1967.

Forrer, G. R. The mother of a defective child. *Psychoanalytic Quarterly,* 1959, *28,* 59–63.

Freidson, E. *Patients' views of medical practice.* New York: Russell Sage Foundation, 1961.

Freidson, E. *Professional dominance.* Chicago: Aldine, 1970.

Glaser, B. G., & Strauss, A. L. *Awareness of dying.* Chicago: Aldine, 1965.

Gliedman, J., & Roth, W. *The unexpected minority: Handicapped children in America.* New York: Harcourt Brace Jovanovich, 1980.

Goffman, E. *Stigma: Notes on the management of spoiled identity.* Englewood Cliffs, N.J.: Prentice-Hall, 1963.

Guralnick, M. J. Early intervention and pediatrics: Current status and future directions. *Journal of the Division for Early Childhood,* 1981, *2,* 52–60.

Guralnick, M. J., & Richardson, H. B. (Eds.). *Pediatric education and the needs of exceptional children.* Baltimore: University Park Press, 1980.

Guralnick, M. J., Richardson, H. B., Jr., & Heiser, K. E. A curriculum in handicapping conditions for pediatric residents. *Exceptional Children,* 1982, *48,* 338–346.

Haug, M. R., & Lavin, B. Public challenge of physician authority. *Medical Care,* 1979, pp. 844–858.

Haug, M. R., & Lavin, B. Practitioner or patient—who's in charge? *Journal of Health and Social Behavior,* 1981, *22,* 212–229.

Kleck, R., Ono, H., & Hastorf, A. H. The effects of physical deviance upon face-to-face interaction. *Human Relations,* 1966, *19,* 425–436.

Kurtz, R. A. Advocacy for the mentally retarded: the development of a new social role. In M. J. Begab & S. A. Richardson (Eds.), *The mentally retarded and society: A social science perspective.* Baltimore: University Park Press, 1975.

Lorber, J. Results of treatment of myelomeningocele. *Developmental Medicine and Child Neurology,* 1971, *13,* 279–303.

Markel, G., & Greenbaum, J. *Parents are to be seen and heard: Assertiveness and educational planning for handicapped children.* San Luis Obispo, Calif.: Impact Publishers, 1979.

Mawardi, B. H. A career study of physicians. *Journal of Medical Education,* 1965, *40,* 658–666.

Mercer, J. R. Social system perspective and clinical perspective: Frames of reference for understanding career patterns of persons labeled as mentally retarded. *Social Problems,* 1965, *13,* 18–34.

Orenstein, A. Organizational issues in implementing special education legislation. Paper presented at the annual meeting of the Society for the Study of Social Problems, Boston, 1979.

Parsons, T. *The social system.* New York: Free Press, 1951.

Powell, F. D. *Theory of coping systems: Changes in supportive health organizations.* Cambridge, Mass.: Schenkman, 1975.

Powers, J. T., & Healey A. Inservice training for physicians serving handicapped children. *Exceptional Children,* 1982, *48,* 332–336.

Powers, J. T., & Rickert, N. Physician perceptions of in-service training needs: A working paper. Evanston, Ill.: American Academy of Pediatrics, 1979.

Pratt, L. V. Reshaping the consumer's posture in health care. In E. B. Gallagher (Ed.), *The doctor–patient relationship in the changing health scene.* Washington, D.C.: U.S. Government Printing Office, National Institutes of Health Publication 78–183, 1978.

Quint, J. C. Institutionalized practices of information control. *Psychiatry,* 1965, *28,* 119–132.

Reeder, L. G. The patient-client as a consumer: Some observations on the changing professional–client relationship. *Journal of Health and Social Behavior,* 1972, *13,* 406–412.

Richardson, H. B., Guralnick, M. J., & Tupper, D. B. Training pediatricians for effective involvement with preschool handicapped children and their families. *Mental Retardation,* 1978, *16,* 3–7.

Richardson, S. A. Age and sex differences in values toward physical handicaps. *Journal of Health and Social Behavior,* 1970, *11,* 207–214.

Richardson, S. A. People with cerebral palsy talk for themselves. *Developmental Medicine and Child Neurology,* 1972, *14,* 524–535.

Richardson, S. A., Goodman, N., Hastorf, A. H., & Dornbusch, S. M. Cultural uniformity in reaction to physical disabilities. *American Sociological Review,* 1961, *26,* 241–247.

Roth, J. A. The treatment of tuberculosis as a bargaining process. In A. Rose (Ed.), *Human behavior and social processes.* Boston: Houghton Mifflin, 1962.

Scanlon, C. A., Arick, J., & Phelps, N. Participation in the development of the IEP: Parents' perspective. *Exceptional Children,* 1981, *47,* 373–374.

Seligman, M. *Strategies for helping parents of handicapped children.* New York: Free Press, 1979.

Shaw, A., Randolph, J. G., & Manard, B. Ethical issues in pediatric surgery: A national survey of pediatricians and pediatric surgeons. *Pediatrics,* 1977, *60,* 588–599.

Slack, W. V. The patient's right to decide. *Lancet,* 1977, *30,* 240.

Spina Bifida Association of America. Mother expresses serious concerns about catheterization program. *Spina Bifida Insights,* 1982, p. 9

Stacey, M. Charisma, power, and altruism: A discussion of research in a child development centre. *Sociology of Health and Illness*, 1980, *2*, 64–90.

Stillman, P. L., Sabers, D. L., & Redfield, D. L. Use of trained mothers to teach interviewing skills to first-year medical students: A follow-up study. *Pediatrics*, 1977, *60*, 165–169.

Stimson, G., & Webb, B. *Going to see the doctor: The consultation process in general practice*. London: Routledge and Kegan Paul, 1975.

Straus, R. Medical education and the doctor–patient relationship. In E. B. Gallagher (Ed.), *The doctor–patient relationship in the changing health scene*. Washington, D.C.: U.S. Government Printing Office, 1978.

Strong, P. M. *The ceremonial order of the clinic: Parents, doctors, and medical bureaucracies*. London: Routledge and Kegan Paul, 1979.

Task Force on Pediatric Education. *The future of pediatric education*. Evanston, Ill.: American Academy of Pediatrics, 1978.

Todres, I. D., Krane, D., Howell, M. C., & Shannon, D. C. Pediatricians' attitudes affecting decision-making in defective newborns. *Pediatrics*, 1977, *60*, 197–201.

Voysey, M. *A constant burden: The reconstruction of family life*. London: Routledge and Kegan Paul, 1975.

Waitzkin, H., & Stoeckle, J. D. Information control and the micropolitics of health care: Summary of an ongoing research project. *Social Science and Medicine*, 1976, *10*, 263–276.

Wolraich, M. L. Pediatric training in developmental disabilities. *Mental Retardation*, 1979, *17*, 133–136.

Wolraich, M.L. Pediatric practitioners' knowledge of developmental disabilities. *Journal of Developmental and Behavioral Pediatrics*, 1980, *1*, 133–136.

Wolraich, M. L. Communication between physicians and parents of handicapped children. *Exceptional Children*, 1982, *48*, 324–329.

Zuk, G. H. The religious factor and the role of guilt in parental acceptance of the retarded child. *American Journal of Mental Deficiency*, 1959, *64*, 139–147.

III

FAMILY DYNAMICS

5

Fathers of Exceptional Children

MICHAEL E. LAMB

BIOGRAPHICAL SKETCH

Michael E. Lamb, Ph.D., is Professor of Psychology, Psychiatry, and Pediatrics at the University of Utah. His research is concerned with social and emotional development (especially in infancy and early childhood) and the development of parent–child relationships. He is the author of numerous articles and chapters on these topics and has written and edited several books, including The Role of the Father in Child Development, Development in Infancy, Infant Social Cognition, Social Interaction Analysis, Nontraditional Families, *and* Sibling Relationships. *His work has earned two national awards from the American Psychological Association.*

ISBN 0-8089-1561-4
Copyright © 1983 by Grune & Stratton

U NTIL a decade ago, students of human development did not think
much about paternal influences on child development. An increasing
focus on early (infantile) experiences had led to a near-exclusive focus on
the formative importance of the mother–infant relationship. In Bowlby's
(1951) classic treatise on institutionalization and social deprivation, the
father's role as a source of emotional and economic support for mothers
was alluded to briefly, and even this limited consideration was rare. Only
after publication of Schaffer and Emerson's (1964) research on infant attachment and Rutter's (1972) reconceptualization of the "maternal deprivation" literature did there emerge a realization that, in emphasizing the
undeniable importance of mothers, theorists had lost sight of the broader
social context in which children are raised. Thanks to this realization, the
imbalance has been redressed somewhat in the last several years. Many
research projects have been undertaken, and these have helped reshape
the traditional conceptualization of the socialization process. Our understanding of socioemotional development in infancy has been revised most
dramatically, but other areas of research have also been affected.

Other important changes in perspective have also occurred in the
past decade or so. One such fundamental change concerns the way in
which the child's role in socialization is portrayed. Formerly, we tended
to view children as malleable organisms waiting to be shaped by exogenous socialization processes. We have become increasingly aware, however, that each child has individual characteristics that not only affect the
way the child is influenced by exogenous forces but also help to shape the
socializers themselves (Bell & Harper, 1977). Socialization, then, is currently viewed as a bidirectional process whereas it was once viewed as a
unidirectional process. Unfortunately, there have been relatively few systematic attempts to explore the ways in which children affect their parents and families (Lerner & Spanier, 1978). Conspicuously lacking are
studies designed to explore the differential impact of different types of
children—boys versus girls, temperamentally easy versus temperamentally difficult children, chronically ill versus healthy children, mentally
retarded versus mentally normal children, and so forth—on marital quality and family interaction.

The topic of this chapter thus stands at the intersection of two areas
of investigation that have received relatively little attention: father–child
relationships and the family relationships of special children. Not surprisingly, therefore, we know very little about the types of relationships fathers have with their mentally handicapped children, the reactions of fathers to the birth of retarded children, and the direct and indirect effects
of these relationships and reactions on children and family integration.
Consequently, this chapter is of necessity brief and uncomfortably specu-
lative. It begins with a review of studies focused on the relationships be-

tween fathers and their normal, nonhandicapped children. Thereafter, the small body of literature on fathers and retarded children is reviewed, and then the reader's attention is turned to evidence concerning family integration and marital satisfaction in families with a handicapped child and to suggestions about the effects this may have on children and on parent–child relationships.

PATERNAL INFLUENCES ON CHILDREN

Let us begin by considering evidence suggesting that the father–child relationship deserves more attention than it has traditionally been accorded. The preponderance of the evidence briefly reviewed here suggests that most children establish emotionally salient relationships with both of their parents early in infancy, and that fathers have a significant impact—which can be either positive or negative—on their children's development. The implication is that fathers may have a significant role to play in the lives of retarded children too.

Father–Infant Relationships

Observational studies of infant–mother and infant–father interactions have demonstrated convincingly that infants form attachments to both of their parents by the middle of the first year of life, even when their mothers are primary caretakers and their fathers spend relatively little time with them (Cohen & Campos, 1974; Kotelchuck, 1976; Lamb, 1976b, 1977c, 1979; Schaffer & Emerson, 1964). Thus infants preferentially seek proximity to and contact with their parents, react with distress to separation from either, and are comforted by the presence of either. When they are distressed, infants turn to whichever parent is present for comfort, although distressed 12- and 18-month-old infants turn to their mothers rather than their fathers when they have the choice (Lamb, 1976a, 1976e). Comparable preferences are not evident in 8- or 24-month-olds, suggesting that they only characterize the first part of the second year of life (Lamb, 1976c, 1976d). Presumably, the preference patterns would be different if fathers were the primary caretakers, although the relevant research has yet to be conducted.

Direct Effects

There are two major ways in which mothers and fathers directly influence their children's socioemotional development. First of all, mothers and fathers are the major sources of stimulation and the primary models of socially approved behavior for their young children to emulate. The fact that both parents are attachment figures increases their salience in the eyes of their children and thus maximizes their impact. Although new parents are initially more responsive to newborns of their own sex (Parke & O'Leary, 1976), it is fathers who remain more likely to accord preferential attention to sons in later infancy (Lamb, 1977a) whereas mothers discriminate less between sons and daughters. Probably as a result of their fathers' behavior, boys develop preferences for their fathers in the second year of life (Lamb, 1977b). Furthermore, although there are many ways in which maternal and paternal behavior is similar, there are some characteristic differences between maternal and paternal interactional styles that ensure that mothers and fathers have distinct and independent influences on their infants' development. Fathers are noted for their playfulness— more particularly their penchant for robust, physically stimulating play— whereas mothers are characteristically associated with caretaking and more conventional, "containing" modes of play (Belsky, 1979; Clarke-Stewart, 1978; Lamb, 1976b, 1977c; Yogman, Dixon, Tronick, Als, & Brazelton, 1977). Infants come to expect their parents to act in these characteristic ways (Lamb, 1981a). They also respond more positively to play bids by their fathers than by their mothers (Clarke-Stewart, 1978; Lamb, 1976b, 1977c) and they initiate playful interaction with their fathers by preference (Lynn & Cross, 1974).

The second way in which fathers affect socioemotional development depends on the security of the infant–father attachment relationships. The security of attachment relationships depends on the meshing of the parent's and infant's behavior, usually expressed in terms of the adult's sensitive responsiveness to the infant's signals and needs (Ainsworth, Bell, & Stayton, 1974; Lamb, 1981a, 1981b). Infants establish relationships of different quality with their mothers and fathers, suggesting that the security of attachment characterizes specific relationships (and reflects the responsiveness of specific adults) rather than the infants' social style (Grossmann & Grossmann, 1980; Lamb, 1978; Main & Weston, 1981).

Most of the studies designed to explore the predictive importance of security of attachment have involved mothers and infants. Nevertheless, the evidence appears impressive. Securely attached infants are more sociable and cooperative with unfamiliar adults than are insecure infants (Main, 1973; Thompson & Lamb, 1983). Securely attached infants are also more socially competent with peers (Pastor, 1981; Waters, Wippman, & Sroufe, 1979) and more persistent and enthusiastic in challenging situations (Gove, Arend, & Sroufe, 1980; Matas, Arend, & Sroufe, 1978) than insecurely attached infants are.

Two groups of researchers have compared the predictive validity of infant–mother and infant–father attachments. Main and Weston (1981) reported that the security of both infant–mother and infant–father attachments affected the infant's sociability but that the security of the relationships with mothers (in all cases the primary caretakers) was most important. The most sociable infants were those who were securely attached to both parents, then came those who were securely attached to their mothers only, then those who were securely attached to their fathers only, and finally those who were insecurely attached to both parents. These results suggested that the predictive validity and formative importance of the infant–*father* attachment would increase depending on the father's involvement in childrearing. However, Lamb, Hwang, Frodi, and Frodi (1982) obtained rather different results in their study of Swedish infants, some of whose fathers were unusually involved in childcare. Only the security of infant–*father* attachment was related to sociability in this study, and there was no relationship between degree of relative involvement in childcare and the relative predictive importance of the attachment relationships. These surprising results raised the possibility that the procedure used to assess security of attachment in the United States is not appropriate in some other cultures.

Indirect Effects

In addition to the direct effects just discussed, fathers also have significant indirect effects on their children's development (Belsky, 1981; Lewis & Weintraub, 1976; Parke, Power & Gottman, 1979). By this I mean that fathers affect child development—adversely or advantageously—by way of their influence on their wives. When the relationships between the parents are warm, fathers provide the emotional support that facilitates the formation of secure and stimulating infant–mother relationships and so they indirectly contribute to healthy socioemotional development. Similarly, in traditional families, the fathers' financial support frees mothers of economic concerns and permits them to devote themselves to their children's needs. By contrast, when the relationship between the parents is hostile and unsupportive, the quality of the mother–infant relationship is adversely affected. Interestingly, hostile marital relationships seem to have more reliably negative effects on child development than does divorce or the permanent absence of one parent (Rutter, 1979).

Cognitive Development

Most of the recent research on father–infant relationships has been descriptive in nature. Consequently, few attempts have been made (save for work on the predictive validity of the security of attachment) to determine how greatly fathers influence the development of their young children. The few outcome-oriented studies that have been undertaken have been concerned with paternal influences on infant cognitive development (e.g., Belsky, 1980; Clarke-Stewart, 1978; Pedersen, Rubenstein, & Yarrow, 1979). These studies have demonstrated positive relationships between paternal involvement and cognitive development, but the interpretation of these relationships remain uncertain. It seems, however, that paternal stimulation can have a beneficial impact on children's cognitive development.

Paternal Influences on Older Children

In comparison with the research on infancy, the research on older children is less programmatic and less concerned with defining the processes whereby parents affect their children's development. With few exceptions, this research has been correlational rather than experimental in nature, and longitudinal investigations have been rare. Consequently, few conclusions can be stated with any confidence.

Processes of Influence

Studies have identified both direct and indirect paternal influences on child development. Most directly mediated parental influences on child development involve either of two processes: behavioral conditioning or observational learning. It is obvious that both parents attempt to shape their children's behavior through the discriminating application of punishments and rewards, and these attempts are often successful—at least in the short-term. Children also learn by imitating their unwitting parents, and they are most likely to imitate models who are warm, nurturant, and powerful (Bandura, 1977; Mussen, 1967). This of course maximizes the tendency to imitate parents rather than other adults.

Whereas psychologists have written about behavioral shaping and imitation for many years, they have only recently come to appreciate the importance of indirect effects (Belsky, 1981). Indirect effects involve influences of one parent or the other, who then behaves differently toward his or her children. The potential for indirect effects is enormous, and we are only beginning to appreciate the diverse ways in which they may affect child development (Lewis & Feiring, 1981; Parke, Power, & Gottman, 1979). Both direct and indirect effects are implicated by the studies discussed in the paragraphs that follow.

Gender Role and Gender Identity

As mentioned earlier, parents (especially fathers) are particularly attentive (and thus salient) to children of the same sex from infancy. This may facilitate the acquisition of gender identity, which seems to occur in the first two to three years of life (Money & Ehrhardt, 1972).

Probably because they are much more concerned about "appropriately" sex-typed behavior then mothers are (Bronfenbrenner, 1961;

Goodenough, 1957; Sears, Maccoby & Levin, 1957; Tasch, 1955), fathers emit reinforcements and punishment for sex-typed behavior more consistently than mothers do (Langlois & Downs, 1980). Boys whose fathers are absent or uninvolved later appear to be less masculine than those whose fathers are psychologically and physically present (see Biller, 1974 and 1981, for reviews). On the other hand, it is not the case that masculine fathers have masculine sons (e.g., Mussen & Rutherford, 1963; Payne & Mussen, 1956). Significant correlations between paternal and filial masculinity occur only when the father is also warm; indeed, nurturance is more reliably related to the masculinity of sons than the fathers' masculinity is (Mussen & Rutherford, 1963; Payne & Mussen, 1956; Sears, Maccoby, & Levin, 1957). Girls whose fathers are masculine tend to be more feminine (Heilbrun, 1965; Johnson, 1963; Mussen & Rutherford, 1963; Sears, Rau, & Alpert, 1965), presumably because these fathers complement and encourage their daughters' femininity. Both boys and girls develop less traditionally sex-stereotyped attitudes about male and female roles when their mothers work outside the home (see Hoffman, 1974, and Lamb, 1982, for reviews) and when their fathers are highly involved in childcare (Radin, 1978; Sagi, 1982). Both of these effects are probably attributable to the fact that these parents provide less traditional models for their children to emulate.

Of course, sex-role acquisition is not only affected by parental behavior. From the preschool years through adulthood, significant influences are exerted by peers (Fagot, 1977; Fagot & Patterson, 1969; Lamb, Easterbrooks, & Holden, 1980; Lamb & Roopnarine, 1979; Nash & Feldman, 1981), teachers (Dweck, 1978; Fagot, 1977; Serbin, Tonick, & Sternglanz, 1977) and the media. Most of these socializing agents have a similarly traditionalizing effect, making it difficult to appraise the relative importance of each.

Achievement and Achievement Motivation

As mentioned earlier, appropriate responsiveness to infant signals and needs appears to foster the development of a sense of personal efficacy or effectance, which is a basic component of achievement motivation (Lamb, 1981b). Other studies show that parents who provide stimulation that is developmentally appropriate and plentiful have more cognitively competent children (for a review see Stevenson & Lamb, 1981). High achievement motivation develops in boys whose parents are warm, not controlling, and encourage independence (Radin, 1976; Rosen & D'Andrade, 1959; Winterbottom, 1958). Girls benefit when they receive less unconditional nurturance than they usually receive (Baruch & Barnett, 1978). In traditional families (i.e., those in which fathers are the primary breadwinners and the instrumental leaders of their families), paternal models are especially important to both boys and girls. Many highly achieving women may benefit from the warm encouragement of their fathers since there are few female role models for them to emulate (Baruch & Barnett, 1978).

Children whose fathers are absent tend to perform more poorly at school than children from two-parent families (Shinn, 1978; Radin, 1981), but these effects are much more consistent in lower-class than in middle-class families (Radin, 1981). Perhaps this is because single mothers in lower-class families are subject to more severe economic and socioemotional stresses that affect their ability to guide and stimulate their children. Interestingly, Blanchard and Biller (1971) reported that qualitatively similar effects occurred when fathers were nominally present but were uninvolved with their sons. By contrast, children with highly involved, nurturant fathers tend to be more cognitively competent and to manifest the internal locus of control that is one aspect of higher achievement motivation (Radin, 1978; Sagi, 1982).

Recently, conceptualizations of achievement motivation have been influenced by attributional theory (e.g., Weiner, 1974; Dweck, 1978). According to this theory, individuals can attribute their successes or failures to either controllable or uncontrollable (external) factors and to either effort or ability. Achievement motivation is enhanced when others (1) attribute the child's successes to his or her efforts and failures to the lack of effort and (2) encourage the child to attribute responsibility in this way. By contrast, achievement motivation is squelched when failures are attributed to a lack of ability and success to the easiness of the task. Although most researchers have studied the ways in which teachers affect the development of attributional styles (Dweck, 1978), it is likely that parents are also influential in this regard.

Moral Development

In recent years, the ascendance of Kohlberg's cognitive developmental theory of moral development (Kohlberg, 1969) has provoked a focus on normative issues and a deemphasis of individual differences. Furthermore, to the extent that environmental influences are explicitly considered, Kohlberg emphasizes interactions with peers rather than parents.

A comprehensive review of research on the determinants of moral development a decade ago concluded that parental disciplinary style was indeed influential (Hoffman, 1970). Children develop internalized controls (consciences) most readily when their parents discipline through induction and least when their parents employ a power-assertive strategy. Induction involves encouraging the child to consider the implications of its behavior (notably, its disobedience) for other people. Although some studies show that boys whose fathers are absent display less moral internalization and are more likely to become delinquent than boys whose fathers are present, the preponderance of the evidence indicates that mothers have a much greater influence on moral development than fathers do (Hoffman, 1981).

Psychological Adjustment

Most of the research on psychological adjustment has been concerned with the antecedents of psychological *mal*adjustment. Many studies show that children whose parents are divorced or whose fathers are absent are more likely to manifest signs of psychological maladjustment (for a review see Biller, 1981), but the mode of influence is unclear. Most likely, the divorce itself has adverse effects that are exacerbated by the inability of some single parents to supervise their children adequately— perhaps because they are themselves emotionally and economically stressed and lack social supports. Other studies reveal that divorce has an immediate destabilizing influence on parents and children, who gradually return to stability and adjustment over the next two years (Hetherington, Cox, & Cox, 1978). Large-scale epidemiological studies (e.g., Rutter, 1973, 1979) show that marital hostility and discord are among the most reliable causes of psychological maladjustment.

In one of the few studies concerned with parental influences on psychological adjustment, Baumrind (1971, 1975) reported that socially competent children (those who are friendly, independent, and assertive with peers and compliantly nonintrusive with adults) are likely to have authoritative parents—that is, parents who provide firm and articulately reasoned guidance for their children. Both authoritarian parents (those who fail to provide explanations for their commands) and permissive parents (those who fail to provide adequate guidance) have less socially competent children.

Summary

It is clear that parents have significant influences on their children attributable to the way they behave toward their children as well as the way they interact with one another. Direct and indirect parental influences on the development of sociability, sex roles, morality, achievement, cognition, and psychological adjustment have been demonstrated, although we can only speculate about processes of influence since they have not been explored very thoroughly.

Both mothers and fathers affect their children's development. In cases where the parents' sex role is important (e.g., the development of sex differences and sex roles), mothers and fathers appear to affect their children differently; but, in the main, they influence their children in similar ways. Single-parent families are "at risk" not primarily because they lack an adult of one gender or the other but because the single adult is socially isolated, without emotional and economic support, and without a partner to help in childrearing. In addition, marital hostility and the divorce process may have adverse effects on psychological adjustment.

In some areas (e.g., sex role development), fathers exert a disproportionate influence, either because they are especially concerned about the issue or because the fact that they are relatively novel (compared with mothers) increases their salience in the eyes of their children. In other respects (e.g., the effects of attachment security on sociability), mothers may be more influential. However, in these cases the relative importance of the fathers' influence may increase as their relative involvement in childrearing increases. Finally, the quality of the marital relationship and other indirectly mediated effects are much more influential than was once believed.

FATHERS AND SPECIAL CHILDREN

Only a handful of studies have considered the relationships between fathers and their mentally handicapped children. None of these studies have involved observations of the fathers and children; at best they have involved interviews with the fathers, and in many cases we have only the impressions of clinicians or professionals on which to base our conclusions.

The consensus is that mothers and fathers initially respond differently to the news that their children are intellectually handicapped. Fathers tend to respond less emotionally and to focus on possible long-term problems (especially financial ones) whereas mothers respond more emotionally and express concerns about their ability to cope with the burdens of child care (Gumz & Gubrium, 1972; Hersh, 1970; Love, 1973). Both parents, however, pass through a similar sequence of reactions, commonly involving disappointment, anger, denial, and guilt lest they unwittingly caused the child's retardation (Holt, 1958a, 1958b; Legeay & Keogh, 1966; Ryckman & Henderson, 1965). According to Kanner (1953), a prolonged period of denial may be especially common among minimally involved fathers, who do not have enough interaction with their children to recognize the evidence of retardation.

As indicated in the preceding section, fathers are typically more concerned than mothers about the adoption of socially approved behavior by their children—especially their sons. Likewise, they are more concerned about the social status and occupational success of their offspring (Lamb, 1981c). Not surprisingly, therefore, fathers are more concerned about the long-term prospects of their retarded children than mothers are, and they are more affected by the visibility of the handicap, presumably because of their greater sensitivity to socially defined norms and evaluations (Tallman, 1965). They also report more concern about the child's behavior outside the home (Farber, 1962; Farber, Jenné & Toigo, 1960; Gumz & Gubrium, 1972; Tallman, 1965). Further, because fathers often have higher expectations of sons than of daughters, they are especially disappointed when they have retarded sons (Farber, 1959; Grossman, 1972). The behavioral consequences of this disappointment may take a wide variety of forms. Extremes of great involvement, on the one hand, and total withdrawal, on the other, have been observed in the fathers of retarded sons (Chigier, 1972; Tallman, 1965), whereas these fathers appear more consistently to have limited, routine involvement with retarded daughters (Tallman, 1965), of whom they are more accepting (Grossman, 1972).

For many parents children are a significant source of fulfillment and self-esteem, but when the child clearly cannot live up to the parents' hopes and expectations, self-esteem suffers (Ryckman & Henderson, 1965). Cummings (1976) noted reduced self-esteem in both mothers and fathers of mentally retarded children, with the fathers being especially concerned that the birth of a retarded child proved that they were, in a biological sense, failures as fathers. Perhaps this is because fathers have fewer prescribed opportunities than mothers to do things with and for their retarded children. They thus have fewer concrete reminders of their value and competence.

Some have argued that the child's handicap is especially hard for parents to bear when they are intellectually talented (i.e., when there is a greater discrepancy between their intellectual skills and those of their children) and when they have high-status occupations (and thus have comparably high expectations for their children) (Holt, 1958a, 1958b; Michaels & Schueman, 1962; Ryckman & Henderson, 1975). This is not necessarily or always the case, however, as both Farber (1959) and Grossman (1972) discovered lower-class parents to be more adversely affected by the birth of retarded children than middle- and upper-class parents were, perhaps because lower-SES parents are under greater financial stress and have less access to resources (such as respite care) that are available to wealthier or more knowledgable parents.

In an attempt to spare their own self-esteem and sense of fulfillment, some parents of retarded children often persist in denying the seriousness and irreversibility of their children's condition. They thus maintain unrealistic expectations about the children's educational attainments and are upset by use of the term "mentally retarded" because it connotes incapacity and irreversibility (Meyerowitz & Farber, 1966; Organist, 1971; Wadsworth & Wadsworth, 1971). This denial is especially profound and problematic when children are only mildly retarded, for there are fewer and less dramatic reminders of the children's limitations (Wadsworth & Wadsworth, 1971).

Fathers' reactions to and feelings about their children's retardation may have implications not only for their own behavior vis-à-vis retarded children (e.g., Tallman, 1965) but also for the response of other family members. Peck and Stephens (1960)—albeit in a small study—found a high relationship between the degree of paternal acceptance or rejection and the amount of acceptance or rejection generally observed in the home. This suggested that the father's reaction might set the tone for the family's reaction.

This possibility is not reassuring, because although Tallman (1965) reported that some fathers became very involved in childcare when their sons were retarded, most other writers have observed that fathers tend to offer very little assistance to their primary caretaking wives, even when their wives are overwhelmed by the daunting task of raising a severely retarded child (Holt, 1958a, 1958b; Andrew, 1968). Presumably this reflects the fact that fathers obtain less satisfaction from retarded than from normal children (Cummings, 1976) and the fact that paternal involvement—unlike maternal involvement—is discretionary. In other words, traditionally the paternal role is defined in such a way that fathers can increase or decrease their involvement depending on their preferences and satisfactions, whereas mothers are expected to show equivalent commitment to all their children—regardless of personal preferences or the individual characteristics of their children.

When fathers choose to withdraw from their retarded children, it is not only the development of these children that is likely to be affected; the entire family is likely to suffer. Changes in marital satisfaction or integration affect not only the personal fulfillment of the two spouses but also the way each interacts with their children, both retarded and normal. Evidence regarding marital satisfaction in families with retarded children is discussed in the next section.

MARITAL SATISFACTION

By far the most thorough and thoughtful study on marital satisfaction in families with retarded children was conducted by Bernard Farber and his colleagues (Farber, 1959, 1960; Farber & Jenné, 1963). Farber (1959) studied 240 intact families, each of which had one severely retarded child and at least one other child. Drawing upon sociological formulations concerning the family life cycle, Farber interviewed and questioned both parents. No comparison group of families without retarded children was studied, so it was possible only to identify the correlates of marital disruption in families with retarded children rather than whether these families on the whole differed from comparable families that did not have retarded children. Farber reported that retarded boys had a greater negative impact on family integration than girls did, especially in lower-class families. Presumably this was because parents have higher expectations of boys than of girls, and so their expectations are most seriously violated when sons are retarded. The family disruption increased as the retarded children grew older, probably because of their inability to meet age-graded expectations became more notable with age. Disruption was lessened when the retarded child was institutionalized. The greater the disruption of the marital relationships, the greater the effect on the parents' communication with their other (nonretarded) children (Farber & Jenné, 1963), and the greater the consequent effect on the siblings' adjustment (Farber, 1959, 1960).

Other studies confirm that marital stability and satisfaction are adversely affected by the birth of retarded children. Indeed this point has been so widely noted that Jordan (1962) cites a paper published in *1673* commenting on the crisis provoked by the birth of a handicapped child! More recently, Holt (1957, 1958a, 1958b) reported extensive marital and family disruption in a study of 170 families in Sheffield, England. This disruption was translated into adverse effects on the development of siblings (Holt, 1957). Holt reported that lower-class parents were less affected than middle-class families, whereas Farber (1958) reported that middle-class parents were less, and lower-class parents more, affected—leaving uncertainty about the effects of social class on family reactions to retardation. In another study conducted at about the same time as Holt's and Farber's studies, Saenger (1957, 1960) was unable to replicate another of Farber's findings. Specifically, Saenger found that family cohesiveness and warmth were inversely correlated with the likelihood of institutionalization, whereas Farber reported that family integration was greatest when retarded children were institutionalized.

These differences aside, several reports confirm Holt's and Farber's findings that retardation has an adverse effect on marital integration and satisfaction (Lonsdale, 1978; Schipper, 1959), with these effects being reflected in higher rates of divorce (Love, 1973), suicide (Love, 1973), and desertion (Reed & Reed, 1965). Fowle (1968) failed to obtain evidence for this effect, however, and a majority of Kramm's (1963) subjects reported that the birth of a Down's syndrome child drew them closer. The birth of a retarded child tends to inhibit future childbearing (Carver & Carver, 1972; Chigier, 1972).

Both parents, of course, react adversely to the birth of retarded children. However, the fathers' reactions—if they are accurately depicted by the evidence reviewed in the previous section—may serve to exacerbate the situation. Instead of increasing their level of involvement, many fathers seem to become less involved in their families, thus leaving their wives to cope alone with the emotionally and physically draining task of raising retarded children. Fathers may thus bear a greater responsibility for allowing the birth of a retarded child to have adverse effects on their marriages, even though, ironically, fathers report more family and marital discord than mothers do (Schonnell & Watts, 1956). If fathers reacted by increasing their involvement, their own satisfaction and the integration of the family might both increase.

Marital problems brought about by the presence of retarded children may also be exacerbated by the fact that families with retarded children become socially isolated (Carver & Carver, 1972; Farber, 1962; Illingworth, 1967; Legeay & Keogh, 1966; Meyerowitz & Farber, 1966; Schonnell & Watts, 1956). This seems to occur for a number of reasons, ranging from the lack of time to socialize and the parents' own unhappiness about their children's condition to the lack of acceptance and understanding by others. Unfortunately, therefore, at precisely the time when these parents most need emotional and social support, they find themselves isolated from social networks, significant friends, and relatives.

CONCLUSION

Because of the scarcity of reports and the manner in which this research has been conducted, we know little about the extent to which paternal reactions to the birth of retarded children affect the reactions and adjustment of their spouses, and we do not know to what extent their reactions and behavior have direct effects on the socialization, happiness, and development of retarded children. We can only speculate on the basis of the limited evidence available. As noted above, it seems that fathers tend to react adversely and rejectingly toward retarded children, and this is likely to set an emotional distance between them, reducing the likelihood of positive effects on child development while increasing the likelihood of deleterious ones. Likewise, rejection and withdrawal by the fathers of retarded children serve to increase the burden borne by their wives. This has the effect of straining the marriage and adversely affecting the personal satisfaction of the mothers, which may in turn have harmful effects not only on the retarded children but on other children in their families as well. A harrassed, unhappy, overextended, and isolated mother is likely to be an impoverished mother of all her children, not only of the retarded child who is the cause of the family strain.

Whether or not the father's reaction in fact exacerbates the family crisis, there is reason to believe that intervention efforts should be directed toward fathers more systematically than they have been up until now. Few family support groups involve or explicitly attempt to involve fathers (Ramsey, 1967). This failure to recognize that fathers, too, are emotionally affected by the birth of a retarded child not only deprives them of the counsel and support that might help them cope with these strains but also conveys the implicit message that they do not matter and that they are not expected to behave or feel differently now that a tragedy has struck their families. This is unfortunate. Both traditional (mother caretaking) and nontraditional families are likely to be strengthened when fathers are emotionally and concretely involved with their families, sharing in the burdens and pleasures of parenthood in whatever fashion is consistent with their mutual attitudes and values. The potential benefits of paternal involvement are greater rather than less when there are retarded children, because in such circumstances both mothers and other members of the family have an increased need for emotional support and understanding as well as for practical assistance.

Although the title of this chapter refers to the broad category, "fathers of exceptional children," all of the studies described have been concerned with fathers of mentally retarded children. This restriction of focus does not result from a decision on my part; it represents the narrow focus of research in this area. Probably because the mentally retarded are numerous and appear to constitute a relatively homogeneous group (or one within which variation can be quantified using IQ scores), most researchers have focused on this group rather than on other types of exceptional children. Although there may be some similarities between the family situations of mentally retarded and otherwise handicapped children, there are surely many dissimilarities, and these deserve further investigation. Studies such as that undertaken by Herbert Leiderman at Stanford University (it is still in progress), in which the visibility of the handicapping condition is considered as a factor affecting the parents' behavior, represent the types of studies that we need. My hope is that the future will bring increased attention to the needs and family relationships of all exceptional children, not only the mentally retarded.

REFERENCES

Ainsworth, M. D. S., Bell, S. M., & Stayton, D. J. Infant–mother attachment and social development: Socialisation as a product of reciprocal responsiveness to signals. In M. P. M. Richards (Ed.), *The integration of a child into a social world*. Cambridge: Cambridge University Press, 1974.

Andrew, G. Determinants of Negro family decisions in management of retardation. *Journal of Marriage and the Family*, 1968, *30*, 612–617.

Bandura, A. *Social learning theory*. Englewood Cliffs, N.J.: Prentice-Hall, 1977.

Baruch, G. K., & Barnett, R. *The competent woman.* New York: Irvington, 1978.

Baumrind, D. Current patterns of parental authority. *Developmental Psychology Monographs,* 1971, *1* (Whole No. 2).

Baumrind, D. *Early socialization and the discipline controversy.* Morristown, N.J.: General Learning Press, 1975.

Bell, R. Q., & Harper, L. V. *Child effects on adults.* Hillsdale, N.J.: Erlbaum, 1977.

Belsky, J. Mother–father–infant interaction: A naturalistic observational study. *Developmental Psychology,* 1979, *15,* 601–607.

Belsky, J. A family analysis of parental influence on infant exploratory competence. In F. A. Pedersen (Ed.), *The father–infant relationship: Observational studies in a family context.* New York: Praeger, 1980.

Belsky, J. Early human experience: A family perspective. *Developmental Psychology,* 1981, *17,* 3–23.

Biller, H. B. *Paternal deprivation: Family, school, sexuality and society.* Lexington, Mass.: Heath, 1974.

Biller, H. B. The father and personality development: Paternal deprivation and sex-role development. In M. E. Lamb (Ed.), *The role of the father in child development.* New York: Wiley, 1976.

Biller, H. B. Father absence, divorce, and personality development. In M. E. Lamb (Ed.), *The role of the father in child development* (Rev. ed.). New York: Wiley, 1981.

Blanchard, R. W., & Biller, H. B. Father availability and academic performance among third grade boys. *Developmental Psychology,* 1971, *4,* 301–305.

Bowlby, J. *Maternal care and mental health.* Geneva: World Health Organization, 1951.

Brazelton, T. B. Mother–father–infant interactions. Presentation to the Conference on Family Interaction, Educational Testing Service, Princeton, N.J., December 1977.

Bronfenbrenner, U. The changing American child. *Journal of Social Issues,* 1961, *17,* 6–18.

Carver, N., & Carver, J. *The family of the retarded child.* Syracuse: Syracuse University Press, 1972.

Chigier, E. *Down's syndrome.* Lexington, Mass.: Heath, 1972.

Clarke-Stewart. K. A. And daddy makes three: The father's impact on mother and young child. *Child Development,* 1978, *49,* 466–478.

Cohen, L. J., & Campos, J. J. Father, mother, and stranger as elicitors of attachment behaviors in infancy. *Developmental Psychology,* 1974, *10,* 146–154.

Cummings, S. T. The impact of the child's deficiency on the father: A study of fathers of mentally retarded and of chronically ill children. *American Journal of Orthopsychiatry,* 1976, *46,* 246–255.

Dweck, C. S. Achievement. In M. E. Lamb (Ed.), *Social and personality development.* New York: Holt, Rinehart & Winston, 1978.

Fagot, B. I. Consequences of moderate cross-gender behavior in preschool children. *Child Development,* 1977, *48,* 902–907.

Fagot, B. I., & Patterson, B. R. An in vivo analysis of reinforcing contingencies for sex-role behavior in the preschool child. *Developmental Psychology,* 1969, *1,* 563–568.

Farber, B. Effects of a severely mentally retarded child on family integration. *Monographs of the Society for Research in Child Development*, 1959, *24*, (Whole No. 71).

Farber, B. Family organization and crisis: Maintenance of integration in families with a severely mentally retarded child. *Monographs of the Society for Research in Child Development*, 1960, *25* (Whole No. 75).

Farber, B. Effects of a severely mentally retarded child on the family. In E. P. Trapp (Ed.), *Readings on the exceptional child*. New York: Appleton-Century-Crofts, 1962.

Farber, B., & Jenné, W. C. Family organization and parent–child communication: Parents and siblings of a retarded child. *Monographs of the Society for Research in Child Development*, 1963, *28* (Whole No. 91).

Farber, B. Jenné, W. C., & Toigo, R. Family crisis and the decision to institutionalize the retarded child. *Council of Exceptional Children Research Monographs*, 1960, *A* (No. 1).

Field, T. Interaction behaviors of primary versus secondary caretaker fathers. *Developmental Psychology*, 1978, *14*, 183–184.

Fowle, C. M. The effect of the severely mentally retarded child on his family. *American Journal of Mental Deficiency*, 1968, *73*, 468–473.

Goodenough, E. W. Interest in persons as an aspect of sex difference in the early years. *Genetic Psychology Monographs*, 1957, *55*, 287–323.

Gove, F., Arend, R., & Sroufe, L. A. Continuity of individual adaptation from infancy to kindergarten. Paper presented to the Society for Research in Child Development, San Francisco, March 1979.

Grossman, F. *Brothers and sisters of retarded children: An exploratory study*. Syracuse: Syracuse University Press, 1972.

Grossmann, K., & Grossmann, K. The development of relationship patterns during the first two years of life. Paper presented to the International Congress of Psychology, Leipzig, July 1980.

Gumz, E. J., & Gubrium, J. F. Comparative parental perceptions of a mentally retarded child. *American Journal of Mental Deficiency*, 1972, *77*, 175–180.

Heilbrun, A. B. An empirical test of the modeling theory of sex-role learning. *Child Development*, 1965, *36*, 789–799.

Hersh, A. Changes in family functioning following placement of a retarded child. *Social Work*, 1970, *15*, 93–102.

Hetherington, E. M., Cox, M., & Cox, R. The aftermath of divorce. In J. H. Stevens & M. Matthews (Eds.), *Mother/child, father/child relationships*. Washington, D.C.: National Association for the Education of Young Children, 1978.

Hoffman, L. W. Effects of maternal employment on the child: A review of the research. *Developmental Psychology*, 1974, *10*, 204–228.

Hoffman, M. L. Moral development. In P. H. Mussen (Ed.), *Carmichael's manual of child psychology* (3rd ed., Vol. 2). New York: Wiley, 1970.

Hoffman, M. L. The role of the father in moral internalization. In M. E. Lamb (Ed.), *The role of the father in child development* (Rev. ed.). New York: Wiley, 1981.

Holt, K. S. The impact of mentally retarded children upon their families. Unpublished doctoral dissertation, University of Sheffield, England, 1957.

Holt, K. S. The influence of a retarded child upon family limitation. *Journal of Mental Deficiency Research,* 1958, *2,* 28–34. (a)

Holt, K. S. The home care of severely retarded children. *Pediatrics,* 1958, *22,* 746–755. (b)

Illingworth, R. S. Counseling the parents of the mentally handicapped child. *Clinical Pediatrics,* 1967, *6,* 340–348.

Johnson, M. M. Sex role learning in the nuclear family. *Child Development,* 1963, *34,* 315–333.

Jordan, T. E. Research on the handicapped child and the family. *Merrill-Palmer Quarterly,* 1962, *8,* 243–260.

Kanner, L. Parents' feelings about retarded children. *American Journal of Mental Deficiency,* 1953, *57,* 375–383.

Kohlberg, L. Stage and sequence: The cognitive-developmental approach to socialization. In D. A. Goslin (Ed.), *Handbook of socialization theory and research.* Chicago: Rand McNally, 1969.

Kotelchuck, M. The infant's relationship to the father: Experimental evidence. In M. E. Lamb (Ed.), *The role of the father in child development.* New York: Wiley, 1976.

Kramm, E. R. *Families of mongoloid children.* Washington, D.C.: Children's Bureau, 1963.

Lamb, M. E. Effects of stress and cohort on mother– and father–infant interaction. *Developmental Psychology,* 1976, *12,* 435–443. (a)

Lamb, M. E. Interaction between eight-month-old children and their fathers and mothers. In M. E. Lamb (Ed.), *The role of the father in child development.* New York: Wiley, 1976. (b)

Lamb, M. E. Interactions between two-year-olds and their mothers and fathers. *Psychological Reports,* 1976, *38,* 447–450. (c)

Lamb, M. E. Parent–infant interaction in eight-month-olds. *Child Psychiatry and Human Development,* 1976, *7,* 56–63. (d)

Lamb, M. E. Twelve-month-olds and their parents: Interaction in a laboratory playroom. *Developmental Psychology,* 1976, *12,* 237–244. (e)

Lamb, M. E. The development of mother–infant and father–infant attachments in the second year of life. *Developmental Psychology,* 1977, *13,* 637–648. (a)

Lamb, M. E. The development of parental preferences in the first two years of life. *Sex Roles,* 1977, *3,* 495–497. (b)

Lamb, M. E. Father–infant and mother–infant interaction in the first year of life. *Child Development,* 1977, *48,* 167–181. (c)

Lamb, M. E. Qualitative aspects of mother– and father–infant attachments. *Infant Behavior and Development,* 1978, *1,* 265–275.

Lamb, M. E. Separation and reunion behaviors as criteria of attachment to mothers and fathers. *Early Human Development,* 1979, *3/4,* 329–339.

Lamb, M. E. Developing trust and perceived effectance in infancy. In L. P. Lipsitt (Ed.), *Advances in infancy research* (Vol. 1). Norwood, N.J.: Ablex, 1981. (a)

Lamb, M. E. The development of social expectations in the first year of life. In M. E. Lamb & L. R. Sherrod (Eds.), *Infant social cognition: Empirical and theoretical considerations.* Hillsdale, N.J.: Lawrence Erlbaum Associates, 1981. (b)

Lamb, M. E. Paternal influences on child development: An overview. In M. E. Lamb (Ed.), *The role of the father in child development* (Rev. ed.). New York: Wiley, 1981. (c)

Lamb, M. E., Maternal employment and child development: A review. In M. E. Lamb (Ed.), *Nontraditional families*. Hillsdale, N.J.: Erlbaum, 1982.

Lamb, M. E., Easterbrooks, M. A., & Holden, G. W. Reinforcement and punishment among preschoolers: Characteristics, effects, and correlates. *Child Development,* 1980, *51,* 1230–1236.

Lamb, M. E., Frodi, A. M., Hwang, C.-P., Frodi, M., & Steinberg, J. The effects of gender and caretaking roles on parent–infant interaction. In R. N. Emde & R. J. Harmon (Eds.), *The development of attachment and affiliative behavioral systems*. New York: Plenum, 1982.

Lamb, M. E., Frodi, A. M., Hwang, C.-P., Frodi, M., & Steinberg, J. Mother- and father–infant interaction involving play and holding in traditional and nontraditional Swedish families. *Developmental Psychology,* 1982, *18,* 215–221.

Lamb, M. E., & Goldberg, W. A. The father–child relationship: A synthesis of biological, evolutionary and social perspectives. In L. W. Hoffman R. Gandelman, & H. R. Schiffman (Eds.), *Parentings: Its causes and consequences*. Hillsdale, N.J.: Lawrence Erlbaum Associates, 1982.

Lamb, M. E., Hwang, C.-P., Frodi, A. M., & Frodi, M. Security of mother- and father–infant attachment and its relation to sociability with strangers in traditional and nontraditional Swedish families. *Infant Behavior and Development,* 1982, *5,* 355–367.

Lamb, M. E., & Roopnarine, J. L. Peer influences on sex-role development in preschoolers. *Child Development,* 1979, *50,* 1219–1222.

Langlois, J. H., & Downs, A. C. Mothers, fathers, and peers as socialization agents of sex-typed play behaviors in young children. *Child Development,* 1980, *51,* 1237–1247.

Legeay, C., & Keogh, B. Impact of mental retardation on family life. *American Journal of Nursing,* 1966, *66,* 1062–1065.

Lerner, R. M., & Spanier, G. B. (Eds.). *Child influences on marital and family interaction*. New York: Academic Press, 1978.

Lewis, M., & Feiring, C. Direct and indirect interactions in social relationships. In L. P. Lipsitt (Ed.), *Advances in infancy research* (Vol. 1). Norwood, N.J.: Ablex, 1981.

Lewis, M., & Weinraub, M. The father's role in the infant's social network. In M. E. Lamb (Ed.), *The role of the father in child development*. New York: Wiley, 1976.

Lonsdale, G. Family life with a handicapped child: The parents speak. *Child: Care, Health and Development,* 1978, *4,* 99–120.

Love, H. *The mentally retarded child and his family*. Springfield, Ill.: Charles C Thomas, 1973.

Lynn, D. B., & Cross, A. R. Parent preference of preschool children. *Journal of Marriage and the Family,* 1974, *36,* 555–559.

Main, M. B. *Exploration, play and cognitive functioning as related to child–mother attachment*. Unpublished doctoral dissertation, Johns Hopkins University, 1973.

Main, M. B., & Weston, D. R. Security of attachment to mother and father: Related to conflict behavior and the readiness to establish new relationships. *Child Development*, 1981, *52*, 932–940.

Matas, L., Arend, R., & Sroufe, L. A. Continuity of adaptation in the second year of life. *Child Development*, 1978, *49*, 547–556.

Meyerowitz, H. D., & Farber, B. Family background of educable mentally retarded children. In B. Farber (Ed.), *Kinship and family organization*. New York: Wiley, 1966.

Michaels, J., & Schueman, H. Observations on the psychodynamics of retarded children. *American Journal of Mental Deficiency*, 1962, *66*, 568–573.

Money, J., & Ehrhardt, A. A. *Man and woman: Boy and girl*. Baltimore: Johns Hopkins Press, 1972.

Mussen, P. H. Early socialization: Learning and identification. In T. M. Newcomb (Ed.), *New directions in psychology III*. New York: Holt, Rinehart & Winston, 1967.

Mussen, P. H., & Rutherford, E. Parent–child relations and parental personality in relation to young children's sex-role preferences. *Child Development*, 1963, *34*, 589–607.

Nash, S. C., & Feldman, S. S. Sex role and sex-related attributions: Constancy or change across the family life cycle? In M. E. Lamb & A. L. Brown (Eds.), *Advances in developmental psychology* (Vol. 1). Hillsdale, N.J.: Lawrence Erlbaum Associates, 1981.

Organist, J. E. *The relationship between parental expectancies and the behavior of mildly retarded adolescents*. Unpublished doctoral dissertation, University of Wisconsin, 1971.

Parke, R. D., & O'Leary, S. E. Father–mother–infant interaction in the newborn period: Some findings, some observations and some unresolved issues. In K. Riegel & J. Meacham (Eds.), *The developing individual in a changing world* (Vol. 2, *Social and environmental issues*). The Hague: Mouton, 1976.

Parke, R. D., & O'Leary, S. E. Father–mother–infant interactions. In J. D. Osofsky (Ed.). *Handbook of infant development*. New York: Wiley, 1979.

Parke, R. D., Power, T. G., & Gottman, J. Conceptualizing and quantifying influence patterns in the family triad. In M. E. Lamb, S. J. Suomi, & G. R. Stephenson (Eds.). *Social interaction analysis: Methodological issues*. Madison: University of Wisconsin Press, 1979.

Pastor, D. L. The quality of mother–infant attachment and its relationship to toddler's initial sociability with peers. *Developmental Psychology*, 1981, *17*, 326–335.

Payne, D. E., & Mussen, P. H. Parent–child relations and father identification among adolescent boys. *Journal of Abnormal and Social Psychology*, 1956, *52*, 358–362.

Peck, J. R., & Stephens, W. B. A study of the relationship between the attitudes and behavior of parents and that of their mentally defective child. *American Journal of Mental Deficiency*, 1960, *64*, 839–844.

Pedersen, F. A., Rubenstein, J. L., & Yarrow, L. J. Infant development in father-absent families. *Journal of Genetic Psychology*, 1979, *135*, 51–61.

Radin, N. The role of the father in cognitive, academic and intellectual development. In M. E. Lamb (Ed.), *The role of the father in child development*. New York: Wiley, 1976.

Radin, N. *Childrearing fathers in intact families with preschoolers*. Paper presented to the American Psychological Association, Toronto, September 1978.

Radin, N. The role of the father in academic, cognitive and intellectual development. In M. E. Lamb (Ed.), *The role of the father in child development* (Rev. ed.). New York: Wiley, 1981.

Ramsey, G. B. Review of group methods with parents of the mentally retarded. *American Journal of Mental Deficiency*, 1967, *71*, 857–863.

Reed, E. W., & Reed, S. C. *Mental retardation: A family study*. Philadelphia: W. B. Saunders, 1965.

Rosen, B. C. & D'Andrade, R. The psychosocial origins of achievement motivation. *Sociometry*, 1959, *22*, 185–218.

Rutter, M. *Maternal deprivation reassessed*. Harmondsworth, England: Penguin, 1972.

Rutter, M. Why are London children so disturbed? *Proceedings of the Royal Society of Medicine*, 1973, *66*, 1221–1225.

Rutter, M. Maternal deprivation, 1972–1978: New findings, new concepts, new approaches. *Child Development*, 1979, *50*, 283–305.

Ryckman, D. B., & Henderson, R. A. The meaning of a retarded child for his parents: A focus for counselors. *Mental Retardation*, 1965, *3*, 4–7.

Saenger, G. *The adjustment of severely retarded adults in the community*. Albany: New York State Interdepartmental Health Research Board, 1957.

Saenger, G. *Factors influencing the institutionalization of mentally retarded individuals in New York City*. Albany: New York State Interdepartmental Health Research Board, 1960.

Sagi, A. Nontraditional fathers in Israel. In M. E. Lamb (Ed.), *Nontraditional families: Parenting and child development*. Hillsdale, N.J.: Lawrence Erlbaum Associates, 1982.

Schaffer, H. R., & Emerson, P. E. The development of social attachments in infancy. *Monographs of the Society for Research in Child Development*, 1964, *29* (Whole No. 94).

Schipper, M. T. The child with mongolism in the home. *Pediatrics*, 1959, *24*, 132.

Schonnell, F. J., & Watts, B. H. A first survey of the effects of a subnormal child on the family unit. *American Journal of Mental Deficiency*, 1956, *61*, 210–219.

Sears, R. R., Maccoby, E. E., & Levin, H. *Patterns of child rearing*. Evanston, Ill.: Row Peterson, 1957.

Sears, R. R., Rau, L., & Alpert, R. *Identification and child rearing*. Stanford: Stanford University Press, 1965.

Serbin, L. A., Tonick, L. J., & Sternglanz, S. H. Shaping cooperative cross-sex play. *Child Development*, 1977, *48*, 924–929.

Shinn, M. Father absence and children's cognitive development. *Psychological Bulletin*, 1978, *85*, 295–324.

Stevenson, M. B., & Lamb, M. E. The effects of social experience and social style on cognitive competence and performance. In M. E. Lamb & L. R.

Sherrod (Ed.), *Infant social cognition*. Hillsdale, N.J.: Lawrence Erlbaum Associates, 1981.

Tallman, I. Spousal role differentiation and the socialization of severely retarded children. *Journal of Marriage and the Family*, 1965, *27*, 37–42.

Tasch, R. J. Interpersonal perceptions of fathers and mothers. *Journal of Genetic Psychology*, 1955, *87*, 59–65.

Thompson, R. A., & Lamb, M. E. Security of attachment and stranger sociability in infancy. *Developmental Psychology*, 1983, *19*, 184–191.

Wadsworth, H. G., & Wadsworth, T. B. A problem of involvement with parents of mildly retarded children. *The Family Coordinator*, 1971, *20*, 141–147.

Waters, E., Wippman, J., & Sroufe, L. A. Attachment, positive affect, and competence in the peer group: two studies in construct validation. *Child Development*, 1979, *50*, 821–829.

Weiner, B. *Achievement motivation and attribution theory*. Morristown, N.J.: General Learning Press, 1974.

Winterbottom, M. The relation of need for achievement in learning experiences to independence and mastery. In J. Atkinson (Ed.), *Motives in fantasy, action, and sociey*. Princeton, N.J.: Van Nostrand, 1958.

Yogman, M. Development of the father–infant relationship. In H. Fitzgerald, B. Lester, & M. W. Yogman (Eds.), *Theory and research in behavioral pediatrics*. New York: Plenum, 1983.

Yogman, M. J., Dixon, S., Tronick, E., Als, H., & Brazelton, T. B. The goals and structure of face-to-face interaction between infants and their fathers. Paper presented to the Society for Research in Child Development, New Orleans, March 1977.

6

Siblings of Handicapped Persons

MILTON SELIGMAN

BIOGRAPHICAL SKETCH

Milton Seligman, Ph.D., is a professor in rehabilitation counseling at the University of Pittsburgh. A former editorial board member of the Journal for Specialists in Group Work, *Dr. Seligman at present serves on the editorial board of the* Personnel and Guidance Journal.

He has edited or authored books and articles in the areas of group counseling and psychotherapy and in working with parents of exceptional children. A recent work, Group Psychotherapy and Counseling with Special Populations, *was published in 1982. An earlier book on parents was entitled* Strategies for Helping Parents of Exceptional Children: A Guide for Teachers.

Dr. Seligman teaches courses in individual and group counseling as well as courses in clinical supervision and working with parents of exceptional children.

A S NOTED in Chapter 1, for the past several decades handicapped children have been receiving considerable attention in the professional literature, in educational settings, and in treatment places such as child guidance clinics, children's hospitals, and the like. Until quite recently, however, the parents of handicapped children were a largely ignored special needs group. With the passage of the Education for All Handicapped Children Act (P.L. 94-142) in 1975, society witnessed an increased emphasis on the parents of these children. Because of this legislation, the growing involvement of parents' organizations, and the interest educators in such fields as special education, child development, and social work have shown, the needs of exceptional parents (especially mothers) have swiftly come to the fore. Thus parents of exceptional children have of late been able to make their special circumstances known.

Nevertheless, two roles within the family structure of exceptional children have gone largely unnoticed: fathers and siblings. As Trevino (1979) notes, "It is indeed surprising that in spite of the available knowledge of family systems, roles, and life cycles, professionals persist in maintaining a fragmented view of families with a handicapped child even when preventive efforts are clearly indicated" (p. 488). The exceptional father is discussed by Lamb in Chapter 5. This chapter explores the other area that has received insufficient attention—siblings—in an attempt to more fully understand the brothers and sisters of handicapped children.

RESEARCH FINDINGS: AN OVERVIEW

Research in the area of sibling reaction and adjustment to a handicapped brother or sister has been regrettably sparse. Even though few have made attempts to study siblings, it would seem important to review existing investigations to provide a foundation for the experiences and observations of others.

One of the more ambitious studies of siblings was conducted by Grossman (1972), who collected data on 83 college students, each of whom had a retarded brother or sister. A matched control sample of students with normal brothers and sisters was used for comparison. Each student was interviewed individually about his or her experiences, and tests were given to obtain additional information. Taped interviews were transcribed and scored on 50 different measures relating to the siblings' experience with their retarded brother or sister. Retardation of siblings raged from mild to severe. Grossman's data revealed the following:

1. A number of subjects appeared to have benefited from the experience of growing up with a handicapped sibling. These students seemed to be more tolerant and more aware of the consequences of prejudice as

well as more certain about their own futures and about personal and vocational goals than comparable young adults who had not had such an experience.

2. There were clear indications that some normal siblings were harmed by the experience: they showed bitter resentment of their family's situation, guilt about the rage they felt at their parents and at the retarded sibling, and fear that they themselves might be defective.

3. Families tended to exempt their sons from the demanding duty of caring for their retarded sibling, whereas daughters were more actively involved in their brother's or sister's care.

4. The strongest single factor affecting the normal sibling's acceptance of his retarded brother or sister was parental feelings and reactions, especially those of the mother.

5. Upper-income families, because of their resources, had more opportunity to relieve their normal children of the burdensome care of the handicapped child, but not without some negative yet manageable consequences, e.g., guilt feelings.

6. Lower-income families experienced more hardship as a consequence of the retarded child, especially as the young normal women were expected to assume a major share of responsibility for their handicapped siblings. Young women from larger families fared better, probably because they had normal sisters and brothers who shared responsibility.

Grossman's research indicates the differential impact of sociocultural status as it affects the family's ability to secure relief from the chronic burden of caring for a handicapped child. Lower socioeconomic class families already enmeshed in a day-to-day struggle to survive were in a poor position, psychologically and financially, to take on the additional responsibilities of a significantly impaired child. The major finding of this investigation was that brothers and sisters of handicapped siblings respond in significantly different ways, negative for some and surprisingly positive for others, and that socioeconomic status appears to have a bearing on the family's ability to effectively cope.

According to Grossman, the family's perception of the handicapped child appears to be related to subsequent sibling adjustment. "It is the family's definition of the problem that most directly affects the ability of individual members of the family to adjust to a retarded child. The presence of a retarded child can enhance a family's normal development, or at least not hinder it" (p. 104).

Farber (1959) wanted to understand to what extent interaction with a retarded child influences the future of normal siblings. Farber suspected that frequent interaction with a retarded sibling has impact on one's life goals. He theorized that such exposure may affect occupation, education, marriage, and parenthood.

Eighty-three boys and girls, aged 10–16, with a retarded sibling living at home were asked to rank a series of life goals in terms of the importance of those goals to them. Data on frequency of sibling interaction with their handicapped brother or sister was obtained from mothers. In the analysis, children who interacted with their retarded siblings every day were compared with children who interacted less frequently. Ten life goals were identified, three of which are to (1) be a highly respected community leader, (2) focus one's life around marriage and the family, and (3) learn not to take life too seriously.

The results of Farber's investigation indicated that *boys* who interacted daily with their retarded sibling

1. Placed a greater emphasis on success in business,
2. Expressed more devotion to a worthwhile cause, and
3. Expressed a concern about making a contribution to humanity and had seemingly decided not to take life too seriously.

The same boys showed *less* interest in

1. Having many close friends,
2. Focusing life around marriage and the family, and
3. Being a respected community leader.

For *girls* who sustained daily interaction, the results showed that they wished to

1. Learn to accept hardships,
2. Devote themselves to a worthwhile cause, and
3. Make a contribution to humanity.

The same girls gave a *lower* rank to such items as

1. Having many close friends,
2. Focusing life around marriage and family,
3. Being a respected community leader, and
4. Attaining business success.

In general, Farber's study suggests that normal siblings came to regard sustained interaction with retarded siblings as a duty. In the performance of this duty, the normal siblings internalized helping norms and turned their life goals toward the improvement of mankind or at least toward goals that require considerable dedication and sacrifice.

A later study by Farber (1960) indicated that the adjustment of normal siblings was unaffected by the sex of the retarded child or the social status of the family but was influenced adversely by a high degree of dependence on the part of the retarded child. Sisters tended to be better adjusted when the retarded sibling was insitutionalized than when he or she was at home, whereas the opposite was true of brothers, who seemed less well adjusted when the retarded child was institutionalized.

Farber's studies contradict Grossman's results, which suggested that family socioeconomic status was indeed related to adjustment. In Grossman's study families falling into the higher SES category were in a better position to secure help for their retarded child, thereby reducing the burden placed on normal siblings, especially the normal girls. Farber's finding that sisters appeared better adjusted when the retarded sibling was institutionalized is coorborated by other reports (e.g., Grossman's) that sisters often take the brunt of the responsibility for a handicapped sibling. This point is further developed in a subsequent section.

Farber (1960) discovered little interest on the part of girls frequently interacting with their exceptional siblings to succeed in business. It is quite possible that if his study were replicated in the 1980s the results would be different, in that at present there is ostensibly less concern about gender roles than formerly. This likelihood suggests the inapplicability of research findings from an era in which values differed markedly from contemporary views. Consumers of research must keep in mind that changing societal values affect study results. Replication of earlier studies, especially in instances where research results have importance for policy or treatment decisions, might therefore be highly advisable.

In interpreting Farber's study of sibling life goals one must consider the age range of the normal siblings, 10–16. Although the helping orientation adopted by normal siblings in Farber's study has not been contradicted by other evidence (indeed, there is a fair amount of support for his findings), 10-to-16-year-old youngsters may not be in a position to declare firm life goals. Many young people at this stage of development are doubtless still struggling with other issues common to preadolescent and adolescent youngsters.

Graliker, Fishler, and Koch (1962) attempted to determine the effect of a retarded brother or sister on adolescents (ages 13–18, mean age 15) in terms of their school, social, and family life. Twenty-one teenagers volunteered to participate in the study with their parents' consent. Six boys and 15 girls were interviewed. The retarded siblings ranged in age from 10 months to 5½ years, and the majority fell into the severely retarded group. All of the retarded children except two were living in the home.

As a result of their interviews, which centered on attitudes toward the mentally retarded sibling and relationships in the home, Graliker and associates reported

1. That the normal siblings felt comfortable in having their friends visit their homes.

2. That all of the normal boys and girls had responsibility for specific chores at home.
3. That parent–normal sibling relationships were healthy.
4. That there was a high degree of acceptance of and tolerance for the retarded youngster.
5. That the majority of the subjects had been told of their brother's/sister's retardation almost as soon as the parents were aware of it.
6. That in almost all cases the teenager had little hesitation about having friends meet the retarded sibling and were willing to explain the situation if asked.
7. That all of the teenagers helped at home in some way with the retarded child and in no case did they feel burdened with responsibility for the retarded child.

The remarkably positive findings of this study run counter to other investigations and observations. The positive outlook and response on the part of these adolescents is not in itself surprising; what is remarkable about this study is the rather universal outlook that characterized these youngsters. The investigators properly speculated that the young age of the retarded children (10 months to 5½ years) may account in part for their unqualified acceptance by the teenager. Further, brothers and sisters often gladly help parents with very young siblings, perhaps regardless of whether a disability exists. The parents in this study appeared to be especially sensitive to the needs of the normal siblings by openly communicating their retarded child's condition and in general being aware of their normal adolescents' needs. In this sense the teenage sample studied by Graliker and associates does not reflect the wide range of parental attitudes and sensitivity (or lack of sensitivity) that others have reported. Also, this study utilized a small sample.

Little is known about the long-range effects of having a mentally retarded brother or sister. Because of the lack of studies of adult siblings of mentally retarded persons, Cleveland and Miller (1977) sought to determine if the life commitments of normal adults had been influenced by the experience of having a mentally retarded sibling.

Ninety men and women, siblings of mentally retarded adults residing in a state institution for the retarded, responded to a questionnaire developed by the researchers. The normal brothers and sisters were 25 years of age or older and in all cases were older than the retarded sibling.

The questionnaire elicited responses about normal subjects' recollections of childhood and adolescent experiences involving their retarded brother's or sister's. It also solicited information about their own adult life commitments and the impact the retarded sibling had on career, marriage, and family.

Sixty-three percent of the retarded siblings were male, averaging 29 years of age, and had lived outside their parents' home an average of 16 years. Most of the mentally retarded adults fell into the severe to profound range of retardation. The normal siblings were primarily middle-class, white, married persons with families of their own. Females outnumbered males two to one.

The results of the research showed the following:

1. The majority of the normal siblings reported a positive adaptation to the retarded sibling and the experiences surrounding a retarded sibling. More specifically, they reported good relationships with their other normal siblings and with their retarded sibling, only on occasion did they miss out on activities because of the retarded sibling, their school experiences were not affected, they had friends visit them regularly at home without embarrassment, and most felt that they had adequate information from their parents regarding the condition of their retarded sibling.

2. The majority of the respondents indicated that their parents approached the problem of raising a family with a retarded child in an adaptive manner. The families led relatively normal, successful lives (recall that the retarded brothers and sisters had resided outside of the home for an average of 16 years).

3. The majority of the respondents reported that their adult life commitments were not affected by having a retarded brother or sister.

4. The researchers noted that some definite patterns were discovered among the *minority* of normal siblings who reported that their life commitments had been affected.

5. Striking differences were revealed for male and female normal siblings. The male siblings' responses revealed a lack of information about the retarded sibling that continued into adulthood (general lack of involvement with the retarded sibling may account for this finding).

6. The demands made on female siblings were heavier than those made on male siblings and were heaviest when the subject was the oldest female sibling in the family. (Female siblings showed a closer relationship to the retarded sibling in childhood and also in the adult years. Being assigned surrogate parental roles, sisters may have acquired more understanding of the retardate's condition and circumstances than less-involved brothers.)

7. Female siblings tended to choose "helping" careers more often than male siblings and not suffer greater adjustment problems, as the researchers had speculated.

8. The female siblings that did seem to suffer some adverse effects were those who were the only or oldest female. (It seems that these siblings are overburdened by parental desires to fulfill expectations through

their normal child(ren) and also by the pressures of assuming parent-surrogate responsibilities.)

Cleveland and Miller (1977) conclude that in counseling exceptional families clinicians should be aware of the sexes of the normal siblings and the parental expectations regarding normal siblings' involvement as caretakers; furthermore, they suggest that the retarded siblings' condition be communicated to normal brothers and sisters and that the family be made aware that normal sibling adjustment to a handicapped brother or sister may be subject to change as both grow older.

In a departure from other studies that examined sibling reaction only to mentally retarded brothers and sisters, Breslau, Weitzman, and Messenger (1981) studied families of children with cystic fibrosis, cerebral palsy, myelodysplasia, or multiple handicaps. These researchers sought to answer the following questions: (1) Do normal siblings of disabled children manifest greater psychological impairment compared to children generally?; (2) Do they manifest more interpersonal aggression?; (3) Do type and severity of disability influence the siblings' psychological functioning?; (4) Are there sex, age, and birth order differences in level of siblings' psychological functioning?; and (5) What are the mother's perceptions regarding the effects of the disabled child on attention to siblings?

Mothers from 239 families with a handicapped child in which there were normal siblings 6–18 years old were interviewed for two to three hours with a structured questionnaire. The siblings were predominantly white, and female siblings slightly outnumbered males. This group was compared to a similar group of siblings with nonhandicapped brothers and sisters.

Breslau et al. (1981) found that in comparison with the control group siblings were not more psychologically impaired, yet a few subscale differences were observed. Siblings of exceptional children had significantly lower scores on "isolation" than the control group, indicating fewer (withdrawl behaviors, yet were higher in "self destruction," "mentation problems," "fighting," and "delinquency," thus suggesting somewhat mixed findings of adjustment.

The picture that emerges from the present study is that older female siblings may be "at risk" of maladjustment and that problems of thinking and concentration (mentation) and interpersonal aggression seem to bear a relation to being the brother or sister of a disabled child. Although the interviewed mothers of disabled children denied that they had spent significantly less time with their normal children—a fact that may account for siblings' aggressive behavior—the answer to this question may have been different had the children been interviewed.

The study failed to uncover a significant effect for type of disability, that is, the diagnostic category of the disabled children had no significant effect on siblings. Likewise, level of disability of the afflicted children did not appear to bear a relation to sibling adjustment.

Among siblings *younger* than the disabled child male siblings had greater psychological impairment than female siblings, whereas among siblings *older* than the disabled child female siblings were more psychologically affected. The researchers considered this finding perplexing and could not find a suitable explanation for it. The only accounting offered for this age-sex interaction is that the finding may be a factor when a brother's or sister's disability is congenital. One may speculate, however, that the older female sibling may indeed experience more stress because of the caretaking activities often ascribed to her and the consequent feelings of resentment, anger, and guilt.

The interviewed mothers felt that the special care given to their disabled children did not adversely effect the relationship they had with their normal children. They also felt that they spent adequate amounts of time with their normal children, a finding that runs counter to other observations that a handicapped child's needs excessively absorb the resources of parents and may adversely effect siblings.

Research limitations. Although the sample of research reported here does provide some preliminary data, one must recognize existing limitations. With few exceptions [e.g., Braslau's (1981) study], most of the studies examined sibling reactions to *retarded* brothers and sisters. The ages of the retarded siblings and the normal brothers and sisters differ from study to study, as does the home versus institutional placement of the afflicted sibling. The focus of the research (e.g., career goals, psychological adjustment) differs also. This variability of research is often a limitation in that results are neither confirmed nor denied by replications of the original study. It is advantageous, though, in expanding knowledge beyond prior research and thereby providing a more comprehensive understanding of sibling experiences.

The reported research is often retrospective and subjective and generally involves selective populations. For example, we have no information on the brothers and sisters who choose not to volunteer for a research study. Perhaps most limiting in terms of making useful and conclusive statements about this population is the remarkably small number of reported studies. Nevertheless, existing research does provide us with a beginning and has begun to tease out suggestive findings that will be tested in time through additional research, experience, and observation.

Fantasy

The American Psychiatric Association's *A Psychiatric Glossary* (1980) defines fantasy as "an imagined sequence of events or mental images, e.g., daydreams, that serves to express unconscious conflicts, to gratify unconscious wishes, or to prepare for anticipated future events" (p. 41). In a therapeutic situation the examination of fantasy activity is useful in understanding the stresses and conflicts that may be just below a client's level of awareness. When one comprehends the meaning of a particular fantasy or series of fantasies, a treatment plan can be initiated to help resolve whatever stresses and conflicts exist.

In addition to the common stresses of everyday life, parents may be additionally burdened by the presence of a handicapped child. Like their parents, normal children also experience stress as the brother or sister of a handicapped child, and these stresses or conflicts often become manifest in fantasies.

Conflicts can also be expressed in dreams, as illustrated in the following dream reported by a brother of a child who suffers from severe developmental disabilities and acute deprivation in his fine motor processes, is mentally retarded, and has a behavior problem.

> You [Josh, the father] die. And then Noah suddenly becomes normal. So Fourmi [the mother] goes and kills the father of the other kids in our day-care center. But those kids stay brain-damaged. And Fourmi gets caught and has to go to jail. (Greenfield, 1978, p. 365).

Featherstone (1980) maintains that a handicapped brother or sister evokes powerful fantasies that are sometimes apparent when observing normal siblings at play, perhaps in creating a drama of some sort. In a radio play that Featherstone transcribed in her book, *A Difference in the Family*, she observes themes of sorrow, frustration, and rage that sometimes is expressed with murderous intensity. In addition to violent and guilt-laden themes, terrifying thoughts about one's future responsibility for the handicapped sibling are expressed as well as ones that rationalize thoughts and behavior or are positive and supportive in nature.

Although parents struggle with dark feelings of their own regarding their handicapped child, they seem to be able to find these more acceptable than similar thoughts held by their normal children. Perhaps it is for this reason that normal siblings sense their parents' uneasiness with their conflicts and therefore keep them hidden from their mothers and fathers. Parents wishing to shield their children from troubling thoughts may be doing them a disservice. Children quickly sense family tensions, making it virtually impossible to camouflage them. Yet in pretending that their children are unaware of underlying family tension an important avenue for communication and understanding is missed. In such instances, fantasy often plays an important role in that it allows the child to express conflictive material, which helps to release pent up tensions. It may be that fantasy also allows for the acting out, through imagination, of solutions to dilemmas thought to be unsolvable.

Siblings of brothers and sisters who are facing death or have died have been studied by Binger (1973). Binger reported feelings of responsibility for the sibling's death, fears that the normal sibling may be next to die, resentment that the parents spent so much time with the ill child, anger at the parents who "allowed" the sibling to become sick, and a preoccupation with inner fantasies about death. A more careful exploration of sibling fantasies by a mental health professional may have proven useful in preventing the psychological difficulties observed, after a sibling's death, in more than half of the children Binger studied.

San Martino and Newman (1974) theorized that one of the most important factors responsible for sibling maladjustment is guilt. They believe that the birth of a retarded child, the presence of that child in the home, or the knowledge that the handicapped child once lived at home greatly increases the normal child's existential guilt. To expiate one's guilt about a retarded sibling and to justify the gratification of one's own needs, normal siblings develop fantasies to explain the retardation. San Martino and Newman point out that for a normal child to fulfill himself becomes, in fantasy, a selfish and guilt-ridden activity that takes something away from the retarded sibling.

These authors believe that a normal child's adjustment to the presence of a retarded sibling is, in part, determined by the "family style," which is reflected in attitudes and fantasies, spoken and unspoken, of other family members. Siblings of retarded children develop fantasies that help explain the meaning of retardation, its possible causes, and what it might mean for themselves.

San Martino and Newman further speculate that fantasies about lack of control of one's aggressive feelings provoke potentially distressing identification with the outbursts of the retarded sibling. Another common fantasy is that retardation and mental illness are related, especially when odd behavior or seizures accompany retardation. In such instances a child may fear for his own mental health. Another fantasy, born of guilt, is the notion that any demands placed on the retarded sibling will lead to further damage to that child.

Professionals who work with exceptional families, and especially with siblings, ought to concern themselves with the fantasy productions of these children. These may provide information required for treatment planning toward the ultimate goal of reducing sibling adjustment problems in later years.

Responsibility

The issue of responsibility appears in most of the writing about siblings. The extent to which a sibling may be made responsible for a handicapped brother or sister bears a strong relation to the perception and feelings normal children, adolescents, and adults have about their

handicapped sibling and parents. The research reviewed earlier in this
chapter tends to support the notion that a child's (especially a female
child's) excessive responsibility for a handicapped sibling is related to the
development of anger, resentment, guilt, and quite possibly subsequent
psychological disturbance.

A handicapped child in the family absorbs a great deal of time, energy, money, and emotional resources. Before they are ready, children
may be pressed into parental roles they are ill-prepared to assume. Such
youngsters may move too rapidly through developmental stages so necessary for normal growth.

> From the time Roger began going to physicians and consultants, it seemed
> to me that I carried a five-hundred-pound lead weight around in the front of
> my brain. Never out of my mind was the idea that my brother was retarded,
> needed special attention, needed special care, and that I had to provide
> some of it.
>
> My role in those days was someone who was always around to help care
> for Roger. That was my mother's phrase. My father called me his "good
> right arm." Roger himself called me "Dad" before he corrected himself and
> called me "Bobby."
>
> I never felt I dressed like a kid, never felt comfortable with the clothes I
> wore, never felt I knew how to act as a boy or a teen-ager. I was a little man.
> (Myers, 1978, p. 36)*

The tremendous burden visited upon normal children as they assume
responsibility of a handicapped sibling is vividly expressed by Hayden
(1974). Insensitive parental comments sometimes reinforce one's guilt and
fear.

> The responsibility I felt for Mindy was tremendous. One year, when my
> "babysitting" duties involved periodic checking on my sister, Mindy wan-
> dered away between checks. After a thorough but fruitless search of the
> neighborhood, my mother hysterically told me that if anything happened to
> Mindy I would be to blame. I felt terrified and guilty. I was seven. (p. 27)†

It is often difficult for adults to accept their circumstances when they
compare their lot to others who appear to be more successful. Children
find their life with a handicapped sibling even less comprehensible when
comparing their family to families with normal children:

> The whole situation is profoundly unfair. It is unfair that one family must
> live with schizophrenia, autism, blindness, or retardation while others do

---

*Reprinted with permission from Myers, R. *Like normal people*. New York: McGraw-
Hill, 1978.

†Reprinted with permission of *The Exceptional Parent* magazine. Copyright © 1974,
Psy-ed Corporation, 296 Boylston Street, Boston, MA. 02116. From Hayden, V., The other
children. *The Exceptional Parents*, 1974, *4*, 26–29.

not. It is unfair that some children must function as adjunct parents even before they go to school, while others successfully avoid responsibilities of all sorts well into their second decade. The brothers and sisters of the handicapped child learn to cope with this unfairness, and with their own response to it, the sorrow and the anger. (Featherstone, 1980, p. 162)‡

Family size seems to be related to the extent to which a sibling experiences caretaking responsibility. This clinical observation is born out by Grossman's (1972) research, namely, that students from two-child families found life with a retarded sibling more stressful than those with a number of normal siblings. It could well be that a "spread of responsibility" effect operates in larger families where more siblings are available to help.

Research also tells us that the sex of normal brothers and sisters plays a part in parental demands. It may well be that in contemporary society there are fewer sex-role-typed activities than there were when most of the research on siblings was conducted. One gets the sense that changes in adult behavior have come about as a consequence of the women's rights movement, among other social forces. It is less obvious how the more liberal interpretation of sex-role behavior affects the development of gender-role expectations parents have of children. It may be that female children are still given dolls to play with, are treated in a more gentle fashion, and are taught sex-role-related nurturance activities that differ little from those taught in years past. Conversely, boys may still often be given sporting equipment early on, tend to be more physically active with their parents (especially their fathers), and be taught to be tough, independent, and nonfeeling, although contemporary children undoubtedly see their parents assuming more varied and flexible roles than they did in years past.

Grossman (1972) found that socioeconomic status is related to the amount of responsibility a normal sibling might assume for a handicapped brother and sister. The more financially able a family, the better prepared they are to secure necessary help from sources outside the family. Families that are less secure financially must rely on resources within the family. Financial problems produce additional stress and can detract from general stability where excessive and unreasonable demands may be placed on family members. In financially struggling families the handicapped child may even be scapegoated as the source of the financial woes. In such instances clinicians must be alert to the potential for abuse of the handicapped child.

In families where the handicapped child is the oldest sibling, as the child grows older, his or her status in the sibling group changes. The re-

---

‡Reprinted with permission from Featherstone, H. *A difference in the family*. New York: Basic Books, 1980.

tarded child is regarded as the youngest intellectually and emotionally yet remains the oldest chronologically. As Farber (1959) points out, normal siblings assume a more superordinate role with respect to the retarded child and tend to take on increasing responsibility for the handicapped child.

As has been noted, sisters seem to assume caregiving roles with greater frequency than brothers. This rather general observation is supported by Farber's (1959) research that disclosed that sisters tended to be better adjusted when the retarded child was institutionalized than when the retarded child was at home.

According to Travis (1976), the burdening of siblings with care of chronically physically ill children seems to be common. Travis reports that siblings who have been excessively burdened often leave home at about age 16. She observes that signs of mounting resentment among such siblings can be seen in hasty or unkind physical care. Travis further notes that in close-knit large families, the care of a handicapped child is viewed as a shared responsibility; school-age siblings help with the physical care of their chronically ill brother or sister.

Travis points out that some chronically ill children enslave their physically normal siblings—"Hand me this, pick up that." Chronically ill children have been observed to be verbally abusive toward their normal siblings, presumably because of envy and confusion. In an informal study by Holt (1958), normal children were reported to have suffered repeatedly from unexpected physical attacks by their afflicted siblings.

Responsibility for the physical well-being of a chronically ill child can be taken to great lengths. In instances where the sick child must be guarded from infection—say, in chronic heart disease—Travis reports that mothers warn their normal children to avoid crowds for fear of bringing home infections. Such responsibility for the welfare of one's ill brother or sister places an inordinate burden on normal siblings with possible implications for their subsequent adjustment.

Siblings in a hemophiliac family, for example, may bear an enormous amount of responsibility in helping the family prevent their brother's or sister's "bleeds." These normal siblings are living an abnormal reality, as they must restrain their natural tendency to want to physically interact with their ill brothers or sisters.

Schild (1976) notes that normal siblings may be burdened by excessively high parental aspirations to compensate for parental disappointments and frustrations about a handicapped child. The responsibility for high achievement may fall on the shoulders of normal siblings, some of whom may intellectually or psychologically not be able to attain in a manner compatible with parental expectations.

Michaelis (1980) cautions that a handicapped child's schooling may fall to normal siblings:

> Although using the services of the siblings to help implement the education programs for the handicapped child may at first seem like an obvious solution, it may be the beginning of more problems for the school, the family, the siblings, and even the handicapped child. It is important that siblings are not expected to be their "brother's keeper" to the extent that their own social and academic learning is hampered by the responsibility. (p. 102)

Children who are given excessive responsibility for a handicapped sibling may, in anger and frustration, strike out physically, especially if their brother or sister is difficult to manage.

> Because my older sister and I were the oldest children, we took on a lot of responsibility for Cathy. We took care of her a lot; we babysat with her a lot. I can remember so many days when I was just so impatient, so indifferent. I wanted to go outside and play. I did not want to sit around and take care of Cathy. I can remember even sometimes while I was changing her clothes, she would start crying or become frustrated and maybe I would spank her. (Klein, 1972, p. 15)§

In spite of the rather negative observations about sibling responsibility and the implied dire consequences of assuming excessive responsibility, Graliker, Fishler, and Koch (1962), as a consequence of their interviews of normal teenage siblings, concluded that "in no case did the teenager feel burdened with responsibility for the retarded child" (p. 841). (Again, one ought to keep in mind that in this study, the handicapped siblings were quite young—10 months to $5\frac{1}{2}$ years.) Whether a child is afflicted or not, parental attention and management is common during the early years and normal sibling involvement is typically minimal and sometimes even only volunteered. The study by Graliker et al. does suggest a promising avenue for subsequent research; namely, at which point in the handicapped child's development are normal siblings likely to become more involved in sibling care? Such information may be beneficial for professionals who counsel parents so that they are alerted to problems that may arise around the issue of responsibility.

All parents think about the future of their children—their education, marriage, and careers. The extent to which parents attempt to direct (or guide) a youngster's future depends on numerous factors—their own history of parental interaction, status factors, and financial security, among

---

§Reprinted with permission of *The Exceptional Parent* magazine. Copyright © 1972, Psy-ed Corporation, 296 Boylston Street, Boston, MA. 02116. From Klein, S. D. Brother to sister: Sister to brother. *The Exceptional Parent*, 1972, *2*, 10–15.

others. Parents of handicapped children worry even more about the future as they fret about many of the same issues parents of normal children do, plus such concerns as to what extent their child will be able to achieve independence, how they will be able to care for their handicapped offspring in their twilight years, and who will care for the child once one or both parents are deceased (Seligman, 1979).

In instances where a sibling needs lifelong care or supervision, normal brothers and sisters understandably look anxiously to the future. They wonder whether the responsibility their parents at present assume will later fall to them. They wonder whether they can cope with the decisions that need to be made in future years, in addition to worrying about whether they can physically or psychologically manage to care for their handicapped sibling. A further, related concern of some significance is the doubt siblings may have about whether their future or present spouse will accept or be able to cope with the handicapped brother or sister.

Catching the Disability

Featherstone (1980) points out that in the wake of a disability, young children may be concerned about "catching" the disability. She notes that anxiety about this is exacerbated when normal siblings learn that the disability was caused by a disease like rubella or meningitis.

Marion (1981) substantiates Featherstone's observations by pointing out that younger normal siblings may have anxieties that they will become blind or deaf in the future. Marion also notes that as children grow into adolescents they may fear that they might become the parents of a handicapped child.

Although different from "catching" the disability, Marion (1981) and Luterman (1979) point out that normal children have been known to develop somatic complaints in their attempts to gain attention from their parents. Luterman observes that in normal siblings of hearing-impaired children it is not uncommon for them to develop a pseudosensory deficit as an attention-getting behavior.

Similarly, Michaelis (1980) notes that as a consequence of a strong identification the normal child may feel overly responsible to the disabled sibling in order to justify psychologically the fact that he or she is not the afflicted one.

In instances of childhood death, healthy children do not escape the fear of contamination by the disease that killed a brother or sister (Travis, 1976). Studying siblings of children dying of leukemia, Binger (1973) found that fears that they will die next are not uncommon. Childhood fears of healthy children of siblings who have congenital heart disease worry that they too may have holes in their hearts or that they are defective in some manner.

Finally, Trevino (1979) relates that young children are more likely to be adversely affected by the presence of an afflicted sibling of the same sex because of the fear of also being disabled, especially if there is no other sibling in the family with whom to identify.

Careers

As noted in the foregoing section on research findings, basic life goals of normal siblings appear to be affected when a handicapped child is present in the family. One's career choice may be influenced by having a handicapped brother or sister. In part a child's career decision may be shaped by having interacted with and cared for a less-able brother or sister. Normal siblings are cognizant of others' reactions toward their handicapped sibling, adding to their sensitivity to interpersonal dynamics. Family attitudes appear to play an important role also. Finally, the continuous act of caring for a handicapped youngster, especially in a loving family, may become internalized to the extent that it influences career decisions in the direction of the helping professions.

As Farber (1959) and Cleveland and Miller (1977) found in their studies, normal siblings internalized helping norms and turned their career endeavors toward the improvement of mankind or at least toward life goals that required dedication and sacrifice. In their interviews of adult siblings, Cleveland and Miller (1977) reported that life commitments were not adversely affected by having a retarded brother or sister.

The following comments by a sister of a mentally retarded, cerebral palsied, and epileptic sibling reflects the thinking behind the decision to prepare for a helping profession:

> Having Robin as a member of our family caused me to undergo a great deal of introspection which led me to insights into certain aspects of my character that needed to be changed. My contact with him, coupled with some sound advice from my parents, also unquestionably influenced my decision to pursue a career in special education. I had originally intended to enter the field of chemistry, and indeed I completed a bachelor's degree in that area. However, something about my choice bothered me. I enjoyed the lab work and the excitement of scientific discovery, but something was missing. It wasn't until my father, during the course of one of our "What are you going to do with your life?" discussions, pinpointed the problem when he quoted the following statement made by the philosopher Kierkegaard: "The door to happiness opens outward." What this meant to me was that one could find true happiness through serving others. The choice of a career then became

obvious to me. What better way was there to serve others than to enter the field of special education where I could help people like my brother lead more fulfilling lives? (Helsel, 1978, p. 112)[11]

Anger and Guilt

Anger is an emotion common to human beings. Some handle the expression of anger better than others, while some deny that they experience anger at all. An indication that many of us manage anger poorly is suggested by the outpouring of recent books and workshop offerings designed to assist in the properly modulated expression of anger.

Siblings of handicapped children may experience anger in larger doses than siblings of normal brothers and sisters. Whether siblings harbor or openly express their feelings of anger and resentment depends on a complex arrangement of the following factors:

1. The extent to which a sibling is held responsible for a handicapped brother or sister.
2. The extent to which a handicapped sibling takes advantage of (manipulates) a normal brother or sister.
3. The extent to which the handicapped sibling restricts one's social life or is considered a source of embarrassment.
4. The extent to which a handicapped sibling requires time and attention from the parents.
5. The extent to which the family's financial resources are drained by services for the handicapped child.
6. The number of siblings.
7. The sex of the siblings.
8. The overall accommodation parents have made to their special circumstances.

As Featherstone (1980) corroborates anger may arise against numerous conditions in the home with an exceptional child:

Children feel angry: at parents, at the disabled child, at the wider world, at God or fate, perhaps at all four. Some blame their mother and father for the disability itself (just as they blame them for any new baby). A handicap creates unusual needs; many children envy their brother or sister this special attention. And older children may rage secretly about the sometimes colossal sums of money spent on diagnosis and therapy—resources that might otherwise finance family comforts and college tuition. (Featherstone, 1980, p. 143)

---

[11]Reprinted with permission from Helsel, E. The Helsels' story of Robin. In A. P. Turnbull & H. R. Turnbull (Eds.), *Parents speak out*. Columbus, Ohio: Charles Merrill, 1978.

Additional causes of anger as well as protective feelings exist. Reactions from acquaintances or strangers to a handicapped brother or sister may lead to open expressions of hostility, as illustrated in the following comments from a college student:

I heard some guy talking in the back about Mark and how stupid he was, and you could make him do anything and he is so gullible, and all this kind of stuff. I walked back to the kid and slugged him in the face. . . . I always felt that I had to protect him from someone, from teasing, from fights, and any other kids trying to put things over on kids who are at a disadvantage to them. If you love somebody you cannot help but get emotionally involved in that. (Klein, 1972, pp. 12, 13)

Normal siblings may be placed in an insufferable triple bind. Parental demands to care for and protect the disabled sibling clash with those of a siblings' playmates who encourage shunning; and then one's own confused feelings (anger, guilt, love, protectiveness) toward the handicapped sibling and resentment toward the parents for *demanding* that one love and take care of a handicapped brother or sister result in a most untenable situation.

Wherever I went, Mindy went too. . . . I was often excluded from neighborhood games because of my sidekick. And then there was the unwritten family rule that I must leave with Mindy whenever my playmates made fun of her. They often did mock her, of course, and we would leave—except for one time which to this day gives my conscience no rest, when I joined in. I lost many playmates by having to side with Mindy. I felt neglected by my family and shunned by my peers. I was a very lonely little girl. (Hayden, 1974, p. 27)

Feeling ignored and unappreciated for one's achievements leaves lifelong scars on normal siblings. Hayden (1974) continues:

Mindy's achievements always met with animated enthusiasm from our parents. In contrast it seemed, mother and daddy's response to my accomplishments was on the pat-on-the-back level. I was expected to perform well in every circumstance. I wanted my parents to be enthusiastic about my accomplishments, too. I didn't want to have to beg for praise. I didn't want to be taken for granted. I wanted to be noticed. (p. 27)

In both of the preceding illustrations one cannot ignore parental insensitivity to the plight of Mindy's normal sister. Anger, resentment, guilt, and competition for parental attention could have been largely averted by parents who shared their time and affection with both of their children. Parents sometimes embrace the myth that their handicapped child is the only needy one.

Angry feelings surface when siblings perceive that their mother (often with their help) must carry the burden of care for a handicapped child without their father's help. Work, business meetings, or committee and community involvement can keep fathers from contributing. In such instances it is useful to distinguish fathers who are legitimately occupied from those who are "too busy" because they wish to deny or avoid their threatening circumstances. Chances are good that normal siblings sense their father's motivations, which adds to their anger toward him.

There are many reasons for normal siblings to experience anger—and the guilt that often follows in anger's wake. Even so, in the literature dealing with counseling exceptional families there exists a deficiency in the area of helping siblings understand, tolerate, or accept and express the anger they so often feel.

Parents and those professionals who serve them would do well to consider the sources of a sibling's anger. In addition, siblings should be made to understand the universality of angry feelings and how such feelings are related to guilt. Siblings need to know that their feelings are normal and that their expression is healthy. They also need reassurance that angry feelings toward handicapped siblings may have some benefits in that disabled children who detect general reluctance on the part of family members to express openly certain emotions toward them alone may interpret this as a further indication of their difference or oddness.

Parents also must allow the expression of anger by their normal children; furthermore, by exercising patience with them on this issue they may discover and hence be better able to deal with their own angry feelings.

Communication

Featherstone (1980) observes that the presence of a disabled child in the family inhibits communication. She believes that the lack of communication within a family over a child's disabling condition contributes to the loneliness normal siblings experience. Siblings may sense that certain topics are taboo and that "ugly" feelings are to remain hidden; they are thereby forced into a peculiar kind of loneliness—a sense of detachment from those one typically feels closest to. Trevino (1979) believes that family secrets or implicit rules forbidding the discussion of a problem force normal siblings constantly to pretend that circumstances are other than they seem.

Chinn, Winn, and Walters (1978) believe that the existence of a child with a handicap is a total family problem and that the normal siblings need to be involved in the total family communication process. Often decisions that bear on the handicapping condition are made without prior discussion or explanation to siblings who may be affected by them. These authors encourage open communication within the family. To help reduce unpleasant side effects, parents are urged to communicate what they plan to do and why.

Pearlman and Scott (1981) acknowledge that communicating the nature of a child's handicap to a brother or sister is difficult yet essential. They also caution that children sense underlying feelings regardless of the actual words used; therefore, open and honest communication is important within the family. Pearlman and Scott believe that what is communicated to children should be based on a child's age and what he or she is able to comprehend and assimilate. They believe that parents should be aware of certain key words in their communication to children. For example, the words *better* and *worse* invite comparisons, whereas *different* and *cannot* convey that limitations are not due to anything anyone did or did not do. Finally, Pearlman and Scott urge parents to begin a dialogue with their children as soon as possible.

Insofar as schoolwork is concerned, Michaelis (1980) notes that siblings may resent that the handicapped child is "playing" when they themselves must work so hard. Communicating the methods used with the handicapped child and the skills that are being taught will help make it possible for the sibling to be supportive rather than critical and resentful.

Wentworth (1974) reports that normal siblings want their parents to be honest with them above all else. Interestingly, parents also desire honesty from the professionals with whom they work (Seligman, 1979). Wentworth believes that normal siblings need to know what caused the handicap, how severe the disability is, and what the prognosis is. He urges parents to answer inquiries as truthfully as possible according to the siblings' ages and level of comprehension. In their description of their guided group experience for siblings of mentally retarded brothers and sisters, Schreiber and Feeley (1965) offer the following insights:

> What the normal adolescents really needed and wanted was accurate, up-to-date information, in language and concepts which they understood, about mental retardation and what they could do to help their families and their retarded siblings. They wanted to know how to manage *now* and what they could look forward to. (p. 224)

Isolation

As noted in the previous section, normal siblings can become isolated from their own family members when they are fearful or anxious about discussing their handicapped brother or sister because the subject is felt not to be acceptable for conversation. Being ignored at the expense of one's handicapped brother or sister leads to angry feelings, as we have already noted, but the siblings' problems are compounded by feelings of distance from one's family when communication is lacking.

Peer reactions may isolate sibling's from their social group. Normal siblings who feel rejected by their peers and are largely ignored by their parents are youngsters at risk. Add the caretaking responsibility siblings may assume and the makings of emotional disturbance may be set in motion.

School may be an environment where isolation is heightened, Michaelis (1980), a special educator, believes that parents should be alert to the possibility that school personnel may treat the normal sibling as if he or she were also handicapped. If school personnel relate to the sibling in a different way, it is likely that other students will do the same, thereby increasing the sibling's sense of difference and isolation.

In instances where a sibling's guilt is unbearable that child can become isolated from his or her own feelings. Guilt over such emotions as anger, hostility, resentment, and jealousy may be so excessive that the sibling's true feelings fail to surface. Such a situation may occur in families where negative thoughts about a handicapped sibling are prohibited or punished. Here the clinician should be sensitive to physical symptoms that may be psychogenic in origin (e.g., ulcers). Anger may seemingly be unattached to a handicapped brother or sister, but hostile feelings may be deflected onto others, such as parents, school officials, or other persons. Indeed, Breslau, Weitzman, and Messenger (1981) noted in their study that siblings of chronically ill children scored higher on aggression than the control group.

A final clue suggestive of suppressed or repressed anger accompanied by guilt is obsequious or subservient behavior toward the sibling. A normal sibling's guilt may be so excessive and unacceptable that it becomes manifest in overly helpful and unrealistically kind actions. Recall that by San Martino and Newman's (1974) analysis one of the most important factors responsible for the disturbed behavior of normal siblings is guilt. Isolation from feelings manifested by extreme servility can suggest serious psychological disturbance and requires professional help.

Featherstone (1980) reports on the frustration and isolation normal siblings feel when they are unable to communicate with a handicapped brother or sister:

> The difficulty of "knowing" an autistic or profoundly retarded child, or the child with a severe communication disorder, can frustrate siblings as much as parents. They yearn for a relationship of equals, for someone with whom they can play and tell secrets, someone who shares their child-view of an adult world. Even when normal siblings perform some of these functions, they sometimes imagine the special relationship they might have with this brother if he were more accessible. The able-bodied member of a two-child family may feel very much alone. (Featherstone, 1980, p. 159)

Parental Attitudes

There appears to be ample evidence that normal siblings are affected by their parents' attitudes toward the handicapped child. Trevino (1979) believes that because children's views are so often extensions of those of their parents, their ability to accept the handicap and cope with the hardship is largely influenced by parental attitudes. Parental attitudes of authoritarianism and overindulgence, augmented by such feelings as anxiety, depression, guilt, and uncontrolled hostility, help color the views, feelings, and behaviors of normal siblings.

One of the factors that help to shape parental attitudes is religion (Zuk, 1959; Seligman, 1979). Some preliminary research tends to support the view that Catholic parents may perceive the birth of a handicapped child as a gift, a blessing that God would bestow only on the most deserving. Such positive sentiments surely influence sibling attitudes.

In her study of brothers and sisters of mentally retarded children, Grossman (1972) concluded that among lower- and upper-socioeconomic status families there was a positive relationship between *open* and *comfortable* family discussion of retardation and the sibling's own acceptance of the retarded child. The degree of open communication about the afflicted child in families appears to be an excellent barometer of parental attitudes.

Many exceptional parents are, at some level, aware of their influence on their normal children. Parents often experience this "influence" with pride, yet some parents of handicapped children consider this an added burden. Depressed, anxious, and guilty parents, aware of their psychological state, worry about the effect they have on other members of the family. Parental concern about their normal children is an added drain on their available psychological resources.

Although depressed and anxious parents may have a negative impact on their children, their awareness of their psychological state often leads them to seek help so that they can better cope with their circumstances. Emotionally disturbed parents who are insensitive to the needs of their normal siblings and largely deny the circumstances that confront them inflict considerable harm on those close to them.

PSYCHOLOGICAL PROSPECTS FOR SIBLINGS

The presence of a handicapped sibling changes the experience of each other child in the family. Families with a handicapped child offer normal siblings unusual opportunities for growth as well as unusual problems. A number of potential areas of difficulty have been noted. How these factors interact to form adjustment problems is difficult to determine, yet an examination of elements that may lead to emotional disturbance should prove useful.

Trevino (1979) is unequivocal in her view that normal siblings are children at risk. She believes that the research, as sparse and inadequate as it is, is suggestive of several factors that contribute to emotional disturbance. We have already touched upon some of the items Trevino considers important: the number of normal siblings, age of siblings, gender of siblings, and parental reaction to the handicap.

Different authors and clinicians view the potential for psychological harm somewhat differently. Poznanski (1969), Trevino (1979), and San Martino and Newman (1974) appear to be the most pessimistic about the effects of a handicapped brother or sister on normal sibling adjustment. Poznanski reports that psychiatrists treat more siblings of handicapped children than handicapped children themselves. Trevino believes that normal children with a combination of certain characteristics and circumstances are, indeed, children at risk who require psychological intervention. For San Martino and Newman, guilt provides the foundation for subsequent difficulties normal siblings are likely to experience. From their interviews of 239 families, Breslau, Weitzman, and Messenger (1981) found conflicting results insofar as sibling adjustment is concerned. They did discern a marked trend toward aggressive behavior and confused thinking by normal siblings.

Both Featherstone (1980), from personal experience and in recounting the experiences of others, and Grossman (1972), from her research on brothers and sisters of retarded children, take a more cautious view of the effects on normal children. They believe that the advent of a handicapped child in the family may have differential outcomes: little impact, negative impact, or positive outcome on subsequent adjustment and coping. Farber's (1959, 1960) research tends to support the same conclusion, which is further reinforced by Klein (1972) and Schreiber and Feeley (1965). Graliker, Fishler, and Koch (1962) did not find *any* adverse effects reported by the siblings interviewed in their study.

From an empirical point of view the question of whether normal siblings are not affected, are helped, or are harmed by the presence of a handicapped brother or sister is unanswerable. Even in nonexceptional families where a normal child experiences emotional difficulties it is difficult to ascertain the factors that have contributed to the situation. Scholars have not yet determined the prevalence of emotional disturbance among siblings residing with a handicapped brother or sister compared with that in "normal" families. The factors that interact and subsequently lead to psychological difficulties are many and combine in complex ways.

Nonetheless, astute clinicians can be relatively accurate in assessing the mental health of normal siblings. Furthermore, although we have relatively little data on which to base solid judgments, existing research and commentary do provide us with a number of factors that seem to contribute to siblings' mental health, factors that have already been noted.

Although some contributors to the professional literature are uncompromisingly pessimistic about the effects of a handicapped child on family members, others are remarkably optimistic, especially exceptional parents who have written about their experiences. In reviewing much of the research and commentary about siblings one may be left with the impression that largely negative effects are to be expected. In this final section it may be useful to be reminded of the differential impact a handicapped child may have on one's brothers and sisters, with a particular focus on positive outcomes.

In her research Grossman (1972) reports that a number of the college students who reported on their relationship with their retarded brother or sister appeared to have benefitted from their growing up with handicapped siblings. The ones who benefitted appeared to us to be more tolerant, more compassionate, more knowing about prejudice" (p. 84). In support of Grossman's findings Miller (1974) found a number of normal siblings who had expressed an involvement in the growth and development of retarded siblings and exhibited a sense of pride that they had been a part of it.

Diane, a normal sibling, said the following in her interview with Klein (1972): "I always felt there was something very different about our family. Of course, you know, Cathy being that difference. Because of her difference there was a degree of specialness or closeness about us that, I do not know, it was sort of a bond that made us all very, very close. We all pitched in and helped each other out." (p. 25)

Another sister, this one of a mentally retarded, cerebral palsied, and epileptic boy, has put her retrospective thoughts as follows:

> I do not mean to imply that life with Robin has been all goodness and light. I have seen the strain that the responsibility of his constant care has placed upon my parents. I worry about the increasing frequency of his seizures and about what would happen to him should my parents become unable to care for him. Robin, himself, like all brothers I suppose, can be truly aggravating. It makes me angry to see him try to weasel his way out of doing things that I know he is capable of doing. Just the other day, I was scolding him for not clearing his place at the table. I guess my sisterly bossing was too much

for him. He pointed at me and angrily made the sign for handcuffs—his way of indicating that I should be put in jail.

All in all, though, I feel that Robin has brought much good into the lives of my family. He has taught us a great deal about acceptance, patience, individual worth, but most of all about love. (Helsel, 1978, pp. 112, 113)

And after a lengthy discussion of brothers and sisters of handicapped youngsters and their adaptation to this special circumstance, Featherstone (1980) remarks:

I have focused, up until now, on the difficulties that the able-bodied child faces. These problems are real enough, and assume major importance in the lives of some children. Nonetheless, the sheer length of my discussion creates a misleading gloomy impression. It may suggest that for the brothers and sisters of the disabled the developmental path is strewn with frightful hazards, that all but the most skillful parents can expect to see their "normal" children bruised irreparably by the experience of family living. The truth is quite otherwise. (p. 163)

Finally, from the book authored by Brown and Moersch (1978), *Parents on the Team,* Sara Brown pens the following letter to siblings—a message laced with compassion, honesty, and good advice:

Dear Friend,

So you have a brother or sister who is different? Your friends call your sister a "retard" or your brother a "cripple?" You are asking, "Why did this happen to me?"

If you answered yes to any of these questions, you're probably feeling sorry for yourself, and you have that right—for a little while. All people feel sorry for themselves and for a handicapped person once in awhile. But feeling sorry for yourself much of the time does not help. "Sorry" does not change things much. "Sorry" does not improve a handicap either.

There is something you *can* do to help yourself and your brother or sister. You can learn to understand. Ask your parents questions such as: "What does mental retardation mean?" or "Will my sister always be crippled?" or "Will my brother ever learn to talk?" Ask your teacher and your brother's or sister's special teachers about what is wrong and what that means for you and your family. You have a right to know. Learn all you can. As you truly begin to learn, you will begin to understand.

You will understand why Mom gets tired after lifting a heavy brother or sister who cannot walk yet, day after day. You will understand why Dad is more worried. (Special equipment or training costs money, and he may be concerned about paying for it.) You will begin to understand why Mom and Dad don't spend as much time with you and why they expect you to do more to help out around the house. You may also understand why it is sometimes difficult for them to talk about handicaps. You see, all parents dream that their children will be healthy, strong, and intelligent. It is very difficult for them to understand why they have a "special" child.

There is one more thing you may be worried about: whether your brother's or sister's handicap is "catching." Sometimes other children get the idea that it's like chicken pox or a virus. But you cannot "catch" a handicap. Many handicaps are determined before a child is born or during the birth process. Others are a result of a severe disease or infection. Other handicaps can be caused by accidents.

When you talk to your friends, it's a good idea to teach them the things you've learned. If they see that you know more about your brother's or sister's handicap than they do, they may begin to ask questions because of their desire to learn and help. Some children will tease you about your special brother or sister because they don't understand. If they hear you using the words *retarded, crippled,* or *brain damaged* to describe your brother or sister in a realistic manner, they will no longer enjoy using these words to get on your back. If you don't get "hairy" about it, they will soon learn to understand, as you have done.

There is one more thing that you can do as you are learning to understand: talk with other kids who have handicapped brothers and sisters. Rap groups and sibling groups may not be available in your community, but why wait until they are? Organize one yourself. Visit with your brother's or sister's teachers and therapists. They can be of help in suggesting others who might join your group.

Sincerely,

Sara L. Brown

P.S. Good luck to you! You are healthy and full of life. Make the most of it. You have the right. (pp. 67–68)[#]

REFERENCES

American Psychiatric Association. *A psychiatric glossary* (5th ed.). Boston: Little, Brown, 1980.

Binger, C. M. Childhood leukemia: Emotional impact on siblings. In J. Anthony and C. Koupernik (Eds.), *The child in his family.* New York: Wiley, 1973.

Breslau, N., Weitzman, M., & Messenger, K. Psychologic functioning of siblings of disabled children. *Pediatrics,* 1981, *67,* 344–353.

Brown, S. L., and Moersch, M. S. *Parents on the team.* Ann Arbor: University of Michigan Press, 1978.

Chinn, P. C., Winn, J., & Walters, R. H. *Two-way talking with parents of special children.* St. Louis: C. V. Mosby, 1978.

Cleveland, D. W., & Miller, N. Attitudes and life commitments of older siblings of mentally retarded adults. *Mental Retardation,* 1977, *15,* 38–41.

Farber, B. Effect of a severely retarded child on family integration. *Monographs of the Society for Research in Child Development,* 1959, *24* (Whole No. 71).

[#]Reprinted with permission from Brown, S. L., & Moersch, M. S. *Parents on the team.* Ann Arbor, University of Michigan Press, 1978.

Farber, B. Family organization and crisis: Maintenance of integration in families with a severely mentally retarded child. *Monographs of the Society for Research in Child Development,* 1960, *25* (Whole No. 75).

Featherstone, H. *A difference in the family.* New York: Basic Books, 1980.

Grakliker, B. V., Fishler, K., & Koch, R. Teenage reactions to a mentally retarded sibling. *American Journal of Mental Deficiency,* 1962, *66,* 838–843.

Greenfield, J. *A place for Noah.* New York: Pocket Books, 1978.

Grossman, F. K. *Brothers and sisters of retarded children.* Syracuse: Syracuse University Press, 1972.

Hayden, V. The other children. *The Exceptional Parent,* 1974, *4,* 26–29.

Helsel, E. the Helsels' story of Robin. In A. P. Turnbull & H. R. Turnbull (Eds.), *Parents speak out.* Columbus, Ohio: Charles Merrill, 1978.

Holt, K.S.The home care of severely retarded children. *Pediatrics,* 1958, *22,* 746–755.

Klein, S. D. Brother to sister: Sister to brother. *The Exceptional Parent,* 1972, *2,* 10–15.

Luterman, D. *Counseling parents of hearing-impaired children.* Boston: Little, Brown, 1979.

Marion, R. L. *Educators, parents, and exceptional children.* Rockville, Md.: Aspen, 1981.

Michaelis, C. T. *Home and school partnerships in exceptional children.* Rockville, Md.: Aspen, 1980.

Miller, S. *Exploratory study of sibling relationships in families with retarded children.* Unpublished doctoral dissertation, Columbia University, 1974.

Myers, R. *Like normal people.* New York: McGraw-Hill, 1978.

Pearlman, L., & Scott, K. A. *Raising the handicapped child.* Englewood Cliffs, N.J.: Prentice-Hall, 1981.

Poznanski, E. Psychiatric difficulties in siblings of handicapped children. *Pediatrics,* 1969, *8,* 232–234.

San Martino, M., & Newman, M. B. Siblings of retarded children: A population at risk. *Child Psychiatry and Human Development,* 1974, *4,* 168–177.

Schild, S. The family of the retarded child. In R. Koch & J. Dobson (Eds.), *The mentally retarded child and his family.* New York: Brunner/Mazel, 1971.

Schreiber, M., & Feeley, M. A guided group experience. *Children,* 1965, *12,* 221–225.

Seligman, M. *Strategies for helping parents of exceptional children.* New York: Free Press, 1979.

Travis, G. *Chronic illness in children: Its impact on child and family.* Stanford, Calif.: Stanford University Press, 1976.

Trevino, F. Siblings of handicapped children: Identifying those at risk. *Social Casework,* 1979, *60,* 488–493.

Turnbull, A. P., & Turnbull, H. R. *Parents speak out.* Columbus, Ohio: Charles Merrill, 1978.

Wentworth, E. H. *Listen to your heart: A message to parents of handicapped children.* Boston: Houghton Mifflin Co., 1974.

Zuk, G. H. The religious factor and the role of guilt in parental acceptance of the retarded child. *American Journal of Mental Deficiency,* 1959, *64,* 139–147.

7

Parenting Moderately Handicapped Persons

REBECCA R. FEWELL
STEVEN A. GELB

BIOGRAPHICAL SKETCH

Rebecca R. Fewell, Ph.D., is Professor of Education in the area of special education at the University of Washington and has been a teacher of deaf-blind and multiply handicapped children. She coordinates the graduate program in Early Childhood Special Education and is Director of the Model Preschool Program. Additionally, she is Project Director of SEFAM (Supporting Extended Family Members), a demonstration project of the Handicapped Children's Early Education Program.

Dr. Fewell is the author of numerous journal articles and book chapters. She served as the coeditor of Educating Handicapped Infants: Issues in Development and Intervention, *and has published two tests, the Developmental Activities Screening Inventory (with Beth Langley) and the Peabody Developmental Motor Scale (with Rhonda Folio).*

Steven A. Gelb, M.Ed., is a Title VII Bilingual Fellow at the University of Washington, where he is enrolled in the doctoral degree program in educational psychology. In addition to teaching at the preschool level, he has been a parent counselor in a wide variety of settings: educational, medical, as well as the home. He is currently preparing a handbook for Washington teachers and administrators who work with handicapped children from non-English-speaking backgrounds.

ISBN 0-8089-1561-4
Copyright © 1983 by Grune & Stratton

A NY MEANS of dividing children with special needs into mild, moderate, and severe categories will be arbitrary and disputable, especially at the confluence of categories. It is not likely that mildly and severely handicapped individuals will be confused with each other, but moderately handicapped children who range from the upper limit of mild and to the lower limit of severe are most open to ambiguity in definition. Having made this admonition, we will begin our discussion by defining the "moderately" handicapped.

One meaning of *moderate,* according to Webster's dictionary (1977 edition), is "keeping within reasonable bounds." Our definition of the moderately handicapped extrapolates from Webster: They are those children whose disabilities obviously are sufficiently substantial to require special services, yet their restrictions are such that substantial areas of normal functioning exist. The moderately handicapped child is markedly deficient in one area (at least) while perhaps normally functioning in others. By contrast, the severely handicapped child's disability is not "within reasonable bounds;" it pervades most if not all areas of functioning. The mildly handicapped child differs from the moderate in the degree of disability. Here the handicap is less obvious and has less impact on the child's life.

The severely handicapped child is one who is generally perceived by others as "abnormal." The mildly handicapped child, despite the existence of a problem, is generally perceived as "normal." The moderately handicapped child occupies a more ambiguous position and may be defined at some times as "normal" and at others as "abnormal." This overlap and its implications for parents and professionals will be a consistent theme in our discussion.

We should note that these designations are functional rather than categorical. That is, an individual seen as severe at one time may, after developing mastery, be (by this definition) moderate at a later time. The nature of the handicap must be marked in aspect yet be "within reasonable bounds" in its effect on the individual's life.

Our major sections elaborate on the theme of ambiguity that pertains to this intermediate level of disability. First, we review the psychosocial aspects of parenting the moderately handicapped child. Parents must cope with the social evaluation of disability made by our culture, as well as the marginality of their child vis-à-vis society.

Secondly, the service needs of these children and their families are discussed. Ambiguity can result in "falling between the cracks" of available services. The moderately handicapped may be too "normal" for services aimed at more severely handicapped children, yet in need nevertheless.

The concluding section of the chapter describes ways professionals may assess family needs and determine strategies that will work to meet identified needs. An emphasis is placed upon identifying and working with the existing strengths of the family unit.

PSYCHOSOCIAL ASPECTS OF PARENTING THE MODERATELY HANDICAPPED

Parents cannot be properly understood in isolation from their social context. Bronfenbrenner (1976) , Brim (1975), and Gordon (1980), as well as others, have helped us to be aware of the many ecological variables that affect parents in general. These are not less potent for the families of moderately handicapped children. These parents are "normal" individuals subject to the same forces and changes in modern life that influence all families. As parents of children with special needs, they must adjust to other factors as well. The first of these is the nature of the disability itself. Equally important, however, is the attitude of the community toward the disabled child. As Roskies (1972) noted, the child's role within the family is inseparable from his or her status in the community.

A disability, whether mental or physical, is of itself not a psychological event. Its impact on a family or individual is determined by its meaning within an ecological context (Grossman, 1972; MacGregor, Abel, Bryt, Lauer, & Weissman, 1953; Myerson, 1963; Wright, 1960). Disabilities are evaluated according to cultural attitudes and the cause (putative or real) of the disability. Myerson (1963) noted that "disability is not an objective thing in a person, but a social value judgment" (p. 11).

Cultures vary in their attitudes toward the disabled. Edgerton (1970, 1981) described a wide range of evaluations of the retarded in traditional societies. They ranged from complete intolerance leading to neglect or outright killing to the granting of the status of "saint." Maisel (1953) provided similar examples of cultural variety in response to physically disabled people. The Palaung of the Malay peninsula, for example, considered a person especially fortunate to have been born with a cleft palate.

The perceived cause of a facial deformity was found to strongly influence its meaning, both to the disfigured and to others (MacGregor et al., 1953). Congenital deformities were evaluated negatively, while war-inflicted injuries were evaluated more highly. The authors concluded that "what the deformity symbolizes for the patient and others around him seems to have in many instances more significance than the specific defect itself" (MacGregor et al., 1953, p. 75).

Haffter (1968) provided an excellent example of the way in which a culture's evaluation of a disability as well as perception of its cause affected parents of handicapped children. In Europe during the Middle Ages children with birth defects were called changelings. They were believed to be the offspring of a woman's union with the devil. A woman suspected of practicing witchcraft would be asked if she had given birth to a changeling, and an admission could result in being burned at the stake. Not surprisingly, families with disabled children were fearful, secretive, and unaccepting of the child (Haffter, 1968). The parents' behavior was not "pathologic;" it was a realistic response to social pressure.

If we study families of the disabled in isolation from their social context, we miss the meaning of their behavior. Our judgments are likely to be unfair to parents and we are likely to wind up "blaming the victim" (Ryan, 1971).

A society's negative evaluation of a child places severe strain on the child's parents. Parental aspirations for the child and the realization of cherished goals can be thwarted by social obstacles as well as by the disability itself. In addition, parents are forced into conflicting roles as providers who desire the best for their children and as members of a society that views the child as socially unworthy. Finally, when the child's handicap is a moderate one, the parent faces the added uncertainty of not knowing in a given situation whether the child will be accepted or rejected. The uncertainty engendered by this marginality is especially stressful.

Parental Aspirations

There is a great variability in human parenting behavior across cultures. Nevertheless, human parents everywhere have some common goals for their children. One of these is the achievement of a culturally valued role within the community (Levine, 1980). The realization of this parental aspiration depends not only on the child but also on the community's assessment of the child. When a society rejects a child it deprives the parent of the possibility of achieving this aspiration. Moreover, parents whose children are devalued by their culture are devalued themselves as parents. If a prime role of parenting is the transmission of culture, those whose children are rejected by the culture are left with a role stripped of its purpose. Such parents must raise their children in what Roskies (1972) described as a "social void."

The American mainstream culture places high values on normal appearance and behavior. Persons (including the disabled) who deviate from the norm are stigmatized (Goffman, 1963). Goffman described the stigmatized person as one who "is reduced in our minds from a whole and usual person to a tainted and discounted one" (pp. 2–3). The stigmatized person is, by this definition, seen as less than fully human. The stigma of disability is linked with shame and inferiority (Wright, 1960). The "handicapped" role expected of disabled people is characterized by incompetence, helplessness, and deviance. The role precludes other more normal social roles, such as friend, lover, coworker, or autonomous adult (Gliedman & Roth, 1980). Sarason and Doris (1979) wrote: "In our society the retarded child has always been a second-class human being for whom one should have pity, and toward whom one should be humane, but for whom society has no use" (p. 77). This statement is also true for children with other disabilities (Gliedman & Roth, 1980).

The magnitude of their disabilities excludes the severely handicapped from assuming normal social roles. But the separation of the moderately handicapped from society has a different cause. The stigma applied to them is a response to their difference from the norm, not to the differing characteristics themselves. Ethnic groups have been stigmatized for different dress, language, or skin color. Midgets and dwarfs are stigmatized although they do not have impairments in mental or physical functioning (Sagarin, 1969). A facial deformity is a handicap leading to inferior status, but not because of any impairment in physical functioning (MacGregor et al., 1953).

The effect of the moderate disability on functioning is, according to our definition, limited. The moderately handicapped are not of themselves socially deviant. They are penalized, however, by virtue of the "handicapped" label. They are identified with the severely handicapped, although they could as easily be identified with the nondisabled. Their social isolation is no less palpable for being undeserved, and it strongly affects their parents.

Roskies' (1972) study of thalidomide-deformed babies and their mothers found social factors deeply enmeshed in parents' reactions to the disabled babies. "Even at the moment of the mother's initial awareness of the fact that she had borne a deformed baby, her attitudes towards this crisis were based not only on her own feelings, or on the physical diagnosis of the child, but also on the social prognosis" (p. 169). Moreover, the importance of social factors upon the mothers' reactions to their children increased as time went on. Their optimism was directly related to the degree of social normalization the child had achieved in the eyes of the community. The mothers strove to believe that "to engage in the maternity of thalidomide children was not a socially futile act" (p. 180).

A measure of social futility is inescapable when societal attitudes deny parents the opportunity to raise a child who will assume a culturally valued role. The denial of this aspiration when the child's disability is of an intermediate rather than severe nature may be the result either of features of the child or of social discrimination. The difficulty in distinguishing between the two factors is one characteristic of the particular quandary faced by the parents of the moderately handicapped.

The Parent in the Community: The Conflict of Roles

The role of the parent of a disabled child is in conflict with the role of the parent as a member of the community (Roskies, 1972). Parents are expected to be selflessly devoted to their child while remaining members of a society that devalues that child. The conflict presents a psychological dilemma to parents and manifests itself in relations with community members and professionals.

As "normal" members of the community, parents share cultural definitions of normality and abnormality with other community members. As parents they have a need to love and accept their child. They must choose between viewing their child through the eyes of the community to which they belong or through the eyes of nurturing parents (Roskies, 1972). Either choice will incur a penalty.

If parents see their child as abnormal and deserving of stigma, they jeopardize their ability to identify with and love the child. A child seen this way will suffer rejection and isolation within the family. The parents maintain their continuity with the community and its values at the cost of their ability to parent their child. Since parents are expected to love and accept their child even when society will not, parents who reject their child may be expected to experience conflict and guilt.

Those parents who reject society's evaluation of the handicapped child also suffer. They find themselves in opposition to their culture's definition of normality. By identifying with the child they will be forced to redefine their values and their relationship to the community. They may become part of a subculture formed around the needs and value of children like theirs (Darling, 1979).

The conflict of roles is keenly experienced in encounters in the community. Strangers stare, make comments, or offer advice upon seeing children who appear different. The comments usually reflect stereotypical negative judgments about disability and often assume that the parents share the same perspective. Darling (1979) reported that a mother was told by a stranger that she would be better off if her child had died. Featherstone (1980) described a woman who began to avoid going out with her child because she could no longer bear hearing people tell her to "put her child away" (p. 9).

The conflict is reexperienced as the parent attempts to obtain professional services for the child. Many professionals share society's evaluation of these children (Finkelstein, 1980). Darling (1979) found that one-half of a group of pediatricians whom she had interviewed had substantially negative attitudes toward disabled children.

In addition to expressing negative attitudes about the child, community members and professionals may treat the parents as if they too are discounted. The "courtesy stigma" (Goffman, 1963) is extended to those closely associated with the disabled. In this way parents experience a loss of status in the community by virtue of parenting a handicapped child.

The family may be seen as a "handicapped family" whose lives revolve around their child's disability. Featherstone (1980) related the story of one family whose child was being helped by volunteers. Several of the volunteers became angry when they discovered the parents were planning to redecorate their home. Redecorating was seen as inappropriate by the volunteers who expected the parents to spend all their time working to enhance the development of the handicapped child.

Professionals may view the parents as "patients" who are in need of treatment (Seligman, 1979; Turnbull & Turnbull, 1978). The parents of one child were threatened with the loss of services if they terminated unneeded and irrelevant psychiatric counseling (Akerley, 1978).

Parents who speak out against condescending treatment by professionals may have their objection trivialized and treated as a manifestation of an underlying pathologic condition (Gliedman & Roth, 1980). They may be labeled "guilty," "conflicted," or "angry."

The conflicted situation of parents vis-à-vis society is unresolvable. A resolution would require either their child to become nondisabled or society to change its evaluation of such children. Family members pay a cost for society's attitude toward the disabled child. The parent unable to find a babysitter because the child is handicapped, or the family whose siblings are teased by other children, may find their ties to the community diminished because of their child. The interests of the child and the interests of the parents are thus placed in partial conflict (Roskies, 1972). This fact may be partly responsible for the higher than average risk of child abuse faced by handicapped children.

Marginality of the Moderately Handicapped

The marginal person is one who may claim partial membership in two worlds but is not completely acceptable to either (Stonequist, 1937). The moderately handicapped are marginal both to the nondisabled world and to the world of the severely handicapped. Their intermediate status creates ambiguity for them and their parents. Uncertainty is experienced in response to overlapping situations in which the role of the disabled is unclear (Barker, 1948; MacGregor et al., 1953; Myerson, 1963; Roskies, 1972; Wright, 1960). Myerson (1963), referring to the physically disabled, said that "the disabled person lives in two psychological worlds. Like everyone else he lives in the world of the non-disabled majority. He also lives in the special psychological world that his disability creates for him" (p. 42). The moderately handicapped person cannot be sure whether he or she will be treated according to "normal" or "handicapped" expectations in a given situation. Wright (1960) provided the example of blind people wishing to find work: They are uncertain as to whether society will accept them for their normal abilities or reject them as fit only for a workshop sheltered for their blindness.

The reaction of the nondisabled to the severely handicapped is more predictable than their reaction to the more moderately, less obviously handicapped person. In their study of facial deformities MacGregor et al. (1953) found that severely deformed individuals evoked consistent (and negative) responses in others. By contrast, the more moderately deformed are "held in a hair trigger and precarious position: they are never quite certain what will happen. They alternate between feelings of relief and tension and adjustment to their situation is made more difficult" (p. 87).

The parents of the moderately handicapped live with the same uncertainty. They may never be completely sure if their child will be seen as alien or acceptable by the community. The more moderate the handicap, the more difficult it becomes to predict the response of others to their child.

The construct of marginality predicts that intermediately handicapped people will have more adjustment problems than more severely handicapped individuals; some studies have substantiated this theory. Sanua (1966) examined the attitudes of adolescents with cerebral palsy in eight countries. Those with fewer physical defects were more prejudiced toward the disabled as a group than the more severely handicapped. MacGregor et al. (1953) reported that the more severely facially deformed persons in their sample were less conflicted than the more mildly deformed. The less-disfigured group experienced anxiety in response to the uncertainty of others' responses to them.

Marginality was a focus in a study of 127 blind and partially sighted adolescents and 140 deaf and hard-of-hearing adolescents (Cowen & Bobrove, 1966). The totally disabled were found to be better adjusted than the more moderately disabled: the partially sighted and hard-of-hearing group scored higher on a scale of perceived pity and lower on perceived acceptance. The total disability group made higher adjustment scores than the more marginal group on 20 of 28 comparisons. The authors concluded that marginality, while an issue for all disabled people, is especially salient to those with intermediate handicapping conditions.

Parents, too, are made anxious by ambiguity. A mother in a parents' discussion group led by one of the authors stated that she was glad to know her child was completely blind rather than visually impaired. She was relieved to be free of the uncertainty of what the future held for her child's visual acuity. She preferred irreversible blindness and its certainty to a less clearly defined situation.

In Grossman's (1972) study of college students who had handicapped siblings, the positive adjustment of some brothers was directly related to the severity of the physical handicap of the retarded sibling. "This result seemed closely tied to the entire family's greater clarity about, and comfort with, a visible defect in their child, in contrast to their discomfort and uncertainty with retarded children who showed no visible evidence of defects" (p. 178).

Uncertainty is the bane of the parents' thoughts about the future. For moderately handicapped children the future may be especially ambiguous. Parents may perceive of it as both a promise and a threat (Roskies, 1972). The promise lies in the hope that the child will be accepted in the world of the "normal." The threat hangs on the fear that rejection and social isolation will result from the disability.

Resolution of the disabled child's marginality in relation to the worlds of the "normal" and "abnormal" is beyond parental control. Ultimately, the social context, through the attitudes and opportunities it presents to the disabled person, will define his or her status as a member of the community or as an outsider.

Our culture is one in which disability breeds social isolation and inferior status (Finkelstein, 1980; Gliedman & Roth, 1980). This important social feature can make "acceptance" of a disability difficult for parents. In this case the locus of the problem is not only in the family but in the community as well.

The adjustment of parents to a moderately handicapped child has been analyzed from a psychosocial perspective. The perspective gives meaning to parental behavior that cannot be wholly understood by studying the family in isolation. A disability has no psychological value of its own: it assumes its meaning within the society in which it occurs. The status of the child in the family is invariably linked to his or her status in the community.

Negative evaluation and rejection of disabled children have a strong impact upon their parents. The moderately handicapped group, because of the intermediate nature of their disability, are especially affected by social definitions of normality and deviance. They and their parents can be caught between two worlds. Parents may be denied their parental aspirations, experience a conflict between their roles as parents and as members of the community, and be caught in the ambiguity created by their child's marginality.

Parents may have good reason to resist accepting the social judgment conveyed by the word *handicapped*. The term is indiscriminately applied to persons who are not similar (Keniston, 1980). Keniston noted that the child with cerebral palsy and the blind child (to give one example) are each more similar to normal children than they are to each other. What they have in common, according to Keniston, are the attitudes of society: they share a stigma and a social destiny. Parents' difficulty with that destiny is inevitable and normal, and not a sign of pathologic functioning.

The psychosocial influences on parents are, however, not the entire picture. The psychology of family members, the existence of support networks, the availability (or lack) of needed services, the family's financial status, and the temperament and disability of the child are all significant factors in family adjustment. We have discussed social influences at length because they are usually ignored and because of their special salience for the moderately handicapped child and family.

We move now from the "macro" level to the "micro," and discuss the impact of handicaps on parenting.

THE IMPACT OF THE HANDICAP ON PARENTING

Throughout this chapter we stress the multiplicity of factors that shape responses of handicapped children and their families to personal and societal demands. Each person's individual history, experiences, talents, goals, and contributions to each situation, along with society's expectations and exploitations through its policies and practices account for the circumstances parents of handicapped children face.

There are some similarities in the experience of all parents of children with exceptional needs. They encounter the dilemmas of finding appropriate services, of marshaling resources, of explaining their child's needs as well as their own needs to a society that tells them in subtle ways that their child is unworthy. Parents enumerate common experiences with service professionals as well: they tell of being forced to interact continually with professionals who do not seem to realize how it feels to be a parent or who view parents as unable to understand what the problems are and yet, nevertheless, expect parents to be understanding and cooperative, passive and appreciative.

While most experiences of domestic life are shared by all families, there are certain experiences that are felt more strongly by parents whose children have one impairment as opposed to another. For a more thorough understanding of the impact of the various individual handicaps on the child and the family, readers will find information in the literature on these handicaps. In the following section we draw on examples across four different areas of impairment in an effort to illustrate, in an abbreviated manner, the impact of various impairments on children and especially on the parents of these children.

Parenting Visually Impaired Children

For most people without personal knowledge of the blind, the condition of blindness conjures up memories of street vendors selling pencils, of beggars strumming guitars for coins in cups, of persons being led on the arms of others or swinging white canes from side to side, of guide dogs leading their masters across busy intersections. Perhaps even more striking are recollections of religious writings that describe the blind as possessed by demons, as subjects of scorn, or left to die in the wilderness. In contrast, positive images of the blind—of the talented Tom Sullivan, musician, songwriter, and frequent television guest star, for example, or of talented musicians such as Ray Charles and Stevie Wonder, may be buried in one's mind. These images, and those of blind persons reading bus schedules with the help of sophisticated mechanical devices or successfully prosecuting criminal cases, might possibly be retrieved from one's memory. More likely, however, the initial information that a parent receives that blindness resides in one's child is more likely to cause the negative images to emerge. At first, with the shocking news of the child's blindness, grief and self-recrimination dominate the emotions, and estrangement from one's own child may result.

Blindness can be caused by many things. Genetic conditions, infections, and diseases are common etiologies. Parents of blind children, like those of other handicapped children, search for the cause of their child's blindness. A genetic cause can result in blame and guilt on the parents' part. Adventitious blindness presents a very different set of conditions. In families where children are born with sight, normal parent–child relationships develop. For the normally sighted infant–parent dyad, the attachment that develops is mediated through vision. Smiling upon recognition, discriminating looks, using call sounds and responses, visual memory, scanning, tracking, and mutual gazing are all signifiers of attachment that are basically visual in the forming of human relationships. If blindness occurs after 18 months of age, early bonding experiences are likely to provide the secure basis for continued emotional growth as well as a basis for many cognitive discoveries that build upon schemas acquired during the attachment phase. If blindness comes later, parents must face the task of not only their own personal adjustment but the child's adjustment as well. Explaining why it happened, what it means, and how it will affect the child now and in the future culminates in stressful interaction, the success of which depends on the many contributory factors described earlier in this chapter.

The severity of the visual loss is a most important factor in any case of blindness. The presence of some sight, despite the fact that it is minimal, makes a difference in parental reactions. It is the opinion of Lairy and Harrison-Covello (1973) that parents of children with some remaining vision can ignore the blindness for a longer period of time or can "valor-ize" the remaining sight. This reaction may be quite similar to the fre-quent reactions of partially sighted children to their own visual competen-cy. They attempt to use it to the best advantage. It is not at all unusual for these children to pretend to see things in the same way as do sighted children, as they are unaware of what others are seeing when they look at images. A teacher may ask the child if he sees a street sign and he may see the diamond-shaped sign and respond in the affirmative, yet the child may never realize that a message is written on the sign. Likewise, parents may not realize the extent of their child's impairment and may treat their child as one whose vision resembles that of nonvision impaired persons.

The strain of trying to "pass" as a normally sighted person is a fre-quent and expected reaction of moderately visually impaired persons. Criddle (1953) described this experience quite insightfully: "That I could keep a girl from knowing about my eyes through the intimacies of court-ship, even a rapid one, seems improbable. That I did seems a little fantas-tic even to me now that I realize how little I could see at that time. This concealment became habitual. I would refrain from exposing my eye con-dition as unconsciously as I would refrain from touching a fire; for it was often just as painful" (p. 76).

Parents, too, are caught in the dilemma of not wanting to identify their children's differences from the sure pain that is so likely to be felt. Parents of visually impaired children must rely on professional judgment to ascertain how seriously the visual loss affects the child's ability to see. Can he see print, large print, or will he need to read braille or use a ma-chine such as the Optacon that converts print to tactile letters? Answers to these questions have serious implications for where and how the child will be educated. Can a student who needs training in braille be accommo-dated in the local public school or will it be best to send the child to a residential school for the blind? Because vision services are needed by very few students, the parents of these children are more likely to face the decision of whether an alternative to the neighborhood school is a more appropriate educational environment.

Parenting Hearing-Impaired Children

As we stated earlier, society is not always kind to its members who are different. Schlesinger and Meadow (1972) report people are more un-comfortable around deaf persons than those with other disabilities and experience a "shock-withdrawal-paralysis" reaction on their first expo-sure.

Many of the parents of deaf children have experienced deafness in their family or are deaf themselves. They are aware before having a child of the possibilities that the child may be deaf. For these parents, there are different reactions, and life experiences that are major problems for hearing parents of deaf children are not problems for deaf parents of deaf children. For example, deaf children of deaf parents consistently have higher language scores than do deaf children of hearing parents, are better adjusted (Brill, 1960, 1969), and receive manual language training earlier, thus benefiting from an earlier onset of receptive and expressive language. Moreover, deaf parents demonstrate greater acceptance of deafness and experience greater ease in childrearing (Schlesinger & Meadow, 1972).

Knowledge that their child is deaf comes to many parents as they notice subtle signs, such as the child not responding to loud noises or to his or her own name or failing to show increasing use of babbling sounds or initial words. Once a suspicion is confirmed, parents experience the disappointment, hurt, guilt, shame, blame, and variable feelings so many other parents of handicapped children share.

With deafness, technology can help if the child's loss is of the kind that will respond to amplification. This modality makes a tremendous difference in that parents can actively help their child. Parents can get help in acquiring aids and, in so doing, they have the satisfaction of knowing they can do something that can make a difference.

With hearing aids come many other problems that are stressful to parents. Aids are expensive; they operate on batteries that must be checked daily and replaced frequently; earmolds do not always fit and they must be cleaned and also replaced; service for the aid is seldom around the corner. Another set of aid problems center around psychological adjustment to the aid, learning to accept it and use it. Just getting the child to tolerate wearing it is a major accomplishment. Many parents have described the frustrations of the early months and years of adjustment to this foreign object, the crying children, the aids thrown down toilets or hidden, earmolds chewed, and cords discarded. Parents have the major responsibility of helping their child cope with the aid and learn to use it. The realization that the important language, listening, and speaking skills are not immediately forthcoming can be disappointing and cause doubt, depression, and more frustration in both the child and the parents.

Accepting the aids as a part of the child is another very difficult experience, so poignantly stated by Norma in the penetrating videotape "Today is Not Forever" (Knox & Chrisman, 1979): "We put the [hearing aids] on [Tracy] and my first reaction was those ugly hearing aids on my pretty little girl. And I just couldn't stand it and I cried."

Grandparents and other extended family members have their own problems with their deaf family member. Relatives find the deafness hard to believe and can be adamant in their expectation of sudden miracles or in their continued belief in misinformation. For those one step removed from parenting, the importance of learning and using signs is less well understood. They have other grandchildren with whom they can communicate. One mother's description of this sadness in relation to her daughter says it well. "My sisters still won't learn to sign. . . . A hug just isn't enough" (Ferris, 1980, p. 68).

Siblings of deaf children, like those of all handicapped children, are also affected. For some the handicap is viewed as a burden, for others, a blessing. Parents express their concerns about female siblings mothering the deaf child, others describe the hearing sibling's loneliness when the deaf child leaves each Monday to return to the school for the deaf. If the sibling is also deaf, the bond between them can be unusually strong, as they indeed have a language to share—one that is not frequently understood by other neighborhood children.

Parents of deaf children, like those of blind children, must make a difficult decision about whether to educate their child in a residential school or a public school. Parents describe this as an agonizing decision and one that they may reverse later. Among the issues raised in such a decision are the following: Where is the better education, the better resources, and can the family tolerate weekly, monthly, or longer separations? If the child goes to a residential school, will he or she be a member of another world, the world of the deaf, for life? If the child stays at home, will mainstreaming work, can a special class be formed or will a resource room be available? The advantages and disadvantages of the child's social life in the deaf community and in the hearing community are another major consideration. One variable that continues to be conspicuous in terms of the child's success or failure is the classroom teacher—that individual's sensitivity to the child, his needs, and his capacities.

Parents of deaf children can look to a future that holds promise of college, employment, and family life. There are many examples of successful deaf persons. This knowledge can be the basis for dreams and long-term goals. Knowing about the success of other hearing-impaired persons and that a productive future is open to their child is indeed an important support in helping parents through the early years. One's view of what the future holds is a major difference for parents of mildly or moderately impaired children as opposed to parents of severely impaired children. For children who have additional or more severe impairments, the future may not be as optimistic, and longer years of dependency are likely.

Parenting Children with Physical Impairments

Parents become aware of a child's physical impairments during the early years, when rapid growth changes and the achievement of familiar motor milestones occur. As in other conditions, the earlier the impairment is noticed the more severe the damage is likely to be. Children with moderate physical impairment achieve motor milestones significantly later than normal children do, and the motor patterns are less efficient and frequently abnormal. Dodge (1976) examined the impact of a cerebral palsy child on the family and described the results of these multiple stresses as "stir crazy syndrome." Chronically ill children present a set of practical care problems, e.g., sleeping, washing, dressing, feeding, and toileting. The extra demands on parental time often result in physical exhaustion as well as psychological and interpersonal strain.

Parents of physically impaired children express their first concerns through attention to the child's physical needs. This usually means frequent hospitalizations, special shoes, braces, and other adaptive equipment. In addition, physical therapy during the early years is almost always recommended. Parents are encouraged to seek early educational programs for their children, as the possibility of developmental delays in other domains is greatly increased when physical impairments are known already to exist. Centers advocate the use of sensory-motor integration procedures in providing physical therapy (Ayres, 1972); others focus on the effects of impaired movement on perceptual development (Abercrombie, 1968; Rosenbloom, 1975), cognition (Campbell, 1974), or motor facilitation as a general aspect of learning (Bobath, 1971).

In some cases parents of physically impaired children are faced with decisions as to which program is best for their child, but more likely they are restricted in their choices by what is available. If choices are to be made, several factors will be taken into consideration: the recommendation of their physician, transportation, related services, program philosophy, and cost.

The heavy emphasis on therapy and early intervention for the child with moderate handicaps provides parents with hope that the hard work and sacrifice will culminate in positive results and that the future will be a happy and productive one for their child. This period of intensive effort provides parents the opportunity to learn more about their child's problems. In public and in parent groups they see other children and their parents with similar problems, some more severe, others perhaps less so, and learn from them things no professional could ever teach them. They begin to learn what to expect when their child is older—the emotional, social, and mobility problems, the academic problems that might be associated with physical impairment, and the continued attention to the child's physical needs. Through this experience they may come to see their child's abilities both to withstand the pain so often endured and to learn very difficult skills and tasks that for others are easily mastered and taken for granted.

A major concern for parents of moderately physically impaired children is the child's educational placement. Many children are quite able to participate in the academic program of their nonhandicapped peers. They may, however, need more time to complete assignments, their speech or writing may be difficult to interpret, they may not be as socially adept; but given an understanding teacher who knows when and how to make appropriate demands, many students can make a remarkable adjustment to the requirements of the regular classroom. Handicapped children nevertheless frequently change schools. Using their scale, *Family Inventory of Life Events and Changes,* McCubbin, Nevin, Larsen, Comeau, Patterson, Cauble, and Striker (1981) found that the two most frequent events experienced by families of cerebral palsy children were child related, namely, "child changing to a new school and child becoming seriously ill" (p. 36). It is interesting to note, however, that the school change was far less stressful to these families than the strain of increased expenses for such basic needs as food and clothing. Moreover, the increase in the cost of special education for their child was also a frequent source of strain.

The presence of a physical handicap is usually obvious to casual observers (less so in cases of deafness, emotional handicaps, mental retardation as well as other impairments). This has both positive and negative effects: observers might assume that other differences in the person are caused by or related to the physical impairment, and thus there may be less curiosity on their part, while on the other hand they make numerous assumptions about the person that are not true. Handicapped persons telling their own stories in Orlansky and Howard's (1981) *Voices: Interviews with Handicapped People* provide numerous examples of such effects.

Parenting Children with Mild Handicaps

Parents of children with mild handicaps (learning disorders, mild mental retardation, mild behavior disorders, etc.) are slow to recognize the problem and to seek the help that the child needs because these handicaps can be easily overlooked or ignored. The child's behavior may be accepted as normal, even if perhaps affected by slow development; such behavior will no doubt change as the child "catches up" in the next five years.

Little help is available from professionals during the early years. Infants and preschool-age children come to the attention of physicians and other health-related persons when impairments are more obvious. Milder handicaps are identified when children are observed over an extended period of time and under conditions that place demands upon them. This time period is needed to answer the question, "Is Johnny immature?" Entrance into organized learning environments means having to cope with the demands of working and playing in groups, responding to many new stimuli, organizing, retaining, retrieving, and producing information, adapting to a preferred learning style, motivating self and others, and regulating one's activity level. These factors interact with each other to increase the impact on the child. In some children this impact is manifested in performance on academic tasks, in others it is more apparent in regard to social relationships.

Parents may suspect that something is different about their child, but the subtle cues appear singly and can always be explained as "immaturity," "takes after his Daddy," "just ornery," "lazy," while the best course of action seems to be to "wait and see."

Teachers are usually the first persons to consistently observe the child over time and to see the many facets of child behavior that collectively suggest a learning problem. To determine whether suspicions are indeed signifiers, the teacher may have a conference with the parents and request their permission to have the child tested. This seldom presents a problem for parents because the school is an appropriate setting for both identifying and dealing with learning problems.

Parental reactions to the news that their child does have a learning disability are quite varied. For some it is relief, for others it is amazement, shock, disbelief, or anger. Osman (1979) reports that parents of children in her clinic go through emotional stages similar to those experienced after a severe loss or death of a family member or someone close—perhaps the loss of the "superchild." Parents invariably seek answers to questions, some of which are quite predictable: Why this child? What were the early signs we should have seen? Whose fault is it? Is it because I have failed as a mother or father? What can be done about it? How long will it last? What differences will it make in his or her education? While answers can be given based on the performances of thousands of children who have previously been identified, it does not necessarily follow that the same outcomes can be predicted for every child.

Wadsworth and Wadsworth (1971) examined parental involvement in educational programs with parents of mildly retarded children and found two interesting differences in responses to questionnaires. Parents whose children had higher IQs were significantly less likely to respond to the questionnaire, and middle-class parents were significantly less likely to respond to the questionnaire than the higher occupational-status parents. The experimenters concluded that the parents with children who had IQs in the borderline area were less reluctant to accept a mental retardation diagnosis, and middle-class parents as opposed to higher-class parents were less accepting of their retarded children. The authors suggested that the higher-status parents were more disposed to respond to the questionnaire and less threatened by the fact of having an intellectually limited child.

In the preceding sections we have discussed four impairments considered to be moderate and some of the particular stresses each has on the
family. In most cases, the presence of a child with a moderate impairment
creates the following concerns: the dilemma of being educated with the
nonhandicapped or the handicapped; the stress of heavy involvement in
physiotherapy; the stress of acknowledging the existence of the handicap
or simply covering it up. In each case, the family members' own contributions to the situation are so critical that they too must be carefully considered.

ECOLOGY OF IMPACT ON THE FAMILY

During the process of diagnosing a problem and planning intervention
strategies, it is important to understand the dynamics of the family, to
appraise how a family copes with the handicap, and to identify family
strengths that can be used to deal effectively with future events. The perspective implied is transactional, in that what happens to one family member affects other family members or persons directly related to the person
most centrally involved. Extending this perspective further, there is a mutual interdependence between persons, their behaviors, and their environments. Insights into individual family members' past experiences in relating to crises, coping with personal stress, accepting role responsibilities,
rearing children, using support networks, making decisions, resolving
conflicts, and setting and achieving goals are crucial for understanding the
ways in which individuals and the family unit cope with the problem now
confronting them. Sarason (1975) describes the reactions of copers and
noncopers. Copers organize the anxiety-provoking situation so that they
and others survive. A second level of copers completes the tasks assigned
to them by others even though they engage in considerable preoccupation. On the other hand, noncopers wallow in their self-preoccupation,
doing nothing for themselves or for others.

How the family operates as a unit and the ways in which family members relate to one another will have a major impact on the outcome of
intervention for the young handicapped child. Belsky (1981) proposes that
the family system be viewed not just in terms of parent–child relations but
also in regard to how the marital relationship and other relationships within the family affect the child. These relationships cannot be studied in
isolation but must be viewed as they influence and subsequently shape
the behavior of all family members. Gabel, McDowell, and Cerreto (1983)
extend the analysis of the second order effects (described by Belsky) to
grandparent–parent relations and other relationships within the context of
the extended family of young handicapped children. The way in which the
family system reacts to the disabling condition of a family member affects

every other member of the family. Osman (1979) has referred to a learning disability, for example, as "a family affair." Any impairment or disabling condition may or may not become a "handicap," depending on the family's interpretation of the child's state.

The importance of involving family members in intervention is well known. Bronfenbrenner (1974) concluded after reviewing intervention programs with and without parent participation that "the evidence indicates that the family is the most effective and economical system for fostering and sustaining the development of the child. The evidence indicates further that the involvement of the child's family as an active participant is critical to the success of any intervention program" (p. 55).

Research with developmentally delayed children (Christophersen & Sykes, 1979), behaviorally disorderd children (Strain, 1981; Christophersen, Barnard, Barnard, Gleeson, & Sykes, 1981), deaf children (Simmons-Martin, 1981) blind children, and physically impaired children supports Bronfenbrenner's contention. Nevertheless, after reviewing parent education programs during the 1970s, Clarke-Stewart (1981) described the contemporary uncertainties: "Parent child-rearing techniques are still embedded in an abiding and persistent socio-cultural context, and there is no evidence that they are easily shaped by expert opinion or educational literature. Although direct educational programs for parents have been successful in changing some of the more superficial kinds of parent behavior, such as caretaking, talking, and teaching, they have been less successful in modifying other more subtle and perhaps more critical aspects, such as responding, caring, and playing" (p. 57).

PERIODS OF FAMILY STRESS DUE TO THE IMPAIRMENT

In previous sections we have discussed the impact of various impairments on family members. Each type of handicap presents problems for the affected family member and related problems for the entire family. The importance of all relationships within the family system to the outcome of the handicapped child has also been discussed. Equally important is the impact of society's reaction to "difference" in everything that happens to the child and to the family. In this section we discuss impact-reduction strategies on two levels: strategies that focus directly on reducing the impact of the handicap (hearing aids, drugs, prosthetic devices, speech therapy, basic care, home instruction, etc.) and strategies that more directly reduce negative impact through changes in a variety of interacting factors (family interactions, economic relief, social policy, litigation, and legislation). Although realizing that these two levels are not entirely separable, we dichotomize for purposes of relating more specifically to the impact and the strategies.

Impact During the Screening and Referral Phase

When physicians, parents, grandparents, teachers, or other observers of children see behaviors that are different than expected they ask questions: Is something wrong with my child? Can Sally see? Shouldn't Lydia be sitting up by now? Have you asked the doctor why Sarah breathes with those noises? Why can't Bill learn to read? These questions are attempts to determine whether a problem exists. Generally, parents of mildly and moderately handicapped children have a longer and lonelier discovery period. Doubts, fears, questions, attempts to link current observations to pregnancy events, guilt feelings, and so forth can date from before the birth and continue for several years, even when parents are assured by authorities that their child is normal. Parents have seen, heard, or read too much to dismiss the possibility that the child may be handicapped in some way (Barsch, 1968). According to Barsch, "the data suggest that the parent is aware of a deviancy from one to four years before someone establishes a diagnostic label to characterize the parental concern" (p. 95). When there is a problem, knowledge comes slowly, bit by bit, until the parent acts to seek an answer. With many moderately handicapped children, parents are unaware, or do not have suspicions confirmed, until the child manifests a learning or adjustment problem in school. Parents sometimes dismiss these problems with such remarks as "He is just like his Uncle Harry" or "That's the way little girls are." These behaviors are easy to overlook if major milestones such as walking and toilet training are accomplished at the appropriate age.

Once problems are recognized by parents, steps must be taken to determine their validity. A variety of professionals in both public and private sectors are available to provide screening services. Answers to assessment questions that confirm the existence of the problem lead to its eventual identification. A process involving several successive steps is usually followed when parents or professionals act to answer these questions. Parental reaction during this phase can be characterized by the desire to move on to the diagnostic phase, which will help them identify the problem and perhaps the cause.

Impact During the Identification and Diagnosis Phase

After referral and screening and if a problem is confirmed, identification and diagnosis are likely to follow, according to a model that medical professionals have used to determine causes for purposes of prescribing treatment. For many impairments, this procedure results in immediate intervention that terminates symptoms or else identifies a very precise plan for intervention. For example, the symptoms of a seizure disorder may be virtually eliminated through identification of the type of seizure followed by chemotherapy designed to control the behavior. While the problem is not likely to be eliminated, it can be controlled, and the stress upon both the child and his family is greatly reduced.

The age of the child is an important factor in assessing the impact of initial diagnosis on the family. When parents of handicapped children rated the importance of categories of concern, there was an important relationship between the age of the child and the impact of initial diagnosis (Bray, Coleman, & Bracken, 1981). When the child's handicap was diagnosed before age two, 44 percent of the parents reported the initial diagnosis to be the most critical event or stress they had faced in their role as parents; when diagnosis occurred at age six, the importance of the initial diagnosis dropped to 26 percent and when it occurred over age six, initial diagnosis was viewed as primary by only 16 percent of the parents. This suggests that the lower the child's age at the time of diagnosis, the more likely the problem will require additional services; it points directly to the need for early intervention. Parents will want to pursue all channels in getting the early educational, medical, and psychological services their child requires.

With the moderately impaired, who in many cases are more difficult to accurately assess, educational and emotional problems are not easily identified nor are treatment avenues as obvious. Testing is not as reliable and treatments not as sure. Opinions regarding diagnosis and treatment sometimes differ widely from one professional to another. These factors cause families to seek a favorable diagnosis from many sources, which prolongs initiation of a treatment plan and thrusts the family into a state of stress. In many cases, several intervention strategies must be tried and results monitored before an appropriate plan for minimizing the impact of the problem can be determined.

Impact of Daily Parenting Responsibilities

Parents of children with learning disabilities, for example, experience stress daily as they face the disability while the child is doing homework. Because the task is painful, the child may delay it or become frustrated and angry. The parent may get upset, and place demands on the child that the child is unable to meet; the confrontation may result in a tearful shouting match that accomplishes nothing but a wider gap between parent and child.

When diet management is an important aspect of a child's medical regimen (for example, in diabetes, kidney disease, or Prader Willi syndrome) parents can find daily responsibilities extremely frustrating. They may feel guilty about withholding certain foods and so yield to the demands of a youngster, who may become defiant and mistrustful if a parent even tries to learn what foods the child has eaten during the parent's absence. The same kind of situation may exist when children are beginning to accept responsibility for their own medication.

Parents of moderately handicapped children may feel caught in a time bind: they have been told that each day in the life of a young child is very important, and that they should be involved each day in the child's educational program. The inability to take an active, daily role can cause guilt and may be a source of stress between staff members who encourage parental involvement and the parent who must respond to other family priorities. On the other hand, parents of the severely impaired child may have realized how much of a difference their involvement really makes, while the parents of the mildly handicapped child may think that present involvement, which staff members consider so crucial for the child, can be easily postponed to some future time. Parents who do become involved in daily activities such as classroom participation may view the experience positively, as a real contribution to the child's development, or negatively, as a drain on their energy and time. Parents' reactions are subject to so many variables that it is clearly impossible to generalize about their perceptions and experiences.

Parents who can realize the kind of facilitative role their child needs at any given point in time have a major advantage over those who cannot. For example, observations of just how the child can best learn new material, along with the use of prompting, modeling, ignoring, and positive reinforcement, can provide a critical plan that the child may adopt for self-direction long after the parents' support has ended.

STRATEGIES FOR HELPING PARENTS

The family that is sufficiently open about a child's problem to discuss it with the child and to help siblings and grandparents to respond in a positive and understanding manner can contribute much to the child's adjustment. The ability of parents to respond in a supportive manner is sometimes difficult; nevertheless, certain factors have clearly emerged as likely to produce positive results.

Family organization is critical. Many mildly handicapped children have difficulty making small decisions, handling emotional extremes, or coping with changes, chaos, and turmoil. It is not uncommon for disorganization to be more frequent in families of learning disabled children than in other families (Osman, 1979). If the family can define and implement a structure for its daily life together, then routine will follow; the children will know what to expect, have fewer decisions to make, and be less vulnerable to environmental changes as they gain better control over their environment. As organizing features become routine in the home as well as the school environment, the process of learning and coping is also made easier.

Clearly, an underlying theme in parent–child relations is consistency. Emotionally healthy children are reared in families that have very different styles of relating. A family's belief system about children and child-rearing techniques contributes significantly to parental teaching and managerial strategies. These belief systems, or values, vary significantly from family to family. They are formulated from the parents' experiences as members of previous family units, by their cultural and social and educational environments. The consistency with which parental reactions can be predicted by children is a major factor in child adjustment.

Parents of a moderately handicapped child can eliminate much confusion for their child (who does not always make decisions easily) by being consistent in their responses. This strategy is based on the premise that both parents are in agreement with what responses are made to a variety of circumstances. The child will learn what to expect if similar situations evoke similar responses. This consistent structure is particularly useful to the handicapped child for whom understanding parental cues may not be easy.

For parents it is a matter of knowing how and when to help, when to reward or withhold reward, and when to respond in other ways. There are no sure answers. Each child presents a different set of problems; the attitudes and experiences that the family members bring to the situation will also determine how the child responds. Nevertheless, the stories of parents (e.g., Featherstone, 1980; Knox, 1981; Murphy, 1981; Schiff, 1980; Seligman, 1979; Turnbull & Turnbull, 1978) consistently convey the sometimes unarticulated but deeply felt empathy that parents express toward other parents who have had the same or similar experiences. Helping parents to get in touch with other parents who share similar concerns is an important professional activity.

Some strategies for professionals to use in their work with parents have been clearly and simply stated by Gorham, Des Jardins, Page, Pettis, and Scheiber (1975). These strategies are summarized as follows:

1. Involve the parents as team members every step of the way.
2. Make a realistic management plan part of the assessment outcome.
3. Inform yourself about community resources.
4. Avoid professional jargon in your reports and communications.
5. Give copies of the reports to parents.
6. Be sure the parents understand that the diagnosis is subject to change.
7. Help the parents to think of life with this child in the same terms as life with their other children.

8. Be sure the parents understand their child's abilities and assets as well as disabilities.
9. Warn the parents about service insufficiencies.
10. Explain to the parents that while some professionals may dwell on negatives, parents should think about the positives. (pp. 183–184)

There are some instances of the use of incentives for the involvement of families in the care of their handicapped members. In the state of North Dakota, families who keep their severely handicapped family members at home rather than place them in institutions are provided monthly compensation. The family reports on how it disperses the funds. In the Extending Family Resources Project (EFR) at the Children's Clinic and Preschool in Seattle, Washington, 16 family support units, who worked as a team and consisted of parents, aunts, uncles or other relatives, friends, or neighbors, signed a unit performance contract to provide care and training for the person in need. For example, an uncle may agree to take the child to community parks for two hours a week and to work on developing motor skills as one portion of the performance contract. In return, the family unit was given up to $200.00 per month to spend to fulfill its contract. These funds were usually spent in three areas: training, equipment, and respite. Evaluation data on this project enabled the staff to support a number of conclusions that have implications for the design of other programs to support families under stress.

The EFR concept provides for individualized family programs which share a common framework, but account for circumstances which are variable among families, such as income, size, and relatives present or absent.

The EFR project demonstrated that family support systems can and should have a variety of participants.

The EFR project showed that parents, relatives, friends and volunteers can be trained to work with a handicapped child as an extended family group.

The EFR project demonstrated that appropriately trained extended family members can provide a range of support services to families of handicapped children.

The EFR project provided a model for reducing family stress related to a child's handicapping condition.

The EFR project was an effective demonstration of how a child's family-based program can be designed to complement the child's school or center-based program.

The EFR service model demonstrated that the goal of implementing a family support network can usually be completed in a time period of six to ten months.

The stipend money was important for removing barriers for families, but its significance was found in combination with other elements of the EFR project.

The role of the Family Clinicians was crucial to the families' successful completion of the program.*

Certainly careful monitoring of other incentive programs will provide more information on the effectiveness of such procedures for helping families in their caretaking roles.

In this chapter we have discussed the psychosocial aspects of parenting a moderately handicapped child, the impact of handicaps on the child and family, and strategies for consideration while working with families of handicapped children. We have focused on the difficulties unique to families of the moderately handicapped, where expectations are more uncertain than certain. We have provided examples of why each handicap must be considered separately in order to understand the community's reaction to it. Finally, we have described selective strategies that are effective with all parents. These guidelines have validity for all professional relations with parents regardless of whether the child is handicapped.

REFERENCES

Abercrombie, M. L. Some notes on spatial disability: Movement, intelligence quotient and attentiveness. *Developmental Medicine and Child Neurology,* 1968, *10,* 206–213.

Akerley, M. S. False gods and angry prophets. In A. P. Turnbull & H. Turnbull (Eds.), *Parents speak out.* Columbus, Ohio: Charles Merrill, 1978.

Ayres, A. J. *Sensory integration and learning disorders.* Los Angeles: Western Psychiatric Services, 1972.

Barker, R. G. The social psychology of physical disability. *Journal of Social Issues,* 1948, *IV*(4), 28–38.

Barsch, R. H. *The parent of the handicapped child: The study of childrearing practices.* Springfield, Ill.: Charles C Thomas, 1968.

Belsky, J. Early human experience: A family perspective. *Developmental Psychology,* 1981, *17*(1), 3–23.

Bobath, B. Motor development, its effect on general development, and application to the treatment of cerebral palsy. *Physiotherapy,* 1981, *53,* 26–33.

Bray, N. M., Coleman, J. M., & Bracken, M. B. Critical events in parenting handicapped children. *Journal of the Division for Early Childhood,* 1981, *3,* 26–33.

Brill, R. G. A study in adjustment of three groups of deaf children. *Exceptional Children,* 1960, *26,* 464–466.

Brill, R. G. The superior IQs of deaf children of deaf parents. *The California Palms,* 1969, *15,* 1–4.

---

*Reprinted with permission from Moore, J. A., Hamerlynck, L. A., Barsh, E. T., Spieker, S., & Jones, R. *Extending family resources.* Seattle, Washington: Children's Clinic and Preschool Spastic Aid Council, Inc., 1982, pp. 40–43.

Brim, O. Macro-structural influences on child development and the need for childhood social indicators. *American Journal of Orthopsychiatry,* 1975, *45,* 516–524.

Bronfenbrenner, U. Development research, public policy and the ecology of childhood. *Child Development,* 1974, *45,* 1–5.

Bronfenbrenner, V. The experimental ecology of education. *Educational Research,* 1976, *5,* 5–15.

Campbell, S. K. Facilitation of cognitive and motor development in infants with central nervous system dysfunction. *Physical Therapy,* 1974, *54,* 346–353.

Christophersen, E. R., Barnard, S. R., Barnard, J. D., Gleeson, S., & Sykes, B. W. Home-based treatment of behavior-disordered and delayed children. In M. Begab, H. C. Haywood, & H. L. Garber (Eds.) *Psychosocial influences in retarded performance.* Vol. 2. *Strategies for improving competence.* Baltimore: University Park Press, 1981.

Christophersen, E. K., & Sykes, B. W. An intensive home-based family training systems program for developmentally delayed children. In L. A. Hamerlynck (Ed.), *Behavioral systems for the developmentally disabled* (Vol. 2). New York: Brunner/Mazel, 1979.

Clarke-Stewart, K. A. Parent education in the 1970s. *Educational Evaluation and Policy Analysis,* 1981, *3*(6), 47–58.

Cowen, E. L., & Bobrove, P. H. Marginality of disability and adjustment. *Perceptual and Motor Skills,* 1966, *23,* 869–870.

Criddle, R. *Love is not blind.* New York: Norton, 1953.

Darling, R. B. *Families against society.* Beverly Hills, Calif.: Sage Publications, 1979.

Dodge, P. Neurological disorders of school aged children. *Journal of School Health,* 1976, *46,* 338–343.

Edgerton, R. B. Mental retardation in non-Western societies: Towards a cross-cultural perspective on incompetence. In H. C. Haywood (Ed.), *Sociocultural aspects of mental retardation.* New York: Appleton-Century-Crofts, 1970.

Edgerton, R. B. Another look at culture and mental retardation. In M. J. Begab, H. C. Haywood, & H. L. Garber (Eds.) *Psychosocial influences in retarded performance* (Vol. 1). Baltimore: University Park Press, 1981.

Featherstone, H. *A difference in the family.* New York: Basic Books, 1980.

Ferris, C. *A hug just isn't enough.* Washington, D.C.: Gallaudet College Press, 1980.

Finkelstein, V. *Attitudes and disabled people: Issues for discussion* (Monograph No. 5). New York: World Rehabilitation Fund, Inc., 1980.

Gabel, H., McDowell, J., & Cerreto, M. C. Family adaptation to the handicapped infant. In S. G. Garwood & R. R. Fewell (Eds.), *Educating handicapped infants: Issues in development and intervention.* Rockville, Md.: Aspen, 1983.

Gliedman, J., & Roth, W. *The unexpected minority: Handicapped children in America.* New York: Harcourt Brace Jovanovich, 1980.

Goffman, E. *Stigma: Notes on the management of spoiled identity.* New York: Jasson Aranson, 1963.

Gordon, I. J. Significant sociocultural factors in effective parenting. In M. D. Fantini & R. Cardenas (Eds.), *Parenting in a multicultural society.* New York: Longman, 1980.

Gorham, K. A., DesJardins, C., Page, R., Pettis, E., & Scheiber, B. Effects on parents. In N. Hobbs (Ed.), *Issues in the classification of children* (Vol 2). San Francisco: Jossey-Bass, 1975.

Grossman, F. K. *Brothers and sisters of retarded children: An exploratory study.* Syracuse: Syracuse University Press, 1972.

Haffter, C. The changeling: History and psychodynamics of attitudes to handicapped children in European folklore. *Journal of the History of the Behavioral Sciences,* 1968, *4*(1), 55–61.

Keniston, K. Preface. In Gliedman, J. and Roth, W. *The unexpected minority: Handicapped children in America.* New York: Harcourt Brace Jovanovich, 1980.

Knox, L. *Parents are people too.* Englewood Cliffs, N.J.: Prentice-Hall, 1981.

Knox, L., & Chrisman, C. *Today is not forever.* Nashville, Ten.: Intersect, 1979. (Videotape)

Lairy, G. C., & Harrison-Covello, A. The blind child and his parents: Congenital visual defect and the repercussion of family attitudes on the early development of the child. *AFB (American Foundation for the Blind) Research Bulletin,* 1973, No. 25.

Levine, R. A. A cross cultural perspective on parenting. In M. D. Fantini & R. Cardenas (Eds.), *Parenting in a multicultural society.* New York: Longman, 1980.

MacGregor, F. C., Abel, T. M., Bryt, A., Lauer, E., & Weissman, M. S. *Facial deformities and plastic surgery.* Springfield, Ill.: Charles C Thomas, 1953.

Maisel, E. Meet a body. Manuscript (1953) cited in Wright, B. A. *Physical disability: A psychological approach.* New York: Harper & Row, 1960.

McCubbin, H. I., Nevin, R. S., Larsen, A., Comeau, J., Patterson, J., Cauble, A. E., & Striker, K. *Families coping with cerebral palsy.* Family Social Science, University of Minnesota at St. Paul, 1981.

Moore, J. A., Hamerlynck, L. A., Barsh, E. T., Spieker, S., & Jones, R. *Extending family resources.* Seattle, Washington: Children's Clinic and Preschool Spastic Aid Council, Inc, 1982.

Murphy, A. T. *Special children, special parents.* Englewood Cliffs, N.J.: Prentice-Hall, 1981.

Myerson, L. Somatopsychology of physical disability. In W. Cruikshank (Ed.), *Psychology of exceptional children and youth.* Englewood Cliffs, N.J.: Prentice-Hall, 1963.

Orlansky, M. D., & Howard, W. L. *Voices: Interviews with handicapped people.* Columbus, Ohio: Charles Merrill, 1981.

Osman, B. B. *Learning disabilities: A family affair.* New York: Warner Books, 1979.

Rosenbloom, L. The consequences of impaired movement—a hypothesis and review. In K. S. Holt (Ed.), *Movement and child development.* Philadelphia: Lippincott, 1975.

Roskies, E. *Abnormality and normality: The mothering of thalidomide children.* Ithaca, N.Y.: Cornell University Press, 1972.

Ryan, W. *Blaming the victim.* New York: Vintage, 1971.

Sagarin, E. *Odd man in.* Chicago: Quadruple Books, 1969.

Sauna, V. D. *A cross cultural study of cerebral palsy.* New York: Yeshiva University, 1966.

Sarason, I. Anxiety and self-preoccupation. In I. Sarason & C. Spielberger (Eds.), *Stress and anxiety.* New York: Wiley, 1975.

Sarason, S. B., & Doris, J. *Educational handicap, public policy, and social history: A broadened perspective on mental retardation.* New York: Free Press, 1979.

Schiff, H. S. *The bereaved parent.* New York: Penguin, 1980.

Schlesinger, H. S., & Meadow, K. P. *Sound and sign: Childhood deafness and mental health.* Berkeley: University of California Press, 1972.

Seligman, M. *Strategies for helping parents of exceptional children.* New York: Free Press, 1979.

Simmons-Martin, A. Efficacy report: Early education project. *Journal of the Division of Early Childhood,* 1981, *4,* 5–10.

Stonequist, E. V. *The marginal man: A study in personality and culture conflict.* New York: Scribner's, 1937.

Strain, P. S. Conceptual and methodological issues in efficacy research with behaviorally disordered children. *Journal of the Division of Early Childhood,* 1981, *4,* 111–124.

Turnbull, A. P., & Turnbull, R. R. *Parents speak out: Views from the other side of the two-way mirror.* Columbus, Ohio: Charles Merrill, 1978.

Wadsworth, H. G., & Wadsworth, J. B. A problem of involvement with parents of mildly retarded children. *The Family Coordinator,* 1971, *20,* 141–147.

Wright, B. A. *Physical disability: A psychological approach.* New York: Harper & Row, 1960.

8

Working with Families of Severely Handicapped Persons

STEVE LYON
ANNIE PREIS

BIOGRAPHICAL SKETCH

Steve Lyon, Ph.D., is Assistant Professor and Coordinator of the Severely Handicapped Program, Special Education Department, University of Pittsburgh. Dr. Lyon has published a variety of articles, book chapters, and curriculum and research monographs related to the education and treatment of persons with severe handicaps. A particular interest of his is the development and implementation of a transdisciplinary team organization whereby professionals and parents can work effectively together.

Annie Preis, Ph.D., is Assistant Professor of Education at Bethany College, Bethany, West Virginia. Prior to completing her education at the University of Pittsburgh, she worked with children and youth in a learning disabilities clinic, as a teacher of severely disturbed and retarded children at Western Psychiatric Institute and Clinic, and as an educational supervisor in a number of schools serving children with disabilities.

Support for this chapter was provided in part by contract #300-82-0368 (Early Childhood Research Institute) from the U.S. Department of Education to the University of Pittsburgh. However, the opinions expressed herein do not necessarily reflect the position or policy of the U.S. Department of Education and no official endorsement by the Department should be inferred.

ISBN 0-8089-1561-4
Copyright © 1983 by Grune & Stratton

O NE OF THE most difficult tasks our society has undertaken in recent years has been to assume a large responsibility for the provision
of comprehensive social services to persons with severe handicaps. Because of what Abeson and Zettell (1979) termed a "quiet revolution,"
educational, residential, health, and a wide variety of other services for
severely handicapped persons and their families have been greatly increased. As a result of pervasive legislation, litigation, and subsequent
"community reintegration" (Blatt, Bogdan, Biklen, & Taylor, 1977), professionals representing a wide array of human service disciplines are now
frequently called upon to interact and intervene with severely handicapped persons and their families. Not only has the influx of this population into mainstream American society created a crisis for professionals
responsible for direct treatment, it has also created a compelling need for
the development of effective ways of understanding and working with
families of severely handicapped persons.

Formerly, the large majority of severely handicapped persons was
incarcerated within large residential institutions where conditions were
often inhumane and services extremely limited (Blatt & Kaplan, 1974).
Traditionally, the largest portion of persons in these large residential institutions were those with the most limited mental, physical, and social abilities—these individuals are referred to in this chapter as severely handicapped (Hewitt & Forness, 1977). Severely handicapped persons have
been classified and labeled in various ways. They generally include persons manifesting severe mental retardation, physical and sensory handicaps, and chronic social and behavioral disorders. Typically, severely
handicapped persons have been regarded as the least capable and most
dependent members of our society, who require the most effort to habili-
tate (Sontag, Smith & Sailor, 1977).

In the past, the predominant approach to habilitation, education, and
treatment of severely handicapped persons was custodial maintenance.
That is, since the prognosis for educational and social learning and independence in these persons was considered so poor, many pediatricians
routinely recommended institutionalization to parents of severely handicapped children at birth (Caldwell & Guze, 1960). Caring parents and
families of these children then faced a difficult dilemma: concede to institutional placement and in all likelihood relinquish the chance for a reasonably normal life for their child, or keep the child at home in the community where few (if any) services to the child or family would be available.
Some professionals have been critical of medical personnel for their role
in creating this dilemma; certainly it was natural for parents to have
looked to physicians for advice, especially when no other help was available. This issue was undoubtedly extremely traumatizing to many parents
and families of severely handicapped children. Indeed, the history of ser-

vices to severely handicapped persons, their parents, and families has been a dark one, typified by only limited assistance, support, and understanding.

In recent years the course of this history has changed with the emerging trends in service delivery. As parents, professionals, and advocacy-oriented organizations join together to affirm the entitlement of basic rights and services for severely handicapped persons, movements regarding institutional reform, deinstitutionalization, right to treatment, nondiscrimination, and mandated educational services have gotten underway (Gilhool & Stuttman, 1978). Importantly, parents and their organizations have played critical roles in leading the way to improved services for themselves and their severely handicapped children (Katz, 1961).

As services began to evolve and expand in the mid-1960s, initial efforts were also made to understand and collaborate with the parents and families of these children. Although methods and approaches to working with families have varied widely over the years (Lillie, 1976), early services were focused primarily on providing parent counseling or parent training. Parents were commonly viewed by professionals as in need of counseling to help them to "accept" their severely handicapped child (Ballard, 1978) or in need of training to better enable them to "manage" their severely handicapped child at home (O'Dell, 1974). Research on families with severely handicapped children was also somewhat narrowly focused. Studies attempted to clarify the psychological stress and adjustment of parents and to assess the allegedly negative impact of a severely handicapped child on the family unit (Jacobson & Humphrey, 1979). While these early trends toward understanding and working with families were certainly useful in many respects, they also, we believe, contributed to a rather circumscribed and even condescending attitude on the part of many professionals toward parents and families. In many cases professionals have made assumptions about the needs of parents and families of severely handicapped children without obtaining solid empirical evidence or even bothering to confirm or refute these assumptions by listening to parents themselves (Roos, 1977).

During the past 10–15 years services and attitudes toward severely handicapped persons and their families have changed dramatically. Institutions have been reformed and depopulated; parent advocacy groups have become well organized and effective; as noted by Strickland in Chapter 2, important legislation has been implemented (Section 504 of the Rehabilitation Act, and the Education of All Handicapped Children Act of 1975); community-based services have been established in many parts of the nation; and many valuable technological advancements in the diagnosis and treatment of severely handicapped persons have been accomplished. These advances have been accompanied by an increased interest in a broader understanding and a more cooperative approach to working with parents and families.

Currently, the services for severely handicapped persons is in a period of adjustment. Sweeping social changes have occurred. Interpretations of and direct administrative regulations for services are finally being implemented and monitored. Although many severely handicapped persons remain within institutions, the trends toward deinstitutionalization and the establishment of services within the community are continuing (Larsen, 1977). Because of these trends, a wide variety of social service agencies (e.g., those in school systems, health clinics, rehabilitation and vocational training centers) are extending their services to include severely handicapped persons who now reside in the community, either in their natural homes or in other community living arrangements. Many new community-based programs are being developed to attempt to meet the needs of severely handicapped persons. This has resulted in a great deal of pressure upon agencies and professionals who, in many cases, have very little training or experience in working with this population. Additionally, community placement of severely handicapped persons has also forced professionals of these agencies to respond to the wishes and needs of parents and families (Kroth, 1978).

Today, most professionals involved in providing services to severely handicapped persons concur that working effectively with parents and families is a vital aspect to the overall program. There are several reasons why it is critical for professionals to attempt to collaborate with the families of severely handicapped persons. The most obvious is that if agencies are to be effective in maximal habilitation of handicapped persons and in fostering their independence, then the families and home lives cannot be ignored. Educational, vocational, or health-related services must be delivered in a manner consistent and congruent with the ongoing structure and ecology of the family. Otherwise services will not be effective in a meaningful and lasting way. A second reason why professionals must work effectively with families is that many of them have important needs that extend beyond the immediate needs of their severely handicapped child (Dornberg, 1978). That is, providing direct treatment to severely handicapped persons without concurrently addressing the needs of the family may have negative effects on the family itself. Professionals must remember that the goals of treatment or intervention should not be exclusive of the goals and needs of the family to which the severely handicapped person belongs. Finally, individual members of these families (parents and siblings) have specific needs, apart from those addressed by the program established for the severely handicapped sibling. It is essential that an approach to understanding and working with these families maintain a balanced perspective so that the individual needs of all family members are accommodated.

As social service agencies and professionals are beginning to realize the importance of meeting the needs of families of severely handicapped persons, more productive networks of parent–professional alliances are being created. Although much progress in this area has been achieved in recent years, parents and professionals alike realize that much more remains to be accomplished. Many more quality community-based services for severely handicapped persons are needed (Kenowitz, Gallagher, & Edgar, 1977). Creative efforts must be directed toward the development and establishment of services that result in meaningful family involvement and participation in service programs (Mattson, 1977). Attempts must also be made to develop coordinated and longitudinal services so that the lifelong needs of severely handicapped persons can be met (Brown, Nietupski, & Hamre-Nietupski, 1976) and so that overburdened families can receive relief from their chronic circumstances. Finally, professionals in a wide variety of fields must become knowledgeable and skillful in working with severely handicapped persons and in understanding and working with their families (Shell, 1981).

This chapter aims to provide information that will help professionals better understand the problems and needs of severely handicapped people and to prepare professionals to communicate and work cooperatively with families of these individuals. Three major areas are emphasized here: the nature and implications of severe handicaps, a discusson of the unique needs of families of severely handicapped persons, and suggestions for working with these families. If severely handicapped persons are to assume their rightful place in society, then professionals will need to take up the challenge of relating not only to the pervasive and complex problems of severely handicapped persons but also to those of their families.

CHARACTERISTIC PROBLEMS IN SEVERE HANDICAPS

In order for professionals to be able to relate with ease and effectively serve severely handicapped persons and their families, a general understanding of the nature and implications of severe handicaps is important. There are several general facts about severely handicapped persons that must be understood.

First, the phrase *severely handicapped,* as used here, refers to a heterogeneous population of persons; their characteristics, needs, and abilities vary greatly. Second, a variety of different classifications and labeling schemes have attempted to describe these persons and their disabilities. Third, severely handicapped persons constitute an extremely low-incidence (by estimation, only 1.5 percent) population (Brown, Nietupski, & Hamre-Nietupski, 1976). Fourth, it is probably at least as important to understand the nature of services required by severely handicapped persons as it is to understand the nature and manifestations of their handicaps. The remainder of this section therefore addresses the classification and definition of severe handicaps, the frequent and characteristic problems and difficulties of severely handicapped persons, the resulting service needs, and a description of the existing service delivery system.

Historically, a wide variety of different classification and definition schemes have been used to describe severely handicapped persons. Generally, our society's agencies and institutions and the services they provide have often been organized around the placement of handicapped persons in certain homogeneous disability categories. Once a handicapped person is diagnosed as belonging to a certain specific group of persons with similar handicapping characteristics, then eligibility is established and services can then be provided (Sailor & Guess, 1982).

Severely handicapped persons have also been viewed in this manner, and several classification frameworks have been used. Perhaps the predominant approach to classification has been intelligence testing, which yields scores related to levels of mental retardation. Through the years the American Association on Mental Deficiency (AAMD) has offered varying descriptive and diagnostic systems for the identification and categorization of mentally retarded persons. Currently, the AAMD recognizes four district groups based upon IQ scores: mildly retarded 70–53); moderately retarded (52–37); severely retarded (30–20) and profoundly retarded (19 and below). This classification scheme requires the "mental retardation" to have been manifested during the individual's developmental years and that "functional retardation" also be present (Grossman, 1977). Although it is probable that a large proportion of severely handicapped children may meet the criteria of severe or profound retardation, clearly this classification scheme is, in and of itself, insufficient to fully understand the severely handicapped population.

A second method of diagnosis and classification used with severely handicapped persons has been a medical–clinical diagnostic approach. Because many severely handicapped persons suffer from congenital anomalies often due to prenatal or perinatal trauma, there is also a relatively high incidence of clearly visible clinical symptoms of central nervous system involvement, resulting in such disorders as cerebral palsy, epilepsy, spina bifida, hydro- or microcephaly, consequences of rubella, and so forth (Black & Nagel, 1975). The medical–clinical approach to description and definition utilizes a disease model: the person is described in terms of the symptoms of a disease or disorder (e.g., severe spastic quadriplegia). Again, while it is true that accurate medical diagnosis and treatment is important for reduction or elimination of the pathologic condition, viewing severely handicapped people solely as medical phenomena may not lead to the most effective habilitation. Classifying a child as "severely retarded with spastic quadriplegia" may not be a great help in the process of teaching the child to feed, dress, play, or even live semi-independently in the community.

Thus the traditional homogeneous classification systems are beginning to give way to a more heterogeneous approach to understanding the nature and implications of severe handicaps. Because the old systems have generally been highly stigmatizing and have nurtured lowered expectations, and in many cases have not been accurate predicators of childrens' abilities and learning potential, more emphasis is now being placed upon gaining an understanding of the functional abilities of severely handicapped people and an understanding of the types of services and treatment that are needed for their maximal habilitation. Sontag, Smith, and Sailor (1979) call for a new approach to understanding and working with severely handicapped persons, one that rejects the idea that people can be neatly classified in homogeneous groups based upon a specific type or combination of disabilities. Sontag, Burke, and York (1973) add that the exact nature of the disability or the degree of mental retardation is less important than understanding the type of services needed to develop functional skills that lead to independence. An approach stressing assessment of functional abilities and the identification of services to promote maximal functional skill development has recently been established as a meaningful way of understanding and working with severely handicapped persons (Guess & Mulligan, 1982; Sailor & Guess, 1982). Even though there is widespread support for such an approach, many state and local service agencies are only beginning to adapt their regulations accordingly. Only a few states currently utilize the definition *severely handicapped,* while many others continue to use such categories as trainable, or profoundly retarded, or multiply handicapped, or deaf-blind (Justin & Brown, 1977).

Although the population of persons with severe handicaps is heterogeneous and is difficult to divide into classifications, there are a number of characteristic problems and difficulties persons in this population experience, and their parents and families in turn also experience. These difficulties are discussed here in terms of characteristics often observed in persons with severe handicaps and in terms of the specific types of learning and living problems often experienced as a result of the handicaps.

As alluded to earlier, the prevalance of intellectual deficits is one general characteristic of the population of severely handicapped persons. Implications of these deficits are that many severely handicapped persons are substantially delayed cognitively, do not acquire even the most rudimentary conceptual abilities, and are extremely limited in the acquisition and use of language (Baumiester & Brookes, 1981). Often severely handicapped children do not readily acquire and perform many of the same skills and abilities as nonhandicapped children. The presence of such limited mental abilities in these persons requires highly specialized and intensive educational programing in order to achieve even the most modest gains.

Another problem common among severely handicapped persons is the presence of physical anomalies. Chief among these is cerebral palsy, a nonprogressive disorder resulting from damage to the central nervous system and manifesting itself by partial or total paralysis of various parts of the body (Bobath & Bobath, 1975). Cerebral palsy and other related disorders may severely restrict physical development as well as the learning or ability to perform very basic movements such as walking, use of the hands, and speaking or eating. Although effective forms of intervention now exist to prevent the long-term deleterious effects of these central nervous system disorders, the presence of such physical problems is extremely restrictive to these persons and also places a great burden on the family, which, in many instances, must provide extensive amounts of assistance and care.

A third general characteristic problem among severely handicapped persons is sensory impairment. Many severely handicapped persons (labeled typically as multiply handicapped or deaf-blind) suffer from various degrees of visual and/or auditory impairment (Lehr, 1982). It is also common for sensory impairments to be accompanied by various degrees of retardation and medical or physical problems. There is little doubt that the presence of multiple severe handicaps is devastating to the health and well-being of those affected and their families, if only in terms of the level of effort required to overcome the loss of these important vehicles for the quality of life. Yet, even with these individuals, experience has proven that with proper services and with support and assistance to their parents and families, many positive benefits can accrue. Severely and multiply handicapped children are at present attending public schools in increasing numbers, living at home with their natural families, and learning many important skills critical to greater independence.

Severely handicapped persons also often experience extreme difficulty in developing and demonstrating typical and appropriate social behaviors. Social problems may be associated with intellectual deficits (Guess & Horner, 1976) or may be a function of such chronic and severe emotional disorders as childhood autism (see Rutter, 1978). Many of these children possess an extremely limited social repertoire and may also demonstrate bizarre behaviors such as echolalic speech, self-stimulation, and even self-destruction. These types of aberrant social behaviors are extremely difficult to treat clinically and often require extensive effort and commitment on the part of parents and family members to remedy or even tolerate (Browning, 1980; and Koegel, Egel, & Dunlap, 1980).

The implications of these characteristic problems and difficulties pose great challenges for professionals and parents: severely handicapped children are often extremely difficult to care for (Tizard & Grad, 1961) and to teach (Liberty, Haring, & Martin, 1981), and seldom generalize skills that are learned (Stokes & Baer, 1977). Additionally, many of these children may never attain total independence and will require extensive assistance all of their lives.

NEEDS OF PERSONS WITH SEVERE HANDICAPS

Not surprisingly, the needs of severely handicapped children and adults are as heterogeneous as the problems they must overcome. As these needs vary, so do the needs of the families of these persons. Some of these requirements stem directly from the problems discussed earlier: medical problems may require treatment from pediatricians or neurologists; sensory handicaps will require treatment from ophthamologists and audiologists; physical problems may require extensive therapeutic intervention from orthopedists, physical therapists, and occupational therapists; cognitive and language deficits will require the expertise of specially trained speech and language therapists and special education teachers; and as these children grow older, vocational trainers, counselors, and engineers will be needed to attempt to aid in the preparation for meaningful vocational experiences. The pervasiveness and relentlessness of the needs of severely handicapped persons seem staggering. However, if one considers that the goals for these individuals are maximal development, health, happiness, and inclusion within the mainstream of our society, it becomes clear that they do not differ substantially from those for nonhandicapped people. It is the realization of these universal human needs that some may find difficult. Our experience has been that just as parents share in the desire for the attainment of these goals for their children, they also often share in the agony of attempting to secure the needed services.

Beyond the more obvious types of services just described, there are some overriding concerns that must also be addressed that transcend day-to-day matters and relate more to the longitudinal needs of severely handicapped individuals. To begin with, severely handicapped persons and their families often need adequate and sometimes need highly specialized health care over a long period of time. As noted by Rubin and Quinn-Curran in Chapter 3 and by Gordon (1977), parents speak of the difficulty they experience in securing adequate health care for their severely handicapped child. Indeed, depending upon the particular physical problems of their child they may need the services of several different specialists. Although professionals have been rather judgmental in terming parents' efforts as symptomatic of denial (see, e.g., "Search for the cure," Rosen,

1955), often parents do need to contact several different agencies and professionals before the proper services can be identified and secured for their child. Additionally, since many severely handicapped persons experience rather brittle medical existences (e.g., congenital heart defects, uncontrolled seizure disorders, acute hydrocephalus), emergency medical treatment may be needed to respond to a variety of life-threatening crises. Now that increasing numbers of severely handicapped persons are residing in the community (rather than in institutions) a wide spectrum of routine maintenance and emergency health care services must be accessible to them.

For many severely handicapped persons, specialized residential services are also needed. As noted earlier, many more severely handicapped children than formerly now reside with their families. These families often need various types of assistance (e.g., in-home professional consultation, respite care services) in order to adequately manage these children so that families' resources and energies are not depleted and so that these families can maintain most of their ongoing normal functions. For other persons with severe handicaps, residential placement in alternate community living arrangements (CLAs) may be more appropriate and even necessary. That is, some parents and families may be unable to provide the needed specialized care at home, some older parents may themselves be unable physically to handle their severely handicapped adolescent or adult, while still others may prefer that their child be placed in a CLA for other reasons. Decisions regarding selection of and placement in an alternative residential arrangement can be extremely difficult and are affected by many different factors unique to individual families. Severely handicapped persons and their families need to know of a variety of options for community living, and they need professionals and agencies who will work with them toward the most appropriate placement (O'Conner, 1976).

Central to the successful maintenance of severely handicapped people in the community is the need for appropriate educational services. Now that appropriate public education has been mandated by federal legislation, most public school districts now serve severely handicapped students. Even so, parents have had to struggle long and hard for the inclusion of their severely handicapped child in such programs (Turnbull & Turnbull, 1978). Even though P.L. 94-142 outlines guidelines for these programs, many parents find themselves assuming adversarial positions toward school personnel in order to exercise their legal right to due process of law to bring about appropriate services for their children. (See Chapter 2.) In many respects the problems public school districts face in serving severely handicapped students resemble those faced by other social agencies: lack of adequate facilities, poorly trained and inexperienced staff, and insufficient funds to pay for services (Semmel & Morrissey, 1981).

Additionally, educating severely handicapped students is a relatively new challenge to the field of education, and although great strides have been made (Sontag, Certo, & Button, 1979), much remains to be learned about how best to teach these children (Burton & Hirshoren, 1979). In a time when available resources from the public and private sectors continue to decrease, it is becoming increasingly difficult to continue to develop and implement new and effective methods and programs for educating severely handicapped persons (Sontag et al., 1979). Under these conditions parents and professionals will need to work closely together if strides in the education and treatment of severely handicapped persons are to be made.

Encompassing each of these types of basic service delivery need of severely handicapped persons and their families is the overall need for continuity, coordination, and consistency of services. As noted from the preceeding discussion, the needs of severely handicapped persons differ in some respect from mildly handicapped persons (see Chapter 7 by Fewell and Gelb)—severely handicapped people's needs are pervasive and may extend across all major aspects of their lives and across all age periods of their lives. At any point in time a severely handicapped person may be receiving services from four to six different agencies and may be in contact with 15–20 different professionals. With each of these different agencies and each of these highly specialized professionals assuming its own role, the attainment of continuity, coordination, and consistency of services can become a problem of considerable magnitude. It is the parents and the family, then, who are left with the primary responsibility of creating order out of what may seem to be a chaotic situation (see Chapter 3). Indeed, lack of coordination of services for children is one of the most frequently heard complaints of parents. For this reason professionals who serve these children and families must be knowledgeable about the different agencies and services available in their local community. If professionals are knowledgeable about these services and willing to work cooperatively with parents and families, then the ultimate goals of habilitation for severely handicapped children can be better realized: maximization of independence, the improvement of ones quality of life, and the preparation for adulthood. From the earliest point at which a severely handicapped child is identified and placed in an early intervention program, to the point at which that child reaches adulthood and is placed in a vocational program, service agencies need to converge around common and reasonable goals for the child and consistent and effective ways of working with the child's family.

Advocacy can be a critical need of the severely handicapped child's family. For the most part, persons with severe handicaps are either unable or ineffective in advocating for themselves. As a result, parents, professionals, and agencies must provide this important function if the rights, opportunities, and privileges of severely handicapped persons are to be protected. Agencies and professionals can play an important role in this area either by assuming advocacy functions or by assisting or supporting parents, who bear the brunt of the burden.

A further overriding concern is the need for services and support to the parents and families. Many parents as well as professionals have described the numerous needs of parents and families of severely handicapped children as falling into three major categories: psychological and emotional support and understanding; information, education, and training; and effective services for their children (Dean, 1975; Turnbull & Turnbull, 1978). Professionals must be mindful that parents and families are, ultimately, the most important advocates, caretakers, and teachers of their severely handicapped children. If the families of these children are not adequately supported, or are disrupted, then these very important functions may be disrupted. For professionals to adequately support and work with parents and families, they must have an understanding of the impact and implications of a severely handicapped child in the family. This understanding will enable professionals better to address the unique needs that these families face.

IMPACTS ON FAMILIES

Attempts to assess the impact of a tragic or traumatic event or circumstance on a family and to determine appropriate courses of action are extremely difficult. The same has been true of attempts to understand the impact of severely handicapped children on their families. Because children and families vary so widely on their specific characteristics and because any number of different psychological, social, and practical day-to-day factors affect each family differently, attempts at a characteristic profile of families of severely handicapped children are impossible. Just as different families react and adjust uniquely to different crises, families react idiosycratically to their severely handicapped child. The research in this area supports this contention—namely, that it is extremely difficult and even erroneous to assume that all families of severely handicapped children are similarly affected, possess similar characteristics, or are in need of similar types of assistance. Just as severely handicapped persons vary widely in their characteristics and needs, so too do families.

With the above considerations in mind, it is likewise important to understand that some parents and families of these children experience feelings, burdens, and stresses that families of nonhandicapped or less handicapped children will not experience. In this section we describe those experiences unique to families of severely handicapped persons and discuss the implications for various family members, as well as for families as a whole. The following paragraphs provide an overview of the impact of a severely handicapped child upon the family. Three areas of impact are discussed: psychological or emotional; financial; and practical and logistical implications on the overall functioning of the family.

One of the most frequently discussed areas pertaining to the families of severely handicapped children has been the psychological or emotional impact upon the family. Literature in this area has been concerned primarily with psychological or emotional reactions and has primarily attempted to describe the deleterious and stressful effects of the presence of a handicapped child on the family. The major areas examined include the impact on the parents, impact on the siblings, and effect on the family unit.

Many authors have described the psychological and emotional impact upon parents, and their reaction and subsequent adaptation to a handicapped child. An early account of parental reactions to the birth of a handicapped child was that of Kanner (1953) who, on the basis of clinical observation of parents, suggested that three types of parental reactions are common: acceptance, disguise, or denial. Rosen (1955) states that parental reactions to a handicapped child occur in a fairly predictable order, generally including the following stages of psychological adaptation: awareness of a problem, recognition of the problem, search for a cause, search for a cure, and acceptance of the problem. Rosen's discussion and interpretation of the mother's understanding and adaptation to the retarded child are widely cited by authors in this field. Baum (1962) adds to Rosen's description of parental reactions without mention of grief, denial, hostility, guilt and shame, and withdrawal. Roos (1963), the parent of a handicapped child, also suggests that many parents experience difficult emotional trauma over having a handicapped child: loss of self-esteem, shame, ambivalence, depression, self-sacrifice, and defensiveness. Menolascino and Egger (1978) describe parental reactions as a series of crises to be resolved: the crises of shock and novelty, the personal values crisis, and the crisis confronted when the daily burden of care is realized.

Research in this area has generally followed along the lines of the above constructs of parental reaction and adjustment to the presence of a handicapped child. Several early studies attempted to assess associated differences in the psychological reactions of parents of institutionalized and noninstitutionalized children (Jacobson & Humphrey, 1979). Caldwell and Guze (1960) surveyed parents of both groups and did not find significant differences in adjustment between mothers of institutionalized and noninstitutionalized children. Fowle (1968), however, noted that fathers of noninstitutionalized children tended to experience more role tension than fathers of institutionalized children, and generally also more tension than mothers. Graliker, Koch, and Henderson (1965) attempted to identify parent and family factors related to the decision to institutionalize. The authors did not find a relationship between institutionalization and social class, religion, education, or age; however, parents of first-born severely handicapped children were more apt to institutionalize their children. Farber (1959, 1960) conducted a series of studies to compare the effects of institutionalization with home care upon families of retarded children. Although these studies were not related specifically to effects on parents, he did find that the overall "family integration" of parents and families who kept their child at home tended to be negatively affected.

Other authors have addressed the difficulties parents face when they are initially informed or counseled about the fact that their newborn is a severely handicapped child. The communication of this event is often traumatic for professionals (see Chapter 4) as well as for parents. Ballard (1978) also notes the difficulty of initial counseling and suggests that professionals responsible for informing and advising parents also need assistance and support. Parents have reported that the specific manner in which physicians handle these situations, as well as how knowledgeable the physician is of the infant's condition, influences initial reactions of parents of severely handicapped infants (Zwerling, 1954). Undoubtedly, the manner in which parents are initially informed or receive counseling about their severely handicapped child is critical in contributing toward their psychological reactions to what is a shocking event. One of the most difficult situations faced by both parents and professionals is the decision of whether to treat medically severely injured neonate. Duff (1981) suggests that this event may be extremely difficult for all involved, and that the resolution of this question (referred to elsewhere as involuntary euthanasia) is an important social as well as personal issue.

Relatively few studies have examined directly whether parents of severely handicapped children actually do progress through a series of predictable stages of reaction to a severely handicapped child. Dunlap and Hollinsworth (1977) reviewed survey studies of parents of severely handicapped children that revealed no serious consequences of adjustment in parents or family members. These reports contradict two clinical case study reports by Taichert (1975) and Menolascino and Pearson (1974). These authors confirm after observational reports that the parents of these children do experience severe negative emotional reactions and tend to follow a fairly predictable sequence of experiences. Drotvar, Baskiewicz, Irvin, Kennel, and Klaus (1975) interviewed 20 parents of congenitally malformed infants and also found support for the existence of a series of stages of emotional reactions. In one of the few experimental studies in this area, Bitter (1963) attempted to improve what were considerable undesirable attitudes and expectations of parents toward their Down's syndrome children. Although the results were inconclusive, the author suggests that counseling may fulfill an important role for those parents who experience difficulty in developing healthy and appropriate attitudes toward their child. Matheny and Vernick (1969) were able to positively change the attitudes of parents toward their handicapped children through a direct approach consisting of providing information and education about their child's handicaps and their implications. These authors note that counseling strategies may, in fact, be less successful than more direct educational approaches with some parents. Gath (1977), who has extensively studied the effects of Down's syndrome children upon their families and parents, found that parents of Down's children tended to evidence more depression, tension, hostility, and lack of warmth than a control group of "normal" parents.

While still others have suggested that the presence of a handicapped child has negative psychological effects upon the parents (Dornberg, 1978; Roos, 1982) the research data in this area are clearly equivocal. Zucman (1982) states that the literature in this area does not lead to · the conclusion that the presence of a severely handicapped child results in necessarily negative or harmful effects on parents. A more reasonable interpretation is that there are a variety of factors that contribute to parental reaction, and it is difficult if not impossible to predict what type of reactions to expect of parents. It is, however, important for professionals to realize that some parents may react strongly, be affected negatively, and in fact need professional counseling to help them adjust or adapt to the birth of a severely handicapped child.

A related area of interest is the impact upon other children in the family (see also Chapter 6 by Seligman). Many studies have consisted either of directly interviewing the handicapped child's siblings or of administering various types of psychological test batteries. Early work in this area was by Farber (1960), who studied families of institutionalized and noninstitutionalized children to assess differences in family integration between the two groups. In a frequently cited study, Farber (1959) reported that for families who kept their retarded child at home, siblings, particularly older female siblings were negatively affected psychologically. Farber's work was an important precursor to later studies in this area, particularly his concept of "family integration" as it related to families of the handicapped. Although Farber did report data supporting the negative effects of handicapped children on their siblings, his accounts were carefully restricted. Unfortunately, it appears that other authors have overstated Farber's results and have failed to carefully interpret findings.

Several others have also suggested that the siblings of these children are negatively affected. Hormuth (1953), in reporting on three case studies, states that often siblings of handicapped children may be prejudiced and that older siblings may be more apt to be than younger siblings. In a study discussed earlier, Fowle (1968) also reported negative impact upon normal siblings, particularly in the form of increased role tension among families who kept their retarded child at home.

In a series of studies, Gath (1973, 1974) attempted to identify the amount and the nature of these negative effects upon siblings. Her studies were similar, methodologically, to those discussed earlier and involved either direct interview or the administration of psychological tests or both to identify the presence of psychiatric disorders. In each study responses of siblings of Down's syndrome children were compared to those of non-handicapped or less handicapped children. Gath reported that older sisters revealed higher levels of psychiatric disorders, siblings of low-SES families were negatively influenced, as were boys of large low-SES families. It should be noted that each of these studies employed rather small samples, and that in an earlier study (Gath, 1972) no significant negative impact upon siblings was noted.

Still other authors have suggested that siblings of severely handicapped children are negatively affected in numerous ways. Grossman (1977) states that the siblings of these children may experience a variety of negative emotional reactions, including fear, death wishes, apprehension, and a lack of understanding. Hunter, Schucman, and Friedlander (1975) found that many siblings may exhibit anger over having a handicapped sibling. It has been recommended that since many different emotional reactions of siblings may be observed, parents must be open and candid about the situation with their children (Wentworth, 1974) and attempts should be made to provide these siblings with opportunities to communicate openly with others so that they can adequately deal with their feelings (Chinn, Drew, & Logan, 1979; Chinn, Winn, & Walters, 1978).

Based upon the literature just discussed, while there is limited evidence that some siblings experience negative impacts owing to the presence of a severely handicapped child in the family (Dornberg, 1978), the research data in this area are far from conclusive. In fact, several authors argue that no assumptions or generalizations should be made about siblings. Caldwell and Guze (1960) for example, found no evidence of such negative impact in studying mothers and siblings of retarded children kept at home. Chinn and his colleagues (1978) suggest that while these siblings may sometimes need assistance from parents or professionals, that it is extremely difficult to predict the type of response a sibling will make to having a handicapped child in the family. Zucman (1982) also states that the responses or reactions of normal siblings may be influenced by a variety of different factors that are difficult to isolate. Wolfensberger (1968), in a review of studies investigating the impact of handicapped children on their siblings, also concluded that the research does not support the notion that all siblings are negatively affected, or that they are affected in similar ways.

Like the literature on the impact of a severely handicapped child, studies of the impact on siblings also lead to few conclusions. The one consistent finding has been that older female siblings may experience difficulty, which is not surprising if these girls are called upon to provide extensive caretaking. Much more research is needed in this area to ascertain the nature of the impact (both negative and positive) that severely handicapped children have on their siblings. Perhaps even more importantly, there is a need for agencies and professionals to identify and to address the special needs of these siblings.

Families of severely handicapped children have also been discussed in terms of the overall psychological and emotional impact they experience. The literature in this area is also mixed, with some authors reporting relatively litle negative impact of severely handicapped children on their families, and others suggesting that the impact is predominantly negative. Many accounts have been reports describing the extremely emotionally and physically exhausting effects of a severely handicapped child on the family (Christ-Sullivan, 1976; Gordon, 1977; Tizard, 1961). In one of the few attempts at describing, specifically, families of severely handicapped children, Odle, Greer, and Anderson (1976) provide a brief review and discussion of the potentially negative effects of these children upon their families. Suggesting that all family members may be affected, these authors also state that other factors outside of the family may also influence the nature of the impact.

Several studies investigating psychological impact upon parents and siblings, which were discussed earlier, also report results of negative impact of a severely handicapped child upon the overall family (Hormuth, 1953; Farber, 1960; and Caldwell, & Guze, 1960). These authors report negative emotionality, role tension, and increased divisiveness within these families. In studying a group of families with Down's syndrome children, Gath (1977) reports that Down's syndrome families evidenced more negative emotions than a group of families of otherwise handicapped children, but that the families of other handicapped children also reported they felt more drawn together emotionally as a result of the event. Farber (1976) has suggested that many of these families progress through a series of adaptation stages to the birth of a handicapped child, and that this adaptation is helpful toward their integration of the family unit. Fost (1981) states that an important and effective approach to counseling these families is to facilitate family members' adaptation and adjustment to these types of emotional stages.

While the evidence in support of the negative psychological impact of a severely handicapped child upon the family is mixed, the research that contradicts this negative impact is even more compelling. Fowle's study (1968) revealed relatively no differences in integration between families that institutionalized their child and those who kept their retarded child at home. Dunlap and Hollinsworth (1977) also reported no serious negative psychological or emotional effects on families, but did report that these families were greatly in need of financial assistance and adequate educational programs for their handicapped children. In a survey study, Dunlap and Hollinsworth (1977) interviewed 400 families of handicapped chldren with disabilities and found their adjustment good and no serious consequences that could be identified. The authors did report, however, that families of children with multiple handicaps and seizure disorders were more burdened with financial concerns and had more time constraints that circumscribed their social life than the other families. In a recent study, Blackard and Barsch (1982) surveyed both parents and professionals to compare their appraisals of the impact of a severely handicapped child upon the family. The results indicated that special educational personnel tended to overestimate the negative impact of the handicapped child upon the family as compared to parents' appraisals. These authors reported that the difficulties these families experienced were centered around practical matters (e.g., obtaining respite care) more than around psychological reactions.

Several authors have summarized the literature in this area and concur that there is little empirical support that families are negatively effected or badly disrupted by the presence of a severely handicapped child in the family. On the basis of their review, Jacobson and Humphrey (1979) drew three conclusions about the effects of a severely handicapped child on the family: that the negative effects have been overstated; that the positive aspects have been ignored; and that many other family variables have been neglected from study. The authors further state that there are differing family responses to be ultimately identified, a much deeper understanding and study of these families is needed. Carr (1974) and Wolfensberger (1968) also reviewed literature and reseach in this area and found many studies so limited by methodological problems that there was a general lack of support for the conclusion that families are negatively influenced.

It appears that much more research in this area is needed before it can be assumed that severely handicapped children do in fact generally influence their families in negative ways. Based upon a review of the above articles several problems or limitations of the literature seem apparent. First, many of the published studies are flawed methodologically (e.g., small or biased samples, lack of valid and reliable measures). Additionally, few of these studies identified their populations in specific and concrete terms. Because the population referred to here as severely handicapped is so heterogeneous in nature, with so many different types of characteristic problems, it is difficult to generalize reported results to any specific family or even to any specific subgroups of severely handicapped children's families. Although studies with more precisely defined populations and more direct and reliable measures might lead to more conclusive results, the appropriateness and importance of this type of research seems equivocal. Rather than to continue to view these families as functioning pathologically we might better and more productively focus upon those practical matters that are of great concern to the families themselves.

Two such areas have frequently been reported by the parents of severely handicapped children: financial difficulties, and the burden on the practical and logistical day-to-day operations of the family. Several survey studies cited earlier stressed that many parents reported difficulty with financial matters stemming from the need to obtain numerous services for their children (Dunlap & Hollinsworth, 1977; Gath, 1973). Christ-Sullivan (1976), a parent of a severely handicapped child, also states that when many different services are needed expenses can be great, sorely burdening the financial solvency of the family.

As discussed earlier, while strides have been made in providing health and educational services to severely handicapped children and their families, there are many other needed services that are not commonly available at public expense. Parents and handicapped children experience difficulty in locating dentists, doctors, opthamologists, and even babysitters who are either willing or able to work effectively with their children. For the parents of low-functioning, multiply handicapped children this problem is even more acute. Abramson, Gravnick, Abramson and Summers (1977) surveyed a large portion of the parents of handicapped children in the state of Connecticut and found that many parents were dissatisfied with the services they were receiving. Blackard and Barsch (1982) also report that most problems of parents of severely handicapped children were related to difficulties in locating and paying for needed services.

In addition to these difficulties, parents of severely handicapped children also epxerience extra expenses in attempting to meet the needs of their children, many of whom need wheelchairs, adaptive equipment, hearing aides, orthopedic shoes, and many other types of equipment. Because many of these items are very expensive, and because government assistance may only partially reimburse for expenses, middle-class parents end up paying for the bulk of the items. Financial burdens are even more devastating to low-income families, who have even fewer resources available to them. One of the most important, expensive, and difficult to secure services is respite care (short-term care and management of the child by trained personnel, usually in the home). This type of short-term care is very important for parents of extremely difficult to manage children, particularly if there are other younger children in the home. In many respects these financial pressures may be much more difficult for parents and families to deal with readily than some of the more subtle psychological or emotional problems they may experience.

A related area of the impact of a severely handicapped child upon the family is the stress involved in the simple, day-to-day logistics of maintaining the family functions. Helsel (1978) provides a frank, and direct account of typical logistical problems families encounter. Meeting the needs of the handicapped child, caring for the other, nonhandicapped siblings, maintaining satisfying marital relationships, and fulfilling professional commitments as well as the more mundane concerns of daily living can sometimes be overwhelming for families of children who need to be fed, dressed, toileted, and so on several times a day, each day, for years. Gorham (1975), the parent of a severely handicapped child, believes that many professionals are often either ignorant or insensitive to the realities of daily living faced by these families. It does seem, then, that the financial and logistical burdens weigh acutely and unremittingly upon most of these families. In many respects the manner in which we professionals have attempted to understand families of severely handicapped children has been influenced by a rather problem-oriented preoccupation with their mental health, to the virtual exclusion of the practical priorities that are close at hand in their daily lives.

Further, while much has been written about the various problems and characteristics of these families, little has been done in terms of viewing these families as systems. Adopting a family systems approach to understanding families of these children might make possible a more meaningful understanding and also allow for the development of more effective means of meeting their needs. Several authors have called for a family systems approach to understanding and working with families of handicapped children (Berkowitz & Graziano, 1972; Chinn et al., 1978; Turnbull, 1982; Zucman, 1982).

Turnbull's account (1982), in particular, lends itself readily to a deeper understanding of families in general and families of handicapped children in particular. Three aspects of the family system are described: structure, functions, and life cycle. From a family systems approach the structure consists of several subsystems between the spouses, parents, siblings, and other extrafamilial persons (e.g., extended family members, friends, neighbors). Within each subsystem, then, different families are expected to vary on several different factors, such as culture, ideology, or role parameters. Family functions are described as including those areas in which every family member receives assistance and support from the total family: financial, physical, rest and recuperation, socialization, self-definition, affect, guidance, vocational, and educational. Finally, Turnbull also describes the life cycle of a family in terms of developmental stages: transitions, changes and catalysts, and sociohistorical context. We believe that this type of ecological approach to understanding families offers the possibility for more meaningful understanding of families in general, and of specific differences among families as well. Undoubtedly, the characteristics and needs of families with severely handicapped children will vary considerably with differences in the various aspects of the family system. This model accommodates the need to view families of severely handicapped children as complex entities with unique ways of responding to significant events in their life.

MEETING THE NEEDS OF FAMILIES OF PERSONS WITH SEVERE HANDICAPS

To work effectively with severely handicapped persons and their families it is important that professionals develop a basic understanding of the common needs of these families as well as the ability to identify specific needs that are unique to individual families. As the preceding discussions indicate, a wide variety of different factors may affect the types of assistance needed or requested.

The literature contains two types of reports about parental needs that are worthy of consideration: individual reports of parents themselves (Gorham, 1975; Greer, 1975); and large-scale surveys of groups of parents (Justice, O'Conner, & Warren, 1971; Kenowitz et al., 1977). Over the years these two sources of information have yielded rather consistent information about the needs of parents and families of handicapped children: support, information, and adequate services are most frequently noted by parents themselves. This section provides suggestions for understanding and meeting these needs, particularly as they pertain to families of severely handicapped persons. Since many of these needs have been previously addressed, only selected additional areas are discussed here.

One of the most important areas of need often reported by parents is for professionals and others to attempt to better understand their problems and provide emotional support in a nonjudgmental manner (Schlesinger & Meadow, 1976; also see Chapter 4). Professionals should understand that the responsibility of parenting a severely handicapped child is often very demanding and may drain the resources of the family. Positive feedback and encouragement can be extremely helpful to parents and family members who feel at times exhausted, overwhelmed, or even uncertain about the care and treatment they are providing to their child. Persons working with these families can be supportive and understanding without having necessarily to assume roles as counselors. When and if family members do need counseling to ease adjustment problems, then this should be left to well-trained professionals.

Informational assistance is also a commonly reported need of families of severely handicapped children (Dean, 1975). One of the most common types of assistance parents need is accurate information. As suggested earlier, the presence of a severely handicapped child in the family often means that parents need to obtain, understand, and utilize all kinds of information. The type of information needed by these parents could include the nature of their child's handicap, characteristic patterns of normal development, methods of parenting and management, agencies providing training and consultation, the availability of health or related services, the selection of an educational program, legal protection and advocacy services, parent self-help and support groups, respite care, and the long-term expectations or implications for the child. Again, these informational needs will vary from family to family and also from time to time. Some families need assistance in obtaining information, some with interpreting or understanding the information, and some with using the information to make decisions. Still other parents may have more information available to them than most agencies and will not need any assistance. In providing parents with information, care should be taken to avoid the use of technical, professional jargon and communicating in a condescending manner.

One of the most important needs of families of severely handicapped children is to obtain the necessary services for their child within the community (Justice et al., 1971; Kenowitz et al., 1977). One of the areas in which parents often experience great difficulty is in obtaining appropriate and effective educational programs. Public educational programs for severely handicapped students are often highly centralized in large, segregated centers far from the student's homes. These types of programs may require students to spend large amounts of time riding buses each day, may restrict the child's recognition and acceptance within the local community, and may fail to offer opportunities for the learning of important socialization skills (Brown, Wilcox, Sontag, Vincent, Dodd, & Gruenewald, 1977). Many parents are calling for more decentralized services located closer to students' homes, to be provided by local school districts in order that many of these problems may be alleviated.

A related need is for meaningful involvement and participation in educational and other services provided to the child. Although federal and state legislation now mandates the protection of certain specific rights of parents' participation (e.g., prior written informed consent, access to records, due process procedures,), there are accounts of circumstances in which these basic rights have been violated or ignored. It has also been noted that professionals or agencies do not make meaningful attempts to involve parents, beyond the minimum letter of the law (Mattson, 1977). Professionals should attempt to work toward overcoming obstacles between themselves and parents (Roos, 1997) and should attempt to establish close working relationships (Perske, n.d.) so that the family and the child can benefit maximally.

One important form of involvement with professionals and agencies that parents and families may need is training. Children with severe handicaps may need extensive supervision, care, and possibly even highly specialized treatment on a frequent basis. Parents (and even siblings) may need specific training from professionals in many different areas related to the care of their severely handicapped child, such as feeding, handling, and positioning, management of severe behavior disorders, and toilet training. Over the years, a variety of different approaches and programs have been used to provide parents with training (Berkowitz & Graziano, 1972; O'Dell, 1974). In fact, it could be argued that training parents has been the predominant approach of professionals. Professionals (particularly in the field of education) have often been quick to assume that they themselves know the best treatment for the child, that parents lack the necessary skills to provide the treatment, and that certain designated training approaches should be provided so that "right" techniques can be used.

There are several problems with this approach to understanding and working with these families. First, while it is often true that parents may need and request specific training to better care for their severely handicapped child, it should not be assumed that all parents want or even need training in all or any areas in caring for their child. Second, the implicit assumption that parents (as well as siblings) are essentially without skills in caring for their severely handicapped child is often blatantly false. Many times parents possess extensive amounts of expertise in caring for their child, and may, in fact, be able to train professionals in the most effective techniques. Vincent, Dodd, and Henner (1978) call for professionals to recognize that parenting is a specialized discipline and that parents bring valuable assets of their own to the care of their child. Third, the preoccupation with training has probably inhibited many parents from selecting other forms of participation and involvement in their child's life. There are many other needs and preferences that parents and families have that cannot be satisfied only by parent training. Fourth (and perhaps most important), in limiting the scope of interaction with families to parent training programs, professionals may fail to understand the family as a system, with its own unique structure, functions, and life cycle. This failure can, and often does, result in families feeling or even actually being compelled to comply with professionals' expectations for home treatment, which may be intrusive to the family itself. Approaches to providing training should be carefully considered by professionals so that the preferences and styles of families are respected.

An additional need of many families of severely handicapped children is for direct home care and assistance, often referred to as respite care. In some families this short-term care may be helpful where both parents work, where several other children are in the home, and when and if the family simply wishes or needs to obtain relief from the intensive and exhausting 24-hour care routines. This type of assistance may also be critical for single parent families or families where no other siblings or extended family members are available to help out. For these families, in-home assistance may make the difference between maintaining the child at home and alternate residential placement. Traditionally, our service delivery systems have been highly centralized, and families in need of services are expected to go to the center, the clinic, the school, or the hospital, for assistance. We believe that professionals working with these families should make every effort to extend their services into the homes where the very important needs of these children and their families exist and must be dealt with on a long-term basis.

CONCLUSIONS

Education and health care professionals must realize several important principles when attempting to meet the needs of families of severely handicapped children. First and foremost is the fact that these children and their families' characteristics, needs, and preferences differ widely; therefore, what may be important or appropriate for one family may not be for another. Second, families are complex units with varying and uniquely different interactional styles. Professionals should not ignore the importance of the differences in family styles, for they are as important in their own right as how family interaction affects the severely handicapped child. Third, the focus of intervention with these families should not be narrowly defined. Parents, in particular, should be respected for their efforts as well as the expertise they possess. Fourth, the focus of intervention around which parents and professionals interact can be broadened and enhanced by extending options for assistance, involvement, and participation from which parents and family members may select. Finally, service agencies and professionals must be more family- rather than individually oriented and must direct more of their efforts toward positively affecting the social system of the family.

Helping families of severely handicapped children may require professionals to do many things, ranging from providing simple encouragement and support to parents, assisting in providing and interpreting information, training parents in caring for their child, providing crisis intervention and assisting in special problems to helping parents clarify goals and needs for themselves, their severely handicapped child, and their family.

Several important areas must be addressed if we as a community of professionals, parents, and families are to fully attain our goals. More naturalistic research needs to be conducted, focusing on the identification, analysis, and development of more effective service delivery models and strategies for helping these children and their families. More and better training must be provided to the many different professionals who are expected to work effectively with these children and their families. More community-based services, such as respite care and in-home assistance, must be made available to assist these families. Finally, we professionals must adopt an ecologically valid approach toward these families as well as to our own particular roles: the child, the family, and the community must be viewed in context with one another.

REFERENCES

Abeson, A., & Zettel, J. The end of a quiet revolution: The Education for All Handicapped Children Act of 1975. *Exceptional Children*, 1977, *44*(2), 114–128.

Abramson, P. R., Gravnick, M. T., Abramson, L. M., & Summers, D. Early diagnosis and intervention of retardation: A survey of parental reactions concerning the quality of services rendered. *Mental Retardation*, 1977, *15*, 28–31.

Ballard, R. Help for coping with the unthinkable. *Developmental Medicine and Child Neurology*, 1978, *20*, 517–521.

Baum, M. H. Some dynamic factors affecting family adjustment to the handicapped child. *Exceptional Children*, 1962, *28*, 387–392.

Baumeister, A., & Brookes, P. Cognitive deficits in mental retardation. In J. Kauffman (Ed.), *Handbook for special education*. Englewood Cliffs, N.J.: Prentice-Hall, 1981.

Berkowitz, B. P., & Graziano, A. Training parents as behavior therapists: A review. *Behavior Research and Therapy*, 1972, *10*, 297–317.

Bitter, J. A. Attitude change by parents of TMR children as a result of group discussion. *Exceptional Children*, 1963, *30*, 173–177.

Blackard, M. K., & Barsch, E. T. Parents' and professionals' perceptions of the handicapped child's impact on the family. *Journal of the Association for the Severely Handicapped,* 1982, *7*(2), 62–69.

Blatt, B., Bogdan, R., Biklen, D., & Taylor, S. From institution to community: A conversion model. In E. Sontag (Ed.), *Educational programming for the severely and profoundly handicapped.* Reston, Va.: Council for Exceptional Children, Division on Mental Retardation, 1977.

Blatt, B., & Kaplan, F. *Christmas in purgatory: A photographic essay on mental retardation.* Syracuse, N.Y.: Human Policy Press, 1974.

Bleck, E. E., & Nagel, D. A. (Eds.). *Physically handicapped children: A medical atlas for teachers.* New York: Grune & Stratton, 1975.

Bobath, B., & Bobath, K. *Motor development in the different types of cerebral palsy.* London: William Heineman Medical Books, 1975.

Brown, L., Nietupski, J., & Hamre-Nietupski, S., The criterion of ultimate functioning and public school services for severely handicapped students. In A. Thomas (Ed.), *Hey don't forget about me! Education's investment in the severely and profoundly handicapped.* Reston, Va.: Council for Exceptional Children, Invisible College, 1976.

Brown, L., Wilcox, T., Sontag, E., Vincent, B., Dodd, N., & Gruenewald, L. Toward the realization of the least restrictive environments for severely handicapped students. *AAESPH Review,* 1977, *2,* 195–201.

Browning, R. M. *Teaching the severely handicapped child.* Boston: Allyn & Bacon, 1980.

Burton, T. A., & Hirshoren, A. Some further thoughts and clarifications on the education of severely and profoundly retarded children. *Exceptional Children,* 1979, *45*(8), 618–625.

Carr, J. *Young children with Down's syndrome: Their development, upbringing and effect on their families.* London: Butterworths, 1974.

Caldwell, B. & Guze, A. A study of the adjustment of parents and siblings of institutionalized and noninstitutionalized retarded children. *American Journal of Mental Deficiency,* 1960, *64,* 845–861.

Chinn, P., Drew, C., & Logan, D. *Mental Retardation,* St. Louis: C.V. Mosby, 1979.

Chinn, P. C., Winn, J., & Walters, R. H. *Two way talking with parents of special children.* St. Louis: C.V. Mosby, 1978.

Christ-Sullivan, R. The role of the parent. In A. Thomas (Ed.), *Hey don't forget about me: Education's investment in the severely, profoundly and multiply handicapped.* Reston, Va.: Council for Exceptional Children, 1976.

Dean, D. Closer look: A parent information service. *Exceptional Children,* 1975, *41*(8), 527–530.

Dornberg, N. L. Some negative effects on family integration of health and educational services for young handicapped children. *American Journal of Orthopsychiatry,* 1978, *39*(4), 107–110.

Drotvar, D., Baskiewicz, B., Irvin, N., Kennel, J., & Klaus, M. The adaptation of parents to the birth of an infant with a congenital malformation: A hypothetical model. *Pediatrics,* 1975, *56*(5), 710–717.

Duff, R. Counseling families and deciding care of severely defective children: A way of coping with medical Vietnam. *Pediatrics,* 1981, *67,* 315–320.

Dunlap, W. R., & Hollinsworth, J. S. How does a handicapped child affect the family? Implications for practitioners. *Family Coordinator,* July, 1977, *26,* 286–293.

Farber, B. Effects of a severely mentally retarded child on family integration. *Monographs of the Society for Research in Child Development,* 1959, *24*(2, Serial No. 71).

Farber, B. Organization and crisis: maintenance of integration in families with a severely retarded child. *Monograph's of the Society for Research in Child Development* (Antioch Press), 1960, *25*(No.1).

Farber, B. Family process. In W. Cruickshank (Ed.), *Cerebral palsy: A developmental disability* (3rd rev. ed.). New York: Syracuse University Press, 1976.

Fost, N. Counseling families who have a child with a severe congenital anomaly. *Pediatrics,* 1981, *67,* 321–324.

Fowle, C. M. The effect of the severely mentally retarded child on his family. *American Journal of Mental Deficiency,* 1968, *73,* 468–473.

Gath, A. The mental health of siblings of congenitally abnormal children. *Journal of Child Psychology and Psychiatry,* 1972, *13,* 211–218.

Gath, A. The school age siblings of Mongol children. *British Journal of Psychiatry,* 1973, *123,* 161–167.

Gath, A. Sibling reactions to mental handicap: A comparison of mothers and sisters of Mongol children. *Journal of Child Psychology and Psychiatry,* 1974, *15,* 187–198.

Gath, A. The impact of an abnormal child upon the parents. *British Journal of Psychiatry,* 1977, *130,* 405–410.

Gilhool, T., & Stuttman, E. Integration of severely handicapped students: Toward criteria for implementing and enforcing the integration imperative of P.L. 94-142 and Section 504. Paper presented at Bureau of Education for the Handicapped Conference on the Concept of the Least Restrictive Environment, Washington, D.C., 1978.

Gordon, R. Special needs of multi-handicapped children under six and their families. In E. Sontag (Ed.), *Educational programming for the severely and profoundly handicapped.* Reston, Va.: Council for Exceptional Children, Division on Mental Retardation, 1977.

Gorham, K. A. A last generation of parents. *Exceptional Children,* 1975, *41*(8), 521–525.

Graliker, B., Fishler, K., & Koch, R. Teenage reactions to a mentally retarded sibling. *American Journal of Mental Deficiency,* 1962, *66,* 838–843.

Greer, B. G., On being the parent of a handicapped child. *Exceptional Children,* 1975, *41*(8), 519.

Grossman H. J. (Ed.). *Manual on terminology and classification in mental retardation.* Washington, D.C.: American Association on Mental Deficiency, 1977.

Guess, P. D., & Horner, D. The severely and profoundly handicapped. In E. Meyer (Ed.), *Exceptional Children and Youth: An introduction.* Denver: Love Publishing Company, 1976.

Guess, D. & Mulligan, M. The severely and profoundly handicapped. In E. Meyer (Ed.), *Exceptional Children and Youth: An Introduction* (2nd Edition). Denver: Love, 1982.

Helsel, E. The Helsel's story of Robin. In A. P. Turnbull & H. R. Turnbull (Eds.), *Parents speak out: Views from the other side of the two-way mirror.* Columbus, Ohio: Charles Merrill, 1978.

Hewitt, F. M. & Forness, S. R. *Education of exceptional learners* (2nd ed.). Boston: Allyn & Bacon, 1977.

Hormuth, R. P. Home problems and family care of the mongoloid child. *Quarterly Review of Pediatrics,* 1953, *8,* 274–280.

Hunter, M. H., Schucman, F. & Friedlander, G. *The retarded child from birth to five: A multidisciplinary program for the child and family.* New York: John Day, 1975.

Jacobson, R. B., & Humphrey, R. A. Families in crisis: Research and theory in child mental retardation. *Social Casework: The Journal of Contemporary Social Work,* 1979, December, 597–601.

Justice, R. S., O'Conner, C., & Warren, N. Problems reported by parents of mentally retarded children—Who helps? *American Journal of Mental Deficiency,* 1971, *75*(6), 685–691.

Justin, J., & Brown, G. Definitions of severely handicapped: A survey of state departments of education. *AAESPH Review,* 1977, *2*(1), 8–14.

Kanner, L. Parent's feelings about retarded children. *American Journal of Mental Deficiency,* 1953, *57,* 375–389.

Katz, A. H. *Parents of the handicapped.* Springfield, Ill.: Charles C Thomas, 1961.

Kenowitz, L. A., Gallagher, J., & Edgar, E. Generic services for the severely handicapped and their families. What's available? In E. Sontag (Ed.), *Educational programming for the severely and profoundly handicapped.* Reston, Va.,: Council for Exceptional Children, Division on Mental Retardation, 1977.

Koegel, R. L., Egel, A. L., & Dunlap, G. Learning characteristics of autistic children. In W. Sailor, B. Wilcox, & L. Brown (Eds.), *Methods of Instruction for severely handicapped students.* Baltimore: Paul H. Brookes, 1980.

Kroth, R. Parents—powerful and necessary allies. *Teaching Exceptional Children,* 1978, *10,* 88–90.

Larsen, L. A. Community services necessary to program effectively for the severely/profoundly handicapped. In E. Sontag (Ed.), *Educational programming for the severely and profoundly handicapped.* Reston, Va.: Council for Exceptional Children, Division on Mental Retardation, 1977.

Lehr, D. Severe multiple handicaps. In E. Meyer (Ed.), *Exceptional children in today's schools: An alternative resource book.* Denver: Love, 1982.

Liberty, K. A., Haring, N. G., & Martin, M. M. Teaching new skills to the severely handicapped. *Journal of the Association for the Severely Handicapped,* 1981, *6*(1), 5–13.

Lillie, D. An overview to parent programs. In D. Lillie & P. L. Trohanis (Eds.), *Teaching parents to teach.* New York: Walker, 1976.

Matheny, A. P., & Vernick, J. Parents of the mentally retarded child: Emotionally overwhelmed or informationally deprived. *Journal of Pediatrics,* 1969, *74,* 953–959.

Mattson, B. D. Involving parents in special education: Did you really reach them? *Education and Training of the Mentally Retarded,* 1977, *12,* 358–360.

Menolascino, F. J., & Pearson, P. H. Beyond the limits in services for the severely and profoundly retarded: A crisis model for helping them cope more effectively. New York: Special Child Publications, 1974.

Menolascino, F. J., & Egger, M. *Medical dimensions of mental retardation.* Lincoln: University of Nebraska Press, 1978.

O'Conner, G. *Home is a good place: A national perspective of community residential facilities for developmentally disabled persons* (Monograph of the American Association on Mental Deficiency, No. 2). Washington, D.C.: American Association on Mental Deficiency, 1976.

O'Dell, S. Training parents in behavior modification: A review. *Psychological Bulletin,* 1974, *81*(7), 418–433.

Odle, S. J., Greer, J. G., & Anderson, R. M. The family of the severely retarded individual. In R. M. Anderson & J. G. Greer (Eds.), *Educating the severely and profoundly retarded,* Baltimore: University Park Press, 1976.

Perske, R. Parent-teacher relationships that go beyond the ordinary. Unpublished manuscript. n.d.

Roos, P. Psychological counseling with parents of retarded children. *Mental Retardation,* 1963, *1,* 345–350.

Roos, P. Special trends and issues. In P. T. Cagelka & H. J. Prehm (Eds.), *Mental Retardation: From categories to people.* Columbus, Ohio: Charles Merrill, 1982.

Roos, P. A parent's view of what public education should accomplish. In E. Sontag (Ed.), *Educational programming for the severely and profoundly handicapped.* Reston, Va.: Council for Exceptional Children, Division on Mental Retardation, 1977.

Rosen, L. Selected aspects in the development of the mother's understanding of her mentally retarded child. *American Journal of Mental Deficiency,* 1955, *59,* 522–528.

Rutter, M. Diagnosis and definition of childhood autism. *Journal of Autism and Childhood Schizophrenia,* 1978, *8,* 139–161.

Sailor, W., & Guess, D. *Severely handicapped students: An instructional design.* Boston: Houghton Mifflin, 1982.

Schlesinger, H. S., & Meadow, K. P. Emotional support for parents. In D. Lillie & L. Trohanis (Eds.), *Teaching parents to teach.* New York: Walker, 1976.

Semmel, D. S. & Morrissey, P. A. Serving the unserved and underserved: Can the mandate be extended in an era of limitations? *Exceptional Education Quarterly.* 1981, *2,*(2), 17–26.

Shell, P. M. Straining the system: Serving low-incidence handicapped children in an urban school district. *Exceptional Education Quarterly,* 1981, *2*(2), 1–10.

Sontag, E., Burke, P. J. & York, R. Considerations for serving the severely handicapped in public schools. *Education and Training of the Mentally Retarded.* 1973, *8,* 20–26.

Sontag, E., Certo, N., & Button, J. On a distinction between the education of the severely and profoundly handicapped and a doctrine of limitations. *Exceptional Children,* 1979, *45,*(8), 604–616.

Sontag, E., Smith, J., & Sailor, W. The severely and profoundly handicapped: Who are they? Where are we? *Journal of Special Education,* 1977, *11*(1), 5–11.

Stokes, T. & Baer, D. An implicit technology of generalization. *Journal of Applied Behavior Analysis,* 1977, *10,* 341–367.

Taichert, L. Parental denial as a factor in the management of the severely retarded child, *Clinical Pediatrics,* 1975, *14*(7), 666–668.

Tizard, J., & Grad, J. C. *The mentally handicapped and their families.* London: Maudsley Monograph No. 7, 1961.

Turnbull, A. Keynote Address to Annual DEC Conference. Council for Exceptional Children, Division for Early Childhood, and the Handicapped Childrens' Early Education Program, Washington, D.C., 1982.

Turnbull, A. P., & Turnbull, H. R. (Eds.), *Parents Speak Out: Views from the other side of the two-way mirror.* Columbus, Ohio: Charles Merrill, 1978.

Vincent, L. J., Dodd, N., & Henner, P. J. Planning and implementing a program of parent involvement. In N. G. Haring & D. D. Bricker (Eds.), *Teaching the severely handicapped* (Vol. 3), Columbus: Special Press, 1978.

Wentworth, E. H. *Listen to your heart: A message to parents of handicapped children.* Boston: Houghton Mifflin, 1974.

Wolfensberger, W. Counseling the parents of the retarded. In A. Baumeister (Ed.), *Mental Retardation: Appraisal, rehabilitation and education.* London: University of London Press, 1968.

Zucman, E. *Childhood disability in the family.* World Rehabilitation Fund—International Exchange of Information in Rehabilitation, Monograph No. 14, New York, 1982.

Zwerling, I. Initial counseling of parents with mentally retarded children. *Journal of Pediatrics,* 1954, *44,* 467–479.

IV

INTERVENTIONS

9

The Uses of Bibliotherapy in Counseling Families Confronted with Handicaps

JUNE B. MULLINS

BIOGRAPHICAL SKETCH

June B. Mullins, Ph.D., is Associate Professor in Special Education at the University of Pittsburgh and has been a teacher of children and youth with many kinds of physical and emotional disabilities. She is an associate editor of Exceptional Children.

Dr. Mullins is the author of journal articles in the fields of special education, rehabilitation, and the art therapies. She has written three books: Special People Behind the Eight Ball: Annotated Bibliography of Literature Classified by Handicapping Conditions *(with S. Wolfe);* Hospital, *a book for deaf children describing the people who work in a children's hospital (with K. Hammermeister); and* A Teacher's Guide to Management of Physically Handicapped Students.

ISBN 0-8089-1561-4
Copyright © 1983 by Grune & Stratton

DEFINITIONS OF BIBLIOTHERAPY

> I was looking in books for a bigger world than the world in which I lived. In some blind and instinctive way I knew what was happening in those books was also happening all around me. And I was trying to make a connection between the books and the life I saw and the life I lived.
>
> You think your pain and your heartbreak are unprecedented in the history of the world, and then you read. It was books that taught me that the things that tormented me the most were the very things that connected me with all the people who were alive, or who had ever been alive.*

The man who related these feelings knew, even in childhood, the value and power of literature. Literature can be deliberately selected to address a reader's particular concerns, such as loneliness and pain. Such a use of literature is therapeutic in that the reader learns, for example, that pain is a human condition shared by all.

A variety of definitions of *bibliotherapy* has been offered by theorists and practitioners in a number of professions. The first use of the word is generally credited to Crothers (1916), who quoted a friend as saying, "Bibliotherapy is such a new science that it is no wonder that there are many erroneous opinions as to the actual effect which any particular book may have."

Shrodes (1949) defined bibliotherapy as the process of dynamic interaction between the personality of the reader and the literature—a psychological field that may be utilized for personality assessment, adjustment, and growth.

Webster's Third International Dictionary (1968 edition) defines bibliotherapy as "the use of selected reading materials as therapeutic adjuvants of medicine and psychiatry; also guidance in the solution of personal problems through directed reading" (p. 212). The *Dictionary of Education* (1959) has a somewhat different definition: "Use of books to influence total development: a process of interaction between the reader and literature which is used for personality assessment, adjustment, growth, clinical and mental hygiene purposes: a concept that ideas inherent in selected reading materials can have a therapeutic effect upon the mental or physical ills of readers (p. 58).

The differences in these definitions are mainly in their emphasis—either toward therapy and treatment or toward education and knowledge—not in their basic meaning. Counselors will undoubtedly be more comfortable with a therapeutic emphasis, and teachers will want to stress

---

*Remarks made in the program "My Childhood," presented over Channel 5, WNEW-TV, New York, May 31, 1964, by James Baldwin.

the educational aspects of bibliotherapy, since their training in counseling and psychotherapy is generally limited.

Mullins (1975) suggested an extension of the concept of bibliotherapy. She noted that the usual definitions do not include a very important component that is assumed in definitions of the therapies of dance, music, and art; namely, the possibility of creative expression in the medium, to enhance growth and understanding or to facilitate healing.

This chapter is limited to a discussion of literature as the written word. Therefore, such forms as film and television are not considered, although some of the points addressed here might very well be generalized to these as well as other artistic media.

WHAT OTHERS HAVE SAID ABOUT BIBLIOTHERAPY

The Healing Place of the Soul

Inscription over a library in ancient Thebes

Research Findings

In reviewing the research on the effects of literature on attitudes, Purves and Beach (1972) caution, "Nearly all of the students . . . fail to consider the work read as one of hundreds of independent variables influencing an attitude" (p. viii). They point out that most research in the area of bibliotherapy is case-study research rather than empirical or survey research. Both points suggest a basic weakness in effectively evaluating the impact of bibliotherapy.

For example, Shrodes' study in 1949 utilized psychoanalytic techniques to probe the responses of individuals to literature. She concluded that psychological diagnosis combined with prescribed reading and free response could alter personality structures of patients. Following Shrodes' investigation, other case studies were conducted by Wilson (1951), Edgar, Hazley, and Levitt (1969), and Osthoff (1970). All support the notion that a skillful mental health professional or teacher, using literature in the form of prose, poetry, and drama, can facilitate personality change. These particular studies tend to focus on helping emotionally disturbed individuals rather than essentially normal persons who are faced with an extraordinary event such as the imposition of a handicapping condition into their lives. They also suggest that people can change basic personality characteristics through psychological treatment, a most ambitious and (according to Blocher, 1982) unrealistic outcome.

Osthoff (1971) and Bass (1977) used bibliotherapy in a counseling practicum to increase the effectiveness of counselor trainees. They found that the utilization of books by these trainees increased empathy toward schizophrenics. Shrank (1977) found that bibliotherapy effected a positive change in children's attitudes toward slow-learning children. However, McClasky (1970) reported that bibliotherapy for emotionally disturbed patients did not positively affect attitude, although the program did result in behavioral gains.

Le Unes (1974) reports the successful use of literature about exceptionality as a good alternative or addition to textbooks for college students. Young adults seem particularly interested in the literature of deviancy, and this can be used to good advantage in coursework. Le Unes writes: "There is a discernible thread of consistency that marks their interests in abnormal behavior, and these readings can constitute the beginning of a master thriller list for students at this level" (p. 213).

Shrank and Engels (1981) provide a recent update of research offered to support the contention that bibliotherapy can be an effective part of counseling. Some of their review was concerned with persons who were handicapped. They cited some studies on the efficacy of bibliotherapy in raising academic achievement with regular elementary and high school students, underachievers, and disadvantaged children. These groups showed a positive effect, although it was concluded that findings of the majority of studies in this category support the notion that bibliotherapy may not be very effective for increasing academic achievement. They found that, in general, bibliotherapy was most effective in bringing about attitude changes, including those toward handicaps and exceptionalities (Amato, 1959, Russell & Shrodes, 1950, Shrank, 1977, Zaccaria & Moses, 1968).

From the research they reviewed on the value of bibliotherapy in counseling, Shrank and Engels (1981) conclude:

1. Bibliotherapy might be useful to counselors and therapists in their work with individuals and groups.
2. Bibliotherapy might be useful to school counselors and teachers who wish to tap the benefits of guided reading for guidance or instructional purposes.
3. Counselors should be aware that positive recommendations of the value of bibliotherapy exceed available documentation of its usefulness. (p. 145–146)

Children's Literature

In considering the effect of literature on children, the Carnegie Quarterly (1974) states the following:

Books, perhaps children's books most of all, are powerful tools by which a civilization perpetuates its values—both its proudest accomplishments and its most crippling prejudices. In books children find characters with whom they identify and whose aspirations and actions they might one day try to emulate; they discover, too, a way of perceiving those who are of a different color, who speak a different language or live a different life. Heroic epics, schoolbook histories, timeless fairy tales all help to inspire pride and ambition, fear, and defeatism. (p.1)

Bettelheim (1977) has written extensively about the power of children's literature, particularly fairy tales, to transmit the cultural heritage and to stimulate and nurture the very young child's resources of mind and personality to cope with his difficult inner problems.

Literature about exceptionalities has been recommended for use in classroom settings at the preschool level. In discussing the education of young children, Strasser (1974) states that

While it is recognized that handicapped children might benefit from rich experiences with all good books for children, it is believed that books dealing with children or animals who are handicapped would have especial value for handicapped children. (p. 2200)

McGuire (1969) describes a program using books that depicted children and animals who were handicapped:

The children come wearing braces, in wheelchairs, or crutches, but their needs and interests differ little from non-handicapped classmates. For both groups, books are helpful in laying a foundation for a worthwhile, satisfying life. (p. 607)

Bettelheim (1981) also takes a strong stand on the use of children's literature, including textbooks, to help them deal with crucial problems of the day. In an interview, Bettelheim (1981) was asked, "If serious problems involved children who were the main characters in the story, wouldn't it seem threatening to children?" He replied, "Yes, but you cannot deal with anything serious without creating some ambivalent feelings or even some anxiety. Children have to learn that a certain amount of anxiety is manageable. They need to know, 'I can get into difficult situations, but I can manage them.' " (p. 32)

Wolfenstein and Kliman (1965) report the case of a youngster who did not cry when his own mother died, but who subsequently cried profusely when he read about the demise of a favored fictional character in Dumas' *The Three Musketeers*. The authors describe this process as "mourning at a distance."

Mullins (1979b) has addressed the need to represent handicapped children and adults in educational materials and has discussed the value for handicapped and nonhandicapped children in the encounter of exceptional persons in these materials.

Educational materials should depict adult life in the working world. Persons with exceptionalities have become teachers, lawyers, and business leaders.

Handicapped people exist in all walks of life, and have been contributors in all fields of endeavor. Children with handicapping conditions need role models in textbooks that reflect appropriate aspiration levels. (p. 21)

In her National Book Award acceptance speech for *The Great Gilly Hopkins* (1979), Paterson said

The wonderful thing about being a writer is that it gives you readers, readers who bring their own stories to the story you have written, people who have the power to take your mythic, unbelievable, ten-foot-high characters and fit them to the shape of their own lives.

Paterson (1981) recounts a visit to a high school where she was to address a class of "gifted" students who had read her much-awarded book, *The Great Gilly Hopkins*. The protagonist of this book is an 11-year-old foster child: wily, tough, brash, prejudiced, and very vulnerable. Paterson arrived at the school to find that the special reading teacher had read the book aloud to her special students and therefore insisted that her classes also be allowed to hear Paterson's presentation. One boy, who she later learned was a belligerent, lonely, nonreader, listened avidly to her presentation and spoke briefly but intensely to her afterward. Subsequently she sent him a copy of the book so that he might own it even though he couldn't read it. His first letter back reported that he was on page 16. He proceeded to become a reader and a learner, and his life was quite literally turned around. This story underscores the fact that literature can inspire adolescents with lower than average reading skills and can serve to increase such skills.

Use of Creative Writing

Kubie (1961) has explored in great depth the relation of artists' "neuroticism" to their creative products, noting as evidence the repetitiveness and pecularity of both themes and archaic symbolism in particular artists' works. It seems equally legitimate to view artistic products as a culmination of a highly constructive process of dealing with inner and outer conflicts and problems by troubled, talented people.

Some therapists have given evidence concerning the benefit of actually writing a journal and discussing feelings or fears. Counselors have made use of their clients' writing for its personal rather than artistic content (Gurman, 1981). Leedy (1969, 1973) has provided readable and informative descriptions of techniques employing poetry therapy. He uses both published work and the creative endeavors of clients in his therapy sessions.

Most parents of handicapped children do not publish books about coping with handicaps, although a number have done so. Some of these have been listed by Mullins and Wolfe (1975) and in Appendix C at the end of this chapter.

Handicapped people have written extensively about their lives. Of approximately one thousand trade books about the handicapped compiled by Mullins and Wolfe (1975), about half were actually written by handicapped persons, and some others were written by parents and spouses.

The meaning of the literary creative process to handicapped persons can be made clearer by a closer examination of the kinds of individuals who write and the nature of their works. By far the largest categories of disability represented in the trade literature of deviancy are the sensory disorders; books in this category are written by the deaf, the blind, and the deaf-blind (Mullins & Wolfe, 1975). In these categories are people deprived of the most important avenues of human communication, the aural and/or the visual. They are often socially deprived far beyond the physical restraints of their impairments by the deeply rooted fears and prejudices of more normal people toward these particular handicaps.

Adventitiously blinded persons, usually of extraordinary intelligence and insight, have contributed a large amount of literature describing the shock and mourning accompanying loss of sight and the gradual rebirth of personality into the new identity of the successfully coping blind person. These writers also explore the attitudes of other people toward them. The books have blindness as a central theme and might be considered therapeutic work as well as communication and good literature.

It is interesting to note that persons who have been blind from birth seldom contribute to the literature of blindness. Such congenitally blind people develop consistent auditory and motor perceptual communication systems that never included visual schema and do not experience loss of that which they have never known. Their particular dilemma is more concerned with social acceptance and opportunity than with physical deprivation.

We can also see differences between congenitally deaf and deafened authors. Adventitiously deaf individuals may find written communication their only means of social contact for some time. Their desperation is often revealed in their literature.

Finally, various writers describe the plight of the misfit, the person who feels like the proverbial square peg in a round hole. The situation may be due to some kind of mismatch between the writer and his environment or between his perceptions and the realities, or it may be due to hidden handicaps or tribal stigma. The dread of the stutterer, the lonely existence of the leper, the terror of the psychotic, the shame of the hard-of-hearing—these experiences, the reconciliation, and even the triumph are richly chronicled by sensitive, sharing people.

Condon (1972) is a psychotherapist and quadriplegic, dependent since college days on a motorized wheelchair. She provides insight into the benefit of written exploration of her feelings of loneliness and isolation in this quotation: "Epilogue: I began unsure of what questions would emerge. I end without any answers. Yet I feel content for I have stated my dilemma so that even I can see it more clearly" (p. 40).

Elizabeth Léonie Simpson (1982) is a professional writer whose brain and body were severly affected by tuberculosis. In her book about her rehabilitation she writes eloquently of the meaning of her creative writing:

> Life is more than the sum of words; but words strive after reality, help us to define it, and give it value. Why does a writer record if it is not to cheat fate, to hinder oblivion, to share and, therefore, to extend experience? Writing is the building of a relationship between the author/maker and the reader; it is a lessening of the distance between each person who suffers and the mind which reports of creates accounts of these sufferings. Direct confrontation of the suffering of others changes a person forever. The doors of possibility are suddenly widened. To write about despair or illness honestly is to begin to conquer them. It is not the event itself that is being communicated, but its acquisition and disposition by the participant, creative mind.
>
> Personal expression in any mode flounders before painful sovereign reality. Viewed as fantasy, it does not have to be confronted; but, as the record of experience, it creates another situation entirely; the fantasy is real, yet the observer, shaken, may have no means of evaluating its dimensions. When you are trying to understand what is there, everyday life can include too much reality and art not include enough to do more than hint at it. Writing, as a medium of art, is an intervention as well as a means of communication. I am trying to build my life today—not just to *re*construct it— by intervening in that reality. As Pirandello wrote, "A fact is like a sack; it won't stand up till you've put something in it." (pp. 6,7).†

THE READER'S RESPONSE

To be able to understand the unique contribution bibliotherapy makes it is useful to explore the nature of the interaction between the reader and the written product. A four-stage description of the process of response of the reader to a published work is suggested by Holland (1969) and supported by others (Shrodes, 1949):

1. Identification of the reader with the work (an affiliation with it).
2. Projection of the self into the work.

---

†Reprinted with permission from Simpson, E. L. Notes on an emergency: A journal of recovery. New York: Norton, 1982.

3. An emotional purging or catharsis.
4. Intellectual or conscious insight.

These stages are discussed in the following sections.

Stage 1: Identification-Affiliation

The affiliation of the client with the situation or character presented in the prescribed book facilitates the objectification and abstraction of the client's situation.

Clients can see that others have been in similar quandaries; they are not alone. They can project themselves into the situations depicted (thereby entering Stage 2) or they can pull back, saying, "My problem is really different" or "I am not quite like that character." (Alternatively, it may be the counselor who will supply the objectivity within the context of a subsequent therapy session).

A piece of literature gives deference to the client regarding the speed of the impact the reader wishes to experience. The process is self-paced; the client can always close the book or decide whether to affiliate or not to affiliate—the book can be put aside or studied further. Clinical experience, however, tends to substantiate a voraciousness on the part of troubled children and adults in consuming literature relevant to their problems (Le Unes, 1974; McWilliams, 1976; Mullins, 1975).

Stage 2: Projection of Self

Positive identification with characters can be very general. Witness the popularity of books about persons who have overcome great odds or endured uncommon hardships, such as Patricia Neal, Roy Campanella, or Christy Brown. But since in the literature of disability there are books written about very specific problems, a book and reader can be matched quite precisely. For example, Plummer's (1970) chronicle of mothering a child with osteogenesis imperfecta would give a parent facing this rather uncommon and uniquely demanding life situation a very appropriate character with whom to identify.

When working with clients who have been burdened with handicapping conditions (either their own or a family member's), therapists not having the disability may be perceived by clients as incapable of understanding the problem. The counselor, by word or attitude, wants to project an empathic attitude to convey a deep understanding of the client's circumstances. When the client has faced or faces an extraordinary crisis that the counselor has not shared, however, the relationship may suffer. The client may envy the counselor's good fortune. The client may legitimately be angry at attempts on the part of the counselor to understand the client's dilemma, when perhaps only those who have suffered similarly can do so. In such cases the positive identification with appropriate literary characters and situations of a client coping with serious disability may prevent a loss of credibility and a resulting negative transference on the part of the client toward the counselor.

Such a psychological impasse can be lessened by the use of nontraditional therapeutic arrangements. Self-help and therapist-led groups of clients confronted with similar problems have been enormously successful (Lieberman & Bormann, 1979; Seligman, 1982). Professionals who have coped with severe problems themselves may be less inclined to stimulate resistance such as denial, envy, and anger in their clients. Hence, talented disabled people are often motivated to enter the fields of rehabilitation, counseling, and psychology.

From the literature on attitudes toward the disabled, one can assume that for most professionals who work with troubled persons, an honest self-appraisal might lead to the following admissions: "Their problems seem overwhelming to me. I don't feel comfortable around them and don't know if I can help." "I am appalled at the continuing burden my client must bear." "I hope I am never in the same shoes. If I were, I'm not sure I would cope any better, or perhaps as well as my client does." "I can't identify with this client who faces such an unrelenting, life-long problem."

A counselor who conveys discomfort with the client's circumstances can, nevertheless, be supportive and honest, thereby establishing the trust with which the therapeutic relationship should begin. The initial step in resolving uncomfortable feelings around disabled or otherwise troubled persons is to become aware of one's internal reactions without self-accusation.

Mullins and Wolfe (1975) state:

> It is often gratuitous for even the most understanding friend, parent, teacher, or counselor to claim understanding of the burden which a handicapping condition places on those persons or their associates, or to foresee the many difficult challenges of their everyday lives. (p. 1)

In such instances the recommendation of literature articulating the thoughts, feelings, and experiences of parents of handicapped children or handicapped authors and those who write about them may be very effective.

In recognizing the limited empathy one may have for another's circumstances, it is honest and helpful for the mental health professional to say or convey in some way, "I really cannot fully appreciate your situation, since your problem is so unique to you, but I do know a book written by [or about] someone who also faced such a crisis. I would be pleased to give you the title and author if you think it would be helpful to you."

Stage 3: Emotional Catharsis

Naranjo and Ornstein (1971) have written,

As to the relationship between art and therapy as ways of expression and liberation, it may be said that art centers in the issue of expression, and therapy in that of removing blocks to expression, but any sharp boundary between the two processes can only be artificial. The shaman was at the same time an artist and healer, and today we seem to be entering a stage of decompartmentalization of disciplines through which we can understand their original unity. More specifically, art-education disciplines are becoming therapies, and therapy is seen as both an art (rather than a medical technique independent of the inner states of the 'patient') and a means of liberating the artist in the 'patient.' (p. 118)‡

Catharsis (emotional purging on the part of the client-reader) is a clinical goal most frequently stressed by therapists who treat troubled persons (Leedy, 1969; Wilson, 1951). Catharsis may be achieved after the reader has addressed his or her problem by choosing to read literature relevant to it (affiliation) and identified with characters and situations that are personally meaningful (projection).

Stage 4: Intellectual Insight and New Personal Integration

Bibliotherapy is an effective and enjoyable aid for those who may not be able to change substantially their situations but who can increase their own awareness and insight. For persons confronted with handicaps, their children's or their own, it may not be possible to alter or remove the disabling condition. What *can* be achieved are peace of mind and the sense of belonging, personal worth, and joy of life that should be the legacy of every human being.

The concepts of normalcy and health and of deviance and abnormality are relative. Perhaps they are differently weighted for those professionals who have chosen to work with those who are troubled and different. Certainly we are not in the business of obliterating pain and struggle in our clients, for that would be a futile task, but rather we can hope to support them as they reckon with their often burdensome reality.

---

‡From Naranjo, C., & Ornstein, R. E. *On the psychology of meditation.* Copyright © 1971 by Claudio Naranjo & Robert Ornstein. An Esalen Book. Reprinted by permission of Viking Penguin, Inc., New York.

MATCHING LITERATURE AND CLIENT

You glance at a thin, flat object made from a tree, as you are doing at this moment, and the voice of the author begins to speak inside your head. (Hello!)

Carl Sagan, *Dragons of Eden*

The Family System Approach

This volume is specifically addressed to mental health professionals who work with families of handicapped children. As noted elsewhere in this book, a handicapping condition impinges on the entire family system regardless of who possesses it.

Seligman and Meyerson (1982) attest to the use of bibliotherapy for all members of a family confronted with a handicapped child. They contend that judiciously selected readings can provide the parents, handicapped youngster, or normal siblings with inspiration, hope, and needed information. Counselors can expect that some parents of handicapped children will also be handicapped and that some exceptional conditions are hereditary.

In speaking of the impact of a deaf child upon the family, Schlesinger (1972) cautions that each parent and other member of the family must make an adjustment to the new realities that are thrust upon them. Further, this adjustment can be facilitated by appropriate guidance and counseling, but it cannot be rushed by platitudinous remarks from the various professionals with whom the parents are likely to come into contact. The counselor can, Schlesinger believes, make careful use of literature to facilitate that adjustment and to strengthen the counseling relationship.

Precautions in Choosing Reading Materials

Professionals have advised the exercise of caution in the use of bibliotherapy. Wylie and McWilliams (1965) discuss the negative effects they have encountered in counseling parents who have read materials about their children's problems. While they were most concerned with popular books, articles, and pamphlets discussing professional concerns, their cautions can also apply to some weightier literary works as well. They cite three main objections to the uncritical use of reading materials for therapeutic purposes:

1. The materials are often so brief as to be misleading.
2. They frequently include more than a parent can absorb emotionally or intellectually.

3. They may be written from the point of view of a specific philosophy that may conflict with what has been planned for a particular child.

Other dangers are also apparent in trade books. In fictional literature it may be that the author has no understanding of the real impact a given disability would have on his character. In others one finds miraculous cures or healing, totally unrealistic and apt to cruelly reinforce vain hopes and fantasies of the reader. Even nonfiction may be less than helpful. For example, a few persons who are both deaf and blind have made monumental contributions to the literature. Helen Keller and Robert Smithdas come to mind. However, such people cannot be used as examples to comfort either parents of handicapped children or handicapped children themselves. Many autobiographies and biographies are written by notable exceptions, who can be admired for their talent; but they are incomparable, handicapped or not. Either the hopes of parents of an ordinary handicapped child are falsely raised or parents are intimidated by accounts of others who seem to be coping so much better than they or upon whom fortune seems to smile so much more.

Therefore, the counselor should take heed of McWilliams' (1976) cogent conclusions:

> Once again, bibliotherapy does not simplify the clinician's responsibilities as reading material for parents is sometimes thought to do. Rather, the use of it requires that the clinician be well versed regarding the offerings in particular fields and that, initially, those things considered to be most objective, least misleading and biased, and most compatible with the overall treatment protocol being projected or carried out be made available. (p. 51)[5]

Selection of children's literature for families confronted with handicaps can be a joint counselor–parent enterprise. Literature about exceptional conditions can be used to promote understanding of all children—handicapped children, siblings, and friends who surround them. The use of a book that can further acceptance and understanding of differences and explores honest feelings and possible courses of action can be therapeutic as well.

Parental Use of Bibliotherapy with Children

It may also be beneficial to counsel parents in the use of bibliotherapy with their own children. (Please keep in mind that bibliotherapy, in keeping with our earlier definitions, can be construed as the sensitive

---

[5]Reprinted with permission from McWilliams, B. J. Various aspects of parent counseling. In E. Webster (Ed.), *Professional approaches with parents of handicapped children*. Springfield, Ill.: Charles C Thomas, 1976.

selection of reading matter and does not necessarily involve therapy). Stein (1974) has written an effective book designed to explore feelings about handicapped persons, with a parents' text and a child's text. Bettelheim (1977), in discussing parents reading helpful literature (fairy tales, in this case) aloud with their very young children, advises that it is always best to follow the child's lead. If the child does not take to a story, it has not evoked a meaningful response and should be dropped. He also feels that even if a parent should guess correctly why a child has become emotionally involved with a story, this knowledge is best kept to oneself.

> The young child's most important experiences and reactions are largely subconscious, and should remain so until he reaches a more mature age and understanding. It is always intrusive to interpret a person's unconscious thoughts, to make conscious what he wishes to keep preconscious, and this is especially true in the case of a child. . . . . If the parent indicates that he knows them already, the child is prevented from making the most precious gift to his parent of sharing with him what until then was secret and private to the child. (p. 19)

It has been suggested that creative writing by the client is an effective technique. Although there is an effort in mental health fields to emphasize health and normalcy rather than defects and disability, persons with extreme life problems need opportunity and encouragement to work through those problems that appear intransigent to them.

A number of family therapists have had their clients prepare written material of a more or less literary nature (Gurman, 1981). This may range from the simple drawing of a family tree to the preparation of a detailed family chronology. While most counselors will probably not wish to require a client bring "homework" to a session, they might use a less onerous approach. They can encourage the writing of free verse or a free association or description of a sad or beautiful event, fictional or factual, to be shared in a counseling session. An examination of the literature written by parents and by handicapped persons themselves seems to bear out the cathartic effect on them of chronicling their experiences.

Since the published literature indicates that handicapped individuals often profit from the exercise of written exploration of their feelings and experiences in relation to their marred lives, this technique might also be of value to children and to others who may never aspire to publish their work.

GUIDELINES FOR JUDGING A LITERARY WORK

Guidelines for the Representation of Exceptional Persons in Educational Material (National Center on Educational Media and Materials, undated) was written to aid publishers in producing and selecting educational materials that would fairly and positively portray exceptional persons. This publication suggests criteria by which a mental health professional might judge the appropriateness of a literary selection.

Guideline 1

In printed and nonprinted educational materials, 10 percent of the content should include or represent children or adults with an exceptional feature.

A bibliotherapeutic work should feature predominantly someone with whom the client can identify in a positive way. The exceptional conditions or problems may not be identical, but a theme of common concern must exist.

Guideline 2

Representation of persons with exceptional conditions should be included in materials at all levels (early childhood through adult) and in all areas of study, such as career education, guidance, health studies, language arts, vocational education, mathematics, physical education, science, and social studies.

This guideline serves to remind the counselor that books selected may highlight many kinds of subject matter in which a reader might find interest. Besides being about handicapped persons, biographies and autobiographies, for example, are about physicists, philosophers, physicians, sports figures, explorers, politicians, and so forth.

Guideline 3

The representation of persons with exceptional features should be accurate and free from stereotypes.

The professional must be sensitive to literature that unrealistically either elevates or demeans the handicapped person, putting him or her beyond the pale of ordinary existence. Such a tendency is all too frequent in mass publications such as in comic books (Weinberg & Rossini, 1978).

Guideline 4

Persons with exceptionalities should be shown in the least restrictive environment. They should be shown participating in activities in a manner that will include them as part of society.

Some literature of a few decades ago espoused the then-prevailing belief in segregation and institutionalization as opposed to normalization and mainstreaming of handicapped persons. Such literature would not be considered appropriate by most counselors today.

Guideline 5

In describing persons with exceptional conditions, the language used should be nondiscriminatory and free from value judgments.

Counselors should be sensitive to patronizing, pitying, or overcheerful tones in books. Such qualities may not always be avoidable, but positive and negative aspects of a work should be weighed and discussed with the reader.

Guideline 6

Persons with exceptional features and persons without them should be shown interacting in ways that are mutually beneficial.

Literature that emphasizes mutual interaction and respect (in which others are not always depicted doing *for* or *to* persons confronted with handicaps) should be selected.

Guideline 7

Materials should provide a variety of appropriate role models of persons with exceptional conditions.

It would not be helpful to recommend a book portraying the success of parents of enormous means in rehabilitating their child to parents who have meager resources. Similarly, it may be counterproductive to have the parents of an ordinary blind or crippled child read of the success of Helen Keller or Charles Steinmetz.

Guideline 8

Emphasis should be on uniqueness and worth of all persons, rather than on the difference between persons with and without exceptional features.

The tone of the work selected should foster an attitude of "one of us" rather than "one of them." The language should imply that deviances, disabilities, and differences are a part of, not apart from, our society and our common human condition.

Guideline 9

Tokenism should be avoided in the representation of persons with exceptional features.

Some ingenuity may be required to find literature not limited to the deaf, blind, physicially handicapped, or mentally retarded. With diligence, materials can be found portraying all types and levels of physical and behavioral variation.

PROCEDURES FOR USE OF BIBLIOTHERAPY

Steps Taken with Clients

While these may vary from person to person, a few general strategies are summarized:

1. Identify a problem about which the client might like to read.
2. Familiarize oneself with literature that might be appropriate in terms of subject matter, the realism and sensitivity of the work, reading level, and level of sophistication. A book should not be recommended unless the counselor is familiar with it.
3. Orient the client to the work. The counselor should discuss the book with the client, telling him or her why it might be a good selection. If a book has been chosen for a parent to read to a child or to suggest for a child, the counselor should discuss with the parents their subsequent orientation of the child to the work.
4. Be available to discuss the work, and make this explicit to the client. If the book is for a child, the counselor should discuss the kinds of questions the parents can anticipate as well as the answers they might offer.

In her discussion of the use of bibliotherapy in counseling parents of exceptional children, McWilliams (1976) underscores this last point: "In addition to these precautions, the parents should be given the opportunity to discuss what they have read and to resolve any conflicts that may have resulted. This interaction with a knowledgeable person should be available also to the parent who seeks and reads on his own, perhaps with insufficient background to be discriminating" (p. 51).

It is a testimony to the power of the technique of bibliotherapy that it must be used with care by those mental health workers, teachers, and others who are in a position to help families confronted with handicaps.

Locating Appropriate Literature

Locating appropriate literature for clients is a challenge for the counselor. Part of the problem has to do with the practices of publishers of literature, both literary and educational, and of works for children and adults.

Bettelheim (1981) decries the failure of stories in children's textbooks in America to address important issues that confront all children. Rather, he says, life in many of these books is nothing but a succession of pleasurable activities at the shallowest level. "If a child takes what he reads seriously, he comes to think his own family is terrible, because no family can live up to the expectations about typical family living raised by these stories" (p. 31).

If this is the situation for relatively normal children, the problem is surely compounded for the family confronted with handicaps. In fact, educational materials and trade books, through neglect and thoughtlessness, seldom portray handicapped persons at all; and where they do so, they often perpetuate stereotypical images and false beliefs. The search for appropriate literature is strongly recommended, however, and counselors should consider undertaking the responsibility to locate literature relevant and appropriate to their clients.

Counselors and teachers whose clients have disabilities must perforce become advocates and resource persons for them:

> It cannot be assumed that other professionals, such as social workers or physicians, actually know or will communicate what resources are available, what benefits are due to disability groups, and what information is available, even though these may relate closely to their professional interests. (Mullins, 1979b, p. 380)

Available Resources

Libraries, public health agencies, universities, and authors of many books in special education and counseling annotate comprehensive lists of names and addresses of organizations serving disability groups. Many of these organizations have extensive bibliographies and often produce literature, films, and the like of interest to their clients.

The members of the Association of Hospital and Institution Libraries have had a long-term interest in bibliotherapy for children through publications and workshops. A subcommittee studying the troubled child yielded nine annotated lists, including a section on adjusting to physical handicaps and several more on various social and emotional problems confronting children (Association of Hospital and Institution Libraries, 1971).

Mullins and Wolfe (1975) have compiled a bibliography classified by handicapping conditions. Their collection includes trade books, indicating appropriate reading level, from preschool through adult, and separates fiction from nonfiction. This reference is valuable in alerting people to many literary offerings available that can be suggested by mental health professionals.

Dreyer (1981) developed *The Bookfinder: A Guide to Children's Literature about the Needs and Problems of Youth,* a reference work that describes and categorizes 1031 current children's books according to more than 450 psychological, behavioral, and developmental topics of concern to children and young adolescents ages 2 through 15. Dreyer says of the book, "It is written primarily for parents, teachers, librarians, counselors, psychologists, psychiatrists, and other adults who want to identify books that may help children cope with the challenges of life. In short, the *Bookfinder* was created to fill the need for a way to match children and books" (p. ix).

Baskin and Harris' (1977) book evaluates juvenile fiction written between 1940 and 1975 portraying the handicapped. The sensitive reviews of such literature can help the professional helper decide whether a certain book might be of benefit.

Fassler (1978) reviewed contemporary children's literature to find books and stories to be used to help children grow, to reduce fears and anxieties, and to initiate open, honest communication between children and adults. The sections dealing with death, separation, hospitalization, and illness are pertinent for handicapped children and their siblings.

Lass and Bromfield (1981) identify factors to be considered in selecting a book about handicaps. In addition, they provide an up-to-date selection of good books to be used with children.

Landau, Epstein, and Stone (1978) have compiled a book of short stories with characters who are physically and behaviorally impaired to be used in a structured manner. The accompanying text of suggestions for planning a program and formulating discussion topics is intended to aid the teacher or mental health worker to develop positive attitudes, understanding, and familiarity with various exceptional conditions.

Illustrative Bibliographies

A book should help us either to enjoy life or to endure it.

Samuel Johnson

There has been an increasing body of adult literature for parents of handicapped children and about handicapped people almost too extensive for a bibliographer to keep up with. Any counselor will undoubtedly build up a personal list or library of the kinds of books from which clients might be likely to profit. The appendices of this chapter list selective bibliographies for counselors, parents, and young people.

REFERENCES

Amato, A. J. *Some effects of bibliotherapy on young adults.* Unpublished doctoral dissertation, Pennsylvania State University, 1957.

Association of Hospital and Institutional Libraries. *Bibliotherapy: Methods and materials.* Chicago: American Library Association, 1971.

Baskin, B. H., & Harris, K. H. *Notes from a different drummer: A guide to juvenile fiction portraying the handicapped.* New York: R.R. Bowker, 1977.

Bass, D. L. *A comparison of Eastern bibliotherapy and Western bibliotherapy in counselor effectiveness.* (Doctoral dissertation, East Texas State University, 1976.) *Dissertation Abstracts International,* 1977, *37,* 6947. (University Microfilms No. 77-09, 621)

Bettelheim, B. *The uses of enchantment: The meaning and importance of fairy tales.* New York: Vantage Books, 1977.

Bettelheim, B. Our children are treated like idiots. *Psychology Today,* 1981, *15,* 28–44.

Blocher, D. H. Human ecology and the future of counseling psychology. *The Counseling Psychologist,* 1982, *9,* 69–77.

Carnegie Quarterly, 1974, *22,*(4). Carnegie Corporation of New York.

Condon, M. A place for an unpaired person. *Voices: The Art and Science of Psychotherapy.* American Academy of Psychotherapists, Spring 1972, pp. 40–42.

Crothers, S. M. A library critic. *Atlantic Monthly,* 1916, *118,* 291–301.

Dreyer, S. S. *The bookfinder: A guide to children's literature about the needs and problems of youth aged 2–15.* Circle Pines, Minn.: American Guidance Service, Inc., 1981.

Good, C. V. (Ed.). *Dictionary of Education* (Series in Education). New York: McGraw-Hill, 1959.

Edgar, K. F., Hazley, R., & Levitt, H. I. Poetry therapy with hospitalized schizophrenics. In J. J. Leedy (Ed.), *Poetry therapy: The use of poetry in the treatment of emotional disorders.* Philadelphia: Lippincott, 1969.

Fassler, J. *Helping children cope: Mastering stress through books and stories.* New York: Free Press, 1978.

Gurman, A. S. (Ed.). *Questions and answers in family therapy.* New York: Brunner/Mazel, 1981.

Holland, N. *The dynamics of literary response.* New York: Oxford Press, 1969.

Kubie, L. S. *Neurotic distortion of the creative process.* New York: Noonday Press, 1961.

Landau, E. D., Epstein, S. L., & Stone, A. P. *The exceptional child through literature.* Englewood Cliffs, N.J.: Prentice-Hall, 1978.

Lass, B. & Bromfield, M. Books about children with special needs: An annotated bibliography. *Reading Teacher,* 1981, *34,*(5), 530–533.

Leedy, J. (Ed.). *Poetry therapy: The use of poetry in the treatment of emotional disorders.* Philadelphia: Lippincott, 1969.

Leedy, J. *Poetry, the healer.* Philadelphia: Lippincott, 1973.

Le Unes, A. Psychological thrillers revisited: A tentative list of 'Master Thrillers.' *American Psychologist,* 1974, *29*(3), 211–213.

Lieberman, M. A., & Borman, L. D. *Self help groups for coping with crisis.* San Francisco: Jossey-Bass, 1979.

McClasky, H. *Bibliotherapy with emotionally disturbed patients: An experimental study.* (Doctoral dissertation, University of Washington, 1970.) *Dissertation Abstracts International,* 1970, *31,* 5205A. (University Microfilms No. 71-08, 523).

McGuire, A. Library program at Case Elementary School. *American Library Association,* 1969.

McWilliams, B. J. Various aspects of parent counseling. In E. Webster (Ed.), *Professional approaches with parents of handicapped children.* Springfield, Ill: Charles C Thomas, 1976.

Mullins, J. B. *Bibliotherapy for people in quandaries.* Urbana, Ill.: *National Center for Teacher Education, 1975. (ERIC Clearinghouse on Reading and Communication Skill).*

Mullins, J. B. *A teachers' guide to management of physically handicapped students.* Springfield, Ill.: Charles C Thomas, 1979. (a)

Mullins, J. B. Making language work to eliminate handicapism. *Education Unlimited,* 1979, *1,*(2), 20–24. (b)

Mullins, J. B. & Wolfe, S. *Special people behind the 8 ball: An annotated bibliotherapy of literature classified by handicapping conditions.* Johnston, Pa.: Mafex Associates, 1975.

Naranjo, C., & Ornstein, R. E. *On the psychology of meditation.* New York: Viking Press, 1971.

National Center on Educational Media and Materials for the Handicapped. *Guidelines for the representation of exceptional persons in educational media.* Westerville, Ohio, no date.

Osthoff, F. I. *Accurate empathy in helping profession trainees as related to reading experiences.* Unpublished doctoral dissertation, University of Illinois at Urbana, 1970. *Dissertation Abstracts International,* 1971, *31,* 4471A. (University Microfilms No. 71-05, 191)

Paterson, K. *The great Gilly Hopkins.* New York: Harper & Row, 1978.

Paterson, K. *The word: Language in children's books.* Presentation at the 1981 Fall Festival of Books, Carnegie Library, Pittsburgh, Pa., November 6, 1981.

Plummer, B. *Give every day a chance.* New York: Putnam Books, 1970.

Purves, A. C., & Beach, R. *Literature and the reader: Research in response to literature, reading interests and the teaching of literature.* Final report to the National Endowment for the Humanities, Project #H69-0-129, University of Illinois at Urbana-Champaign, January 1972.

Russell, D. H., & Shrodes, C. Contributions of research in bibliotherapy to a language arts program. *School Review,* 1950, *58,* 335–342.

Schlesinger, H. S. Diagnostic crisis and its participants. *Deafness Annual, 2,* 1972, 29–34.

Seligman, M. (Ed.). *Group psychotherapy and counseling with special populations.* Baltimore, MD: University Park Press, 1982.

Seligman, M., & Meyerson, R. Group approaches for parents of exceptional children. In M. Seligman (Ed.), *Group psychotherapy and counseling with special populations.* Baltimore, Md.: University Park Press, 1982.

Shrank, F. *A semantic differentiated study concerning attitude change of fourth grade children toward slow learning children utilizing imaginative literature as a psychological field.* Unpublished educational specialist thesis, University of Tennessee, 1977.

Shrank, F. A., & Engels, D. W. Bibliotherapy as counseling adjunct: Research findings. *Personnel and Guidance Journal,* 1981, *60,* 143–147.

Shrodes, C. *Bibliotherapy: A theoretical and clinical study.* Unpublished doctoral dissertation, University of California at Berkeley, 1949.

Simpson, E. L. *Notes on an emergency: A journal of recovery.* New York: Norton, 1982.

Stein, S. B. *About handicaps: An open family book for parents and children together.* New York: Walker, 1974.

Strassler, M. G. For the handicapped. *Library Journal,* 1974, *99,* p. 2200.

Webster, E. (Ed.). *Professional approaches with parents of handicapped children.* Springfield, Ill.: Charles C Thomas, 1976.

Webster's Third New International Dictionary. Springfield, MA: G. & C. Merriam, 1968.

Weinberg, N., & Rossini, S. Comic books: Champions of the disabled stereotype. *Rehabilitation Literature,* 1978, *39,* 327–331.

Wilson, J. W. Treatment of an attitudinal pathosis by bibliotherapy: A case study. *Journal of Clinical Psychology,* 1951, *7,* 345–351.

Wolfenstein, M., & Kliman, G. *Children and the death of a president.* New York: Doubleday, 1965.

Wylie, H. L., & McWilliams, B. J. Guidance materials for parents of children with clefts. *Cleft Palate Journal, 2,* 1965, 123.

Wylie, H. L., & McWilliams, B. J. Mental health aspects of cleft palate: A review of literature intended for parents. *ASHA, 8,* 1966, 31. Vol. 8 #2 Feb. 1966 p. 31–34.

Zaccaria, J. S., & Moses, H. A. *Facilitating human development through reading: The use of bibliotherapy in teaching and counseling.* Champaign, Ill.: Stipes, 1968.

APPENDIX A: BOOKS FOR PROFESSIONALS

These books are intended to help professionals develop (1) an understanding of the circumstances surrounding exceptional parenthood, (2) a greater awareness of the complex nature of parent–professional relationships, and (3) productive communication skills helpful in working with parents.

Arnold, L. E. (Ed.). *Helping parents help their children.* New York: Brunner/Mazel, 1978.

Berger, E. H. *Parents as partners in education—the school and home working together.* St. Louis: C.V. Mosby, 1981.

Chin, P. C., Winn, J., & Walters, R. H. *Two-way talking with parents of special children.* St. Louis: C.V. Mosby, 1978.

Michaelis, C. T. *Home and school partnership in exceptional education.* Rockville, Md.: Aspen, 1980.

Paul, J. L. (Ed.). *Understanding and working with parents of children with special needs.* New York: Holt, Rinehart & Winston, 1981.

Seligman, M. *Strategies for helping parents of exceptional children: A guide for teachers.* New York: Free Press, 1979.

APPENDIX B: BOOKS TO HELP PARENTS COPE

Aspar, V., & Beck, J. *Is my baby all right?* New York: Pocket Books, 1972.

Ayrault, E. V. *Helping the handicapped teenager mature.* New York: Association Press, 1971. (A guide to common problems, this book includes listings of directories of rehabilitation services, camps, colleges, and universities accepting the physically handicapped.)

Brutten, M., Richardson, S., & Mangel, C. *Something's wrong with my child.* New York: Harcourt Brace Jovanovich, 1973. (Practical information on various aspects of raising a child with learning disabilities.)

Finnie, N. R. *Handling the young cerebral palsied child at home.* New York: E.P. Dutton, 1975.

Heisler, V. *A handicapped child in the family: A guide for parents.* New York: Grune & Stratton, 1972. (A handicapped professional author frankly and perceptively discusses what it means to be the parent of a handicapped child.)

Henderson, M., & Synhorst, D. *Care of the infant with myelomeningocele and hydrocephalus: A guide for parents.* Iowa City: University of Iowa Press, 1975.

Strauss, S. *Is it well with the child? A parent's guide to raising a mentally handicapped child.* New York: Doubleday, 1975. (A professional writer tells of her own experiences as the parent of a mentally handicapped child and gives general advice for parents and professionals.)

Ulrich, S. (with Wolf, A. W. M.). *Elizabeth.* Ann Arbor: University of Michigan Press, 1972. (A mother describes the first five years of her blind child's life and provides many useful ideas for home care.)

APPENDIX C: BOOKS WRITTEN BY PARENTS

Brown, H. *Yesterday's child*. New York: New American Library, 1976. (A mother writes openly about the emotions and realities she faced in raising her multiply handicapped daughter.)

Featherstone, H. *A difference in the family: Living with a disabled child*. New York: Basic Books, 1980. (A professional exceptional parent writes about her profoundly handicapped child and her experiences with other parents who have similar problems.)

Greenfield, J. *A child called Noah*. New York: Warner Paperback, 1973. (A father writes of the family's experiences in coping with their autistic son.)

Gunther, J. *Death be not proud*. New York: Harper & Row, 1979. (A father's story of his brave and spirited boys' fight against a brain tumor.)

Massie, R. & Massie, S. *Journey*. New York: Knopf, 1975. (Parents write of their son's chronic, debilitating disease, hemophilia, and have much to say to families of children with other handicapping conditions.)

Park, C. C. *The seige: The first eight years of an autistic child*. Smythe, 1967. (A mother writes sensitively about raising her autistic daughter.)

Turnbull, A., & Turnbull, H. *Parents speak out: Views from the other side of the two way mirror*. Columbus, Ohio: Charles Merrill, 1978. (Insights from professional parents of handicapped children.)

West, P. *Words for a deaf daughter*. New York: Harper & Row, 1970. (Novelist-poet-critic tells the story of his brain-damaged daughter.)

White, R. *Be not afraid*. New York: The Dial Press, 1972. (A father chronicles his family's 14 years following the diagnosis of epilepsy in his eight-year-old son.)

APPENDIX D: BOOKS FOR CHILDREN AND YOUTH

Probable reading and interest level of these books is given below, although some coded for children and youth may be suitable for adults, and some books considered adult literature may be of interest to younger readers.

Preschool level. Books that can be read aloud to children ages 2–5, usually with pictures that also tell the story.

Primary level. Books that can be read aloud or by beginning readers, of interest to kindergarten through third graders. Usually illustrated.

Elementary level. Books on a third- to eighth-grade level of interest and reading.

Intermediate level. Books on approximately a seventh- through ninth-grade reading level.

Youth. Books of interest to those of high school age (and often to adults) with a relatively uncomplicated literary style.

Campanella, R. *It's good to be alive.* Boston: Little Brown, 1959. (The well-known baseball star tells of his life after being paralyzed as a result of an automobile accident.) *(Youth)*

Gordon, S. *Living fully: A guide for young people with a handicap, their parents, their teachers and professionals.* New York: John Day, 1975. (This special educator has a no-nonsense and compassionate approach to disabled kids.) *(Youth)*

Griese, A. A. *At the mouth of the luckiest river.* New York: Crowell, 1969. (Tatlek, the hero, is an Athabascan Indian child in Alaska who has an orthopedic handicap but deals with this difference in natural, pragmatic fashion.) *(Elementary)*

Hickok, L. A. *The story of Helen Keller.* New York: Grosset & Dunlap, 1958. (A biography of the famous deaf woman.) *(Elementary* and *Intermediate)*

Kellogg, M. *Tell me that you love me Junie Moon.* New York: Farrar, Straus, & Giroux, 1968. (A group of "rejects" leave the rehabilitation institution and learn to live and love in the world. *(Youth)*

Krents, H. *To race the wind.* New York: G.P. Pulnarus, 1972. (An autobiography of an undaunted blind young man, both moving and humorous. *(Youth)*

Ominsky, E. *Jon O. A special boy.* Englewood Cliffs, N.J.: Prentice-Hall, 1977. (Photographs and text describe the life of a young boy with Down's syndrome.) *(Preschool* and *Primary)*

Robinson, V. *David in silence.* Philadelphia: Lippincott, 1966. (A deaf boy in industrial Birmingham, England has many adventures, and his thoughts and feelings are sensitively chronicled in this story.) *(Intermediate* and *Youth)*

Sobol, H. L. *My brother Steven is retarded.* New York: Macmillan, 1977. (The photographs and text tell a poignant and sensitive story from the perspective of a younger sister.) *(Elementary)*

Southall, I. *Let the balloon go.* New York: St. Martin's, 1968. (This compelling story portrays an intelligent, imaginative boy with cerebral palsy in Australia as he learns to assert himself and overcome the expectations of family and peers.) *(Elementary* and *Intermediate)*

Warfield, F. *Keep listening.* New York: Viking Press, 1957. (The author tells of her struggles as a hard-of-hearing adolescent.) *(Youth)*

White, P. *Janet at school.* New York: Crowell, 1978. (Text and photographs portray appealing five-year-old Janet, who has spina bifida, in many school experiences.) *(Preschool* and *Primary)*

10

Individual Counseling with Parents of Handicapped Children: Rationale and Strategies

PETER RANDELL LABORDE
MILTON SELIGMAN

BIOGRAPHICAL SKETCH

Peter Randell Laborde is Research Graduate Assistant in the Rehabilitation Counseling Program at the University of Pittsburgh. Prior to returning to the University of Pittsburgh for doctoral study he was Program Director of the Pennsylvania Direction Service, a federal research and demonstration project designed to learn how best to match families with handicapped children with appropriate human services.

Mr. Laborde is principal author of the Pennsylvania Model Individual Individual Written Program Plan for Vocational Rehabilitation Programs *written for the Pennsylvania Department of Public Welfare and* Resource Manual: Information and Referral *written for the Pennsylvania Department of Education.*

Milton Seligman, Ph.D. is a professor in rehabilitation counseling at the University of Pittsburgh. A former editorial board member of the Journal for Specialists in Group Work, *Dr. Seligman at present serves on the editorial board of the* Personnel and Guidance Journal.

He has edited or authored books and articles in the areas of group counseling and psychotherapy and of working with parents of exceptional children. A recent work, Group Psychotherapy and Counseling with Special Populations *was published in 1982. An earlier book on parents was entitled* Strategies for Helping Parents of Exceptional Children: A Guide for Teachers.

Dr. Seligman teaches courses in individual and group counseling as well as courses in clinical supervision and working with parents or exceptional children.

ISBN 0-8089-1561-4
Copyright © 1983 by Grune & Stratton

C HILDREN can be born with or develop a vast array of disabling conditions. Estimates of the number of disabled children and youth have been as high as 12 percent of the population (Brewer and Kakalik, 1979). While accurate information of the actual incidence of disabling conditions is not currently available, one can be certain that the number of children who are disabled in some way is quite high.

The conditions that result in a handicap are complex and diverse and their manifestations are not always apparent. Some handicapping conditions are readily apparent and can even be detected prior to birth. Others may not become known for months or years or even until the child begins attending school. As a consequence of illness or of physical trauma, handicapping conditions may occur at any time in a person's life. Handicapping conditions include deficits in cognitive development, perception, sensory acuity, neurologic functioning, expressive or receptive language, behavior control, memory, or other areas. A handicap may consist of one or more functional deficits.Handicapping conditions can vary markedly in the degree to which they impair functioning. The child who is handicapped to a mild degree faces different obstacles than the child who is moderately or severely handicapped by the same condition (see Chapter 7 and Chapter 8). Families may suffer serious consequences from a child's handicap regardless of the type or severity of the condition if not treated early and appropriately. We believe that individual counseling with parents is one form of intervention that is well suited to helping parents of handicapped children deal with their unique circumstances.

PROFESSIONALS WHO COUNSEL PARENTS

It is essential that conseling be a helping process for parents. Misguided or inneffective counseling pursued for too long may make counseling unnacceptable to parents in the future when it might be even more critical for their adjustment (Freeman & Pearson, 1978). Parents of children with disabling conditions typically come into contact with a wide range of professionals and can develop a rather cynical view of those who offer help. Some of the reasons for the tension that exists between parents and professionals are discussed in some detail by Darling in Chapter 4. However, several salient issues relevant to parent–professional relationships deserve attention here.

Professionals with varying backgrounds are called upon to provide counseling to parents. Physicians who make the initial diagnosis of disability, ministers who are consulted in an hour of need, therapists who attempt to intervene during personal difficulties, and educators who teach the disabled child may be called upon to provide supportive or in-depth counseling to parents. A broad range of professionals, then, functions in a helping capacity to parents of disabled children. The need for trained professionals to assist parents will become even greater in the future as the public policies of mainstreaming and normalization act to keep disabled children in the community.

There is a growing number of reports related to the training, experience, and attitudinal deficiencies of professionals who work with parents. Fox (1975) observes that "some parents react to [meetings with professionals] so strongly that individual meetings with professionals and group staffings become major traumatic events to be dreaded and avoided" (p. 36). Wolraich (1982) notes that physicians are often ill-prepared to work with parents. Some of the factors that impede physician–parent communication are (1) the physician's inadequate knowledge of developmental disabilities (2) the physician's negative attitude toward handicapped children, and (3) the physician's inept skills in communicating with parents. Wolraich believes that all three factors are interrelated: deficiencies is one area affect the physician's abilities in other areas.

The areas of deficiency that Wolraich believes are important considerations for physicians can easily be attributed to other professionals as well. It should be noted, however, that the parent–physician relationship in particular has been under considerable scrutiny in recent years (Darling & Darling, 1982; Guralnick, 1980; Howard, 1982; Jacobs & Walker, 1978; Powers & Healy, 1982), whereas in the 1970s the major emphasis was on the parent–teacher relationship (Chin, Winn, & Walters, 1978, Kroth, 1975; Seligman, 1979).

In terms of the personal feelings and attitudes of professionals, Seligman and Seligman (1980) note the following professional factors that account for the adversarial relationship with parents:

1. Feelings of sympathy, pity, fear, or hostility toward parents.
2. A pervasive feeling of hopelessness or hostility about the parent's situation.
3. Overidentification with the parents' circumstances, which reinforces parental denial.
4. Viewing parents' observations as untrustworthy and meaningless.
5. Viewing parents as emotionally disturbed.

Ross (1964) states unequivocally that professionals who work with parents should have certain qualities:

A mental health professional may be able to develop these in the course of closely supervised experience but some people lack these qualities in sufficient measure that they should probably not enter a profession whose central task is helping other people. No amount of exhortation can make a rejecting person accepting, a frigid person warm, a narrow-minded person understanding. Those charged with the selection, education and training of new members of the helping professions will need to keep in mind that the presence or absence of certain personality characteristics makes the difference between a truly helpful professional and one who leaves a trace of misery and confusion in the wake of his activities. (pp. 75–76)

To be able to effectively engage in counseling with parents, it is essential that the professional's characteristics, attitudes, and biases be taken into consideration *and* that he or she be trained in the rudiments of counseling, at minimum. This view has gained the support of professionals representing several disciplines (Bissell, 1976; Kroth, 1975; McWilliams, 1976; Paul, 1981; Reynolds & Birch, 1982; Seligman, 1979).

FACTORS THAT AFFECT PARENTAL REACTIONS

Professionals who work with a potentially troubled human system (in this case, the family) must recognize the many complex and interacting variables that affect psychological adjustment. Many of these factors are discussed in other chapters. Those that are particularly amenable to individual counseling are the focus of this section.

The perceptions of others contribute to the degree of impact the handicapped child has upon the family. A study of parents of children with cystic fibrosis found that half of the parents perceived community attitudes as negative and as a result felt some degree of social isolation (Meyerwitz & Kaplan, 1967). Walker (1971) found that mothers of children with spina bifida expressed concern about exposing their child to normal children *and* to more severely disabled children as this might adversely affect their child. Parents also have differing perceptions about their child based on their experiences and expectations of disabled and nondisabled children. Indeed, Darling and Darling (1982) observed that parents of handicapped children often harbor *negative* attitudes toward deviance that resemble those held by the general public. As a result, parents experience quite a jolt when a handicapped child is born. Not only must parents deal with their feelings about their handicapped offspring, but they must also confront their previously held negative attitudes toward those who are different.

Parents have a need to understand what happened to their child; what the condition is; why it occurred (this is not always known); how it can be treated; and what the prognosis is. Answers to their questions should be given in a factual *and* compassionate manner, with the child's strengths and weaknesses both addressed. Fellendorf and Harrow (1969) reported that only one-half of the parents they surveyed expressed satisfaction with the manner in which the diagnosis of their child's handicap was conveyed. Parents have reported incidents in which inaccurate information was presented in a harsh and uncaring manner. Springer and Steele (1980) reported that a majority of parents of children diagnosed as having Down's syndrome felt that physicians were unduly pessimistic in their assessment of their child's potential. While professionals must be careful not to paint an unrealistically rosy picture regarding a child's future, they must be equally wary against burdening parents with negative prospects for their child's development, especially when the child's future development is equivocal. In such instances, contact with a professional only leads to needless anguish.

As stated previously, not all handicaps are identified immediately. Parents may not become aware that their child is experiencing difficulties until months or years after birth. Many parents are not knowledgeable about developmental milestones and thus may not realize that their child is experiencing delays in development (Jordan, 1971). When a disability is detected later, parents may experience difficulty in perceiving their child as "handicapped" having for some time perceived their child as "normal."

Barsch (1969) describes parents of handicapped children as falling into one of two categories: parents who become aware soon after the birth of their child that the child has special needs, and parents who discover their child's special needs at a later point in the child's development. Barsch states that the second category of parents is presented with special challenges, as these parents must undergo gradual changes in their thinking about their child and about themselves. These changes often occur concurrently with the child's adjustment to new and, at times, traumatic experiences, such as starting school. Professionals should be aware of the confusion that parents experience in feeling that their child is not developing normally, while lacking information about the nature of their child's problem. This confusion, compounded by the normal, everyday problems of parenthood, can be most distressing to parents. The couselor can be of assistance at this time by being a source of emotional support and as a provider and clarifier of information.

Accurate information is of paramount importance to the parent of a handicapped child. Parents do not expect professionals to have complete knowledge of the handicapping condition, although they do expect rudimentary knowledge (Schwartz, 1970); but, as noted earlier, parents are very concerned about *how* information is provided (Pueschel and Murphy, 1976). For example, Telford and Sawrey (1981) quote a mother who characterized her professional conferences as "a masterful combination of dishonesty, condescension, misinformation and bad manners" (p. 143).

The mental health professional can help parents cope with the initial period of ambiguity until a definitive identification of the child's handicap is made (assuming that an informed explanation can be made at all). Information, even if inconclusive, must be presented in a compassionate, empathic, personal way that conveys the professional's concern to parents.

Shopping for Services

Once informed of their child's handicap, parents often wish to have further evaluations of their child. Professionals frequently view this desire as a form of denial in which parents search for a "cure" to their child's condition. This parental behavior may not, however, be as common as the literature would suggest. Keirn (1971) investigated the prevalence of "shopping" behavior by parents and concluded that it is an overstated problem. Only three percent of the parents in Keirn's study were considered to be "shoppers." Seeking opinions from other professionals is an option that the parents have a right and often a need to exercise. Indeed, as Seligman and Seligman (1980) note, parents may wish another opinion, or they may want to have the initial diagnosis or current problems reviewed, especially as the child achieves certain developmental milestones and the nature of the handicap changes. Also parents may "shop" because they feel they have been treated with little respect by professionals. They wish to see professionals who both have the required expertise and treat them compassionately. Keirn (1971) also found that parents who shop for services often are looking for evaluations that will permit their child to receive services provided to children with specific diagnoses.

On the other hand, Davidson and Schrag (1968) found that over half of the recommendations presented as part of a psychological consultation were not carried out by parents. This lack of follow-through by parents may be a consequence of parental denial. Alternatively, it may either be the result of misunderstanding on the part of the parents as to what is expected of them or reflect disagreement with the professional's judgment as to what is best for their child. Davidson and Schrag (1968) found that parents were much more inclined to follow recommendations that were mutually agreed upon. The mental health professional, acting as a broker, can help parents understand recommendations made in behalf of their child and can assist the parent in negotiating with professionals. If agreement between parent and professional can be achieved, the likelihood of treatment implementation should increase.

Gorham, Des Jardins, Page, Pettis, and Scheiber (1975) surveyed 500 parents whose children were identified as handicapped and found that 56 percent of the children had been labeled at different times with different diagnoses. The authors indicate that this multiple labeling is a major source of parental frustration. Adroit parents may shop for "good" labels that may help their child obtain needed services to replace "bad" labels that deny their child entrance into highly regarded but limited-enrollment programs. Professionals must determine why parents shop before they conclude that denial is the motivating factor. If parents are, in fact, denying the existence of their child's condition, the counselor can assist the parent in recognizing this, especially if parental denial is having an adverse effect upon the child. If they shop for services because of the desire to obtain the best possible treatment for the child and they have a realistic appraisal of the child's condition, professionals should assist parents in establishing a plan of action that will accomplish this desired goal.

Related Factors Affecting Family Functioning

Parenting any child is a challenging endeavor. As noted previously, parents of handicapped children experience challenges that other parents may not face. For instance, parents may not receive cues or feedback from their child that provides them with negative as well as positive reinforcement regarding their actions as parents (Hart, 1970). This lack of feedback may result in reduced interaction with their child. Decreased interaction limits the opportunities the child has of developing necessary social skills that are typically learned from parents, and the child may experience a diminished sense of self-worth. A vicious circle of limited parent–child interaction results—one that is difficult to disrupt. It is important for the sake of both the child and the parent to break this pattern as early as possible. Much progress has been made in the past several years in providing early intervention and infant stimulation programs. Early intervention programs can help parents counteract the parent–child distancing that has negative implications for child development (Brassel, 1977).

Increased marital conflict may accompany the presence of a handicapped child in the family. Ross (1964) believes that latent conflicts in the family may erupt with the added stress of providing for a mentally retarded child. The child is often not the cause of these conflicts—the potential for conflict may lie within the pre-existing structure of family relationships. The counselor can help parents distinguish such family problems from those arising from their feelings toward their handicapped child. Parents may need help in realistically appraising their circumstances. While it is true that a handicapped child can disrupt family equilibrium, parents can be helped to become more aware of the causes of their frustration and so learn to diffuse it with more gratifying activities. If the counselor senses that the parents unrealistically intend to devote their lives to their handicapped child, he or she should help them examine their own needs, such as professional development and leisure-time pursuits.

Mothers may feel special stress from raising a handicapped child. Love (1970) notes that mothers of handicapped children may experience jealousy toward other mothers who do not have a handicapped child. Mothers of the disabled not only are reminded that their children are different from others but also anticipate more extended periods as primary caregivers than other mothers. If a handicapping condition is severe, mothers generally perceive their caretaker role as perpetual, and their future may appear bleak as they anticipate increased hardship during their child's later years. Cummings, Bayley, and Rie (1966) found that mothers with a mentally retarded child had significantly greater feelings of depression, were more preoccupied, and had more difficulty in handling anger toward their child than did a matched sample of mothers with no handicapped children. A clear implication of this study is that mothers felt burdened by the demands of caring for their mentally retarded child and had more difficulty expressing their feelings about their child and being a mother.

Fathers also experience increased feelings of depression as well as preoccupation with their handicapped child (Cummings, 1976). Cummings reported that fathers, like mothers, indicated little enjoyment from their interactions with their mentally retarded child. The same study also reported that fathers indicated less enjoyment in their other children as well. There appears to be a qualitatively different type of interaction between fathers and sons and fathers and daughters. Fathers are more disappointed with a mentally retarded son than daughter and tend to act in a more rejecting manner toward handicapped sons. This suggests that their expectations of what their sons should achieve exceeds fathers' expectations of their daughters—a probable reality that effects their differential reactions. In this regard, Lamb (see Chapter 5) suggests that exceptional fathers tend to withdraw from the family, which weakens the mother's support system and increases her burdens as well as those of the siblings.

Parents are confronted with many practical problems in raising a handicapped child. Because of the special services the child may need, the family's financial resources may be strained, thereby limiting opportunities for other family members, such as college for other children. Family social and recreational patterns may be altered considerably owing to the added care needed by the child or by the perceived societal stigma parents attribute to their child. Available time for parents to pursue personal interests may be markedly reduced. Sexual relationships may be hindered by negative feelings about oneself or one's partner or fear of producing another handicapped child. Boles (1959) surveyed mothers of cerebral palsied children and a matched sample of mothers with no handicapped children and found significantly more marital conflict in the families with a cerebral palsied child.

Boles' research on parents, along with that of others, is typically conducted on specific populations characterized by unique features that may not be representative of parents of handicapped children in general. Indeed, Medinnus and Johnson (1969) and Trevino (1979) raise serious questions about the adequacy of the research in this area. Further research into parental response to a child's handicap is needed in order to understand the specific problems that confront parents. Investigations must take into consideration such variables as the nature and severity of the child's handicap, the number of other children in the family, the support system available to parents, and the nature of parental reaction to stress in the past, among others.

Siblings of handicapped children have special concerns. Older sisters, for example, may display unfavorable attitudes and behaviors toward their handicapped sibling and toward others when given the major responsibility of care for their handicapped brother or sister (Fowle, 1968). Their responsibility may be so overwhelming as to reduce their opportunities for development in other areas of life. The female sibling may fall victim to the "Cinderella syndrome" (i.e., leaving home) as the only escape from her situation. Parents often do need help in caring for the handicapped child; however, the developmental needs of the nonhandicapped siblings cannot be ignored. In attending to the needs of their nonhandicapped siblings, parents should facilitate communication between themselves and their children. For example, Grossman (1972) reported that adolescents found talking with their parents about their sibling's mental retardation as difficult as talking with them about sex.

Siblings may develop fantasies or dreams about their handicapped sister or brother that greatly disturb them. Siblings may fantasize or dream about taking some unduly harsh or cruel action against their handicapped brother or sister, an experience that is frightening to them and results in increased feelings of anxiety and guilt. They may also believe that something is wrong with them, just as something is wrong with their sister or brother. As noted earlier, siblings may also become resentful about the inordinate amount of parental fiscal and emotional resources absorbed by the handicapped child. Just as parents have unfulfilled needs, so do the family's other children. Parents may need assistance in recognizing that all family members require expressions of caring and attention so often characterized as necessary for positive growth (see Chapter 6 by Seligman for more on siblings).

Having a handicapped child in the family is a burden, a burden that must be shared by all family members if adjustment problems are to be held to a minimum. Although "normal" family members must contribute, parents must learn that the handicapped child should also be given reasonable responsibilities for the management of the household and for providing support to other family members. Such responsibilities allow the handicapped child to assume an important, contributing role in the family. They also allow the child to help others and not be confined to dependent roles within the family. The handicapped child should be expected to play a significant part in the general well-being of the family. Professionals may wish to enlighten parents to this important altruistic function, which any person—and especially a handicapped family member—may take great pride in.

THE COUNSELING PROCESS

The counseling process can be viewed as having three main components: educative counseling, facilitative counseling, and personal advocacy counseling. Each function has unique aspects.

Educative Counseling

Parents have a need for information concerning their child's handicap. Parents who receive complete and accurate information from the time they are first informed of their child's handicap tend to seek out more information as their child grows (Burton, 1975). The professional must be prepared to explain the handicap, its prognosis, and its impact on the child to the parents in order to help reduce confusion.

Parents often have little knowledge about handicapping conditions until confronted by their own child's handicap. Freeston (1971) found that fewer than one-half of the parents of children diagnosed as having spina bifida had heard of the condition prior to the birth of their child. Only a few of the parents felt that they fully understood the initial explanation of their child's condition that was given to them. There is, then, a great need for professionals to help parents be better informed about their circumstances, about where they may receive additional information, and about available services.

The professional cannot expect to be an expert on every handicapping condition or even on all of the ramifications of any one condition. One can, however, refer parents to written materials (see Chapter 9) and to organizations with specialized information about handicaps. Often special education centers have libraries or media centers that have materials of interest to parents. Professionals should review information and materials to which parents are referred to be sure that it is both accurate and appropriate (McWilliams, 1976). Some information can be so misleading that parents under- or overestimate the seriousness of their child's handicapping condition. Mutual exploration of appropriate materials by parent and professional can ensure that accurate information is obtained, although the professional should attempt an initial screening of such materials before recommending them.

Children with handicaps often need to learn special techniques or require special equipment for their care. The physically handicapped child may need to be fed differently than other children or require equipment that encourages maximal mobility. The hearing-impaired child may need to learn different communication methods than do other children. The parents must also learn these techniques if they are to communicate successfully with their child. A number of professionals have produced materials to assist parents to develop such techniques (Berko, 1970; Caplan, 1972; Finnie, 1968; Pitt, 1974). As noted previously, such materials are generally available through special education centers and organizations such as the Association for Retarded Citizens and the Association for Children with Learning Disabilities. Organizations of professional and lay persons typically have a wealth of information for families with a child who has a specific disability. Such organizations, often very specific in focus, exist for a variety of handicapping conditions, such as epilepsy, retardation, learning disability, arthritis, blindness and deafness, among others.

In general, professionals can serve as interpreters of available materials and techniques and can encourage parents to carry through on suggestions that are described in the materials or are prescribed by other professionals working with the child.

Parents may also need information regarding their rights for service and education. Laws such as P.L. 94-142, the Education for All Handicapped Children Act, have had a significant impact upon the rights of the handicapped child and his parents (see Chapter 2). The Developmental Disabilities Bill of Rights Act of 1975 has established mechanisms administered by each state to assist developmentally disabled individuals and their families in resolving disputes concerning needed services. Counselors can refer parents to professionals who specialize in the rights of handicapped individuals when legal issues emerge and provide support to parents if they decide to exercise their rights. Professionals should also be aware that they may be called upon to help substantiate parental claims during legal challenges.

One final word of caution. Ferhold and Solnit (1978), although strongly supportive of helping parents locate resources, believe that educative counseling should be facilitative, not advisory:

> The counselor is more a facilitator of learning and problem-solving than a teacher of facts or an instructor in child-rearing effectiveness. Although a counselor should be a competent source of advice and information, specific child-rearing practices are rarely advised. The counselor avoids too many

specific directions, even when they appear to be helpful in the short run, because they dilute the process of enabling parents and child to be active on their own behalf. Optimally, the counselor helps with practical problems of child care by helping parents to be aware of alternatives from which they can choose what they prefer for their child and themselves. (pp. 160, 161)*

Ferhold and Solnit (1978) further make the intriguing statement that "the counselor needs to have faith that parents will make sound choices allowing for some mistakes along way; when the counselor can no longer accept the parents' decisions, he should withdraw" (p. 162).

Facilitative Counseling

In addition to providing practical help, counselors are often called upon to provide support and to help clarify feelings parents may have toward their child or regarding events associated with the presence of a handicapped child in the family. As noted earlier in this chapter, parents of handicapped children may experience a variety of feelings toward themselves and their child as their relationship evolves. In addition to being knowledgeable about parental feelings, the mental health professional can view the parent–child relationship in terms of the particular stage (of the adjustment process) parents are experiencing. In Chapter 11 Meyerson elaborates on Kubler-Ross' stages of mourning as they apply to parents. Specific to the parents of handicapped children, McDowell (1976) discusses several aspects of parental adjustment to their child's handicapping condition. A few of these aspects or reactions are elaborated below along with appropriate intervention strategies.

Disbelief

When first told about their child's condition, parents cannot believe that they have a handicapped child. The mental health professional can help the parents see their child in a realistic light by providing information the parents request, being careful not to thrust too many realities on them before they are ready. The counselor should acknowledge that their dreams and plans for their child may be severely shaken while reminding them that they can still, to a large degree, live normal, productive, and comfortable lives. During this state of shock the parents may fantasize that their child is perfect or that problems are momentary and will vanish in time. When the counselor senses that the parents are ready to cope

---

*Reprinted with permission from Ferhold, J. B., & Solnit, A. Counseling parents of mentally retarded and learning disordered children. In E. Arnold (Ed.), *Helping parents help their children.* New York: Brunner/Mazel, 1978.

comfortably with their reality, he or she can provide information concerning the child's handicapping condition in a realistic, positive, and empathic manner. Information may bear repetition on several occasions so that parents understand both the possibilities and potential limitations inherent in their situation. Repetition may also be useful in that parents may feel overwhelmed the first time an emotionally charged issue is broached and, as a result, do not fully hear what is said. It is important for parents to hear optimistic, yet realistic, appraisals of their child's potential and that they be encouraged to seek help as soon as possible. Pines (1982) reports that when some Down's syndrome children receive adequate infant stimulation, receive appropriate medical intervention for physical anomalies, and are monitored for imbalances (such as thyroid deficiency) the degree of mental retardation experienced by the child can be minimized.

Guilt

Parents may blame themselves for their child's handicap. While an occasional handicapping condition, such as fetal alcoholism syndrome, is associated with the behavior of the parent, most conditions are not. The counselor can assist parents in understanding that their child's handicap is not their fault. Some parents nevertheless begin an endless search for the cause of their child's handicap at this point. Feelings of guilt may center on past "misdeeds," focusing on events that cannot be changed and over which parents have no control. Such parents should be redirected to thoughts about the present and to the needs that they and their children currently have. It is in the parents' best interest to work on those aspects of their lives over which they do have some control (Prescott & Hulnick, 1979). The counselor can empathize with the parents' feelings of guilt and also be sensitive to parental grieving but should redirect discussion to more active, forward-looking issues. Parents may be tempted to "make up" for supposed inadequacies by trying to be overprotective and not permitting their child to experience the usual viscissitudes of childhood. The counselor can explore guilt feelings with parents, help them understand their source, and assist them in enabling their child to function as normally as possible.

Kogan and Tyler (1973) explored a technique of working with mothers of handicapped children using playrooms with one-way observation mirrors. The therapist observed the interaction between mother and child and provided immediate feedback to the mother by wireless microphone. This procedure resulted in mothers easing their tight grip on their child and led to a more normalized relationship between mother and child.

Rejection

Parents may withdraw from their child and attempt to dissociate themselves from the imperfection their child manifests. Ferhold and Solnit (1978) note that some parents appropriately use counseling to help them separate from their child. Generally, though, the counselor assists parents in separating their feelings of anger over the handicap from their feelings toward their child. Parents may need to express the hopes and dreams they had for their hoped-for "normal" child before they can work on developing new life goals that take the child's handicapping condition into consideration.

It is important that parents find appropriate outlets for expressing anger and rejection so that it is not directed toward the child, their other children, or their spouses. Individual counseling is, of course, an appropriate vehicle for the expression of anger and the exploration of feelings of rejection and guilt. Another excellent source of help is peer-conducted groups, where parents who share similar problems assemble for purposes of mutual support and practical help. The mental health professional should not overlook this potent resource for parents—it is an excellent adjunct to individual counseling and one that is gaining momentum as a viable mental health alternative (Seligman, 1982).

The professional must be aware that a parent's feelings of rejection are not all-or-nothing, or a one-time occurrence. Parents may deeply love their child but may find one aspect of their child's condition difficult to accept. Also, feelings of rejection, similar to other emotions, tend to be cyclical, that is, they come and go over time. It is important for the professional to help parents realize that feelings of anger and occasional or limited rejection are normal and that their expression is likewise acceptable.

Shame

Parents may withdraw from their child and attempt to dissociate They may pick up both subtle and less-subtle cues from family, friends, and neighbors that they are different from other people.

Guilt and shame are often confused. Telford and Sawrey (1981) discuss the feelings and behaviors that characterize shame:

> Shame refers to the "what will other people think and say" reaction whereas guilt refers to the individual's feelings of self-reproach or self-condemnation. Shame is more other-people oriented; guilt more self-directed. Shame involves the expectation of ridicule or criticism from others, while guilt involves self-blame. personal regret, and a feeling of decreased self-worth. (pp. 174–175)

In regard to others' reactions Mark Twain (Clemens, 1963) once wrote, "there is something that he [man] loves more than peace—the approval of his neighbors and the public. And perhaps there is something which he dreads more than he dreads pain—the disapproval of his neighbors and the public (p. 344).

Parents may feel that they have let others down, especially other family members such as a spouse or grandparent. In individual counseling the parent can learn that their sense of being different in some fundamental way and of being ashamed of their handicapped youngster in certain social situations is acceptable and that they are not alone in suffering from such feelings. As already mentioned, the counselor can direct parents to groups where they can discover that their situation is not unique and others have developed strategies for successfully dealing with their feelings of difference and shame.

Denial

Denial is a frequently cited phenomenon in the exceptional family literature. Denial is a defense mechanism that operates on an unconscious level to ward off excessive anxiety (in this case the frightening reality that one's child is exceptional). It is noteworthy that reality may serve the cause of denial to some extent. For example, a mildly handicapped child may be an only child, making the opportunities for comparison of development limited. In addition, accurate intellectual evaluation of children with severe motor and sensory deficits is admittedly difficult, enabling parents and even professionals to believe whatever they need to believe about the child's true ability. As noted previously, in searching for a more favorable diagnosis and prognosis, parents may hop from one professional to another, often wasting time, energy, and money. For some parents this activity is essential during the denial phase, and unless it reaches the point of absurdity, professionals should be cautious about dissuading parents from seeking additional advice. Such behavior is not always caused by denial but may reflect a realistic appraisal and necessary behavior due to the nature of the disability or the quality of professional assistance available.

A general rule is never to try to force parents to cast aside a defense mechanism; the abrupt unveiling of what is being kept from conscious awareness can have a devastating effect. The strategy of encouraging parents to become aware of their child's handicap is necessary but results in painful insight; this step is never to be attempted when one senses that the parents are desperately tenacious of their unrealistic view of the child. Denial that is chronic, however, requires professional attention. Chronic denial can have severe consequences if parents fail to seek assistance for or make unrealistic demands of their child.

There is some danger in having only one parent involved in the process of overcoming denial. Additional strain is placed on the family when one parent begins to realize a child's serious handicap and the other continues firmly to deny it. Sympathetic friends, relatives, and professionals unintentionally support the parent's denial of the child's shortcomings by stressing assets and minimizing limitations. Also, some parents never completely leave the denial stage. They may accept the diagnosis but reject its prognostic implications by holding out the possibility of a miracle drug cure, a new operation, or a radically new diet.

The denial stage is generally seen as a parental reaction to a handicapped child shortly after birth and is thought to give way to more realistic appraisals as the child grows older. Even so, parents may return to feelings of denial when their child reaches significant developmental milestones.

Helplessness

McDowell (1976) believes that when parents reach the stage of feeling helpless and hopeless they will nevertheless reach out and seek help. They may feel that they can do little for their child or for themselves, so they seek assistance from others. The counselor can assist the parent in seeking help from others and in identifying personal strengths that may at present be hidden to them.

It has been the authors' experience that parents must be ready for help before counselors can be effective. If help is offered before parents are ready to accept it, he or she may enter into the therapeutic relationship only superficially. When their motivation to seek help is weak, it may be judicious to terminate counseling while assuring parents that counseling is available in the future when their need is greater. If counseling is a mandatory component of programing for their child (although it is ethically questionable whether service should be denied a handicapped child because full family cooperation is not forthcoming), the counselor should "work through" this requirement and the parental lack of motivation cautiously so that parents do not become overly resistant.

As the child grows older and passes milestones, such as beginning school or graduation from school, parents may re-experience many old feelings. The counselor must recognize the dynamic nature of the parents' feelings toward their child and not be alarmed if parents need to cover "old territory" at different times of their child's development. Indeed, the counselor should, at minimum, be aware of four major turning points in the developmental cycle of families with a handicapped child:

1. When parents first learn about or suspect a handicap in their child.
2. At about age five or six, when a decision must be reached regarding the child's education.
3. When the time has arrived for the handicapped child to leave school.
4. When the parents become older and may be unable to care for their handicapped child.

As the child matures into adolescence and young adulthood, parents may have a difficult time giving up their child, either to a residential treatment setting or to independent living, when such a living arrangement is indicated. Parents may be so invested in their child that they may find it exceedingly difficult to "let go." "Letting go" is especially difficult for overprotective parents who view their son or daughter's growing independence with apprehension. In such instances the counselor can emphathize with their apprehension and feelings of loss and help parents redirect their desire to nurture to other outlets. It may also be useful to remind parents that contact between them and their child will not cease.

Gordon (1970) writes that parents of children with handicaps must deal with thoughts and feelings they find unacceptable. The counselor can assist the parents in the exploration of disturbing thoughts and puzzling, unacceptable feelings. Depressive thoughts, such as wishing their child were dead or that they themselves were dead, may occur and need to be expressed and explored. Counselors can only be effective with parents during such emotionally charged moments when they themselves have come to terms with feelings often condemned by society.

The fact that a handicap exists is not as important as how the handicap is perceived. Phenomenologically oriented professionals argue that identical events are perceived differently by different people, a point of view that must not be lost on those who work with exceptional parents. The discovery that one has an ulcer may be taken in stride by one person and may throw another into a chronic state of depression. According to the phenomenological point of view, to which we ascribe, it is possible that parents with a severely retarded child may be considerably more accepting and exhibit better coping behaviors that another set of parents who have a moderately or mildly handicapped child. These individual differences make it imperative that the counselor view the parents' circumstances from *their* point of view. Although many factors contribute to highly individualized reactions to stress, the substance of people's accumulated experiences predisposes them to respond in certain ways to specific life events.

While handicapped children are different from their nonhandicapped counterparts in some ways, they are alike in other ways—a point of view that the counselor may wish to share with parents. The counselor can assist parents in assessing their child in terms of normal child development, which may help them focus more on similarities than on differences. As noted earlier parents may become so protective of their child that the child is not given the opportunity to learn by experimenting, a normal requisite of child development. Wolfensberger (1972) speaks of "the dignity of risk" in asserting that the taking of risks is crucial to the development of all people. The counselor can assist parents to decide what is reasonable and what is unreasonable to expect from their child. The counselor can also encourage parents to support their child's positive efforts and generally promote *early* cognitive and socioemotional parent–child experiences.

As previously mentioned, parents may have difficulties that are rooted in their past and are not the direct result of the presence of a handicapped child. The counselor can explore these difficulties with the parents, helping them to separate these concerns from problems more clearly associated with their child. The counselor can also help parents become aware of how the child aggravates pre-existing problems.

Childrearing is a challenging task for any parent, yet parents of special needs children are generally burdened by additional stresses. The counselor can assist the parents of a handicapped child to cope by providing the support and understanding they need to see that their child has value and potential and by helping them handle their pain.

Personal Advocacy Counseling

Parents have the ultimate responsibility and authority for the welfare of their children unless they are removed by legal means. Parents want what is best for their child, yet they may not know how to obtain it. Additionally, parents of handicapped children may become involved with professionals from many different agencies who provide parents with advice and recommendations that may be conflicting or confusing. Parents may therefore be puzzled after receiving well-meaning, yet confusing and sometimes misguided advice from several sources.

Personal advocacy counseling refers to the process of assisting parents to actively and purposively work for their own and their child's welfare by obtaining the support and service necessary. Personal advocacy counseling helps parents to become their own case managers, a point of view expressed by Rubin and Quinn-Curran in Chapter 3.

Realistically, providing help to handicapped children and their families can be a formidable task. Conflicting opinions exist as to which treatments or courses of action are most beneficial. For example, one professional may recommend bracing for a child with cerebral palsy, while another may recommend intensive physical therapy. Conflicting professional opinions leave parents in a quandary: Who should they believe? How do they decide which method is likely to achieve the best results?

In addition to differing opinions of their child's diagnosis, prognosis, or rehabilitation, parents may have to juggle advice from a variety of sources, such as a health agency, a mental health/mental retardation center, a school, a child welfare agency, a respite care service, and a homemaker service, as well as others. Each may have their own perspective regarding what is in the best interest of the child. It is little wonder that parents seeking appropriate and adequate care for their child find the maze of professional services so confusing.

Brewer and Kakalik (1979) found that, while many services are available for handicapped children and their families, parents often are not aware of them. These researchers found that even when parents knew of services they often did not know how to access or coordinate services to meet their own and their children's needs. While parents bear responsibility for their child, they rarely have the sophistication to take the initiative in deciding what services are best or most appropriate. They therefore need assistance in deciding which problems require their attention and what services will best meet these needs. The counselor can assist parents in becoming their own case managers. Parents are, after all, the logical choice for chief coordinators and evaluators of service, with the assistance of the counselor.

To fill this role adequately the counselor must become familiar with general referral procedures and must be knowledgeable about how the various human service systems available to parents and their handicapped child operate. The counselor should not be expected to become familiar with *all* of the specific services available. For example, one of the authors found that over 800 human service providers were extending services to individuals living in an area with fewer than half of a million people (Laborde, 1979). In this area, services changed rapidly, with at least one significant change (moved, new programs added, old programs deleted, new phone number) occurring in one-fourth of these services every three months. With such rapid change, the counselor cannot be expected to keep abreast of the details of all specific services. Even so, professionals who work with parents should be generally aware of available resources.

The counselor must be wary of referring parents to the same few agencies. Agencies that are well known to one counselor are most likely well known to others. These agencies are often overutilized while other agencies with similar services and comparable expertise remain underutilized.

Brewer and Kakalik (1979) propose that direction be provided to parents with handicapped children in regard to acquiring appropriate services. Counselors should be familiar with several resources within their community that can perform this function, such as information and referral services, associations concerned with specific disabilities, and municipal or county human service consortia. The counselor may act as a "broker" of these services by assisting the parent in formulating a clear idea of which needs they wish to have met and deciding where to receive services. The professional, for example, may contact information clearinghouses to obtain complete, accurate, and up-to-date information on available services to meet specific needs. With information on hand, the professional may assist the parent in developing a plan of action for obtaining needed assistance. Kakalik and Brewer note that this type of help can be an important component of personal advocacy counseling and decision making.

The primary goal of personal advocacy counseling is to assist parents to experience a sense of control over events in their own lives and their child's life. Parents, by experiencing this sense of potency, may act with greater confidence and purposefulness when confronted with choices or situations not to their liking. Choices must be made from a sense of purpose rather than from futility or guilt. Personal advocacy counseling can help parents to work for their family's welfare in a positive, determined manner.

The professional must, however, be sensitive to parents who may become so involved in advocacy issues that little energy is left for meeting the needs of their child. The professional can assist the parent in identifying both social and personal issues of concern and help parents place these issues in perspective. At the same time, he or she must keep in mind that many advances in the treatment of handicapped individuals have been due to the tireless efforts of parents of handicapped children. Handicapped individuals need the help of all concerned people, parents as well as professionals, if their voice is to be heard and if their social conditions are to continue to improve.

CONCLUSIONS

Individual counseling is a valuable method of treating parents experiencing problems associated with raising a handicapped child. Individual counseling may be the treatment of choice for parents who are uncomfortable with group experiences. Parents with specific informational needs or specific difficulties may find individual counseling more beneficial than group or family treatment approaches. The professional may also utilize individual treatment in conjunction with groups or self-help (group) experiences. In considering the most useful strategy, the professional must take into consideration the nature of the parent's difficulty, the parent's willingness and preference for various treatment modalities, and the availability of counseling services.

The professional, by helping parents meet their child's particular educative, interpersonal, and personal advocacy needs, will have provided a valuable service. Counseling can provide the catalyst parents need in order to become more independent, confident, and productive and thus be able to reach out to their child and others more easily. Parents with handicapped children have burdens other people do not share. These burdens may, at times, seem overwhelming to those who carry them. The professional can provide the caring and guidance parents need in order to feel more capable of coping with their circumstances during such periods.

The professional faces a challenging task in counseling parents of handicapped children. Counseling parents may be long-term and it may be recurring. Parents receive advice from many well-meaning sources, including other professionals, which may complicate the counseling process. Parents grow frustrated and cynical about the daily demands of a handicapped child, and inflexible and confusing human service deliver systems may add to their problems.

While the professional must keep these difficulties in mind, rewards to both the parent and the professional can acrue. The professional who assists parents in becoming more capable of meeting the special demands of parenting a handicapped child has provided a service of considerable value. The professional helps not only the parents and child to grow but also helps himself to become more aware of the potential that exists in each individual. From a larger perspective, as so-called "deficient" children, youth, and adults become more able, society benefits also. Successful counseling permits greater participation by the handicapped child and his family in all aspects of community life.

REFERENCES

Barsch, R. H. *The teacher–parent partnership.* Arlington, Va.: Council for Exceptional Children, 1969.

Berko, F. *Management of brain damaged children: A parent's and teacher's guide.* Springfield, Ill.: Charles C Thomas, 1970.

Bissel, N. E. Communicating with the parents of exceptional children. In E. J. Webster (Ed.), *Professional approaches with parents of handicapped children.* Springfield, Ill.: Charles C Thomas, 1976.

Boles, G. Personality factors in mothers of cerebral palsied children. *Genetic psychology Monographs,* 1959, *59,* 160–218.

Brassel, W. Intervention with handicapped infants: Correlates of progress. *Mental Retardation,* 1977, *15,* 18–22.

Brewer, G., & Kakalik, J. *Handicapped children: Strategies for improving services.* New York: McGraw-Hill, 1979.

Burton, L. *The family life of sick children: A study of families coping with chronic childhood disease.* London: Routledge and Kegan Paul, 1975.

Caplan, F. *The first twelve months of life.* New York: Grosset & Dunlap, 1972.

Chinn, P. C., Winn, J., & Walters, R. H. *Two-way talking with parents of special children.* St. Louis: C. V. Mosby, 1978.

Clemens, S. L. What is Man? In C. Neider (Ed.), *The complete essays of Mark Twain.* Garden City, N.Y.: Doubleday, 1963.

Cummings, S. T. The impact of the child's deficiency on the father: A study of fathers of mentally retarded and chronically ill children. *American Journal of Orthopsychiatry,* 1976, *46,* 246–255.

Cummings, S. T., Bayley, H. C., & Rie, H. Effects of the child's deficiency on the mother: A study of mothers of mentally retarded, chronically ill, and neurotic children. *American Journal of Orthopsychiatry,* 1966, *36,* 595–608.

Darling, R. B., & Darling, J. *Children who are different: Meeting the challenge of birth defects in society.* St. Louis: C. V. Mosby, 1982.

Davidson, P. O., & Schrag, A. R. Prognostic indicators for effective child psychiatric consultations. *Canadian Psychiatric Association Journal,* 1968, *13,* 533.

Fellendorf, G. W., & Harrow, I. If I had to do it over . . . *Exceptional Children,* 1969, *36,* 43–44.

Ferhold, J. B., & Solnit, A. Counseling parents of mentally retarded and learning disordered children. In E. Arnold (Ed.), *Helping parents help their children.* New York: Brunner/Mazel, 1978.

Finnie, N. R. *Handling the young cerebral palsy child at home.* New York: United Cerebral Palsy Association, 1968.

Freeman, R. & Pearson, P. Counseling with parents. In J. Apley (Ed.), *Care of the handicapped child.* London: Laverham Press, 1978.

Freeston, B. M. An inquiry into the effect of a spina bifida child upon family life. *Developmental Medicine and Child Neurology,* 1971, *13,* 456–461.

Fowle, C. M. The effect of a severely mentally retarded child on his family. *American Journal of Mental Deficiency,* 1968, *73,* 468–473.

Fox, M. A. The handicapped family. *Lancet,* 1975, *2,* 400–401.

Gordon, T. *Parent effectiveness training.* New York: Wyden, 1970.

Gorham, K. A., Des Jardins, C., Page, R., Pettis, E., & Scheiber, B. Effects on parents. In N. Hobbs (Ed.), *Issues in the classification of children.* San Francisco: Jossey-Bass, 1975.

Grossman, F. K. *Brothers and sisters of retarded children.* Syracuse: Syracuse University Press, 1972.

Guralnick, M. J., & Richardson, H. B. (Eds.) *Pediatric education and the needs of exceptional children.* Baltimore: University Park Press, 1980.

Hart, N. W. Frequently expressed feelings and reactions of parents toward their retarded child. In N. R. Bernstein (Ed.) *Diminished people: Problems and care of the mentally retarded.* Boston: Little, Brown, 1970.

Howard, J. The role of the pediatrician with young exceptional children and their families. *Exceptional Children,* 1982, *48,* 316–321.

Jacobs, F. H., & Walker, D. K. Pediatricians and the Education for All Handicapped Children Act of 1975 (Public Law 94-142). *Pediatrics,* 1978, *61,* 135–137.

Jordan, T. E. Physical disability in children and family adjustment. In R. L. Noland (Ed.), *Counseling parents of the ill and handicapped.* Springfield, Ill.: Charles C Thomas, 1971, 10–26.

Keirn, W. C. Shopping parents: Patient problem or professional problem? *Mental Retardation,* 1971, *9,* 6–7.

Kogan, K. L., & Tyler, N. Mother–child interaction in young physically handicapped children. *American Journal of Mental Deficiency,* 1973, *77,* 492–497.

Kroth, R. L. *Communicating with parents of exceptional children: Improving parent–teacher relationships.* Denver: Love, 1975.

Laborde, P. R. Annual Report, Pennsylvania Direction Service (Contract No. 300-77-0458). Washington, D.C.: U.S. Department of Health, Education and Welfare, Bureau of Education for the Handicapped, 1979.

Love, H. D. *Parental attitudes towards exceptional children.* Springfield, Ill.: Charles C Thomas, 1970.

McDowell, R. L. Parent counseling: The state of the art. *Journal of Learning Disabilities,* 1976, *9,* 614–619.

McWilliams, B. J. Various aspects of parent counseling. In E. J. Webster (Ed.), *Professional approaches with parents of handicapped children.* Springfield, Ill.: Charles C Thomas, 1976.

Medinnus, G. R., & Johnson, R. C. *Child and adolescent psychology: Behavior and development.* New York: Wiley, 1969.

Meyerwitz, J. H., & Kaplan, H. B. Familial responses to stress: The case of cystic fibrosis. *Social Science and Medicine,* 1967, *1,* 249–266.

Paul, J. L. (Ed.), *Understanding and working with parents of children with special needs.* New York: Holt, Rinehart & Winston, 1981.

Pines, M. Infant-stim: It's changing the lives of handicapped kids. *Psychology Today,* 1982, *16,* 48–53.

Pitt, D. *Your Down's syndrome child: You can help him develop from infancy to adulthood.* Arlington, Tex.: National Association for Retarded Citizens, 1974.

Powers, J. T., & Healy, A. Inservice training for physicians serving handicapped children, 1982, *48,* 332–336.

Prescott, R. & Hulnick, P. Counseling parents of handicapped children: An empathetic approach. *Personnel and Guidance Journal,* 1979, *58,* 263–266.

Pueschel, S. M., & Murphy, A. Assessment of counseling practices at the birth of a child with Down's syndrome. *American Journal of Mental Deficiency,* 1976, *81,* 325–330.

Reynolds, M. C., & Birch, J. W. *Teaching exceptional children in all America's schools* (Rev. ed.). Reston, Va.: Council for Exceptional Children, 1982.

Ross, A. O. *The exceptional child in the family: Helping parents of exceptional children.* New York: Grune & Stratton, 1964.

Schwartz, C. G. Strategies and tactics of mothers of mentally retarded children for dealing with the medical care system. In N. R. Bernstein (Ed.), *Dimin-*

ished people: Problems and care of the mentally retarded. Boston: Little, Brown, 1970.

Seligman, M. *Strategies for helping parents of exceptional children.* New York: Free Press, 1979.

Seligman, M. (Ed.), *Group psychotherapy and counseling with special populations.* Baltimore: University Park Press, 1982.

Seligman, M., & Seligman, P. A. The professional's dilemma: Learning to work with parents. *The Exceptional Parent,* 1980, *10,* 511–513.

Springer, A., & Steele, M. Effects of physicians early parental counseling on rearing of Down's syndrome children. *American Journal of Mental Deficiency,* 1980, *85,* 1–5.

Telford, C. W. & Sawrey, J. M. *The Exceptional Individual* (2nd ed.). Englewood Cliffs, N.J.: Prentice-Hall, 1981.

Trevino, F. Siblings of handicapped children: Identifying those at risk. *Social Casework,* 1979, *60,* 448–493.

Walker, J. H. Spina bifida—and the parents. *Developmental Medicine and Child Neurology,* 1971, *13,* 462–476.

Wolfensberger, W. *Normalization: The principle of normalization in human services.* Toronto: National Institute on Mental Retardation, 1972.

Wolraich, M. L. Communication between physicians and parents of handicapped children. *Exceptional Children,* 1982, *48,* 324–329.

11

Family and Parent Group Therapy

ROBERTA C. MEYERSON

BIOGRAPHICAL SKETCH

Roberta C. Meyerson, Ph.D., is Assistant Professor in counselor education at the University of Pittsburgh. She previously has been a special education teacher who has worked with handicapped children and adults and their families. Dr. Meyerson coauthored the chapter "Group Approaches for Parents of Exceptional Children" (with Milton Seligman) in Group Psychotherapy and Counseling with Special Populations, *edited by Dr. Seligman.*

A RECENT proliferation of literature on counseling parents and families of exceptional children reflects the growing concern of helping professionals that the needs of the entire families of disabled children, and not just those of the affected child, be considered and addressed. Not only does the optimal development and management of the disabled child depend upon a supportive, competent family structure, but the well-being of all family members rests upon it. In a greater sense, the movement toward treatment of the family is consistent with the increasing emphasis in counseling on a systems approach, i.e., viewing and helping the individual from the perspective of the reciprocal interactions between that person and the system (in this case the family) within which he or she operates (Fogarty, 1976). In the case of the "exceptional family," the birth of (or accident or illness of) a handicapped child clearly affects the feelings, attitudes, and consequent behavior of the parents and other children in the family. Conversely, the handicapped child's feelings, attitudes, and behavior, including his or her self-concept, are influenced by messages, both verbal and nonverbal, received from parents and siblings.

This chapter focuses, in a general sense, on some of the concerns and needs of the parents and families of disabled children. More specifically, family therapy and parent group counseling will be explored as useful vehicles for addressing and meeting the needs of this population. An examination of treatment modalities, which vary in both function and structure, ensues, followed by a discussion of the relative merits of the different approaches. In addition, a plan for family treatment, which incorporates elements of family and parent group therapy, will be proposed.

The birth of a handicapped child into a family is usually an unexpected and devastating event. Although many prospective parents encounter fleeting fears that something might "go wrong," that their baby may not be born perfect, most parents not only hope for but expectantly await a healthy, fully developed infant. When parents are informed, sometimes in the most insensitive of ways, that something is in fact wrong with their infant, their world, at least for the moment, collapses. It is similarly traumatic for parents whose once healthy and normal child suddenly becomes incapacitiated or may even face death due to serious accident or illness. Although the circumstances, timing, and expectations may differ, having a disabled child affects parents and other family members in a variety of critical ways. As counselors, we strive not only to help others cope with their particular set of circumstances but also to help them to expand their awareness and behavioral options in general. In working with families of handicapped children, we must first understand some of the specific feelings, concerns, and considerations that these families confront and must work through before individual and family growth is possible.

Prior to the popularization of Kubler-Ross' (1969) work on death and dying, little professional attention had been devoted to the grieving process that accompanies one's own impending death or the death of a significant other. On the basis of work with dying patients and their families, Kubler-Ross determined five stages that occur in the normal grieving process: denial, anger, bargaining, depression, and acceptance. Movement through these stages is rarely smooth; progression from one stage to the next is often followed by some form of regression to an earlier stage. Fixation at a particular stage may also occur. Viewing Kubler-Ross' work from a broader perspective, grieving is actually a universal phenomenon, something that we all experience when we encounter the loss of somebody or something very important to us. Death is not the only experience that robs us. Loss of the healthy, normal child that parent's once hoped for and expected initiates a similar mourning process (Solnit & Stark, 1961). With the grief comes a myriad of emotions, often commencing with shock and disbelief and progressing in an uneven manner through fear, guilt, resentment, and sorrow.

At first, parents in their disbelief feel that this cannot be happening to them, to their child, to their family. Denial assumes many outward forms, depending in part upon the parents' general ability to cope and in part upon the nature and severity of the child's disability. One of the more common manifestations of denial is the relentless search for a more benign diagnosis (or, better still, a total rejection of the original diagnosis). This quest, commonly referred to as shopping behavior, is a response that may also occur for more rational reasons. Prolonged denial is certainly more likely when the child's physical appearance is normal and the symptoms of the disability are subtle and ambiguous, as in the case of some mildly retarded or emotionally disturbed children. There can be no real denying of a major crisis when the child is born multiply or severely handicapped.

Denial ultimately gives way to the experience of anger. In its most blatant form, anger is expressed as an attack on just about everyone and everything that exists in the parents' world. The question "Why me?" is subtly embedded in the dissatisfaction and blame expressed toward physicians and other medical personnel, relatives and friends, even God. There may be unconscious anger and resentment toward the handicapped child during this stage. These emotions, because of their unacceptablity, rapidly dissolve into guilt. In many respects, the inevitable guilt that parents of handicapped children experience is really self-directed anger, a feeling or even a conviction that if they had done something differently their child would have been all right.

The struggle to accept the reality of the child's condition and prognosis continues, with the parents pushing beyond their anger and attempting to bargain for a better deal for their child. At this stage, parents believe that if they only do the right things, engage in the right activities, their child will improve appreciably (Duncan, 1977). During this time, one finds some parents involved in volunteer work for organizations that may benefit their handicapped child. Other parents may assist with advocacy work for a particular disability group while neglecting the needs of their own child. Active participation in religion and religious organizations is likewise common.

Sooner or later parents come to the realization that their bargaining tactics are not effective in altering their child's condition. The depression that follows is terribly painful and perhaps unavoidable. A positive aspect of the depression is that it signals that parents are finally beginning to confront realistically the fact of their child's disability and its implications. But the acceptance is wrought with immense suffering, and depression hovers like a cloud of doom over the parents' heads. More than at any other time, parents chastise or even torment themselves about how things might have been had they done something differently. This guilt is accompanied by strong feelings of shame and embarrassment, which are, in reality, self-blame projected onto others around them. And there are also the inevitable feelings both of helplessness and hopelessness that arise during this phase.

Eventually, most parents reach a time when they are able to accept the reality of their handicapped child and his or her limitations. There are some parents who find meaning in their difficult situation by seeing their child as special, e.g., a gift of God, or their own destiny as special, e.g., a call from God to contribute to this world in some exceptional way. Most parents simply reconcile themselves to their situation. Parents who have reached this stage of acceptance are able to engage in constructive interaction with the community agencies and educational institutions that provide services to their child. They begin to make and act upon decisions that will benefit not only their disabled child but other family members as well, including themselves. In other words, they accept what they must and do what they can to cope effectively with the situation.

As mentioned earlier, grieving tends to be an uneven process. Parents may experience depression for a time and then suddenly turn the blame outward to the physician caring for the child, who never seems to do enough or do the right thing. Hope and optimism give way to tears and withdrawal when a new drug or new treatment plan fails to work. Parents frequently report feeling like they are on an emotional merry-go-round, up one moment, down the next. Even after the parents have come to terms with their situation, emotions concerning their handicapped child's condition flare periodically, especially at critical developmental stages. Those who have worked with parents of handicapped children, know that, even with acceptance, some parents continue to feel an omnipresent sadness for a long time; some live with it their entire lives.

Siblings of the handicapped child, like their parents, experience a myriad of emotions during the process of mourning and of learning to accept their handicapped brother or sister (see Chapter 6). The siblings' developmental levels as well as their positions in the family constellation determine in part how they will respond and what particular issues will arise. However, there are certain common concerns and considerations with children in the family of a handicapped child. Perhaps the most primary concern is the potential for loss of quality time and care by overly stressed parents, parents who are already stretched to their limit by the heavy demands of a disabled child. At the same time that "normal" children are receiving less attention from the parents, they are often asked to assume additional responsibilities, both in the household in general and for their handicapped sibling specifically. This combined loss of attention and increase in responsibility often leads to resentment toward the parents and anger toward the handicapped child. Children's feelings of anger may be accompanied by fantasies of hurting or even killing their disabled brother or sister, which, in turn, naturally generates immense guilt and remorse.

Brothers and sisters of handicapped children may also experience shame and embarrassment about their handicapped sibling when encountering friends, classmates, and neighbors. Depending on their level of maturity, these youngsters may be very sensitive to the reactions of others and may even seek to avoid others when with their handicapped sibling. Anger may be felt toward the handicapped child for drawing such negative attention, but anger may also be directed toward peers who ogle, bully, or ridicule the disabled child. In the face of such insensitivity, siblings frequently express great protectiveness of their less fortunate brother or sister.

Fear is another strong emotion that may arise in siblings of a disabled child. Where a brother or sister has been incapacitated by an accident or a sudden, devastating illness, anxiety may arise concerning the possibility that this could happen to them. Sleep may be fraught with nightmares in which siblings imagine themselves damaged or even killed in some frightful way. Siblings who are at a preadolescent or adolescent stage of development when a handicapped infant is born into the family may fear that they too will bear abnormal children when their time comes for a family. This fear, if repressed, may lead to future sexual or relationship problems.

Then, of course, there are the day-to-day inconveniences that accompany the growth of a handicapped child in the family. Small mishaps such as spilling liquids or dropping and breaking objects in the home are common, and it is often the "able" children who must mop or pick up the pieces. Handicapped children whose behaviors are immature or inappropriate also tend to invade the personal space and personal belongings of their brothers and sisters, causing the latter to feel angry and violated.

Let us not ignore the fact that there are often moments of great satisfaction, delight, and triumph in the lives of handicapped children and their families. Even during the emotionally tumultuous mourning period, there are times when the handicapped child takes a small step, smiles, or achieves some other developmental milestone and thereby brings pleasure and joy to his or her brothers, sisters, and parents. There is something very special about even the smallest of accomplishments of a handicapped child. As the handicapped child develops, siblings often take pride in helping him or her to learn new skills, such as self-feeding, toilet training, or identifying common objects. According to Chinitz (1981), siblings of cerebral palsied children with whom she worked "showed insight into cuing in to their sibling's level of functioning" (p. 22).

In helping members of families of a handicapped child to cope with and accept the child's condition, professionals must realize not only that emotional states fluctuate during the mourning process within each individual but that differences in timing, form, and degree of mourning exist among family members as well. In fact, a considerable amount of family tension and stress results from the asynchrony with which individuals experience various feelings and emotional phases. For example, the father may be out eagerly searching for some new form of treatment or cure while the mother is home, despairing of her child's fate and feeling both helpless and hopeless. Or a sibling may experience a great deal of resentment at the fact that mother seems to be spending all of her time either managing the disabled child or eagerly volunteering at the agency where the child is being habilitated. Whether the mental health professional is working with the parents, the siblings, or the entire family unit, he or she must assist individuals in gaining awareness of their feelings. Equally important, the professional can serve as a "family facilitator" (Sourkes, 1977), helping to improve overall communication among family members and sensitizing individuals not only to their own experiences but to those of the others in the family.

Overprotection of the disabled child, both by parents and by siblings, is one way of attempting to cope with feelings of fear, guilt, and anger that arise. Fife (1978), in her article on parents of leukemic children, states that "overprotection . . . has been found to be a commonly used parental coping behavior that results in decreased cohesiveness with the family, behavioral problems in the child and his [or her] siblings, and the disruption of the normal patterns of family living" (p. 117). The same often holds true for families of mentally retarded, physically handicapped, and emotionally disturbed children. Not only are family dynamics generally disrupted, but the handicapped child's self-esteem is undermined in the process. Nobody's needs are appropriately attended to when the bulk of time and energy is channeled into indulging and spoiling the handicapped child.

Another problem encountered in families of handicapped children that hampers effective coping is the tendency for parents to ignore or neglect their own needs. Included are the parents' needs for privacy, time away, and social contact with the outside world. In addition, there are the very important needs of the marital relationship, in particular those of intimacy and sexuality. Parents often feel that they must either think of their handicapped child at all times or include him or her in all plans and activities. In doing so, however, they rob the child and themselves of a certain vitality that can only be gained through self-nourishment, which requires attending to their own needs. Parents, in focusing single-mindedly on the handicapped child, also deprive other children in the family of much needed time and care. A future ramification of this form of neglect may be that these children learn that their needs are not valid or important.

With increasing acceptance of the handicapped child's plight by both the parents and siblings, the entire family becomes more functional in terms of both daily problems and future concerns. As with most families, a routine is established in which each family member has a role and responsibilities to fulfill. By this time, family members are acquiring competency in basic caretaking skills. Collectively, they grow increasingly adaptive in meeting the daily challenges presented by their particular family circumstances. They begin to engage the social world in a constructive manner once again. They are clearer in their thinking and can make decisions based less on confused feelings than on balanced consideration of alternatives. Once again the needs of family members other than the handicapped child can be addressed without undue feelings of guilt. It is toward these goals that helping professionals strive with families of handicapped children. Family therapy provides one vehicle for accomplishing these goals.

FAMILY THERAPY

Currently there appears to be a professional trend toward increasing use of family intervention in the treatment of a variety of disorders that either are rooted in or seriously affect the family. In discussing the treatment of childhood psychopathology, Masten (1979) states that "there is some evidence that family and behavioral strategies are gaining preference over traditional individual child psychotherapy approaches" (p. 323). One of the clearest reasons for the growing popularity of family therapy is that it addresses the impact that a child's disability can have on all family members. It likewise emphasizes the family's role in the creation, perpetuation, or aggravation of the child's dysfunction.

Family therapy is by no means a singular, unified treatment modality. Rather, the term is used as an umbrella for a diversity of philosophies and approaches that include the systems, interactional, analytic, and behavioral models, to name but a few. There is considerable controversy over what, exactly, constitutes family therapy—who should be seen and when (Fox, 1976). In a review of family therapy as a treatment for child psychopathology, Masten (1979) established as one of her criteria studies that evaluated the effects of conjoint family therapy, i.e. therapy in which the disturbed child was counseled together with at least one parent. The term *family therapy* is employed in this chapter to discuss strategies in which the handicapped child is seen in the context of either part or all of his or her family. The theme that pervades all family therapies is that the optimal treatment of the child derives from a broad-based intervention strategy, one that encompasses the intra- and interpersonal dynamics of all family members. Once again, the concern rests not only with the well-being of the handicapped child but with that of other individuals within the family and with the family unit as a whole.

It is with families where a child has been labeled as emotionally or behaviorally disturbed (neurotic, schizophrenic, delinquent, etc.) that one frequently encounters family therapy as a recommended therapeutic approach. Many professionals agree that it is appropriate or desirable to work with the child and his or her family conjointly when the primary derivation of the affected child's problem lies in a highly conflicted or dysfunctional family situation. From a family therapy perspective, the disturbed child usually represents a manifestation or symptom, rather than a cause, of family distress. According to Cutter and Hallowitz (1962), "the child's mode of adjustment to home and to society, whether this is normal, psychopathological, or sociopathological, is seen as a mirroring or reflection of the emotional strength of the milieu in which his [or her] ego development has occurred" (p. 153). The child's disruptive or abnormal behavior may provide the impetus for the family to seek treatment, but within the therapeutic context the entire family unit is regarded as the patient. In general, parents are encouraged to help their troubled child by revising dysfunctional patterns of communication with each other, in particular, as well as with children in the family.

Family therapy may also be a desirable intervention strategy with families of children who are intellectually, sensorily, or physically impaired. In these families, it is more likely that the child's handicapping condition is viewed either as creating new family problems or exacerbating already existent family disturbance. However, problems that rest directly with the parents may be partially responsible for negatively affecting the child's condition. White (1970), in discussing parents of mentally retarded children, states the following:

It is interesting to note . . . the way in which the initial focus on the child's problems has been directed back toward consideration of underlying parental attitudes which frequently are an essential part of the child's difficulties and may actually prevent his [or her] functioning at his [or her] maximum capacity, despite inherent limitations. (p. 195)

Warnick (1969) discusses the importance of parental attitudes from another perspective. She suggests that attitudes of parents toward their handicapped children are essentially the same as those toward any child in the family. The primary difference is that the disability and its accompanying problems elicit feelings that otherwise might be less pronounced or even suppressed.

In the preceding discussion it has been implied that it is the family, in general, that is the focus in family therapy and the parents, specifically, who are the pivotal members of the family. In any family system, the relationship between the parents largely determines the climate and overall effectiveness of family life. If the parents' communication is ongoing, open, and honest, then communication between parents and children and among children in the family is also likely to be productive and healthful. If the balance of power in the parental relationship shifts fluidly between mother and father, depending on the demands of a given situation, then issues of control are not as likely to plague other relationships in the family. In families with problems in the areas of communication and power, the weakest member is apt to be greatly affected. Handicapped children sometimes are used unconsciously or scapegoated by parents whose relationship with one another is, in one way or another, severely impaired. Parental misuse of children manifests itself in a number of different ways that include overprotecting, overindulging, and generally spoiling the child at one extreme and neglecting and or physically abusing the child at the other. Where communication between parents is inadequate and struggles for control persist, other children in the family may suffer as well. For example, the anger and frustration of one parent toward the other or toward the handicapped child may be displaced onto the more "able" children; or children may be incorporated into alliances with one parent against the other. Problems in families of handicapped children are essentially no different from those in any family. The primary difference between normal and exceptional families is that, in the latter, the additional stresses and strains may highlight existing problems or force them to a higher level of awareness.

Family therapy provides a vehicle for helping the families of handicapped children to work out the difficulties that interfere with effective emotional coping and successful management of the family system. The major goal of treatment is to assist each family member in learning more adaptive behaviors that will enhance both self and others in the system.

According to Noland (1972), the factors that most critically affect the parents' ability to adapt to their child's disability are past successes and failures in important challenges, present mental and physical health, age, socioeconomic standard, and selective perception (seeing what they choose to see). Frequently, the initial focus of therapy is on helping the handicapped child. Parents enter therapy desiring to discover ways of providing relief or improvement for their child. During this time they also solicit assistance in adjusting to their new set of circumstances. As therapy progresses, the focus and goals gradually broaden to include support and aid for other family members and for the entire family unit.

There are several ways in which mental health professionals help family members to cope and adapt effectively. First, they attempt to improve communication among family members as well as between the family and the professionals involved in the care and treatment of the disabled child (Sourkes, 1977). This is accomplished by teaching and modeling facilitative, appropriate interactional behavior and by calling attention to nonfacilitative, counterproductive communication. As in many families, communication in families of handicapped children is often inhibited or otherwise impaired. There may be either generalized or selective lack of communication. Emotional expression may be suppressed, wherein it is acceptable to talk about a concern as long as one's feelings do not emerge. At times, the communication blockage specifically relates to the disabled child. Messages pertaining to the child and his or her condition may be incongruent. For example, a parent verbally may express great hope for a "cure" for his or her child while walking around with a sad face all day long. The family therapist helps family members to verbalize what they feel and believe in a way that can be heard by others in the family.

Improved communication in the family goes hand-in-hand with increased self-awareness in its members. Family therapists attempt to help individuals in the family to gain access to their feelings and attitudes, primarily by emphatically listening and responding. Through this process each person comes to understand him- or herself better. In turn, family members grow clearer and more honest in what they communicate to others. Modeling of behavior also occurs. As parents and children observe the therapist responding empathically, they learn to hear one another more accurately and to respond more caringly. In other words, increased self-awareness is accompanied by heightened other-awareness. In the process, genuine trust among family members develops. As individuals experience greater and greater emotional safety, they begin to take risks and expose their vulnerabilities. "Unacceptable" emotions come to the foreground and are expressed openly. As one parent shares his or her pain—the disappointment, fear, and anger about the disabled child that has remained submerged—the other may feel relief that he or she has not been alone in these feelings. Siblings, likewise, are more apt to express hidden emotions and various stress reactions when they observe the therapist and then their parents doing so.

Along with increased awareness and effectiveness of communication, family members develop in the ability to understand their particular family dynamics. Structural dynamics, in terms of intrafamilial alliances, and power dynamics, in terms of who exercises control over particular decisional domains, naturally become apparent during the course of treatment. Through well-timed interventions (usually interpretation and confrontation), the therapist assists family members in gaining insight into their own patterns of interaction. He or she might help both parents and children to explore dysfunctional patterns by delving into the origins of these patterns or by aiding individuals in seeing how these patterns are currently manifested. Equally important, the therapist encourages and reinforces adaptive family dynamics and interpersonal interaction. Parents and children need feedback about what they are doing right as well as what they are doing wrong.

Family therapists also help parents and children to develop emotional coping skills. The ability to cope effectively is contingent upon the continuous monitoring of needs and feelings. Parents are often reluctant to take the time to meet their own individual needs (Fife, 1978) and frequently overlook the needs of siblings of the handicapped child as well. As a general rule, distress can be minimized when individuals receive enough rest, relaxation, and recreation. Time for play and other forms of diversion should be encouraged. Solitary, dyadic, and family activities are all important for the well-being of each family member. In addition, parents must give high priority to the needs of the marital relationship, specifically those of privacy, intimacy, and sexuality. Kivowitz (1977) discusses the ways in which parents' sexual relationships can be affected by a handicapped child and the importance of helping parents to deal with feelings of guilt and blame that hinder positive sexual expression.

In summary, family therapists serve in a variety of roles as they help the exceptional family to function effectively. During the initial contacts, they provide emotional support for parents and siblings who have been shocked by the birth or illness or accident of an exceptional child. Therapists provide information about the child's condition, prognosis, and management as well as about community resources—as the parents and children become ready to hear and integrate this data. They encourage and facilitate emotional expression, especially during the painful grieving process. As a part of this process, family counselors assist family members in dealing with the asynchrony of their feelings. When a reasonable level of acceptance has been reached by the family in general and the parents in particular, therapists engage in helping family members to see,

understand, and alter their interactional behaviors. In this way constructive behaviors are maximized and defensive maneuvers are minimized.
Finally, therapists aid the family in learning basic coping and management
skills. Buscaglia (1975) summarizes some of the specific goals of work
with parents of the exceptional child. His suggestions may be applied to
other family members as well:

1. To help the parents to see that the special child is a child first and a
   child with a disability second.
2. To understand the issues and facts involved in the disabling condition
   so as to best be able to help the child in a constructive manner.
3. To assist the parents and child to understand their unique feelings
   which have been aroused by the advent of a disability.
4. To aid the parents and child to accept the disability emotionally and
   intellectually without devaluing the individual possessing it.
5. To help the child and parents in continuing to develop their unique
   potentials together, and independently, toward their own self-actuali-
   zation. (pp. 277–278)*

Therapists who provide treatment for families of handicapped children require not only "generic" therapeutic skills but some specialized
skills as well. Because work with families tends to be more complex than
work with individuals, family therapists must thoroughly understand family dynamics and know how to diagnose dysfunctional interactions. They
must also be competent in employing a variety of strategies for altering
destructive, disruptive, or otherwise faulty patterns of relating. In addition, family therapists must be particularly sensitive to the special needs
and problems that exceptional families encounter. As was mentioned earlier, these families, in many respects, are not different than any other.
They frequently do, however, live with the pressure of additional emotional, social, and economic stressors that would tax any system to the
limit. They need understanding and guidance from the therapist in elicit-
ing and capitalizing upon individual and family strengths.

Most family therapy is relatively brief, often lasting from 10 to 20
sessions scheduled once a week. The length of treatment depends, in
part, on the needs of the family. However, the brevity of therapy is also a
function of the increasing use of more directive approaches to family therapy. These approaches emphasize active direction and control on the part
of the therapist (Safer, 1966). Transference reactions, although they certainly occur, are minimized owing to time constraints and the well-defined
role of the therapist; and interventions are clearly focused on problems

---

*Reprinted with permission from Buscaglia, L. *The disabled and their parents: A coun-
seling challenge.* Thorofare, N.J.: Charles B. Stack, 1975.

and problem-solving rather than on in-depth exploration of intrapersonal or intrapsychic dynamics. The stages of treatment progress rapidly from diagnosis to intervention to termination. Final sessions become more a time for consolidating learning than for dealing with issues of separation as happens in traditional one-to-one and group therapy.

Family therapy provides one avenue for dealing with the problems that exceptional families face. Another viable approach to helping parents and siblings as well as the handicapped child is parent group therapy.

PARENT GROUP THERAPY

Parents of handicapped children, like everyone else, live in a social world populated by relatives, friends, neighbors, coworkers, as well as people encountered in day-to-day transactions of living. Yet the prevailing experience of many of these parents is one of isolation. This sense of aloneness and separateness, of feeling cut off from others, is generally coconstitued. That is, while the parents withdraw from others to hide their shame and embarrassment, their relatives, friends, acquaintances and strangers often tend to avoid the parents rather than confront their own discomfort. As a result, parents of disabled children sometimes feel alienated from the mainstream of society.

Parent groups provide parents of exceptional children with a bridge to other parents like themselves. Regardless of the type of group, most parents are initially relieved to meet with others who have traveled similar roads, experienced similar obstacles, and felt similar anxieties. The realization that one is not alone is most potent. In addition, the support derived from other parents provides a foundation from which real growth and change can take place. Support takes many forms in parent groups. It may be nonverbal expression—a sigh, a nod, a look that suggests "I know what you mean" or "I know what you're going through" that helps another feel connected and understood. It may also be the important verbal swapping of life experiences, whether directly related to the handicapped child or not, that touches a chord of empathy in group members. It may be the sharing of advice, based on practical experience, or the communication of some insight gained from the daily struggles of managing a handicapped child. Very often, parents will express that it is the sense of universality, the sharing with others like them, and the feelings of being supported as well as reaching out that are of greatest benefit in the parent group experience.

With the potential for sharing and support as a common denominator, parent groups take many forms and assume a variety of purposes and goals. Traditionally, these groups are either educational/informational or counseling/therapeutic in focus and direction; some are a combination of educational and therapeutic. Educational/informational groups emphasize the acquisition of knowledge and skills necessary to understand and facilitate the development of the handicapped child. Group sessions often include presentations, lectures, and films on the nature of a particular disorder, discussions on the implications of the disorder for the child and the family, and suggestions and tools for managing the day-to-day problems in raising the exceptional child. Parents commonly share feelings and experiences in these groups; however, the emphasis remains that of learning effective ways to help the handicapped child.

Counseling/therapeutic groups, on the other hand, tend to focus more specifically on the feelings and attitudes of the parents, toward the child in particular and toward their world in general. These groups help parents to explore their own intra- and interpersonal dynamics and how these dynamics affect not only their handicapped child but others as well. Self-reflection and self-exploration are the mainstays of these groups, with feedback among group participants serving as the primary vehicle for learning and change. Although many professionals use the terms *parent group counseling* and *parent group psychotherapy* interchangeably, Blatt (1957) considers the former more child-focused than the latter, in which an array of parental emotions and feelings are more deeply explored. Heisler (1974), in discussing parent therapy groups, focuses on "the goal of promoting the actualization of the parents as individuals, with the expectation that this would enable them to relate to the problem of their child's handicap in healthier and more constructive ways" (p. 330).

The vast majority of parent groups lie somewhere on the continuum between the educational and therapeutic parent groups just described. These multipurpose groups are usually structured sufficiently flexibly to encourage parents to deal with a wide variety of issues, some of which pertain to the handicapped child directly and some of which deal with other concerns, attitudes, and feelings that the parents might have. These combination groups may focus on a particular feeling one week, e.g., anger toward professionals, and a seemingly unrelated concern the next, e.g., dealing with educational considerations for the handicapped child. As participants become increasingly familiar with and trusting of each other, feedback as well as confrontation increase in frequency and helpfulness.

The degree of structure and the general format of a parent group depends in large part upon the purposes for which the group has been established. Educational/informational groups tend to be highly structured, with both content and format predetermined. Group discussion, which is limited from the beginning by time constraints, is continually directed toward the particular topics of concern during a meeting or session. Conversely, therapy groups tend to be more open and flexible. Participants, rather than the leader, create the agendas for the sessions as the needs of the members, both individually and collectively, change and evolve over time. Once again, combination groups fall somewhere in the middle and are structured to the extent that specific content, introduced most often by the leader, is incorporated into the sessions. The degree of structure and formality of a parent group depends upon factors other than the purpose and goals of the group, including the theoretical orientiation and specific methodology of the leader, the personality "style" of the leader, and the demands or expectations of the sponsoring agency.

The vast majority of parent groups, regardless of how they are designated, meet once a week, usually for 1 1/2- to 2-hour sessions. The frequency of meetings as well as the time allotted for each meeting provide for adequate continuity from session to session and enough time to explore important issues and concerns. Generally, educational groups are limited to a predetermined number of sessions (as a rule, not more than 10) and are flexible in terms of group composition. Therapy groups, however, are often more long-term, may or may not have an agreed-upon termination date, and are concerned with group composition to the degree that members commit themselves to staying and working in the group.

Parent groups are most often made available through agencies or educational institutions that provide services to physically, mentally, or emotionally disabled children. Occasionally parent groups are offered on a private basis as well. Generally speaking, the recruitment process is an informal one. Parents are informed about groups through the professionals with whom they are in contact, through notices posted on bulletin boards, or simply by word of mouth. If they wish to participate and are available at the times that meetings are scheduled, they simply sign up or show up for the group. There are agencies or programs within agencies that do, however, make the child's involvement in treatment contingent upon parent involvement in specified groups (Philage, Kuna, & Becerril, 1975). Many professionals believe that the handicapped child cannot derive maximum benefit from treatment or educational endeavors unless the parents actively confront their own attitudes and feelings toward their children.

For the most part, parent interest is the primary if not the only criterion for membership in parent groups. Prospective participants are self-selected rather than formally screened for suitability to a particular group. In practice, it is frequently assumed that parents who are not able to benefit from a particular group will opt out of the group at such time that their discomfort level becomes intolerable. When addressing the issue of screening of potential group members, group leaders must first consider the type of group that they are proposing. If they are planning a group that is educational/informational in its focus and intent, little if any screening is necessary. This type of group, which tends to be large in size, emphasizes the individual's use of his or her cognitive resources—information-processing and problem solving; and while strong feelings and intra- or interpersonal conflict material may spontaneously arise, delving into this material in any depth is discouraged. Hence, educational/informational groups tend to be emotionally "safe" and demand relatively little of the parent psychologically.

For groups that are more therapeutically oriented, screening of prospective members is highly advised. These groups require at least a minimal degree of emotional stability and openness, and participants should be interviewed prior to the first group meeting. Consideration should be given both to what a parent (or couple) might gain as well as what he or she might contribute to a therapy group. According to Seligman and Meyerson (1982), the screening interview should serve the functions of "(1) exploring expectations that the parent has concerning the group; (2) imparting information pertaining to group process and goals; (3) evaluating whether the parent could both benefit and contribute to the group; and (4) seeking a commitment from the parent to attend and participate in group sessions" (pp. 106–107). Although screening interviews provide no guarantees that a group will function effectively and reach its goals, this procedure does increase the likelihood that the group will be a productive one.

Parent group compositions vary considerably, depending upon the availability of participants as well as their interest in attending a group. Combining factors of interest and availability, it should not be surprising to find that groups populated primarily if not exclusively by mothers are still most common. However, there is a growing trend toward the establishment of couples' groups, fathers' groups, and groups that are mixed in composition. Aside from issues of convenience and willingness to attend, mothers and fathers do tend to respond to their disabled children in different ways (Cummings, 1976; Price-Bonham & Addison, 1978), which provides some rationale for separate mothers' and fathers' groups. For example, fathers of mentally retarded children are more likely to distance themselves emotionally from their affected children than are mothers (Love, 1973; see also Chapter 5). As a function of distancing and the denial that frequently accompanies it, fathers tend to focus on long-term concerns more than the day-to-day difficulties of child care and management, concerns that tend to dominate the mother's thoughts and feelings. From the meager writing that has been published on fathers' groups, it appears that men in these groups generally resist or have difficulty sharing and exploring their feelings about their handicapped children (Smith, 1981; Strean, 1962). In the experience of the author, men often invest a great deal of psychological energy in maintaining their image as one of strength, rationality, and practicality, which can work to the detriment of a therapeutic group. It is not uncommon for fathers' groups to be designated as discussion rather than counseling or therapy groups; in these groups, progress toward in-depth exploration of attitudes and feelings is frequently difficult and slow.

This discussion on fathers' groups should not be taken to imply that all fathers of handicapped children have trouble sharing feelings whereas all mothers do so with ease. In groups composed of mothers, there can certainly be straining and reluctance to express feelings and concerns. Nevertheless, mothers, whether employed outside the home or not, are generally still the ones who assume primary responsiblity for the care of their young children. They are usually the ones who, whether inherently more emotionally expressive or not, grapple with the daily frustrations of managing a child with special needs. So it seems natural that mothers' fears, trials, and joys would rise to the surface with greater ease and frequency than those of their husbands. An alternative to the notion of either mothers' or fathers' groups has been proposed by Westman, Kansky, Erikson, Arthur, and Vroom (1972) who, in working with parents of emotionally disturbed children, initiated closed, parallel groups of mothers and fathers. These groups, each with its own therapist/facilitator, would periodically merge for purposes of discussion and sharing of feelings.

More and more agencies are arranging couples' groups for parents of exceptional children. The advantages of having both mother and father involved together in the treatment process are numerous, including the emphasis on sharing of responsibility and, perhaps more important, the encouragement of open communication between partners. Blatt (1957), from his experience in working with couples groups, stated that "it was felt that by having husband and wife in the same group, we could possibly establish personal communication, emotional rapport, consistency in the handling of the child and a deeper appreciation of each other's feelings. It was also felt that placement of the parents in the same group would enable them to utilize the group therapist positively and not as a weapon against each other" (p. 134).

Another group composition issue is that of homogeneity versus heterogeneity of the group's participants. The vast majority of parent groups that have been reported in the literature are homogeneous in that participants all have children with a particular disability or handicapping condition, e.g., mental retardation or cerebral palsy. The assumption seems to be that parents in these groups can best identify with the plight of parents whose children suffer similar afflictions. Maizlish (1957), however, in discussing a diversified selection of parents in a child guidance setting, states that "homogeneity in the group in terms of similarity of problems of the referred children does not appear essential, provided the problems are not extremely deviant or atypical for the given group" (p. 177). Homogeneity in terms of parental qualities such as intelligence, education, or economic circumstances is another consideration. Demographic data on parents in particular group experiences is sparse, although it appears that parents from a broad socioeconomic range participate in and benefit from group experiences. In further addressing this issue, Maizlich asserts that such homogeneity among parents is not necessary. According to him, however, "a certain degree of sophistication appears to be needed in order to overcome initial apprehension and resistances" (p. 177).

Regardless of the type of parent group, effective leadership is an essential ingredient for the ultimate success of a group. The education and training of the leader is of utmost importance and should include cognitive understanding of group processes and dynamics as well as sufficient training experience in both member and leadership capacities. In addition, because parent groups are designated for specific populations and purposes, extensive knowledge of handicapping conditions is necessary. Therapists must be aware of the diagnoses, manifestations, and prognoses of these conditions and must also be familiar with community resources available to assist parents and their families. Most important, parent group leaders must be trained to be sensitive to the psychological needs of these parents as they struggle to accept and effectively cope with their child's disabling condition and what that means for the entire family.

Optimally, group leaders assume a variety of roles within the group context. According to Rapp, Arnheim, and Lavine (1975), leaders should be able to alternate flexibly among three roles—facilitator, teacher, and resource person—depending upon the needs of the group members at any given time. As facilitator, the leader encourages exploration and open communication of feelings and attitudes, guides the group in establishing norms and goals, and assists members in examining alternative solutions to problems. As teacher, the group leader shares his or her expertise pertaining to particular disabilities as well as teaches and models problem-solving skills that can be useful in negotiating the many difficulties that arise in raising a family that includes a handicapped child. Finally, as resource person, the leader helps to refer parents to appropriate professionals and agencies in the community which provide services to exceptional families. Parent education groups emphasize the teaching role, while parent therapy groups emphasize the facilitating role, but regardless of the type of group, leaders should be equipped to assume comfortably each of the three roles.

Whether or not a group leader chooses to label or address them as such, some transference and countertransference issues are bound to arise in parent therapy groups. Given a reasonably safe therapeutic climate, members will inevitably begin to respond emotionally to the group leader, displacing onto him or her both fantasies and unconscious conflicts. It is not unusual for group members to question both the expertise (authority) and understanding (nurturance) of the leader. For instance, if the group leader is himself or herself a parent of an exceptional child, a member may wonder out loud about the leader's ability to be "objective." If, on the other hand, the group leader does not have a handicapped child, a member may challenge his or her ability to appreciate fully a parent's emotions in this situation. Dependency issues are also projected onto the therapist. For some group members, this may take the form of hoping that the therapist will rescue them from this most difficult of situations. Others may resist any assistance on the part of the leader/therapist and may strive desparately to maintain their independence. Competition among members for the leader's attention is common. According to Maizlich (1957), in describing one of his groups, "among the most prominent indications of possible transference feelings was the sibling rivalry for the therapist's approval or special favors" (p. 173).

The sex of the therapist may, to some degree, influence the group dynamics. In most instances, female leaders facilitate groups composed entirely of mothers whereas men facilitate fathers' groups in order that an easy identification with the leader be established. In mixed groups, cofacilitation by a male and a female therapist often seems most desirable. Gottschalk, Brown, Bruney, Shumate, and Uliana (1973) and Loeb (1977) encourage the use of male and female coleaders with couples, for the purpose of both modeling effective interactional behavior and serving as identification figures. Although the sex of the leader(s) is a consideration in planning a parent group, other factors, such as availability of therapists, often take precedence. It is far more important that the leader be well-trained and competent than that he or she be male or female, regardless of the composition and nature of the group.

Just as members of the group transfer some of their issues onto the group therapist, so does the leader at times displace some of his or her conflicts onto either the entire group or certain members of the group (countertransference). A therapist, for example, may become overly identified with the frustration that a particular group member is expressing toward a particular family member. In this case the therapist may be reminded (perhaps unconsciously) of some unresolved conflict with someone in his or her own family or origin. If he or she is also the parent of a handicapped child, the therapist may have difficulty separating his or her own issues from those of a group member during a particularly emotional therapeutic encounter. As was suggested earlier, transference and countertransference both occur naturally in the group process, especially when the group is therapeutically oriented. It is important for group leaders to be aware of these processes as they occur in order to help parents to understand better their own dynamics and to diminish the possibility that the leader's own conflicts will contaminate or, worse yet, damage the therapeutic endeavor.

Parent therapy groups move through more or less well-defined stages as their members progress toward achieving the group's goals. These stages are congruent with the stages of most general therapy groups as they evolve and change over time. During the initial stage of the group, parents grapple with the issue of trust—specifically, their willingness to trust the leader and fellow group members. There is a great deal of dependency on the leader during this stage, and the leader is often beseiged by questions concerning the children's conditions. The parents want answers and at times look desparately for them in the authority figures with whom they are in contact. At some time during this stage, conflict usually arises in the group. Conflict may manifest itself as negativism toward the group leader and distrust of his or her concern or competency. Conflict may also take the form of disagreement among group members as to the priorities and direction that the group is assuming. As members continue to progress through this stage, they eventually grow to trust one another and become increasingly open in their sharing of feelings of grief and disappointment over their child and his or her disability.

The second stage of parent therapy groups is the time during which group members actually do their therapeutic "work." After working through the mourning that normally accompanies the birth or accident of the handicapped child, parents are ready to begin exploring and examining their own intra- and interpersonal dynamics, vis-à-vis the child and other family members. Parents now more closely examine their own interactions and relationships and gain insight into the ways in which these contribute to the problems in their home life. This new growth in awareness in facilitated by the therapist/leader, who through direct and indirect interventions reflects, interprets, and confronts the members as well as encourages the sharing of feedback. With an expansion of awareness comes increased behavioral efficacy in the form of active problem solving and decision making. During this second stage, parents become progressively more confident and competent in handling both the daily and long-term problems of raising a handicapped child.

At some agreed-upon time the group must come to an end, and group members, with the help of their leader, must confront termination issues. It is important that the leader anticipate the end of the group in order to allow adequate time for group members to deal with feelings concerning separation from the group. At this time a diversity of reactions are likely to arise from group members. Some individuals express anger that the group didn't do its job or didn't allow enough time to complete its task.

Others share sadness that they must say good-bye to a group of people with whom they have become close. Some participants may feel abandoned by the therapist and relate persistant fears that they cannot do a decent job of parenting their child without continued support. The responses to termination are as unique as the individuals who constitute the group, complicated by the fact that most members experience general ambivalence upon closing. The leader must both assist in the process of separating and inform parents of professional resources that are available should they need additional help.

CONCLUSIONS

Both family and parent group therapy, in all of their varieties, can assist families in adjusting to and coping with a handicapped child. Each type of treatment has its strengths and its weaknesses, and what may be helpful to one parent or sibling may be inappropriate or ill-advised for another. Group therapy offers some advantages that family therapy cannot, and vice versa. For example, parent groups offer, first and perhaps foremost, an opportunity for parents to experience a sense of universality, i.e., a commonality of feelings and experiences with group members. This universality is frequently coupled with feelings of support from members of the group; both may help to diminish the isolation that an exceptional parent may experience. Parents in group situations need not depend on feedback from the facilitator alone; in fact, for some individuals, it may be easier to receive and incorporate communication from peers than it is from the therapist. There are, however, some parents who may feel threatened at the idea of self-disclosing in a group of strangers or with anyone, for that matter. The group experience may be perceived as overwhelming, and the parent may not be prepared to deal with the deluge of feelings that emerge in what can be a very emotional experience. Family therapy offers the benefit of more individualized and focused attention from the therapist in the safety of a private, controlled context. This means that even marginally functioning persons or family units can benefit from treatment, for the therapist is free to intervene at the individual or family's current level of functioning without worrying about losing the attention of other participants.

A particular advantage of family counseling is that it potentially includes all members of the family, not just the parents. The importance of dealing with the feelings and needs of the handicapped child's siblings cannot be overstated. Although most parent groups devote some attention to concerns about other children in the family and effective means of helping them to cope, direct therapeutic intervention with these children may at times be more beneficial. In family therapy the therapist has an opportunity to directly observe and involve him- or herself with the children. If they are old enough to verbalize, the therapist can learn a great deal about how well the entire family is functioning. The therapist can support children who may crave attention and affection but are deprived of it in an overburdened family system. Equally important, the therapist can observe family members interacting with each other, including the handicapped child. Communication patterns and dynamics can be assessed objectively and interventions can be made immediately. In contrast, parents participating in groups communicate information *about* their family situations, e.g., how individual members are coping or how well the family system is working as a whole. The information is frequently distorted since parents, like any other human being, sometimes see what they want to see. Even when the reporting is accurate, second-hand interventions are more difficult to effect.

Parent groups do, however, offer another clear advantage: that of providing participants with a multitude of examples of coping behavior— both positive and negative. Members rapidly learn from one another's experiences of what works and what doesn't, practically speaking. Individuals may gain courage to try new experiences and take risks when they observe others modeling such behaviors. Family therapy, on the other hand, provides family members with multiple opportunities to learn from each other while at the same time learning about each other. Each person comes to understand the others in a new way, and individual strengths, which may have gone unseen or unacknowledged, can be appreciated. With this new-found positive regard for others in the family, the entire unit is likely to begin operating more effectively for the benefit of all.

In closing, the author would like to propose that parents of handicapped children be offered an opportunity to receive both family therapy and a parent group experience. The following treatment plan provides benefits of both types of intervention without unduly taxing the financial resources or time of the parents or the agency involved: Upon diagnosis of the affected child, the parents are invited to talk with a therapist about any feelings, concerns, or questions that they may have. During the initial visit(s), the therapist works at helping the parents to express themselves while at the same time assessing their suitability and readiness for a parent group, if one is available. At the time that the parents seem likely to join a group, they are prepared by the counselor for the experience. This preparation includes discussion of anticipated family changes and the possible need for adjunctive family therapy. Generally, family therapy is offered on an as-needed basis, with the therapist and parents both responsible for ascertaining the need. One or two family therapy sessions may be scheduled during the course of the group for the purpose of assessing parent or family progress and targeting any particular problems that may be emerging. At the termination of the parent group experience, the entire family is seen once again and evaluated for further family therapy.

Every family member is strongly affected by the presence of a handicapped child, who, likewise, is strongly affected by the feelings and attitudes of the family. Exclusive focus on treatment of the child is clearly inadequate. Parents need to learn ways of effectively coping with the additional stresses and demands that arise in the family. It is especially important that family members—parents and children alike—learn to communicate openly with one another. In this way, feelings and needs are made explicit and can be dealt with in a healthy manner. There are a variety of ways of helping families of handicapped children, including individual counseling of family members, counseling of the parents as a couple, family therapy, and parent groups. This chapter has focused on the latter two approaches. Yet no method of intervention is inherently better than the others in all cases. Each has its strengths and its weaknesses. Combining the better features of more than one type of counseling intervention may provide the optimal solution in helping families of handicapped children.

REFERENCES

Blatt, A. Group therapy with parents of severely retarded children: A preliminary report. *Group Psychotherapy,* 1957, *10,* 133–140.

Buscaglia, L. *The disabled and their parents: A counseling challenge.* Thorofare, N.J.: Charles B. Stack, 1975.

Chinitz, S. P. A sibling group for brothers and sisters of handicapped children. *Children Today,* 1981, 21–23.

Cummings, S. T. The impact of the child's deficiency on the father. *American Journal of Orthopsychiatry,* 1976, *42,* 246–255.

Cutter, A. V., & Hallowitz, D. Different approaches to treatment of the child and the parents. *American Journal of Orthopsychiatry,* 1962, *32,* 918–926.

Duncan, D. The impact of a handicapped child upon the family. Paper presented at the Pennnsylvania Training Model Sessions, Harrisburg, Pa., May 1977.

Fife, B. L. Reducing parental overprotection of the leukemic child. *Social Science and Medicine,* 1978, *12,* 117–122.

Fogarty, T. F. System concepts and the dimensions of self. In P. J. Guerin, Jr. (Ed.), *Family therapy: Theory and practice.* New York: Gardner Press, 1976.

Fox, R. E. Family therapy. In I. B. Weiner (Ed.), *Clinical methods in psychology.* New York: Wiley, 1976.

Gottschalk, L. A., Brown, S. B., Bruney, E. H., Shumate, L. W., & Uliana, R. L. An evaluation of a parents' group in a child-centered clinic. *Psychiatry,* 1973, *36,* 157–171.

Heisler, V. Dynamic group psychotherapy with parents of cerebral palsied children. *Rehabilitation Literature,* 1974, *35,* 329–330.

Kivowitz, J. Counseling parents whose sexual relationship has been affected by a handicapped child. *Medical Aspects of Human Sexuality,* 1977, *11,* 79–80.

Kubler-Ross, E. *On Death and Dying.* New York: Macmillan, 1969.

Loeb, R. C. Group therapy for parents of mentally retarded children. *Journal of Marriage and Family Counseling,* 1977, *3,* 77–83.

Love, H. *The Mentally Retarded Child and His Family.* Springfield, Ill.: Charles C Thomas, 1973.

Maizlish, I. L. Group psychotherapy of husband–wife couples in a child guidance clinic. *Group Psychotherapy,* 1957, *10,* 169–180.

Masten, A. S. Family therapy as a treatment for children: A critical review of outcome research. *Family Process,* 1979, *18,* 323–335.

Noland, R. L. (Ed.). *Counseling parents of the emotionally disturbed child.* Springfield, Ill.: Charles C Thomas, 1972.

Philage, M. L., Kuna, D. J., & Becerril, G. A new family approach to therapy for the learning disabled child. *Journal of Learning Disabilities,* 1975, *8,* 22–31.

Price-Bonham, S., & Addison, S. Families and mentally retarded children: Emphasis on the father. *The Family Coordinator,* 1978, *27,* 221–230.

Rapp, H. M., Arnheim, D. L., & Lavine, B. J. The roles of a parent discussion group leader. *Personnel and Guidance Journal,* 1975, *54,* 110–112.

Safer, D. Family therapy for children with behavior disorders. *Family Process,* 1966, *5,* 243–255.

Seligman, M., & Meyerson, R. Group approaches for parents of exceptional children. In M. Seligman (Ed.), *Group psychotherapy and counseling with special populations.* Baltimore: University Park Press, 1982.

Smith, K. The influence of the male sex role on discussion groups for fathers of exceptional children. *Michigan Personnel and Guidance Journal,* 1981, *12,* 11–17.

Solnit, A. J., & Stark, M. H. Mourning and the birth of a defective child. *Psychoanalytic Studies of the Child,* 1961, *16,* 523–537.

Sourkes, B. Facilitating family coping with childhood cancer. *Journal of Pediatric Psychology,* 1977, *2,* 65–67.

Strean, H. S. A means of involving fathers in family treatment: Guidance groups for fathers. *American Journal of Orthopsychiatry,* 1962, *32,* 719–727.

Warnick, L. The effect upon a family of a child with a handicap. *New Outlook for the Blind,* 1969, *63,* 299–304.

Westman, J. C., Kansky, E. W., Erikson, M. E., Arthur, B., & Vroom, A. L. Parallel group psychotherapy with the parents of emotionally disturbed children. *International Journal of Group Psychotherapy,* 1963, *13,* 52–60.

White, B. L. Clinical team treatment of a mentally retarded child and his parents: Group counseling and play observation. In R. L. Noland (Ed.), *Counseling parents of the mentally retarded.* Springfield, Ill.: Charles C Thomas, 1970.

Index

Page numbers followed by *t* indicate tables.